Z
305
.059
D47
1996

De St. Jorre, John,
  1936-

Venus bound.

$27.00

DATE			

The Brothers' War: Biafra and Nigeria
The Patriot Game (coauthor)
A House Divided: South Africa's Uncertain Future
The Guards
The Marines
The Insider's Guide to Spain

VENUS BOUND

JOHN DE ST JORRE

VENUS
BOUND

*The Erotic Voyage
of the
Olympia Press
and
Its Writers*

RANDOM HOUSE

NEW YORK

Owing to limitations of space, acknowledgments of
permission to quote unpublished and published materials
will be found following the index.

This work was originally published (in slightly different form)
in Great Britain, as *The Good Ship Venus*, by Hutchinson,
a division of Random House UK, London, in 1994.

The chapter-head illustrations, by Norman Rubington,
were kindly supplied by Ann May Green.

Library of Congress Cataloging-in-Publication
data is available.
ISBN 0-679-44336-3

Printed in the United States of America on acid-free paper

24689753

FIRST U.S. EDITION

Book design by Carole Lowenstein

For Norman Rubington
and his alter ego, *"Akbar del Piombo,"*
and for Helen,
who always liked the idea, and made it happen

'Twas on the good ship Venus
By Christ you should have seen us;
The figurehead was a whore in bed
And the mast was a rampant penis . . .

FROM *Count Palmiro Vicarion's*
Book of Bawdy Ballads (The Olympia Press)

Where are you going to, my pretty maid?
"I'm going to publish, sir," she said.
Perhaps you've a fortune, my pretty maid?
"My verse is my fortune, sir," she said.
Then you'd better not try it, my pretty maid;
There's an item for printing, and, when it is paid,
There's "Commission on sales," oh innocent maid!
In your rural retreat have you heard of THE TRADE?
Oh, where are you going to, my pretty maid?

FROM "Measured Steps," by Ernest Radford
(quoted in Stanley Unwin's *The Truth About Publishing*)

Preface

Censorship of the printed word in the West these days is rare; to most people it appears ludicrous, even obscene. Yet, just over a generation ago, many books—some great, others less than great—were banned in much of Western Europe and in the United States. They were condemned as erotic, pornographic, corrupting—obscene.

Victorian tastes, style, and standards were largely matters of historical interest—or radical-chic revival—that had lost their power. Yet the Victorians' view of obscenity lived on, enshrined in law and upheld by governments, parliaments, and the arbiters of public morality. Writers, publishers, printers, booksellers, dealers—all faced stiff legal sanctions if they breached regulations that were a living legacy of the Victorian era.

Censorship was especially paradoxical in Britain and the United States, countries that prided themselves on their long-entrenched democratic institutions and liberal values. Yet confiscated books, regardless of their literary merit, were burned, just as heretics had been burned in earlier times and just as drugs would be later. Words were contraband, more dangerous than drugs. Books, after all, could in theory reach every literate member of the population and "deprave and corrupt"—Britain's definition of obscenity—all who read them.

"Those were the days when books had *power*," said Iris Owens, the American novelist who wrote some pretty powerful books herself in Paris under the pseudonym "Harriet Daimler." Words on the printed page in that early television, prevideo era had enormous power: the power to shock, to excite, to ignite a reader's sexuality and produce a palm-sweating, stomach-fluttering, orgasmic state of arousal. Words were powerful because they targeted human beings' most sensitive sexual organ—the brain. Clandestinity heightened the drama. These were forbidden, banned, censored, secret books that you were not supposed to know about, let alone read.

To young readers, it may seem that all this was a long time ago and, anyway, what was all the fuss about? The rapid change in public mores, attitudes, and awareness that took place during the 1960s, and became loosely known as the "sexual revolution," made the earlier age look archaic. But it wasn't so long ago after all. *Lady Chatterley's Lover* was a banned book in Britain as recently as 1961, when a famous, lengthy, and costly trial struck off its chains. Henry Miller's *Tropic of Cancer* was not published in his own country until the same year. J. P. Donleavy's bawdy but hardly pornographic *The Ginger Man* was not fully available to British readers until 1965. Lawrence Durrell's *The Black Book* did not appear in the United Kingdom until 1973.

As for the fuss, it was real enough at the time, involving a bitter struggle across a deep cultural divide. It was, in a sense, a clash of cultures within a common culture. A group of angry young men and women, many with talent and most with fire in their bellies, had something to say, but the laws, the literary establishment, the appointed and self-appointed upholders of public morality opposed them. A series of running battles took place; each side registered victories and defeats. But, in the end, the establishment retreated, and although serious skirmishes still occur, it is hard to imagine that there will ever be a full-blown counterrevolution.

The famous novels and the pornography published in Paris—the literary ammunition of the sexual revolution—look pretty tame by modern standards. A glance at any bookstall in a British railway station or in an American airport will reveal much hotter—or, as they say in the trade, "stronger"—material. I recently saw a paperback called *The Nun's Delight* with a cover photograph of a startlingly beautiful woman in a nun's habit drawn up waist-high to reveal a shapely gartered thigh, in the airport of Catholic Ireland's capital city. Four-letter words that had writers like D. H. Lawrence and Henry Miller branded as outcasts crop up daily on film, in journalism, and even on television. In some cases, yesterday's "dirty book"—*Lolita*, for instance—has become today's school textbook.

The effect of censorship in those not-so-distant days was to deprive a large number of Irish, American, and British writers of an outlet for their work. Authors like James Joyce, D. H. Lawrence, Henry Miller, Lawrence Durrell, Samuel Beckett, Vladimir Nabokov, J. P. Donleavy, William Burroughs, and many others had to look beyond their native shores if they wanted to see their work in print.

Fortunately, there was one haven: Paris, a city of culture and tolerance. Even better, it was a city that seemed to breed adventurous English-language publishers who had no qualms about nailing their anticensorship colors to their imprints.

Most of the better-known outlawed writers, plus a host of lesser ones, found salvation with two Parisian publishers. They were Jack Kahane of the Obelisk Press in the 1930s, who was followed by his son, Maurice Girodias, who ran the Olympia Press in the 1950s and 1960s, embarking on a series of erotic adventures with a mixed crew of serious writers and artisan pornographers. Kahane and Girodias published a remarkable collection of books that played a major role in undermining the ramparts of censorship, as well as a supporting part in the staging of the sexual revolution itself.

THIS IS THEIR STORY. It is also the story of the last great flowering of Paris as a crucible for creative expatriate talent, when books had power and everything was possible. And it is the story of cultural and social change, the time when literary censorship ended in the United States and Britain.

Censorship nurtured the Obelisk-Olympia experience, while the new freedom, ironically, brought it to an end. Philip Larkin put a date on it:

> *Sexual intercourse began*
> *In Nineteen sixty-three*
> *(Which was rather late for me)*
> *Between the end of the*
> Chatterley *ban*
> *And the Beatles' first LP.*[1]

Once writers like Miller, Beckett, Nabokov, De Sade, Donleavy, Genet, and Burroughs could be published in Britain and the United States, buccaneering bookleggers like Kahane and Girodias were obsolete. Sex emerged from its musty Victorian closet and into the bookshops, the libraries, and even the schools. At the same time, the love affair between Paris and its literary outlaws came to an end. The shabby, ramshackle, freewheeling Fourth Republic was replaced by the discipline of Charles de Gaulle and the puritanism of his wife, "Tante Yvonne." Jack Kahane died in 1939 not knowing what he had started; Maurice Girodias died in 1990 knowing that a major battle had been won.

The war, of course, is not over. While sexual censorship has retreated, other forms have advanced. The British government has tried to prevent its secrets from being published; Islamic fundamentalists have imposed a death sentence on an author whose writing they regard as blasphemous; and a form of censorship has been exercised by the tenets and prejudices of "political correctness." But that is another voyage, in another vessel.

JOHN DE ST JORRE
Mallorca, Spain, 1996

Acknowledgments

The idea for this book came from the fecund mind of Norman Rubington, a painter of talent and a friend of long standing. In another life, in Paris, he had been "Akbar del Piombo," the creator of highly original and witty collage books. He was also a pornographer, writing to arouse, a fast and fluent pen for hire. Norman died before the book was finished, but I like to think that he was keeping an eye on things, wreathed as always in black tobacco smoke and nodding from time to time in his sardonic way.

I never met Maurice Girodias. We did, however, have a brief and spirited correspondence. I wrote to him in Paris from New York describing my book and requesting an interview. He replied, pointing out that he was currently writing his second volume of memoirs and "the danger of conflict and interference between our two projects seems very real to me." Someone, without my knowledge or consent, had sent him my book proposal, and this evoked great ire. He said the outline contained "many errors" and an "absolute lack of knowledge . . . about the period involved." He would, he ended, be "forced to take all necessary measures" to protect his interests.

I replied, cheerfully enough, admitting my state of ignorance, saying that I did not see a conflict of interest (he was, after all, the leading actor while I was a mere scribe) and that surely he, the flail of censorship, would not stand in the way of a serious reporting endeavor about an important subject. A terse response noted that nothing in my second letter was going to change anything in his first. If I insisted on proceeding, he warned, "it is easy to predict that this venture of yours will cause you more trouble than profit."

The same day that he wrote to me he sent a letter to Hutchinson, my publisher in London. He made it clear he was determined to defend his father's and his own public images against the "probable distortions and over-simplifications inherent in Mr. de St Jorre's venture." My outline was "silly, abusive and fraudulent." He warned Hutchinson, obliquely but unmistakably, of the dangers of publishing my book. "The rest is in your hands," he concluded.

Maurice Girodias died in July 1990, and since then I have circled around him and grown fond of him. Perhaps it was as well that we never met. Distance nourishes objectivity and allows the excitement of discovery, and Girodias's absence has been eased by the generous help of his relatives. I would like to thank Laurette Kahane, Juliette Kahane, Eric Kahane, and Lilla Lyon for granting me access to his papers, for reading my manuscript, and for their trust, patience, and insights.

I would also like to express my gratitude to many people who set aside time and shared their memories and their expertise with me. In Sommières in the south of France, my thanks are due to Françoise Kestman and her daughter Nadine at the Centre d'Études & de Recherches Lawrence Durrell. In Paris, grateful thanks to Dominique Aury, Georges Belmont Pelorson, Thomas Quinn Curtiss, Jean-Louis Faure, Michèle Forgeois, Jim Haynes, Odile Hellier, Juliette and Couquite Hoffenberg, Georges Hoffman, Holly Hutchins, Charles Kircorian, Elliot Klein, Karl Orend, Claire Paulhan, Jean-Jacques Pauvert, Monique Sindler-Gonthier, Pierre Ter-Sarkissian, George Whitman, Miriam and Jean-Pierre Worms, and Michael Zwerin.

In the United States, my thanks to Victor Bockris, Georges Borchardt, Mary Briault, Baird Bryant, Gideon Cashman, Gregory Corso, Robert Cowley, Alan Davis, Mary Dearborn, Edward de Grazia, Judith Douw, Ed Ferraro, Leon Friedman, Jay Gertzman, Allen Ginsberg, James Grauerholz, Ann May Greene, Seymour Hacker, Mary Harron, Roger Jackson, Fred Jordan, James Jurgens, Suzanne Kallich, Seymour Litvinoff, Claire Lord, Jim McKinley, Walter Minton, Ted Morgan, Iris Owens, Ann Patty, Michael Perkins, George Plimpton, Bob Rosenthal, Barney Rosset, Earl Rubington, Richard

Seaver, James Sherwood, Norman Singer, Patsy Southgate, Marilyn Meeske Sorel, Carol Southern, Terry Southern, Lyle Stuart, Austryn Wainhouse, Gerald Williams, Andrew Wylie, and Walter Zacharias.

In Britain, I would like to thank Lanny Aldrich, James Armstrong, Jane Bown, John Calder, James Campbell, John Coleman, Paul Cross, Hugh Ford, Mary Guinness, Guy de Jonquières, James Knowlson, Christopher Logue, Barry Miles, Frank Monaco, Michael Rubinstein, Nile Southern, Paul Spike, John Stevenson, Gritta Weil, Patti Welles, and Alan Wesencraft. In Ireland, my thanks are due to J. P. Donleavy.

I would also like to express my gratitude to Paul Bowles in Tangier for seeing me on his sickbed and to Gavin Young, efficiently assisted by Abdul Lateef, for the comforts of Dar Sinclair.

During my research I came to depend heavily on the literary detection skills and goodwill of a small coterie of bibliophiles, all of whom turned out to be interesting individuals. My thanks to Michael Neal, indefatigable researcher and veteran *plongeur* ("I'd rather wash dishes in France," he says, "than lead Her Majesty's Government"); Patrick Kearney, bibliographer of the Olympia Press and scholar of erotic literature, in California; Clifford Scheiner, book collector and dealer, and physician, in New York; and Michael Goss, book dealer and publisher, in London.

Several librarians deserve a special mention. I am indebted to Jane Lowenthal, former chief librarian of the Carnegie Endowment of International Peace and an old friend and colleague; Mary Jane Ballou of the Ford Foundation; Terrance Keenan, in charge of Special Collections at the Library of Syracuse University, New York; and the Special Collections Library, Arizona State University.

I would also like to thank Kate Lewin in Paris and Maggie Berkvist in New York for their invaluable and highly efficient photographic and other research.

Grateful acknowledgment is due for the use of extracts from *Evergreen Review*, *The Paris Review*, *Grand Street*, and *The New York Writer* and to several excellent biographies: Michael Baker's portrait of Radclyffe Hall, *Our Three Selves*; Ted Morgan's book on William Burroughs, *Literary Outlaw*; Barry Miles's on the same subject, *El Hombre Invisible*; and the second volume of Brian Boyd's biography of Vladimir Nabokov, *The American Years*. Several books became constant companions, providing material and enlightenment. These were Hugh Ford's enduring *Published in Paris*; Edward de Grazia's magisterial *Girls Lean Back Everywhere: The Law of Obscenity and the Assault on Genius*; and Patrick Kearney's bibliographies of the Paris and New York Olympia presses. Finally, posthumous homage to Maurice Girodias's own writing, his two volumes of autobiography, countless articles, and, above all, his inimitable letters.

During my travels I was fortunate in being able to stay with hospitable friends who provided logistical support while tolerating mounds of paper and books and constant use of their telephones. My gratitude to Paul Crotto, Hortensia de Hutten, and Paul and Marcelle Webster in Paris; to Nik, Pamela, and Rose Marie Wheeler for a productive and monastic spell in their house in Le Bosc, Languedoc; to Lawrence and Edith Malkin, and Peter Pringle and Eleanor Randolph in New York; to Sallie Quirk and Ira Gasman in Sag Harbor, Long Island; and to Touna and Farid Kioumgi, Tony and Sylvette Hodges, and Dick and Gaby Fyjis-Walker in London.

Several people helped me in various ways that proved indispensable. I am grateful to Jonathan Boulting and Jean-Paul Iommi-Amuntégui for putting me in touch with Dominique Aury; to Patrick Kearney, Clifford Scheiner, Richard Seaver, Michael Neal, James Knowlson, James Armstrong, Karl Orend, Mary Dearborn, Ed Ferraro, and Barney Rosset for reading all or parts of the manuscript. Elinor Bowles, talented editor and former colleague, came up with a number of helpful suggestions. I owe much to Lawrence Malkin and Paul Spike for their useful advice and constructive commentary throughout the research and writing of this book.

Good fortune also brought Gillon Aitken, my literary agent, when the subject of Girodias and the Olympia Press first appeared. He suggested that it was worth a book and urged me to get on with it. His understanding of writing and writers, his tactical judgment, and his unwavering support have been—and continue to be—indispensable. It seemed fitting that he also came up with the title for the Hutchinson and Pimlico editions in Britain, the result no doubt of an early grounding in the literary oeuvre of Count Palmiro Vicarion.

For the American edition, I am grateful to Andrew Wylie, who amongst his other accomplishments is an Olympia Press author, and to his associate Bridget Love, for handling the agenting side of things in New York. My editor at Random House, Samuel S. Vaughan, brought a new title and suggestions that reflect understanding, subtlety, and style; all these have improved the book. I thank him and his assistant, Karen McGuinness, for their enthusiasm and their patience.

Contents

Prologue

It was in the late 1950s, shortly after Easter, when a young Oxford undergraduate arrived in Dover after spending a holiday in Paris. As he walked toward the Immigration and Customs, he was stopped by a man a little older than himself.

"Look," said the stranger, "you don't know who I am but I know who you are. We're both at Balliol. I've got a bit of a problem and I wonder if you can help me?"

Slightly nonplussed, but intrigued, the young student said he would do what he could.

"The thing is," the stranger continued, "I always get stopped at Customs. I've got that sort of face, you see. Now, you've got a totally different face, an honest face. I bet you have never been stopped."

The owner of the honest face admitted that it was true. He had never been stopped, anywhere.

"Would you mind taking something through for me," the other man asked, "and I'll pick it up on the other side."

"What is it?"

"This bag."

He opened a large duffle bag and offered it for inspection.

The young student looked inside. It was full of books.

"All right," he said. "I'll take it and meet you on the other side."

He walked to the control point and was waved through. He turned and looked back. His mysterious accomplice approached the barrier and was immediately whisked inside.

He sat down to wait. He waited for half an hour, an hour, an hour and a half. After nearly two hours, he decided he could wait no longer. He picked up his luggage, swung the bag of books over his shoulder, and boarded the train to London.

It was only when he was back in his Oxford rooms that he examined the contents of the bag. The books were paperbacks, in uniform but distinctive plain green covers. Each bore the legend: The Traveller's Companion Series. The imprint was the Olympia Press, Paris. The titles were eye-catching: *White Thighs, Lolita, Classical Hindu Erotology, The Sexual Life of Robinson Crusoe, Tropic of Cancer, Naked Lunch, Under the Birch, The Loins of Amon, The Ginger Man, Scream, My Darling, Scream*, and so on. Even the authors' names had allure, either because they were well-known renegades whose work was beyond the reach of most readers or because they sounded bizarre and exotic: Vladimir Nabokov, Samuel Beckett, the Marquis de Sade, William Burroughs, Count Palmiro Vicarion, Akbar del Piombo, Greta X, Bernhardt von Soda, Carmencita de las Lunas. What was inside the covers made the young student's knees tremble. He had unwittingly smuggled into Britain a hoard of forbidden "dirty books."

Roderick Bloomfield, involuntary book smuggler and later a seasoned publisher who commissioned this book, never saw the owner of the duffle bag again. But, for a brief period, he was the most popular man in his college as the Olympia titles circulated, exciting Britain's best and brightest with their double freight of prohibition and sexual arousal.

VENUS BOUND

1

Booklegger Jack and the Obelisk Press

ONE SUMMER'S DAY IN 1932 a neophyte publisher, after a good lunch, settled down under a giant copper beech tree in the grounds of his country house. He opened a bulky manuscript, which had been given to him in Paris the day before, and began to read. The publisher was Jack Kahane, an Englishman, who had recently launched the Obelisk Press. The manuscript was *Tropic of Cancer,* by an impoverished and unknown American writer called Henry Miller.

It was dark by the time Kahane finished reading. He walked back into the house "exalted by the triumphant sensation of all explorers who have at last fallen upon the object of their years of search. . . . I had read the most terrible, the most sordid, the most magnificent manuscript that had ever fallen into my hands; nothing . . . was comparable to it for the splendour of its writing, the fathomless depth of its despair, the savour of its portraiture, the boisterousness of its humor."[1]

Kahane's enthusiasm for Miller's book, which he records in *Memoirs of a Booklegger,* was not matched by either his publishing skill or his resources. He had been in business for only a short period, most of which coincided with the onset of the Great Depression, and his hands were tied by an unimaginative partner who believed in playing safe. Kahane's health was poor, the result of being gassed and concussed on the Western Front in World War I; his finances, mangled in the stock-market crash, were equally fragile.

Nevertheless, over the next seven years this unlikely figure—dilettante and dandy, political idealist and literary enthusiast—was to publish a number of groundbreaking books that could find no other way into print. His list included Henry Miller (*Tropic of Cancer, Black Spring, Max and the White Phagocytes,* and *Tropic of Capricorn*), Anaïs Nin (*The Winter of Artifice*), Lawrence Durrell (*The Black Book*), James Joyce (a fragment of *Finnegans Wake* and *Pomes Penyeach*), Radclyffe Hall (*The Well of Loneliness*), Frank Harris (*My Life and Loves*), and Cyril Connolly (*The Rock Pool*). "Only war and the publisher's death finally toppled the Obelisk," commented Hugh Ford, the historian of English-language publishing in Paris between the wars. "But by the time those calamities occurred Kahane's Obelisk logo had been affixed to some of the most controversial books of the past half century."[2]

Kahane was born in Manchester in 1887, the year of Queen Victoria's diamond jubilee, the seventh of eight children. His parents died when he was young and with them disappeared much of the wealth that their Jewish forebears had accumulated in the Lancashire cotton business. Brought up by an elder sister, Kahane was educated at Manchester Grammar School, during which time his family "seemed to be in a chronic state of impecuniosity."

After leaving school he worked in a cotton trader's office. But his mind was elsewhere. Describing himself as a "romantic born in an age of realists," Kahane directed his energies to writing plays, joining literary clubs, and taking an active part in the artistic debates of the day. For this was Edwardian Manchester at its commercial and cultural zenith, crowned by the twin glories of *The Manchester Guardian* newspaper and the Hallé Orchestra under the direction of the German maestro Hans Richter.[3]

Already a Francophile, the young Kahane led a campaign against Richter, who kept to a musical diet of mainly German composers and refused to play French music. Kahane used one jeweled Manchester institution to attack the other. He had become secretary of the Manchester Musical Society and wrote a letter to *The Manchester Guardian* assaulting "the bullying intolerance" of Richter and calling for his retirement. Fearing that the letter was so harsh that it might be dismissed with silent contempt, Kahane wrote a response demolishing its arguments and signed it with the name of a lawyer friend who gave him permission to do so. He then wrote letter number three, under his own name, trashing letter number two. After that the public took over and battle was royally joined. The result was Richter's resignation and return to Germany.[4]

Kahane left the cotton office and set up a small business with another young man making and selling velvet. They prospered, and Kahane indulged his taste for the good life in Manchester, London, and, finally, Paris. He was the archetypal Edwardian dandy: over six feet tall, clad in a fashionably cut Savile Row suit, a monocle screwed into his eye and a cane swinging from his hand. At the height of his good fortune, he owned fifty pairs of trousers, seven bulldogs, and a half share in a racehorse called Algernon.

With the outbreak of war in 1914, Kahane rushed to offer his services against the Germans. He tried to join the French Foreign Legion and was rebuffed; an application to the Grenadier Guards suffered a similar response. Finally, he was accepted as an interpreter, although his knowledge of French was minimal. Once in France he found himself drafted to a cavalry unit, where it was soon discovered that his mastery of riding was as rudimentary as his command of the French language. His picaresque military career took on a more somber tone when he was switched to logistics and sent up to the front. As part of his preparations, he stowed away six spare monocles in his pack. At Ypres he was first gassed and then blown high into the air by a German shell. He lost a lung and many of his teeth but survived and spent the rest of the war behind the lines.

It was during this time that Kahane met his future wife, Marcelle Girodias. The story goes that he spotted her on a beach in the south of France and, peering at her through his military binoculars, fell head over heels in love. He went over to where she was sitting and, in halting French, asked her to marry him. She obliged, and they were married on one of his furloughs in 1917.

Marcelle's father was an empire builder, an engineer who had constructed ports in South America, bridges in North Africa, and railways in Spain. His wife was of Spanish origin, and they had three daughters and a son, Maurice. The war devastated the Girodias family, as it did many others. Maurice was killed on his first day at the front by a bullet through the head, and the two elder daughters died in the Spanish influenza epidemic that swept postwar Europe in 1919. With three out of four children gone, Marcelle's father began to look more benignly upon his recently acquired son-in-law, whose sudden and unorthodox arrival in the family had received mixed notices.

Jack Kahane's response was to provide his parents-in-law with a son to replace the one they had lost. Born on April 12, 1919, the boy was inevitably named Maurice. Three more children arrived over the next seven years: Nicole, Sylvie, and Eric. To make ends meet Kahane wheeled and dealed with surplus military stocks in Paris and did rather well out of it. But his wife's family money also helped to set him up in a style his prewar life had led him to expect.

In the early 1920s the Kahane family moved into a house romantically named Le Fond des Forêts (The Depth of the Forests) in a village some forty miles east of Paris. "The house," he later recalled, "was commonplace enough, a big square edifice, of the style which I believe is known as bastard Gothic, containing about twenty rooms, many of enormous size."[5] It was surrounded by thirty acres of land, and it was here that, a decade or so later, Kahane would spend a long afternoon absorbed in *Tropic of Cancer.*

Meanwhile, a bout of tuberculosis that led to a prolonged stay in a sanitorium turned out to have a silver lining. While Kahane was there he began writing a light, slightly risqué novel called *Laugh and Grow Rich,* which was based on his postwar experiences. He sent it to a British publisher and, to his surprise, received a contract in return. The book did badly until it was banned by lending libraries. A letter of outrage from the author was published in a London newspaper, good and bad reviews followed, and the book took off. Jack Kahane had learned an important sequential lesson about publishing: spice between the covers invoked censorship, which triggered protest, which produced sales.

More novels followed, their titles as frothy as their content: *The Gay Intrigue, Suzy Falls Off, The Browsing Goat,* and so on. "It was the Gallic sexual morality that animated Kahane,"[6] writes Hugh Ford, and it appealed to sexually suppressed English readers. Writing books led to an interest in publishing them, and in 1928 Kahane formed a partnership with a French publisher named Henri Babou. Specializing in expensive illustrated books, Babou was a small, dapper man who had a goatee, wore high-heeled shoes, and in general maintained a sartorial standard that matched Kahane's own. The deal was more than a little one-sided. "Monsieur Babou was in complete control," Kahane noted, "and I was only the most somnolent of sleeping partners."[7] Babou continued publishing his own books while his new partner made the requisite investment and went out to look for new talent.

It was an exciting time to be in Paris, where expatriate literary energy and renown had turned the city into a mecca for the followers of the arts. *Ulysses* was out, and Joyce was a celebrity and a much sought-after figure. Sylvia Beach, his publisher, had made her bookshop, Shakespeare and Company, an essential port of call for writers, poets, playwrights, and painters living in or visiting Paris. Gertrude Stein and Alice B. Toklas were running their famous literary salon. Scott and Zelda Fitzgerald were in and out of town, and Ernest Hemingway, a resident, had just published *The Sun Also Rises* to great critical acclaim. There was a host of small English-language magazines and presses ebbing and flowing across the shifting sands of changing tastes, shaky finances, and quirky personalities. Paris was romantic, creative, unexpected, and full of talented and eccentric Americans, British, and Irish.

Jack Kahane was convinced that another Joyce was out there, just waiting for someone like himself to come along and say: "I publish what others fear to publish. Now, let's have a look at that bulging manuscript I see sitting there." But first he decided to have a go at Joyce himself, so he paid a visit to Miss Beach in her bookshop at number 12 rue de l'Odéon:

"She received me, I am bound to confess, with a certain perplexity and without great warmth. I still wore an eyeglass, a dandiacal attribute the ascetic lady could hardly have been expected to approve. But I explained my ambition [to publish something, anything, by Joyce] in spite of her persistent aloofness and faintly humorous incredulity, and at last . . . [she] promised to take me to the Master."[8]

Kahane describes the great day when Sylvia Beach led him into the "Presence." "I was very nervous, and when at last I clasped his tenuous hand and looked into the (almost) sightless eyes, I had an excess of reverence that is customarily foreign from my nature. Joyce was very gracious, and introduced me to the people who seemed to form his court. . . . I drank and ate and listened to the Master and his disciples, and when the feast was done and the libations poured, repaired with him and Miss Beach to another room, where after a short discussion I respectfully handed to her for his account a cheque for fifty thousand francs in payment of the right to publish a fragment of five thousand words from the work he had in progress in a de luxe edition to be entitled *Haveth Childers Everywhere*."[9]

Kahane left the Presence floating on air. "I could now count myself

amongst the Elect Few having the honour to publish him [Joyce]
who was then freely admitted to be the greatest writer of our time."[10]
He quickly came down to earth, however, when he recounted his
triumph to his partner:

"Babou was proud but very frightened. First I must tell him what
the manuscript was all about. Snag number one.

" 'I am afraid I can't tell you. You see, Joyce is a writer of such
eminence that it is a privilege to publish anything he writes.'

" 'Admitted, in principle. But now you have bought the manuscript
I suppose you have read it?'

" 'No, I am afraid I haven't.'

"His eyebrow ascended in a circumflex direction. All I could tell
him about it, I stammered, was that it was a fragment from a work
in progress. He remained dissatisfied.

" 'But surely you have sufficient literary interest in it to read it?'
Babou continued.

" 'I have tried to read it, and—well—I can't understand it.'

" 'The subject is so abstruse?'

" 'No, the language.'

" 'The language? But—surely you do not tell me it is written in
Irish?'

" 'No, in English.'

" 'And you can't understand—your own language?' "[11]

At this point the two partners seem to have agreed that publishing
a work neither of them understood, and at great financial risk to
themselves, was preferable to the alternative: facing the Presence and
his cohort, the formidable Miss Beach, and committing an act of lèse-
majesté by refusing to publish this incomprehensible and deeply un-
profitable book.

So they published it, beautifully. Five hundred copies were printed
on "a gorgeous Vidalon vellum, and a hundred copies, which Joyce
signed, on the iridescent miracle called Japon Nacre, literally mother-
of-pearl Japanese vellum paper." Later, Kahane was delighted to see
a copy of the signed edition in a publisher's catalogue with the paper
described as "indecent Japan."[12]

All this cost another Frs. 50,000. The book was published but sold
so poorly that Babou and Kahane faced financial ruin. Kahane saved
the day, however, by managing to off load half the print run on an
American publisher who was a Joyce enthusiast. The deal turned potential disaster into a profitable triumph and brought tears to the di-
minutive Babou's eyes.

In her memoirs, Sylvia Beach recalls Jack Kahane driving up to the bookshop "in his convertible Voisin, a sort of glass-enclosed station wagon. . . . He would ask, 'How's God?' (meaning Joyce). He admired me 'no end' for my discovery of such an 'obscene' book, as he termed it, as *Ulysses,* and never relinquished the hope of persuading me one day to let the Obelisk Press take it over. Meanwhile, he was obliged to be content with an extract from Joyce's new work entitled *Haveth Childers Everywhere,* which Kahane thought lacking in sex interest. Kahane and his partner, M. Babou, brought out a very fine edition of *H.C.E.* and, some time later, of *Pomes Penyeach* with Joyce's daughter Lucia's lettering decorations of the text. . . . I liked him [Kahane] for his good humor and scorn of pretenses."[13]

Kahane did not publish any more of Joyce's work, but the two men became friendly and visited each other. Eric Kahane, Jack's youngest son, who is now one of France's leading translators—he has done everything from Nabokov's *Lolita* to subtitles for the entire "Monty Python" television series—remembers two of his father's star authors less than fondly.

"I had two enemies whom I am very proud of now: Henry Miller and James Joyce," he says in a deep bass voice, enriched by alcohol and tobacco, with an inflection that mirrors his travels—a pinch of Cockney, a dash of Australian, a soupçon of his native French. "Henry Miller became quite a figure around the house. I hated his guts. I thought he was gross. He patted my mother's arse—she was sacred to me—and I could have killed the bastard."

But why Joyce? "Because he spoke French better than my Dad and I, as a young kid, thought that was bad manners. I remember one lovely day in June we picked Joyce up in an old car from the Luxembourg Gardens, where he lived. He and my father got into the backseat and started arguing about French slang—something about is it '*ma cul sur la commode*' or '*mon cul sur le buffet*'?

"Since I spoke French better than either of them I knew the answer, but I didn't want to get involved. But then my father tapped me on the shoulder with his cane and said: 'You tell us what it is.' For a fleeting second I felt total panic. I knew the answer, and I knew that Joyce was right. But I couldn't bear to tell my father that he was wrong so, in a very cowardly way, I said I didn't know. Then they tapped on the glass partition and told the driver to stop the car. He did so and rolled back the glass.

"'Do you say "*ma cul sur la commode*" or "*mon cul sur le buffet*"'? they enquired. The man turned round, a huge black leather cap, enormous blue eyes, bushy white mustache, pink cheeks. He said solemnly:

"'*Barin* ["My lord" in Russian], *moi pas connaître France depuis trois mois*' ["me not know France for three months"].

"He was one of those bloody grand dukes who had left Russia after the revolution!"[14]

Eric Kahane has a more frightening childhood memory of Joyce: "One day I was in his apartment in a long corridor, where I was playing with my toys. Suddenly, the door at the far end opened and Joyce came out to go to the loo at the other end of the corridor. He was just about blind by then, and those huge glasses he wore made him a little frightening. The corridor was very narrow, and he was touching the walls on both sides. I felt trapped and did not want to be seen or touched by him. Thanks to French plumbing there were plenty of lead pipes running up the walls. So I climbed up to the ceiling and hung on for dear life. Just as he passed under me, he reached up, pulled me by the ankle, and threw me down on the floor. 'You shit,' he said, and went on to the toilet."[15]

Not long after he published Joyce, Jack Kahane received a telephone call from D. H. Lawrence. The writer had heard about Obelisk and was calling to see if Kahane would take over the publication of *Lady Chatterley's Lover,* which Lawrence had recently published himself in Florence. Its notoriety and lack of copyright had led to the book being pirated in a number of cheap editions, and Lawrence was desperately seeking a legitimate publisher to produce an inexpensive edition and stop the pirates.

He first tried Sylvia Beach, but she decided against publishing the book. In her memoirs she cites lack of capital, space, personnel, and time. But she also added: "It was difficult to tell him that I didn't want to get a name as a publisher of erotica, and impossible to say that I wanted to be a one-book publisher—what could anybody offer after *Ulysses*?"[16]

Kahane was excited about the idea of publishing Lawrence. *Lady Chatterley's Lover* encapsulated his own notions of sexual freedom as well as representing the struggle of a writer who was fighting the good fight for freedom of expression. But Kahane himself was not a free agent, his hands tied by an increasingly erratic and spendthrift partner. While Kahane had been convalescing at his country home after another bout of illness, Babou had been spending Obelisk's capital and profits in Paris. This was compounded by the stock-market crash of

1929, in which Kahane's father-in-law lost much of his personal fortune.

Kahane thus reluctantly decided that he could not take on *Lady Chatterley's Lover* because he could not guarantee to publish it properly. He explained this to the author and "heard Lawrence's disappointment even over a very bad [telephone] line." Lawrence, who was ill and depressed, assumed that Kahane turned the book down because he was frightened of being prosecuted. It was a misunderstanding that was never cleared up because Lawrence died shortly afterward.[17] Kahane did eventually publish the novel in 1936, thus becoming its third Parisian publisher.

The difficulties with Babou convinced Kahane that he had to find a new partner. His choice was a long-established and well-regarded English printer in Paris called Herbert Clarke. In the summer of 1931 a deal was arranged. Unfortunately, just as it was about to be signed, Clarke died and his French partner, Marcel Servant, took over. The terms of the partnership were promptly tightened, permitting Kahane to publish only two or three books a year, one of which he was expected to write himself.

Under financial pressure and eager to be closer to his business, Kahane put his country house on the market and moved his family into Paris, first to Auteuil and then to the suburb of Neuilly. He was later to set up his office in the elegant Place Vendôme, where, from his window, he had a perfect view of the square with its giant obelisk that was made from melted-down cannons captured in Napoleon's crushing defeat of the Austrians at Austerlitz.

"With the agreement signed," writes Hugh Ford, "Kahane christened the press the Obelisk, thus distinguishing it from Servant's printery known as the Vendôme Press, and . . . designed a colophon for the new press that consisted of an obelisk standing on a book, which, seen in perspective, assumed a vaguely yoni-like shape."[18] The logo was the work of Marcelle Girodias, who was a talented amateur painter.[19]

Obelisk's list was meager: Joyce's slim volume; an outspoken novel, *Sleeveless Errand,* by a young Englishwoman depicting dissolute Bohemian life in London that had been banned in Britain and snatched up by Kahane in Paris; a mediocre French novel that he had taken over from Clarke and translated into English himself; and a new confection called *Daffodil* by himself, which he used to launch the new press.

For his "Gallic" novels, Kahane used the pseudonym "Cecil Barr," a name inspired by drinking in a bar called The Cecil. These books were an easy read, sexually suggestive rather than explicit, and concentrated on the appurtenances of erotic titillation (feminine underwear got plenty of space).

At the start of the new venture, Kahane devised a double-sided strategy. Obelisk would be there for "the convenience of those . . . English and American writers who had something to say that they could not conveniently say in their own countries. The next Lawrence or Joyce who came along would find the natural solution of his difficulties in Paris."[20] The other element was what he called his "flower" books; *Daffodil* and the like would finance the serious books that he intended to find and publish: "I didn't want to be dominated by one type of book, or one literary creed. But I had the curious mental quirk of wanting to make it pay. In which I seemed to be alone amongst publishers in Paris, whose habit, so far as I could see, was to begin a publishing business with or without capital and then run its nose into the ground with all possible speed."[21]

It was this simple formula that underpinned Obelisk and its successor, Olympia, run by Kahane's son, Maurice Girodias, after World War II. The critical factor was the existence of censorship in Britain and the United States and the relative lack of it in France. The formula, applied with vigor and panache by both men, within that highly restrictive context, enabled them to publish a unique and formidable list of great books and dirty books and to carve out their own special niche in literary history.

2

Lesbian Love and Male Fantasy

F OR A TIME, the second part of Kahane's strategy worked better than the first. *Daffodil* sold well and was reprinted many times. But where were the geniuses? Kahane tried Hemingway without success: "He was friendly, he was encouraging, but he was sorry, he was just off to Havana or Central America or the North Pole, for the fishing or the shooting or the fighting, and he did not know whether he would have time to write any more books just for the present. In fact an elusive heavyweight. Hemingway's attitude to all publishers is one of consistent suspicion; they want something he has got and he likes to give them the pleasure of the chase."[1]

Kahane tried Ford Madox Ford, novelist, former editor of the *Transatlantic Review,* and literary man–about–town. Ford introduced him to Gertrude Stein, "complete with her poodle but without Miss Toklas." Kahane was impressed by that redoubtable woman's personality but not by her writing. "I have struggled with Gertrude Stein (strictly figuratively) and have even conjured up a puzzled smile as my eyes have fallen upon such titles as *As a Wife Has a Cow a Love*

Story or *Lucy Church Amiably,* but I am bound to confess that they lie beyond the narrow limits of my comprehension."[2]

The doldrums at Obelisk deepened when Britain went off the gold standard three months after the press began operations. This meant the franc strengthened against the pound and the dollar, making Kahane's books more expensive for British and American tourists, who were his main customers. The tourists were thinning out anyway as political difficulties between France and the Anglo-Saxons developed. Ever resourceful, Kahane concocted a scheme to persuade the French government to back an ambitious advertising scheme to promote France in Britain. He was close to success, having reached the upper levels of the bureaucracy, including the head of the French railways, when antigovernment riots shook Paris and the government fell.

The search for new talent, however, was beginning to produce results. A manuscript from the United States entitled *The Young and the Evil* reached Kahane by a circuitous route in 1932. It was an interracial homosexual novel—thus breaching two taboos—set in Greenwich Village and Harlem in New York. Written as a collaboration by two Americans, Parker Tyler and Charles Henri Ford, the book was enthusiastically endorsed by Gertrude Stein, who compared it somewhat extravagantly to Scott Fitzgerald's *This Side of Paradise.* The manuscript made the rounds of publishers and was universally rejected until it arrived at Obelisk. Kahane liked it and published it the following year. The British Customs seized a shipment of five hundred copies and burned them; the United States government also disapproved and turned back several shipments destined for the American market.

The book gained further attention when Waverley Root of the *Herald Tribune* in Paris criticized the authors for being insensitive about how homosexuals lived. Those looking for dirt, Root warned, would find it. But it would be "very dull dirt" and certainly not new. The authors' friends and admirers of the book, who included the Paris-based novelist Djuna Barnes, struck back. From New York, Parker Tyler suggested that what Root deserved was "simply an old-fashioned thrashing."[3]

That year—1933—was a bumper one for Obelisk. In addition to *The Young and the Evil,* Kahane published *Boy* by James Hanley, *The Well of Loneliness* by Radclyffe Hall, and *My Life and Loves* by Frank Harris. These books had been banned in Britain and the United States. To round the year off, Kahane produced one of his titillating potboilers—*Amour = French for Love*—under the Cecil Barr pseudonym.

Boy, another novel with a homosexual theme, was banned in Britain because it had "pederastic tendencies," notwithstanding a spirited defense of the book by Richard Aldington, the British writer and critic. Aldington argued that the novel had "a poetic sensibility achieved by nobody since Lawrence."[4] Kahane's opinion of the book's quality is not on record, although he described the author somewhat opaquely as "that fine, rugged writer" and had no qualms about publishing the book in 1935.

Radclyffe Hall's famous crusading lesbian novel, *The Well of Loneliness,* had first appeared in Britain in 1928, the same year D. H. Lawrence published *Lady Chatterley's Lover* in Italy. The story mirrors much of Radclyffe Hall's own life. The heroine, named "Stephen" (the author liked to be called "John" by her friends), has an unhappy childhood; she slowly accepts her lesbianism and becomes a successful writer; she has two major love affairs and sets up house with her second lover. But society refuses to accept the couple and the relationship deteriorates and finally collapses. Stephen's lover goes off with a man, leaving the heroine alone and in despair.

Although the entire book is about lesbian love, Radclyffe Hall studiously avoided describing the physical details of lovemaking. The most daring passage is when Stephen has a quarrel with her lover, Mary:

"Stephen stared at her, white and aghast. Then all in a moment the restraint of years was shattered as though by some mighty convulsion. She remembered nothing, was conscious of nothing except that the creature she loved was going.

" 'You child,' she gasped, 'you don't understand, you can't understand—God help me, I love you!' And now she had the girl in her arms and was kissing her eyes and her mouth: 'Mary, Mary.'

"They stood there lost to all sense of time, to all sense of reason, to all things save each other, in the grip of what can be one of the most relentless of all the human emotions. . . .

"Stephen bent down and kissed Mary's hands very humbly, for now she could find no words any more . . . and that night they were not divided."

The book ends with an anguished plea for recognition and tolerance: "Acknowledge us, oh God, before the whole world. Give us also the right to our existence!"[5]

Radclyffe Hall had a miserable childhood. She was an only child who was abandoned by a selfish and feckless father and brought up by an unloving and increasingly hostile mother. But by the time she wrote *The Well of Loneliness,* her fifth novel, she had firmly established herself as a writer. She was also a colorful and prominent figure in London's homosexual demimonde of the 1920s and 1930s.

Inheriting her grandfather's fortune, she was conservative and patrician in most things—she loved riding and hunting—except her sexuality. She always dressed like a man—well-cut suits, bow ties, short hair, and a monocle—and, with her adopted name "John," projected herself as the stereotypical "mannish" lesbian. Living openly with her lovers, she was a fearless if at times overweening campaigner for what would now be called lesbian and gay rights but was then known as "sexual inversion."

Published by Jonathan Cape in 1928, *The Well of Loneliness* appeared to mixed reviews, and early sales were encouraging. But then a storm of protest erupted, led by the editor of the *Sunday Express.* (Curiously, the same paper was to lead the attack on Vladimir Nabokov's *Lolita* almost thirty years later.) A long fire-and-brimstone article was headlined A BOOK THAT MUST BE SUPPRESSED. Flaunting "sexual inversion" in the form of a novel was provocative and inadmissible, the editor wrote. Perversion had already gone too far: "I have seen the plague stalking shamelessly through great social assemblies. I have heard it whispered about by young men and young women who do not and cannot grasp its unutterable putrefaction. Both aspects of it are thrust upon healthy and innocent minds. The contagion cannot be escaped. It pervades our social life. . . . I would rather give a healthy boy or a healthy girl a phial of prussic acid than this novel. Poison kills the body, but moral poison kills the soul."[6]

Radclyffe Hall's biographer, Michael Baker, describes the presentation of the article: "A large photograph of John accompanied [it], showing her in one of her more masculine poses—one hand in the specially-made pocket of her skirt, the other languidly holding a cigarette at waist height—and wearing a gentleman's silk smoking jacket, a high collar and black bow tie. The picture was cut off at the knee, thereby eliminating the stockinged ankles and low heeled shoes which would have softened the severe image."[7]

Other newspapers joined in, and Jonathan Cape wilted under the onslaught. Without telling the author, he offered to submit the novel to the Home Office for approval, effectively stopping publication of the book pending an official reaction. However, while he was hedging his bets in Britain he secretly sent the book's type molds to the Pegasus Press, a Cape associate in Paris. Such was the importance of the mission that Cape's partner made the journey himself, the molds stowed safely in his suitcase. They were handed over to Pegasus, and the French printers began to print a new edition.[8]

A new lease on life for *The Well of Loneliness* in Paris was offset by its extinction in the United States. Alfred Knopf had bought the rights and was planning to publish it when he heard the book had been withdrawn in Britain. Knopf's wife, Blanche, argued that its withdrawal completely changed its image in America: the work would now be viewed as a "dirty book," as pornography. Knopf thus turned it down and advised the author not to seek another publisher in the United States. "The Knopfs were afraid that the heat would now be turned on them," writes Michael Baker. "Rather than face it out, they were prepared to cut their losses—although they wanted no one to take their place."[9]

In Britain the author and publisher were formally charged. In the trial that followed, the defense drummed up writers, editors, sexologists, and even a member of Parliament as expert witnesses, foreshadowing the defense strategy in another celebrated book trial (*Lady Chatterley's Lover*), still thirty years in the future. The writers included E. M. Forster, who had also written a novel on homosexual love— *Maurice*—but not published it, Virginia Woolf, Hugh Walpole, A. P. Herbert, Rose Macaulay, and Storm Jameson.

Havelock Ellis, the eminent psychologist and author of *Sexual Inversion,* a controversial study of homosexuality which argued that homosexuality was inherited and inborn, wrote a "commentary" praising the book. He noted that it was "the first English novel which presents, in a completely faithful and uncompromising form, one particular aspect of sexual life as it exists among us today. . . . The poignant situations which . . . arise are here set forth so vividly, and yet with such complete absence of offence, that we must place Radclyffe Hall's book on a high level of distinction."[10] Ellis allowed his remarks to be published with the book as a preface, but he declined to be a witness.

The trial was a gala affair with forty witnesses for the defense lined up and Radclyffe Hall every inch the star, dressed in a leather motoring coat with astrakhan collar and cuffs and wearing a dark blue Spanish riding hat. One newspaper report described her features as "refined and well-chiselled, the expression in the eyes being one of mingled pain and sadness."[11]

In the final judgment, the magistrate stuck closely to the definition of obscenity that dated back to an act passed in 1857. This meant that a book could be judged obscene on the basis of its theme or intent, even though it contained no indecent words or phrases. Earlier in the trial the magistrate had made it clear whose side he was on by dismissing all forty defense witnesses before they had given their testimony. He did this on the grounds that no *opinion* could constitute evidence and that it was his duty alone to decide whether the book was obscene or not.[12]

During the judgment, the magistrate's own personal prejudice against homosexuality became clear when he referred to "these horrible practices," to "these two people living in filthy sin," and to "acts of the most horrible, unnatural and disgusting obscenity." He concluded by declaring *The Well of Loneliness* an obscene libel and ordered the seized copies to be destroyed.[13]

In Paris Pegasus kept the book in print until the company went out of business in the early 1930s. It was then that Jack Kahane moved in with a sprightly step and published the novel in 1933 under the Obelisk imprint. He sensed that he would not make any money out of it, and he also thought it overrated: "It was not a book that in a literary sense deserved anything like its reputation. . . . But it was a courageous if long-winded defence of a subject the literary discussion of which is still taboo in England."[14]

He was right on both counts, but it did Obelisk no harm because it nourished the growing reputation of Kahane's imprint as the standard-bearer of fearless publishing and sexual liberation. More important, the book's social importance compensated for what it lacked in artistry. It raised the issue of lesbianism in particular, and less directly male homosexuality, in a society that was reluctant to accept either. Its roller-coaster career through the courts and publishing world made a significant contribution to liberating the written word in Britain and the United States. The book also came to be regarded as a groundbreaking work in the feminist canon.

The Well of Loneliness was not published again in Britain until 1949, six years after Radclyffe Hall's death, at which time the book was selling about 100,000 copies a year worldwide. The long road from the 1928 trial to a British seal of acceptability finally came in 1974, when "John"'s painful manifesto was read in seventeen episodes on the BBC's "Book at Bedtime" program.

It had better luck in the United States, where another publisher, Covici Friede, took it on after Knopf backed down. The publisher was prosecuted, lost, and then won on appeal. Gallimard put it out in French, thus making Radclyffe Hall its first woman author.[15]

• • •

Kᴀʜᴀɴᴇ's ꜰɪɴᴀʟ ᴘᴜʙʟɪᴄᴀᴛɪᴏɴ ɪɴ 1933 was a totally different affair. After publishing James Joyce's *Ulysses,* Sylvia Beach discovered that she had, quite unintentionally, acquired a reputation for being interested in erotica. She remembers a day when "a small man with whiskers" drove up to her bookshop in a carriage—"a barouche and pair hired for the occasion to impress me, as he afterward confessed. His long arms swinging apelike in front of him, he walked into the shop, deposited on my table a parcel that had the look of a manuscript, and introduced himself as Frank Harris."

Sylvia Beach was familiar with some of Harris's work, notably books on Shakespeare and Oscar Wilde that she had read and liked. She asked Harris what his manuscript was about: "He undid the parcel and showed me a thing called *My Life and Loves,* which he assured me went much further than Joyce. He claimed he was really the only English writer who had got 'under a woman's skin.'" He certainly got under hers, for Miss Beach was neither interested nor amused. "I suggested that he try Jack Kahane, who was always looking for 'hot books,' and *My Life and Loves* found a happy home at the Obelisk Press."[16]

I remember first reading parts of Harris's notorious autobiography—certainly one of the "hot books" of my generation—and thought the author was as fictional as the content. The four volumes recount the putative adventures of Frank Harris as intrepid traveler, historical eyewitness, interlocutor and confidant of the great and the powerful, and swordsman extraordinary. His sexual adventures across the globe, which leave nothing to the imagination, alternate regularly and with increasing monotony with the rest of the material. The chapter titles alone give a good idea of Harris's style: "Student Life and Love"; "Some Study, More Love"; "Goethe, William I, Bismarck, Wagner"; "The Ebb and Flow of Passion!"; "Memories of Guy de Maupassant"; "A Passionate Experience in Paris"; "Queen Victoria and Prince Edward"; "Dark Beauties"; "Sex and Self-Restraint."

It was a surprise to learn later that Harris was a real person, something that his talent for distortion and obfuscation does much to disguise.

"Frank Harris was born in two different countries on three different dates and his name was not Frank Harris," writes Vincent Brome, one of his biographers, his ire beginning to rise as early as page nine. (This book, incidentally, is entitled *Frank Harris: The Life and Loves of a Scoundrel* and turns out to be more sympathetic and understanding than it initially sounds.)[17]

Harris was born in Ireland in 1856 and baptized "James Thomas Harris." He did travel widely as he recounts in his autobiography, and he did become a successful journalist, reviewer, and writer in late Victorian London. He was a notable editor of the *Saturday Review* and the *Fortnightly Review* and also edited the London *Evening News*. Sylvia Beach's praise for two of his nonfiction books is noteworthy; he did hobnob with the famous, the rich, and the influential in London's literary and political salons, and he was erudite and witty.

"There were many Harrises," writes Vincent Brome. "There was the serious writer and editor; there was the man who could play the lover, politician, actor and man of action, when he chose, with equal conviction; and when he chose, above all, he could enthrall an audience, pouring out wit, ideas, comments, throwing off long quotations from the poets and the Bible in a voice, which, if it did not please everyone, could not be ignored. It was an extraordinary voice."[18]

Oscar Wilde recalled staying in the same Paris hotel as Harris, who was lodged four floors above. He wrote: "Frank Harris is here thinking about God, Shakespeare and Frank Harris at the top of his voice."

Harris had to be noticed. His appearance was one way of ensuring a sighting. "Short of stature, he wore two inch heels on his shoes to increase his height and compensated for other inferiorities with a voice like thunder and a Napoleonic vehemence," wrote Brome. "He clothed his barrel-chested body in carefully tailored suits, butterfly collar, spats, and a gold watch chain, and his moustaches swung twelve inches apart like those of a vintage movie villain."[19] (Harris's tailor in New York was Henry Miller's father.)

Harris cut a swath through society. George Bernard Shaw called him "the most impossible ruffian on the face of this earth."[20] Oscar Wilde observed that Harris had been to "all the great houses of England—once."[21] Although a social misfit and rebel, Harris had talent, Vincent Brome points out, not as a novelist but as an editor: "He was remarkable and brought those uneasy bedfellows literature and journalism into a synthesis seldom realized since his day."[22] Another biographer, Philippa Pullar, highlights his human qualities: "the loyal friend and companion, risking his reputation to support Oscar Wilde;

obsessed totally by his wife, Nellie; and acting as a catalyst for young writers."[23]

Harris's most lasting way of drawing attention to himself was the work that tragically eclipsed his human and literary qualities, his autobiography. Pullar wrote: "When one learns that the [four] volumes were dictated between 1921 and 1927 to a series of secretaries most of whom were in love with Harris (who was by then impotent), all of whom he hoped to titillate, it becomes clear that most of the sexual scenes are fantasy, a requiem for lost youth and virility. Nor is the autobiography helped by its author's tone, which is earnest and without humor, making much of the writing delightfully (if unintentionally) comic."[24]

Harris did not take Sylvia Beach's advice immediately. Instead, he published, distributed, and marketed his own book. The dirty bits were printed in detachable chapters that could be easily removed for concealment or destruction. The whole exercise was a disastrous experiment, as Hugh Ford comments: "Besides seeing his profits drastically reduced by pirates whose clandestine editions of the books he was powerless to halt, he had watched, with alarm, the steady depletion of his capital, the decline of his reputation, the loss of his friends, and the erosion of his once-substantial reading public."[25]

Harris then turned to Jack Kahane, who had met him just before World War I. They had had dinner in a notable French restaurant in London. Harris greeted the maître d'hôtel warmly. "You remember, Henri," Harris roared, "that dinner I gave at Monte Carlo to the Grand Duke Dimitri?" They chatted for a while, Kahane listening to their brilliant conversation, "half daft with admiration and envy."[26] The next day Henri confided to Kahane that he had never seen Frank Harris in his life nor had he ever been to Monte Carlo.

Kahane thus knew what he was dealing with when he signed a contract with Harris to publish *My Life and Loves* in 1931. Harris died the same year, and Obelisk published his book two years later. A fifth, unfinished installment was included in the deal. This, however, was not to appear until the 1950s, when Maurice Girodias, who described Harris as "a cosmic monument of sexo-journalistic literary bombast," enlisted one of his star pornographers to do some creative editing and published it as the fifth volume.

It seems that Harris's main reason for writing these overblown and largely apocryphal memoirs was financial, and the best way to succeed was to make them sensational. "If Frank did the things he describes in his books," his wife once said, "he did them on the running board of our car as we drove across France together."[27] A second motive was an attempt to put the record straight about his role in the great events of his time. But, as Philippa Pullar puts it, the result was a double failure:

"His fear, paranoia and disappointment obliterated everything but his posturing in more and more fabulous scenes. His fantasies rose superior to self-interest, flew independent of copyright. However tall his stories, they were brought down at every frontier—then pirated. . . . Ironically, he castrated his own life."[28]

3

Henry, Anaïs,
Larry & Co.

KAHANE'S REVELATORY EXPERIENCE with Henry Miller's manuscript on that summer's day under the copper beech tree in 1932 turned out to be the beginning of a long and arduous publishing saga. *Tropic of Cancer* had reached Kahane through William A. Bradley, an influential American literary agent based in Paris. Miller gave Bradley two books to handle, *Crazy Cock,* which he had written in the United States, and *Tropic of Cancer,* written in Paris. Bradley thought *Cancer* "magnificent" but was silent about *Crazy Cock.* He warned Miller that there would be problems publishing *Cancer,* but he knew one man who would be courageous enough to take it on. Bradley passed the manuscript to Jack Kahane.

Kahane, however, immediately ran into difficulties. By his own account, the main problems were the reluctance of Marcel Servant, his new printer-partner, and a shortage of money. Servant said the book, which people would think was a medical treatise, would not sell. What the public wanted was sex, dressed up, or in the gradual process of being undressed. *Tropic of Cancer* would be an expensive book to produce and a risky one to sell. The tourist market had dried up, and who was Henry Miller anyway?[1] Servant answered his own question with the conjecture that Miller was a "down-and-out Montparnasse reject who would demand advances on royalties and make scenes because his book was not selling a thousand copies a week."[2]

Seeking ammunition to convince his partner that *Cancer* deserved to be published, Kahane showed the book to an editor friend at the large French publisher Hachette. The editor confirmed that Miller was unquestionably "a powerful and formidable writer," and *Cancer* made *Ulysses* and *Lady Chatterley's Lover* look like "lemonade." He advised Kahane to publish the book but replace the Obelisk colophon with the words "Privately Printed." "Obelisk Press" could appear, in minute letters, at the back of the book.[3]

Miller's first reaction to Kahane's enthusiasm was brimming confidence, sensing that his years of obscurity were ending and fame and fortune were around the corner.[4] He told Anaïs Nin, whom he had met at the end of 1931 and who was to become by turns companion, lover, and literary soulmate, that he felt he was not going to like Kahane. "I'm not going to let the book go for a song . . . I'm not going to let Kahane get the idea that he's doing me a favor by publishing it. I expect to treat him rough."[5]

Kahane eventually prevailed over his partner's doubts, and in the autumn of 1932 a deal for *Tropic of Cancer,* with an option on Miller's next two works, was concluded. Miller had already carried out some revisions of the book, which both Bradley and Kahane liked. Publication date was set for February 1933. "It would hardly make a good Christmas gift,"[6] Kahane noted.

Miller had arrived in Paris in 1930. Nearly forty years old, he was a writer who had never been published, a man who had worked at many jobs but had no money, a husband whose second marriage was failing, in short, a man whose life seemed adrift without navigational aids or moorings. Two years later he was to comment, "I hate Montparnasse, being referred to as an intellectual, being forty, wearing glasses, and being bald."[7] Nevertheless, the alchemy of Paris and the expatriate crowd among whom he lived fused inspiration, material, and style.

Tropic of Cancer poured out, an explosive burst of creative energy, a flood of idiosyncratic prose chronicling his experiences, his fears, his joys, his rage, his friends (none of them favorably portrayed), and his obsessions. The voice is powerful, the language rough, tough, and crude. There is plenty of sex in *Tropic of Cancer,* but that is not the central point. Miller said that *Cancer* was not a book "in the ordinary sense of the word. No, this is a prolonged insult, a gob of spit in the face of Art, a kick in the pants to God, Man, Destiny, Time, Love, Beauty . . . what you will. I am going to sing for you, a little off key perhaps, but I will sing. I will sing while you croak, I will dance over your dirty corpse." He explained later that what he was trying to do was different from other writers, who were struggling to get down what they had in their heads. He was struggling to get down "what was below, in the solar plexus, in the nether regions."[8]

It also turned out to be a struggle to get into print. Having overcome his partner's doubts, Kahane seems to have been afflicted by a rash of his own. The financial and censorship implications of publishing *Tropic of Cancer* held him back, so he prevaricated. Before going ahead with the book, he suggested that Miller should write an essay on D. H. Lawrence or James Joyce to make the point that he was a literary figure, not a pornographer.

Miller at first angrily rejected the idea but then decided not only to do it but to turn it into a full-fledged book about both Lawrence and Joyce, with Proust and other writers added for good measure. He called this ambitious enterprise the "*Brochure*" and threw himself into the project with characteristic energy. When Kahane told him that the exercise might not be necessary after all, Miller declared that he was determined to go ahead with it, which he did, only to abandon it finally a decade later.

During these delays Miller was revising, editing, and polishing *Tropic of Cancer*. The book was reduced to a third of its original length; sentimentality was pared down and action beefed up. "Weeding out shit. Putting in new shit" was how Miller described it to a friend.[9] Miller had also begun work on a new book called *Black Spring*. Meanwhile, his relationship with Anaïs Nin deepened. She was a constant presence—at his side, in his bed (or, more often, in her bed with him), writing to him (and, of course, in her diary), plotting and planning ways of having *Cancer* published.

Since he had not brought *Cancer* out within the year specified in the contract, Kahane asked Bradley for a six-month extension, which was granted. Whenever Miller complained, Kahane would explain that the worldwide economic depression—not to mention his own— made it impossible for him to publish *Cancer*. Relations between publisher and author fluctuated as Miller, after showing considerable patience, began to wonder if the book would ever be published. The problem was the lack of an alternative; there was nowhere else to go.

After another six months had gone by, Miller became desperate.

He broke with his agent, denouncing him as an old man who got sadistic pleasure out of criticizing younger men.[10] His frustration was shared by Anaïs Nin. "Jack Kahane has failed in business as well as in true loyalty to Henry," she wrote in her diary. "I will pay for publication of Cancer."[11]

Before matching deed to word, however, she went to London in April 1934 to look for another publisher. She returned to Paris empty-handed. Two months later she walked into Kahane's office and said she would pay all the printing costs if he would publish Cancer. He agreed, and she paid him an advance of Frs. 5,000 (about $330). Nin told Miller that the money had come from her wealthy banker husband, Hugh Guiler. But he learned later that Otto Rank, the Austrian psychologist who had worked with Freud in Vienna and then broken with him, had provided the money. Nin had started analysis with Rank in 1933, sessions that began on the couch and ended in the bed.[12]

Before the book was published, Kahane thought it should have a preface to warn the reader about its inflammatory nature. Miller wrote it himself, probably in collaboration with Nin, and she signed it:

"In a world grown paralysed with introspection and constipated by delicate mental meals this brutal exposure of the substantial body comes as a vitalising current of blood. The violence and obscenity are left unadulterated, as manifestation of the mystery of pain which ever accompanies the act of creation. . . . This book brings with it a wind that blows down the dead and hollow trees whose roots are withered and lost in the barren soil of our times. This book goes to the roots and digs under, digs for subterranean springs."[13]

The cover design, depicting a huge crab holding a naked woman in its claws, was as startling as it was original. Keeping things in the family, it was drawn by Kahane's fifteen-year-old son, Maurice, who recalled that his father's "progenitive pride must have blinded him when he decided to use that foolish piece of schoolboy art . . . for a book he regarded so highly."[14] At the bottom was the legend "Not to be imported into Great Britain or U.S.A." Each copy carried a paper band that said the book was not to be displayed in booksellers' windows.

In September 1934, over two years after Kahane had first read the manuscript, Tropic of Cancer was published. Miller set to work to help his publisher promote the book. Wholesalers would not distribute it, booksellers treated it as though it were "a lump of gelignite," and sales were disappointingly slow. "But Henry Miller did not mind,"

Kahane recalls. "He was serenely confident. He would come and encourage me. He did not want money, he had solved the question of living without money. . . . Only one thing interested him, that people should read his book. He wrote thousands of letters. . . . He was the most useful collaborator a book publisher ever had."[15]

Hugh Ford recounts in his book *Published in Paris* that Kahane "spent the post-publication months in a state of unrelieved apprehension."[16] But any fears he had of proscription by the French authorities proved to be groundless. It was different in Britain and the United States, where *Cancer* was promptly banned. Like many of the Obelisk titles, the book became a piece of contraband to be smuggled into both countries and distributed clandestinely from hand to hand, in brown paper wrappers, and sold furtively from under bookshop counters.

Miller himself mailed off copies to scores of influential literary people. The general response was favorable. T. S. Eliot called it "a rather magnificent piece of work"; Aldous Huxley thought it "a bit terrifying but well-done"; Ezra Pound hailed it as "a dirty book worth reading." He pronounced Miller "sane and without kinks." Within a year of its publication, *Cancer* had become an underground classic.[17]

But there it was to remain for almost thirty years. It was not until 1961, when Miller was approaching seventy years of age, that *Cancer* was published by Grove Press in the United States, and not until 1963 when it was put out by John Calder in Britain. Even then, Miller's American publisher had to fight a titanic legal battle, involving sixty lawsuits, to save the book. The struggle ended in victory at the Supreme Court in 1964, a landmark case in the history of freedom of expression that virtually ended censorship of the written word in the United States.

Miller lived for another eleven years, made a lot of money, and became a celebrity in his lifetime. After his death the manuscript of *Tropic of Cancer* was sold for $165,000, the highest price ever paid for a twentieth-century literary work. "Financial homage was paid to the victory of literature over censorship at Sotheby's in New York on Friday," wrote a London *Times* correspondent describing the sale.[18] Obelisk first editions of *Cancer* have also become valuable, commanding as much as $9,000 a copy.

A FTER *Cancer,* Kahane published three more of Miller's books, *Black Spring* (1936), the most overtly autobiographical of his works; *Max and the White Phagocytes* (1938), a collection of short stories and essays; and *Tropic of Capricorn* (1939), which was set in the United States and centered on his relationship with his second wife, June. The Miller connection brought Kahane two more new authors, both of whom were to achieve literary fame. They were Anaïs Nin herself and a young British writer named Lawrence Durrell.

In the early 1930s, Nin had begun work on a novel that she was to call *House of Incest,* which was loosely based on her triangular relationship with Henry and June. As industrious as Miller himself, she began a second book, *The Winter of Artifice,* before she had finished the first. This novella was a strongly autobiographical story of a man who abandons his wife and young daughter for twenty years and then returns to seek reconciliation with the daughter.

She approached Kahane in 1935, after the publication of *Cancer,* with a view to having both her novels published by Obelisk. He accepted *The Winter of Artifice* but declined *House of Incest.* Nothing happened, however, until 1939, when the first book was finally published and then only after Durrell had agreed to pay the printing costs. Nin published *House of Incest* herself under the Siana imprint—Anaïs reversed—which she had established with Miller and other friends.

Kahane and Nin are strangely silent about each other in print. In her voluminous diaries, she only mentions him briefly in connection with Miller and *Cancer.* In *Memoirs of a Booklegger,* Kahane does not mention her at all. The only possible, oblique reference occurs when he writes: "I would like one day to publish the correspondence of one woman writer I had the misfortune to publish. As a specimen of concentrated, virulent hysteria it must be unique. This woman had nothing against me except that I refused her second book."[19] Kahane's own days were to come to an end, alas, before that day arrived.

Lawrence Durrell was living on the island of Corfu in Greece when he read *Tropic of Cancer.* He was so impressed by the book that he wrote to Miller in Paris, thus launching a forty-five-year correspondence, an enduring literary friendship, and a chain of events that would lead to the publication of Durrell's first serious novel.

Twenty years younger than his hero, Durrell believed that Miller had surpassed all his contemporaries, including Eliot and Joyce. "Dear Mr. Miller," he wrote in 1935, "I have just read *Tropic of Cancer* again and feel I'd like to write you a line about it. It strikes me as being the only really man-size piece of work which this century can really boast of. It's a howling triumph from the word go; and not only is it a literary and artistic smack on the bell for everyone, but it really gets down on paper the blood and bowels of our time. . . . I did not imagine anything like it could be written; and yet, curiously, reading it I seemed to recognise it as something which I knew we were all ready for. . . .

"I salute *Tropic* as the copy-book of my generation. . . . [It] goes straight up among those books (and they are precious few) which men have built out of their own guts."[20]

Miller replied immediately: "Dear Mr. Durrell: . . . You're the first Britisher who's written me an intelligent letter about the book. For that matter, you're the first anybody who's hit the nail on the head. I particularly prize your letter because it's the kind of letter I would have written myself had I not been the author of the book. That isn't just sheer vanity and egotism, believe me. It's curious how few people know *what* to admire in the book.

"The phrase that struck me particularly, in your letter, was—'I seem to recognise it as something we were all ready for.' That's just it. The world is ready for something different, something new, but it seems that it requires a war or some colossal calamity to make people realize it.

"Your letter is so vivid, so keen, that I am curious to know if you are not a writer yourself."[21]

Durrell was indeed a writer, an aspiring novelist, but at that point his only published work was a small booklet of poetry. Later that year, however, his first novel, *The Pied Piper of Lovers,* was published in Britain, and a second, *Panic Spring,* under the pseudonym Charles Norden, appeared in 1937. (The last name was taken from a character called Van Norden in *Tropic of Cancer.*) Durrell was not proud of either book—the first he dismissed as "a cheap romance, wishy-washy stuff"—but he seemed eager to cut his writer's teeth and get into print.[22]

Durrell's main preoccupation was reworking a manuscript that he called *The Black Book* or *A Chronicle of the English Death.* It is the story of the lives, loves, and lusts of an assorted group of seedy and Bohemian people set in a residential London hotel in the early 1930s. Durrell paints a bleak urban landscape: "Fog over the gardens. Fog, marching down among the pines, making dim stone those parcels of Greek statuary. In the distance trains burrowing their tunnels of smoke and discord. Lights shine out wanly against the buildings. The red-nosed commercials will be lining up in the bar for their drinks. I can see the whisky running into their red mouths, under the tabby whiskers, like urine. I sit here . . . smoking, and eating the soft skin on the sides of my cheeks. The customary madness of the suburban evening comes down over us in many enormous yawns. . . . The clock whirrs inside its greenhouse of glass and the Japanese fans breathe a soft vegetable decay into the room. There is nothing to do, nothing to be done."

The novel was strongly influenced by *Tropic of Cancer,* and Durrell wrote to his literary mentor saying that he was trying to "demillerise" it. "Unhealthy influence you are, whatever positive virtues you have. Sticks like fluff."[23] When it was finished, he sent his only typescript of the novel to Miller with the advice to "pitch it into the Seine" after reading it.

Miller responded: "*The Black Book* came and I have opened it and I read goggle-eyed, with terror, admiration and amazement. . . . You are *the* master of the English language—stupendous reaches, too grand almost for any book. . . . You have written things in this book which nobody has dared to write. It's brutal, obsessive, cruel, devastating, appalling. I'm bewildered still."[24] Durrell wrote back, "Your praise rings in my ear like the silver hammers of quinine, and I'm covered in sweat and glory."[25]

Durrell had a contract with Faber & Faber in London for his next two books. He thought *The Black Book* would be rejected out of hand, but, to his surprise, the firm liked it and wanted to publish it, providing the author would assent to "an altered edition" for the British market. T. S. Eliot, a director of the firm, went out of his way to praise the book, describing it as "the first piece of work by a new English writer to give me any hope for the future of prose fiction."[26]

Miller told Durrell that only one publisher would take the book on as it stood: Jack Kahane. Unfortunately, he added, Kahane "is rather set against you. . . . Seems he doesn't like anyone who admires me too much. Curious thing that, but a fact. Sort of professional jealousy. (He writes too you know, under the name of Cecil Barr— vile vile crap, the vilest of the vile—and he admits it, but with that English insouciance that makes my blood creep.) But, if you assent, I will try him. I will wheedle and cajole and jig for him, if necessary— because I believe in it wholeheartedly. And I see no one else on the horizon."[27]

Durrell decided to accept Faber's offer for an expurgated version in Britain with the hope that Miller's jigging with Kahane would result in the publication of the undoctored version in Paris. But when he told Miller of his plan, the older man vehemently opposed it:

"Frankly, I am not in accord with you about accepting Faber's plan, just because it is a *pis aller* [last resort]. No, with that logic, that attitude, you'll always be fucked good and proper. Don't you see, according to *their* logic, you *must* conform—because they control the situation. But the moment you say the hell with that and decide to do as you damn please you find the man to sponsor you. Yes, as you say, our fancy weathercock [Kahane] may turn down your book—it will be Greek to him, that I can tell you in advance. But, canny bugger that he is, he may decide to publish and blow you to the skies because a few others have seen merit in your work. One never knows with such guys. But, anyway, whether he refuses or rejects, whether you lose out permanently with Faber or not, all that is beside the point— that is their affair. Yours is with your own conscience. On that grain of faith on which you built your book you must rest. You stand firm and let the world come round."[28]

Durrell took Miller's advice and rejected Faber's offer. But then agonizing delays with Kahane followed. Miller kept up the pressure and wrote regularly to Durrell in Greece: "I have had many a talk with Kahane, good ones and bad ones, and I see into the whole situation realistically, I think. *You* couldn't do much better yourself. His way, which is the cunning English way of watching and waiting and nibbling off a piece here and there—is perhaps the *only* way in these times."[29]

In August 1937, Durrell and his wife went to Paris and he had his first joyous and boisterous meeting with his mentor. (Miller was to make a return visit to Greece a year later, a trip that produced *The Colossus of Maroussi,* for many his finest book.) Durrell also met Anaïs Nin and the rest of the Miller-Nin entourage. Kahane, meanwhile, had read *The Black Book* and declared that he was "impressed." But he again wanted someone else to put up the printing costs, and again Nin came to the rescue. (Durrell, of course, was to return the favor later when he financed the publication of *House of Incest.*) Durrell finished editing the book; Miller put aside *Tropic of Capricorn,* and, with Nin's help, retyped the manuscript with copies for Herbert Read and T. S. Eliot in London. Kahane followed through, and *The Black Book* was published in 1938.

The novel was reissued in Paris in 1959 by Kahane's son and successor, Maurice Girodias, under the Olympia imprint, and first published in the United States in 1960 after Durrell's *Alexandria Quartet* had become a best-seller. Faber & Faber, who remained Durrell's British publisher all his life, finally "came around" to doing it in 1973.

A year after Obelisk put out the first edition in Paris, Kahane commented: "I have no doubt that Durrell will go far indeed. He is very young and has not yet shaken off all the traces of the influences that have gone to form him, but to my mind he will in a very short time indeed be looked upon as one of the most important of living English writers, as Henry Miller is abundantly one of the most important of Americans."[30]

Durrell fulfilled Kahane's prediction with the success of his *Alexandria Quartet* in the 1950s, his marvelous Mediterranean books on Corfu, Rhodes, and Cyprus, his poetry, essays, and other novels. But *The Black Book* always held a special place for him. In the Olympia edition Durrell wrote a preface explaining why. The novel was "a two-fisted attack on literature by an angry young man of the thirties. With all its imperfections lying heavy on its head, I can't help being attached to it because in the writing of it I first heard the sound of my own voice, lame and halting perhaps, but nevertheless my very own. . . . I did not wish for notoriety, and was content simply to have heard my own voice."[31]

The Oxford Companion to English Literature later described *The Black Book* as "a mildly pornographic fantasia, peopled by prostitutes and failed artists." But as the poet and writer David Gascoyne has pointed out, this judgment ignores "the exceptional vitality, virtuosity and zest of its language."[32]

A similar view was taken by John Unterecker in a critical study of Durrell's work. "The writing of [*The Black Book*] was in an odd way both a consequence of spiritual agony and a labour of love. For Durrell had no expectation that any publisher would risk bringing out a book so savage in spirit and so uncompromising in language."[33]

Henry Miller put it more succinctly: "*The Black Book* was not his first book. But it was the first book he wrote with his right hand."[34]

Kahane published one other book of note and one curiosity before war and death ended the Obelisk adventure. The first was Cyril Connolly's novel *The Rock Pool*. Kahane was in England discussing the possibility of publishing some letters of Henry James when he met Connolly, who had been suggested as an editor for the letters. Kahane thought Connolly "a lovely talker, with a great appreciation of hospitality, and a robust interest in the finer facets of cooking."

The James project did not materialize, but before he left, Connolly whispered to Kahane that he had written a "forbidden" book, which had been rejected by publishers in Britain.

"I at once offered to put it out," Kahane records, and Connolly duly sent him the manuscript. This reversal of the normal decision-making process in publishing typified Kahane's unorthodox methods. He was not disappointed, however: "It was as sweet a piece of writing as I ever have seen, the work of an exquisite, steeped in the classics, and in certain ways a model of impropriety. Its only fault was that it dealt with a period that was no longer of any interest—the raffish days of 1929 amongst the inhabitants of Montparnasse during their summer migration to the south of France."[35] Connolly's novel-writing debut met with disappointing sales, but it elicited a two-column-long review by Desmond MacCarthy in the *Sunday Times* of London, which did Obelisk no harm.[36]

The second book was *To Beg I Am Ashamed* by Sheila Cousins, the memoirs of a London prostitute. The book had been accepted by a respected British publisher, attacked by the popular press before it appeared, and withdrawn. It was a classic Obelisk scenario. Kahane moved in and published the book in 1938. It proved to be a great success, going into many printings and still selling well after the war.

The interesting thing about the book, a straightforward and only mildly salacious account of London lowlife in the 1930s, is that a theory has been put forward that it was ghostwritten by Graham Greene. His involvement was only recently mooted, but it has already enormously enhanced the value of the book. In the mid-1980s the original Obelisk edition was selling for five pounds ($7.50); today the book fetches five hundred pounds ($750).

JACK KAHANE died on September 2, 1939, a day after war was declared. Rebuffed in his attempt to rejoin the army, he took to his bed, where, it is said, he downed a bottle of one of his adopted country's finest brandies and expired.

Kahane was not the greatest of publishers. His formula of mixing books banned or in trouble in Britain, manuscripts picked up in Paris, and his own frothy potboilers produced an unorthodox list marred by dubious taste and of uneven literary quality. ("One publisher's poison is another publisher's meat," he was fond of saying.) He was neither as brave nor as perceptive as his rambunctious, albeit engaging autobiography would have the reader believe.

With his authors he was often economical with the truth, leading them to believe something was happening when nothing was, and he was careful not to put his own money on the line when he could find someone to take the financial risk. He was more worried about the possibility of being prosecuted by the French government than he ever admitted, although his fears were never realized.

That said, Booklegger Jack and the Obelisk Press constituted a unique and remarkable phenomenon that led the *Bookseller* to call the press "the most adventurous publishing house in the world." The evidence lies in the literary core of the Obelisk list: Joyce, Hall, Miller, Nin, Durrell, Connolly. Kahane knew a good book when he saw one, although he himself—as he was the first to admit—wrote bad ones. He believed in his self-appointed crusade to seek out and publish new authors who had something new to say and the talent to say it well.

Money was important, but it was not the driving force behind his publishing venture. He exploited books that appealed to the prurient for the benefit of authors who challenged contemporary morality and literary orthodoxy. For that, Jack Kahane deserves a headstone in the pantheon of the written word.

His most famous authors, especially Miller, Nin, and Durrell, often said unpleasant things about their publisher—what author does not?—or were silently dismissive. But in retrospect they gave him credit for what he had done when no one else would publish their work. Talking many years later about the birth pangs of *Tropic of Cancer,* Miller said: "It was something of a miracle that I found in Paris the one publisher in all the world courageous enough to sponsor such a book: Jack Kahane and the Obelisk Press."[37]

4

Enter Maurice Girodias

JACK KAHANE'S DEATH was a double shock to his family. It was unexpected—he was only fifty-two years old—and a war, with all its uncertainties, had just begun. The Kahanes had been living precariously since Marcelle's father lost most of his money in the stock market and in other financial ventures. Jack had been the only breadwinner and with him disappeared the family's principal source of income. In addition to her four children, Marcelle Kahane had her aged parents to look after. The new paterfamilias was the eldest son, Maurice, a slim, solemn twenty-year-old who was a vegetarian, a theosophist who believed in reincarnation, and a rebel. He was half English, half Jewish, and the Germans were coming.

A new world had to be created out of what was left of the old one, Girodias recalled later in his life. His mother's "twenty-four-year-old affair with a stranger whose language she never really understood had come abruptly to an end. The man to whom she had devoted all the power of her love had now abandoned her for the last time. . . . And so she was left with those children, their children; including myself, a semi-grownup, an undecipherable individual who was at the same time a partial replica of Jack, her husband, and the resurgence of Maurice, her brother. The two men in her life, the first love and the last: This had given as a product Maurice, her son."[1]

Describing his early years, Girodias wrote that he "awoke to the light of life under the sign of Aries with Leo in the ascendant . . . in the mellow comfort of my French grandparents' apartment on Avenue du Bois, now the Avenue Foch." His first years were "spent in the quiet luxury of drapes and lace, velvet and gilt, Louis XV furniture and Chinese art, rich smells of Sunday roasts and the whiffs of lavender coming from the linen closet. Far below, under the tall trees bordering the Avenue, red-faced nurses from Auvergne or Brittany were pushing baby carriages filled with the hope of France, and eyeing gauche soldiers from under their bonnets; immaculate horsemen were torturing their mounts for the benefit of a pale lady, mysterious in the shade of a frilly parasol."[2]

Growing up in the Kahane country house, Maurice seems to have been a lonely child, notwithstanding the company of three younger siblings and a caring mother. In his autobiography, *The Frog Prince,* he tells two stories that provide an insight into his character and, in an uncanny way, foreshadow events in later life. The first one occurred at about eight years of age at the time, he claims, when he first discovered the joys of masturbation through a serendipitous hole in his trouser pocket. This had happened as he was strolling in the garden on a particularly sunny and sensuous day.

When his mind was not on sex, however, it was on building houses. He began by constructing a wooden hut, added another floor, liked the look of it, added a third floor, and, to round it off, put a loggia on the roof. Before inviting guests, he tested the house by persuading his two sisters (aged four and three) to join him on the top floor. Once there, they hauled up baby Eric (eighteen months), who, "drooling and philosophical," accepted this treatment "with equanimity." Whereupon the wind rose, it began to rain, and Maurice Girodias's first castle in the sky crashed to the ground. Fortunately, nobody was hurt, but that night his parents opted for the British solution and packed their sexually and architecturally precocious son off to boarding school.[3]

The second escapade happened at this school, where Maurice spent four difficult years. Appalled at the chauvinistic way of teaching history between the world wars, Girodias persuaded two other boys to join him in a secret society to fight war propaganda. He devised an unusual form of protest that would involve removing the offensive history books during the night and replacing them with an antiwar, antinationalist manifesto and a sum of money equal to their value.

Girodias provided the money, and the campaign began. Everything proceeded according to plan, but instead of the expected uproar— "the local press would be informed and would give our manifesto the publicity it deserved; then the Paris papers would break the story"— there was no reaction at all. Becoming suspicious, he accused his partners of sneaking back to the classrooms, replacing the books, destroying the pamphlets, and pocketing the money. They denied it and accused him of being the traitor. And so it ended: the revolution a failure, good intentions thwarted, betrayal by those in whom you placed your trust.[4]

When the family moved to Paris, Maurice was reprieved and sent to the local lycée. Now a callow teenager, he joined the Theosophical Society and became interested in Buddhism. This did not go down well with his father, who had been brought up as a Protestant but was not much interested in religion of any kind. "My father was deeply irritated by any reference whatever to things spiritual, just as he could hardly bear having a son who was a total vegetarian, whereas he himself was such a dedicated meat-eater that he refused to touch vegetables. He had found me once or twice in the lotus position, in my room, and had flown into a rage. An impotent rage that is, because how can you forbid your son to meditate? It's not like stealing old ladies' purses."[5]

Marcelle Kahane, brought up as a Catholic, had also become interested in theosophy but kept it to herself for the sake of domestic peace. This was not the case with her mother, Mamita. She, according to Maurice, saw her grandson not only as her own dead son's reincarnation but also as "the avatar of some celestial personality."

" 'My son the Bodhisattva,' my father would fulminate, overcome with exasperation. 'The thirteenth sign of the zodiac. He's a dunce at Latin, mathematics, Greek—at everything. You don't find this extraordinary, Mamita, for a demigod to be the last of his class?'

"My grandmother would then look at me inquiringly, uncertainly. Her need to believe was stronger than the flickering flame of her modest intelligence."

The only thing that seems to have given Jack Kahane some hope was Maurice's proficiency at French, a language that he still spoke imperfectly but which he admired. His father's enthusiasm for publishing, Girodias recalls, had taken a more concrete turn at this time: "perhaps he was dreaming of a dynasty of publishers?"[6]

Laurette Buzon, who was later to become Girodias's first wife, remembers him as a teenager: "I went round to their house once and his father told me that Maurice had run away from home. He was very shocked by the fact that he had not even taken his toothbrush. He put his monocle in his eye when he said this, as he often did when there was a problem. I think Jack loved Maurice a lot but there was no tenderness. Even the family photographs with his children on his knees seem to lack tenderness. Maurice was very silent at home. He hardly ever spoke. When he used to come home, his mother would turn to Jack and say: 'Voilà, le vieux qui rentre!' ["Look, the old man is back!"]."[7]

Girodias did nevertheless learn something from his father about two subjects for which both men had a natural affinity: publishing and women. Kahane encouraged his son to visit him at his office, and the young Maurice designed the Obelisk covers not only for Henry Miller's first book, *Tropic of Cancer,* but also for the second, *Black Spring.*

This was before Kahane had moved into the Place Vendôme, and he was still working out of his partner's office, which was also a printing works. Kahane made his visits as short as possible and then, seizing his hat and cane, would take Maurice off to "one of the elegant tearooms of the neighborhood where literary countesses held court."

"How embarrassing to be fourteen," Girodias lamented, "no longer a child and not yet a man! My father would introduce me gently to one or two of his countesses, always a little anxious about my hand-kissing style, and over the chances of my dropping my *tartelette aux fraises* on the lady's illustrious lap. I was not expected to say much and was soon left to my enjoyment . . . but I was passionately feeding on the effluvia, on the mixed aroma of rare teas and precious skins, on the soft intensity of women speaking to one another, communing with one another over that secret they all share, whose existence I could sense vividly but whose nature no male creature will quite understand. . . .

"Womanhood was like a vast sea caressing my soul under silent waves; my father was a lucky dog, and he knew it well. He seldom spoke to me, and the only education I ever received from him had to do exclusively with the appreciation of women, for which words are no use—and indeed undesirable. 'Don't overdress, there's never any need for that,' he would say, or: 'Always keep your nails short and well-trimmed.' And it was clear that those small items of advice came straight from his lady-killer's fund of knowledge."[8]

. . .

AFTER KAHANE'S DEATH, the family moved out of Paris, leaving Maurice to look after what was left of the Obelisk Press. He discovered that his father's bank account was virtually empty, and his first visitors at the Obelisk office were the owners of Kahane's two favorite bars, where he had conducted much of his publishing business and many of his amorous liaisons. Along with their murmured condolences, the bar owners presented Girodias with his father's accumulated debts, which he signed with a brace of swiftly executed IOUs.

Fortunately, Girodias's grandfather had settled some money in trust on his four grandchildren and it was agreed that Maurice should have his share immediately. With this modest sum, and the remainder of the Obelisk Press, he launched his career as a publisher. But it was hard going. First the threat of war and later its reality had eviscerated the publishing house. Most of the readers and authors had disappeared. English-speaking tourists no longer browsed in Brentano's, W. H. Smith, and the other bookshops where Obelisk's books had their largest sales, and virtually all the American and British writers had left Paris.

Since Obelisk was moribund, Girodias began a small venture printing popular American and British books, in English, in preparation for a rapidly expanding market in France once the war was over. Hachette was to provide much of the capital and take care of the distribution. The new firm was called the Unicorn Press, and *The Grapes of Wrath* by John Steinbeck was chosen as the first title.

But events were moving too fast. The French government was in disarray, Girodias's partner had gone to fight the Germans; his secretary, who was Jewish, decided to leave Paris and advised Girodias to do the same; his mother had made the opposite decision—to return to the capital with her children, feeling that she was no less safe there than in the south of France; and the young publisher had fallen in love with Laurette Buzon, who had no intention of leaving the city.

Then came France's crushing defeat at Sedan and the German invasion. Refugees poured into Paris from the north and east and flowed out to the south and west. The city waited for the arrival of the German army. Girodias went to the Place Vendôme, which was deserted, and sat alone in his father's inner sanctum. Conscious of his Jewishness for the first time in his life, he made a mental note to remove the sign on the door that read OBELISK PRESS, JACK KAHANE.

His father's absence manifested itself, Girodias later recalled, "in a feeling of profound calm that accentuates the visual impact of every object, the letters lying open where he had left them, the scattered books he was the last to touch. Pinned to the gray burlap that covers the walls are the actors of the past, each one looking into the dim, dusty room from his or her place in space and time. The mysterious eyes of Anaïs; a photo of Joyce, the sour-faced magister; Durrell's profile, chubby and pugnacious; . . . And other, gayer spots: Miller's water colors, . . . book jackets, crank letters, Christmas cards. Gone are the passengers of this ship, and few remember the stop they made at this port of call. . . . The owner of this room is gone, and the faces all around the room appear disconnected from their purpose."[9]

The German army entered Paris in June 1940 and was to remain in the city for four years. Girodias realized how exposed he was with a Jewish name and a British passport as his only identity document, so he set about changing both. It seems that he had opted for his British nationality to avoid conscription into the French army. He says, however, he had promised his father that he would make an effort to enlist in the British army. At the British embassy, he was told it would take some time. With filial pledge fulfilled and honor secure, Girodias swiftly obtained forged papers identifying him as a French citizen called "Maurice Girodias," a name that he was to keep for the rest of his life.

In the early days of the German occupation, the young Girodias seems to have survived by dealing in black-market goods. He bought and sold whatever he could lay his hands on, rather as his father had done at the end of World War I. Sometimes he did badly, as when he unwittingly bought five tons of canned celery roots, while on other occasions he did better, notably when he cornered a huge stock of fine printing paper.

Throughout, however, he managed to continue publishing. The bitter winter of 1940–41 was hard on the undernourished and under-heated Parisians, who turned to the cinema as a welcome—and relatively warm—escape from the rigors of the Occupation. Girodias noticed filmgoers lacked a guide, so he turned out a weekly publication called *Paris-Programme,* which listed films and other entertainments. He also pursued his Unicorn Press paperback project but scaled it down to "safe" educational textbook material.

Girodias's office was close to the German High Command in Paris, a sensitive area where passersby were often stopped and had their papers checked. He managed to avoid scrutiny on the streets, but his *Paris-Programme* guide attracted the Germans' attention and he was summoned and interrogated. An anonymous letter, signed "A Patriot," accusing him of being Jewish, British, and a Freemason, had been received. He was told that if he could prove that at least one of his grandparents was Aryan, there would be no further difficulties. Grandfather Girodias, much to his surprise, was called in, testified to his non-Jewish, non-British, and non-Freemason heritage, and his half-Jewish theosophist grandson was promptly released.[10]

Around this time Girodias met an experienced editor called André Lejard, who had worked on an art magazine and was looking for a job. With him were two women, an art historian and a book designer, who had worked on the same magazine. This ready-made and experienced team gave Girodias the idea of starting a publishing venture that would specialize in high-class art books. He managed to raise the necessary money, to organize distribution for the first book (on French furniture), and to buy thirty-five tons of high-grade coated paper at prewar prices. In early 1941 Éditions du Chêne was formally established and Maurice Girodias, twenty-one years old, became a full-fledged publisher.

This was also the time when, by his own account, he became a full-fledged man, having pursued and finally bedded a luscious Greek woman called Marina, who was ten years older than himself. He had encountered her at the same theosophical ashram where he had met Laurette, his future wife. This duality of publishing and women, established early in his life, would provide the central axis of Maurice Girodias's *Une Journée sur la Terre* (*A Day on Earth*), the title he gave his autobiography and the epitaph his brother placed on his tombstone.

The relationship with Laurette was a curious one. Notwithstanding Girodias's attraction to other women, he was passionately in love with her and constantly pressed her to marry him: "I felt as if I were bound to her by an umbilical cord through which she was instilling in me an erotic secret, the mysterious fragrance of her own desire. I knew that my boundless love for her had become important to her, that she depended more and more on it as an emotional food necessary to her sustenance, just as I depended on her soft presence to reach a curious form of ecstasy of my own that always left me weak with wonder and frustration."[11]

For her part, Laurette treated him more like a brother or an old friend. During the early part of the war, her primary loyalty was to her ashram, which was led by a charismatic guru called Vivian, who had quarreled with Maurice and ejected him from the group. ("The sun has set for you" were the guru's parting words to the apostate.)[12]

"I was two years older than Maurice," she said. "When I first met him he was sixteen and he used to call me '*Maman*.' I don't know how to describe that form of affection—it was partly maternal, partly fraternal, it was everything at once, a serious feeling that required contact and communication. But I had no desire to marry him. Not at all!"[13]

The ardent Girodias thus had to be content with what he called a "chaste passion like Tristan and Iseult."[14] But he continued to court Laurette, and when he invited her to come and work with him, she accepted. She gave up her Egyptology studies and remained at Éditions du Chêne until the end of the war.

THE PUBLISHING VENTURE began well, albeit with a mistake. Lacking commercial experience, Girodias drastically underpriced his first book. But it sold so well that it made money for the firm and impressed the distributors and booksellers. Production increased with the emphasis on art books—books on French castles, on the Loire valley, on famous painters. They were elegant, carefully produced volumes printed on fine paper, and they caught the reading public's attention in the drab world of wartime publishing. The most ambitious book was one on Delphi (*Delphès*), which was printed on the finest prewar art paper and weighed seven pounds. The edition of three thousand copies was a sellout, largely by subscription.

Girodias mentions all this in his memoirs. What he does not reveal is that he also published two politically controversial books that were to get him into trouble after the war. The first was a pro-Pétain government booklet by Georges Pelorson, an old friend of Girodias. Called *De l'Enfant à la Nation* (*From Childhood to Nationhood*), it was an upliftingly nationalistic appeal for a radical reform of the educational system in France and was published in January 1941. Before the war Pelorson had been a highly respected figure in literary circles, and he fought against the Germans in the brief period of hostilities. But after the collapse of France he joined Marshal Pétain's Vichy government and became head of propaganda in the department responsible for youth affairs.[15] The second was a virulent tract, originally published as a two-part magazine article in 1928, which attacked the well-known French writer André Maurois, who was Jewish. Entitled *Un Écrivain Original: M. André Maurois,* the essay accused him of plagiarism and sought to undermine his literary reputation. The author, writing under the pseudonym of "Auriant," was Alexandre Hadjivassiliou, a literary critic and historian who was also a notorious anti-Semite. The cover depicted Maurois as a vulture, his claws clutching a book, with small Stars of David scattered in the sky. This was put out under the Éditions du Chêne imprint in February 1941.

The Éditions du Chêne's first two years were remarkably successful, with Girodias making his mark as a publisher of fine art books. "I was not only succeeding," Girodias recalled later, "I was becoming terribly respectable."[16] Then the paper began to run out.

That year—1943—began badly, Girodias reported, with a fight between him and his younger brother. Eric was seventeen years old, lively and combative in spirit but puny and undersized in appearance. The fight ended with Eric on the floor, his back broken. For four months he lay prone in the hospital, and no one knew if he would recover. But he did, and as he took his first hesitant steps, his family noticed with surprise that he had grown eight inches since the accident. "He looked down on his mother," Girodias writes, "and was astonished to find himself in an unaccustomed stratosphere."[17]

Paper was one of the most vital commodities in occupied France. The Germans maintained strict controls over supplies as a way of monitoring and controlling what went into print. Girodias, however, had his connections and knew that he could get his hands on ordinary printing paper. But what he needed was coated paper for his art books. A little research revealed that the paper could be treated with a milk product called casein, the principal ingredient in cheese. Three trips to Normandy with a knowledgeable friend produced a huge supply of casein, which was soon stacked in bags in Girodias's office alongside the slowly dwindling supplies of canned celery roots.

The last two years of the war were a busy time for the young publisher. With the success of the art books at Éditions du Chêne, Girodias developed new projects. He published a series of English classics, in English, produced a book on French racehorses for a private German client, and had a few of his art books translated into German.[18] In 1943 he led a successful group protest by French publishers over a Vichy government directive that would have drastically restricted the allocation of paper. Then came the liberation of Paris, followed by the settling of accounts known as *l'épuration,* the purge.

A LARGE QUESTION MARK attached itself to Girodias during the years of the German occupation and has remained there ever since. Laurette, a French Catholic, was interrogated and held for several days, as were thousands of Parisians during that period. Similarly, many able-bodied men were deported to Germany to work in factories and labor camps. How did Girodias, a Jewish British national, survive? He was the first to admit that his forged identity documents were a flimsy cover. Any proper check at the Paris Préfecture de Police, he reckoned, would have revealed that they were false.

But apart from that single summons by the German authorities, Girodias had no trouble. He did not hide; he did not leave Paris, except for a few business trips to the provinces; he did not even bother to keep a low profile. Quite the contrary, he became a clearly defined presence in the Parisian publishing world. He prospered and he lived high on the hog. "The art of living had been replaced by the art of survival," Girodias remarked in the early days of the Occupation. By the end of it, he was an accomplished practitioner of both. Maurice Girodias had, without a shadow of a doubt, a good war.[19]

Charles Kircorian, a close friend of Girodias, saw him almost daily during the war. "I was working as a tailor in the avenue de l'Opéra, close to Place Vendôme, where Maurice had his office," he said over a coffee in the bar of the Grand Hotel in the same neighborhood. "He had paper—that was the key thing—and he made money. After work he and Laurette used to take me to dinner at one of those black-market restaurants where you could eat and drink anything you wanted and it cost a hundred times more than a normal meal. He had American cigarettes, Lucky Strikes. He had a lot of money. For him, the war was a fantastic time, he built up another life for himself, as if the war didn't exist."[20]

Like many young men in Paris during the Occupation, Charles Kircorian received orders to report for work in Germany. But he went into hiding instead and stayed out of the way until the Liberation. He was luckier than another of Girodias's Armenian friends, Pierre Ter-Sarkissian, who was deported to Berlin and spent over a year working in Germany. "When I was ordered to go," he said in the study of his quiet apartment overlooking the Montparnasse cemetery, "Maurice tried to help me. I was working for him, and he went to the Germans to try to persuade them not to send me."[21]

Girodias's intervention with the German bureaucracy was a failure. He says he lost his temper, yelled at the official, banged on his desk, and fled. He and another Armenian friend then took "Petit Pierre," as he used to call Ter-Sarkissian, to a brothel, where they all got royally drunk. The next day the two men saw Ter-Sarkissian off from the Gare de l'Est. "He helped my family when I was in Germany," said Ter-Sarkissian, recalling the moment as if it were yesterday and not half a century earlier, "and Laurette used to come round to my parents' apartment with parcels of food and cigarettes for me."[22]

"How did Maurice survive?" Laurette raised her eyebrows. "By a miracle. He was very lucky. He was particularly lucky to have André Lejard working with him. Lejard spoke fluent German and had lots of contact with Germany before the war. He helped Maurice get the paper."[23]

Muffie Wainhouse, who worked with Girodias after the war and often talked with him about the Occupation, said: "How did he do it? By being imaginative and clever. There was help from his father's connections, discovery of a warehouse of hoarded paper, appeals to the German love of *Kultur*. And then, he didn't notice obstacles."[24]

Seymour Hacker, the New York art-book dealer, had a different view of Girodias. A small pixielike figure, now in his seventies, with white hair and gold half-framed spectacles, Hacker was not in Paris during the war. But he knew Kahane before it and Girodias after the conflict ended: "I met Girodias in Brussels in 1946 and bought some art books from him. Loose portfolios with tipped-in plates—good for their time. It was quite well known in publishing circles that he had played footsie with the Nazis. He had plenty of paper that the Germans tightly controlled, and he published books in German. He was very tight with them. He was quite arrogant about all this. His father was a bit of a rogue, but I liked him better than the son—more charming, more interesting."

Why were there no reprisals against Girodias if he had been such an obvious collaborator? Hacker's eyes twinkled over his half-frames. "Look, everybody knew about his collaboration, but he played both sides of the road so there were no reprisals from the Resistance."[25]

Aside from whatever relationship Girodias had with the German authorities, his publication of Auriant's anti-Semitic tract attacking André Maurois and Pelorson's pro-Pétain booklet on education appear to sully his publishing record. Girodias makes matters worse by ignoring both of them in his voluminous autobiographical writings.

The Auriant booklet is particularly mysterious. The survivors who knew Girodias during the war deny any knowledge of this obnoxious publication. The most obvious explanation is that a half-Jewish, half-British publisher, who was trying to hide his identity from the Germans, might include such a book on his list to establish his credentials with the new regime. The timing is significant. Auriant's monograph and Pelorson's essay were published back-to-back in the first two months of 1941, when Girodias was finding his feet and devising ways of surviving.

The pro-Pétain pamphlet on education by Georges Pelorson is easier to explain. Pelorson was a close friend of Girodias and knew the Kahane family before the war, having taught the three younger children at a Montessori-type school that he ran for a time. He was well known in French literary circles as a poet, writer, editor, and educator. He also mixed with the expatriate artistic community, where he became friendly with James Joyce, Samuel Beckett, and Henry Miller. In the late 1930s Pelorson started up an avant-garde literary magazine called *Volontés*. Contributors included Raymond Queneau, Henry Miller, Leopold Senghor, and even the young Girodias, who wrote an article on gold and economics.

Pelorson's decision to join the Vichy government did not interrupt the friendship between the two men, and they remained in contact throughout the war. After the liberation of Paris, Pelorson, who had been decorated by Pétain, was blacklisted and lay low in the countryside for a time. He also changed his name to Belmont, the name of a village in the Jura mountains. During the postwar period, he established a reputation as a translator, notably of Miller's works but also of Henry James, Evelyn Waugh, Graham Greene, and Anthony Burgess. He had a successful career as a journalist working for *Paris Match* and editing *Marie Claire*.

Hearing that Pelorson was alive and well in Paris, I went to visit him. As I approached his apartment I wondered how to handle his names. That was resolved in the lobby by the plate next to his doorbell, which read: G. BELMONT PELORSON. A vigorous, distinguished-looking man in his early eighties, with silver hair and blue-rimmed glasses, greeted me. The lair of a man of letters lay beyond: books and magazines on every available shelf, table, and chair; a contented cat; photographs of Joyce, Beckett, and Miller; a bottle of Jameson whiskey and glasses in attendance.

We talked about Girodias and the war. Pelorson believes that it was a denunciation by another French publisher, probably out of jealousy, that led to Girodias's interrogation by the German authorities. "He asked me to come with him to the rue de Rivoli and tell his mother if he didn't come out again. But he came out, waved to me briefly, and disappeared under the arcades."

Pelorson said he and his wife lent Girodias some money—which was repaid—when he founded Éditions du Chêne. "I had written an essay before the war on the need to revolutionize the educational system in France [*De l'Enfant à la Nation*]," he said. "Girodias liked it, so he published it. . . . Pelorson was my name in those days. I changed it later. At one point in my life I got fed up with myself and changed it. It's very personal. You can go through terrible events, like a flower—you let yourself be carried along. That's what happened to many of us during the Occupation."

And Girodias? "He was a great gambler. Not with money but with life. I remember him coming over to our house one Sunday and sitting down with a big sigh. 'What's up?' I asked.

" 'Things are going too well,' he said. 'It's boring.' "

As for survival, Pelorson thinks that he played games with both sides, bribing German officials and passing information to the Resistance.

A survivor himself, Georges Belmont Pelorson sipped Irish whiskey and told me about his conversation with his friendly ghosts. "When Beckett died, I put his photograph on that chair where you are sitting and a bottle of Jameson between us. I drank and we talked. Sometimes I do the same with Miller. We have good talks."[26]

THE ARRIVAL of the Germans in Paris not only focused Girodias's mind on survival but turned his thoughts to his own identity. Like his father, he grew up in a family without any strong religious convictions. His father was against religion in general, and his mother was a Catholic but only in a nominal sense. Girodias says he declared himself a Protestant at boarding school because most of the other boys were Catholics, an act of rebellion rather than a road-to-Damascus religious conversion.

"I had rejected the Jewish thing for so long that it had become a mental habit, as well as a self-protective device, to continue doing so. I didn't even want to admit to myself my curiosity for that half of myself that I had thought I could erase simply by denying it."[27]

The Occupation changed all that. "Hitler will never stop winning," Girodias lamented. "The very day after my father's death, my own grandfather, whom I had never dreamed could entertain any racist feelings, blurted out angrily to my mother: 'Remember, I told you not to marry a Jew!' . . . How does one function as an ethnic centaur, when you don't even know which part is Jewish, the front or the rear?"[28]

But what the wartime experience did develop—or, perhaps more accurately, strengthen—was his sense of self, of where he stood in relation to his background and to the schizoid, treacherous, seductive, dog-eat-dog world of wartime France: "I find myself compelled to think for myself, and to generate my own environment."[29]

After the liberation of Paris in August 1944, the activities of French writers, journalists, and publishers during the Occupation were closely scrutinized. Auriant and Pelorson were designated collaborators and blacklisted by the Conseil National des Écrivains [National Council of Writers], an act that effectively deprived them of their livelihoods. Girodias was denounced by other French publishers, who accused him of collaborating with the enemy, and was summoned to appear before the courts.

The charges, however, proved to be nothing more serious than publishing books in German and English and leading the campaign against the Vichy government's attempt to limit the amount of paper available to publishers, a campaign that did not have the blessing of the pro-Resistance writers' group. Girodias defended himself spiritedly in court, the charges were dropped, and the case closed. It was his first encounter with the legal system and the beginning of a long and complex relationship with the world of lawyers, litigation, and the law courts.[30]

It seems likely that Girodias covered his bets with both sides during the Occupation. He had good contacts in the Resistance (one of his closest friends was a decorated Resistance hero), as well as among Vichy sympathizers. The result was that at the end of the war he emerged unscathed, if not smelling like a rose. Collaboration was, after all, not a clear-cut issue. In the broadest sense, many people "collaborated" with the Germans simply in order to survive. A number of French publishers, including some of the most famous firms, cooperated closely with the Germans.

The critical questions center on how active was an individual's collaboration, what was the motivation, and how damaging were the effects, especially to those who were actively opposing the Germans. No evidence has come to light to show that Girodias's dealings with the enemy damaged French national interests, or caused harm to individual people, during a murky period of French history.

One of Girodias's favorite films was called *Cochon à Travers Paris,* the story of getting a live, contraband pig across wartime Paris. Shot in black and white, in perpetual drizzle, the adventure focused on concealing the pig from other Frenchmen rather than the Germans. Girodias felt it perfectly evoked the miserable grayness, meanness, and grudging compromises of the war years.[31]

After the war, he was honest enough to admit that he was not proud of all that he did during the Occupation. When one of his friends later mentioned Éditions du Chêne's publication of Auriant's anti-Maurois book and the Pelorson pamphlet, he replied: "I blush whenever I think of them."[32]

IF WAR BROUGHT Girodias trouble, it also saw him successfully through the rites of passage of manhood and starting a career. It was ironic that the early postwar years carried with them disappointment in both love and business. Initially, however, things went well. Éditions du Chêne started publishing some of the old Obelisk titles, notably Henry Miller's books. Miller's work was still banned in the United States and Britain, so Girodias was in a good position to exploit it, especially since France was full of British and American troops hungry for the "hot stuff."

The end of World War II saw a rapid expansion in Girodias's business affairs. He rented larger and more sumptuous premises in the rue de la Paix and spent a great deal of money on renovation. He moved his publishing office there and turned the Place Vendôme space into an art gallery for modern paintings. To run the gallery Girodias hired a Ukrainian called Georges, who became known immediately as "Georges-Galerie-Vendôme." As with the new office, no expense was spared on the gallery, and together they represented the young Girodias's second foray into architecture and design. These elegant structures did not collapse, but they ran their creator into serious debt.

Peace also brought marriage. In 1945 Girodias married Laurette Buzon in the mayor's office in the sixth arrondissement, ending a ten-year courtship. The day they chose happened to be a time when marriage fees were waived, giving the mayor's office the appearance of a Hieronymus Bosch painting with all the blind, the crippled, and the pregnant of the neighborhood waiting their turn. After a large reception at his mother's home in Neuilly, the couple went to Nice for a honeymoon that was not a success.

Girodias admitted later that the marriage, from the beginning, was not the glorious culmination to his passion that he had cherished and had indeed expected.[33] Laurette, for her part, says she had no intention of marrying him: "I told him I loved him and was happy to work with him and help him but not as his wife."

Why then did she marry him? "Because he took me by surprise." She laughed at the strangeness of it all. "In December 1944, he became annoyed with me and said, either we get married or you go away. He couldn't bear the situation anymore. I said, fine, and left Éditions du Chêne. But we missed each other a great deal. He was part of my life.

"Anyway, my brother-in-law arranged a lunch and left us alone. Maurice said how happy he was to see me again and then said: 'Let's get married.' That evening I telephoned his house to tell him that it wasn't on. His mother answered and said she had heard that we were getting married, how wonderful it was, and so on. I adored her and I didn't dare say it wasn't on. You understand how things can happen that way? I didn't dare tell her that I was not going to marry her son. C'était drole, n'est-ce pas?"[34]

It was strange. It was as if the marriage had never taken place, although they did live together and had two daughters, Valérie and Juliette. (Laurette and her daughters, as well as Girodias's brother, Eric, all kept the family name, Kahane.) Girodias reflected later that he had spent almost a third of his life—he was twenty-six years old when he married Laurette—adoring her, but when she finally gave herself to him, he lost her forever.[35]

Success and the pressures of wartime living had changed Girodias's lifestyle. Vegetarianism, meditation, and abstention from alcohol had been abandoned. He now enjoyed good living, restaurants with fine table linen and crystal, gourmet food, vintage wines, fashionable clothes. He also had developed an eccentricity or two. In a moment of great emotional stress, for instance, he once picked up his whiskey glass and, in front of astonished onlookers, began to eat it.

By the same token, he tolerated oddities in others. Georges Pelorson remembers the time when Girodias invited him out to lunch and he went wearing his wife's hairnet, "a red one, if I remember correctly." Girodias did not bat an eyelid when they greeted each other and never mentioned it throughout the meal. "He was very British in this respect," Pelorson says.[36]

The late 1940s and early 1950s were a difficult and frustrating period in Girodias's life. His marriage failed, and the couple separated in 1950, with Laurette taking the two young daughters. "Yes, it's true," she says, "it was really over before it began. . . . After five years I decided to leave. I wanted a clean break."[37]

On the publishing front, Girodias had a few more successes, a couple of fights, and a disaster. He launched a monthly review called *Critique* that was devoted to literary and philosophical topics and edited by the writer Georges Bataille. He reissued some of Miller's Obelisk titles in English and had his friend Georges Belmont Pelorson translate two of them (*Tropic of Capricorn* and *Max and the White Phago-cytes*) into French. He also published a new Miller book, *Sexus,* in 1948. Eclectic as ever, Girodias published a new version of John Cle-land's eighteenth-century erotic classic *The Memoirs of a Woman of Pleasure* (*Fanny Hill*), Nikos Kazantzakis's *Alexis Zorba* (*Zorba the Greek*), a series of Russian classics in French, and a journal devoted to the art of knitting.

The first battle came with a controversial book attacking the gov-ernment for corruption, which he published in 1947. This was *Le Pain de la Corruption* (*The Bread of Corruption*), by Yves Farge, which tar-geted the minister responsible for food and caused a scandal. The minister sued the author and publisher, and a well-publicized trial ended in a victory for Farge and Girodias.

The second tussle occurred when Girodias reissued Miller's *Tropic of Capricorn*. The French government prosecuted Girodias and two other firms, which had also published Miller's work, under a law against obscene publications passed in 1939. "L'Affaire Miller," as it came to be called, was the first time the French government had moved publicly against a published work since the famous cases against Flaubert's *Madame Bovary* and Baudelaire's *Fleurs du Mal* in the previous century. Writers, publishers, and other intellectuals rallied to the defense of Miller and his publishers; committees and pressure groups were formed, and, after two years of sporadic litigation, the government dropped the case.

The disaster came when Girodias got into serious financial diffi-culties and lost control of Éditions du Chêne to Hachette. "It was a cruel lesson," he wrote later, "as Éditions du Chêne had become part of my flesh and blood, and losing it made me feel like King Saud must have felt being suddenly deprived of all his wives."[38]

In Paris in 1992, I picked up, quite by chance, a glossy publisher's brochure. It had been issued by Hachette to celebrate the fiftieth anniversary of the founding of one of the firm's cherished imprints, Éditions du Chêne. The name of the publishing house's creator and owner for ten years, Maurice Girodias, was not mentioned.

5

Great Books, Dirty Books: Olympia Gathers Steam

IF A BOOK LOVER, browsing in Paris in the spring of 1953, had dropped into the bookshop at number 13 rue Jacob on the Left Bank, a curious tableau would surely have caught the eye. Perched on a sagging mattress behind a trestle table in the back of the shop sat a slim, well-dressed man in his mid-thirties up to his elbows in man-uscripts, letters, scraps of paper, and bills. At his side was an attractive young woman with jet black hair, green eyes, and skin the color and luminosity of fine porcelain.

The man, of course, was Maurice Girodias, the woman, Lisa Ro-senbaum, originally from Danzig, and their low-tech enterprise, the Olympia Press. After losing Éditions du Chêne to Hachette in 1950, Girodias had floundered for the next three years. On top of the failure of his marriage came the suicide of one of his women friends and a series of unsatisfactory relationships and business ventures. "My only companion," he says, "was my brother Eric, who was in nearly as bad shape as I; but he was 27 and I was 34, and I felt utterly senile."[1]

Desperate, Girodias returned to the source—his father's bookleg-ging formula. He borrowed some money, obtained credit from a printer, and wrote to Henry Miller in Big Sur, California, asking him, did he, by any chance, have something ready for publication? Miller did, a massive manuscript entitled *Plexus,* and he dispatched it to Paris forthwith. Girodias found office space in the back of the rue Jacob bookshop—space that had to be evacuated promptly in the evening so that the owner could sleep on Girodias's directorial throne—and treated himself to a secondhand car, a large, lush, midnight-blue Citroën.

Girodias named his new venture the Olympia Press, partly to preserve an alliterative allusion to his father's Obelisk Press and partly because he was paying homage to Edouard Manet's famous painting *Olympia.* This picture of a young naked woman with a black bow around her neck, and a knowing look in her eye, had caused a scandal when it was first exhibited in Paris in the middle of the nineteenth century. Both the subject matter of the painting and its iconoclastic impact appealed to Girodias and formed a perfect metaphor for the erotic content and the rebellious spirit of the new enterprise.

The Olympia Press's inaugural publications in the summer of 1953 were a strange but impressive mixture. Accompanying Miller's *Plexus,* issued in two volumes, was a raft of translated sado-erotic French classics that included the first English rendering of the Marquis de Sade's *La Philosophie dans le Boudoir* (*The Bedroom Philosophers*); Guillaume Apollinaire's *Memoires d'un Jeune Don Juan* (marketed in English with the upbeat title *Memoirs of a Young Rakehell*); and Georges Bataille's *L'Histoire de l'Oeil,* translated as *A Tale of Satisfied Desire* but retaining Bataille's original and mellifluous pseudonym, "Pierre Angelique."

Girodias had by this time met a group of expatriate writers, poets, translators, and editors who were to play an important part in the fortunes of the Olympia Press. Their common interest was a small avant-garde literary magazine called *Merlin,* which they had founded a year earlier and by whose name they came to be collectively known. Denizens of the Left Bank, their favorite cafés were the Old Navy in the Boulevard Saint-Germain and the Café Tournon in the street of the same name.

The "erratic pope of that pagan church" was Alexander Trocchi, a Scot of Italian origin who had come to Paris from Glasgow to write and escape the bourgeois confines of Britain. A tall, powerfully built man, he had a large Roman nose, a resonant voice, and a commanding presence. He and his American girlfriend, Jane Lougee, the daughter of a banker from Maine, had set up *Merlin* with her money and the couple's collective energy. He was, by common consent, primus inter pares in the Merlin group.

The magazine, which declared itself a vehicle for "innovation in creative writing," brought together a collection of colorful individuals. One of them was Austryn Wainhouse, an American writer and translator who had toured Europe with his wife, Muffie, on a motor scooter before settling in Paris. Austryn, like many of his expatriate contemporaries, was passing through an intensively romantic and experimental phase of his life. He spoke excellent French but surprised his French literary friends by conversing in an archaic eighteenth-century form of the language. He wrote with a quill pen on foolscap paper.

Another American in Paris was Richard Seaver, who had come to study at the Sorbonne but also worked on translations. Dick married a Frenchwoman, Jeannette, and became a great fan of Samuel Beckett's work, which was virtually unknown at that time. Christopher Logue, a British poet, was also a central figure in the Merlin group. Girodias described him as "pale, ill-fed, and ill-garbed." Logue's response to that description was "not ill-fed."

More peripheral but still part of the group were John Coleman from Britain, who came to write and became *Merlin*'s business manager. Baird Bryant, another American writer, coedited *Merlin* with Trocchi when the review was in its terminal stages. He was particularly interested in the drug and jazz subcultures that flourished in Paris at the time. John ("Steve") Stevenson, a British journalist and writer, arrived in Paris with his wife two years after Merlin had started. He inherited the business manager job from Coleman and was set to work selling the highly literary and often intensely obscure magazine to tourists in Left Bank cafés, a task that surely provided an early definition of "the hard sell."

All these "Merlin juveniles," as Beckett called them, were to become involved at different levels with Girodias and the Olympia Press. In the vanguard were Wainhouse and Seaver, who translated the first French books (Wainhouse did de Sade and Bataille and Seaver took care of Apollinaire). Then Trocchi, Logue, Coleman, Bryant, and Stevenson joined the team as writers of what Girodias liked to call the "DB" (dirty book) side of Olympia's operations.

This marriage of talent to lubricity, however, took place after a more decorous union had been established between the Merlin group and Girodias. Two years earlier, Richard Seaver had come across two books, written in French by someone called Samuel Beckett. On an impulse he had bought *Molloy* and *Malone meurt* (*Malone Dies*) and taken them to his abandoned warehouse home in the rue du Sabot, where *Merlin* was soon to establish its headquarters. He later described his reactions:

"Before nightfall I had finished *Molloy*. I will not say I understood all I had read, but if there is such a thing as a shock of discovery, I experienced it that day. The simplicity, the beauty, yes, and the terror of the words shook me as little had before or has since. And the man's vision of the world, his painfully honest portrayal thereof, his anti-illusionist stance. And the humor; God the humor. . . . I waited a day or two, then reread *Molloy,* tempted to plunge into *Malone* but resisting the temptation, as one resists the seductive sweet. The second reading was more exciting than the first. I went on to *Malone*. Full worthy of the first. Two stunning works. Miracles."[2]

Seaver rounded up all Beckett's published works and attended the first radio recording of a section of *Waiting for Godot*. He told Trocchi about his discovery. "Stop talking, mon, and put it on paper!" was the Scotsman's response. "There's a deadline next Thursday." Seaver's piece on Beckett was published in *Merlin's* second issue. A little later, Seaver heard from Beckett's publisher, Jerôme Lindon of Les Éditions de Minuit, that the writer was sitting on a novel called *Watt* that he had written in English during the war. A request to the author to publish an extract in *Merlin* was greeted by silence.

Seaver had just about given up when, one rainy afternoon, there was a knock on the door of the *Merlin* office. "A tall gaunt figure in a raincoat handed in a manuscript in a black imitation-leather binding, and left almost without a word." That night the Merlinois—Girodias's name for them—sat up late reading *Watt* aloud to each other. An extract, firmly selected by Beckett himself, was published in the next issue of the review, a leap of faith that resulted in several angry letters and the cancellation of five subscriptions—5 percent of *Merlin*'s fragile paid-up readership.[3]

Undeterred, the Merlinois decided that they would publish the whole novel under their own imprint, Collection Merlin, a venture that was still in the blueprint stage. French law required a French manager for such an enterprise, and there was also the problem of financing. The solution came in the shape of Girodias, who offered his services as manager and his own tenuous financial resources for publishing operations. Collection Merlin would have editorial control over Beckett's work and several other titles that the Merlinois had acquired.

In return, Girodias would put the books out under his Olympia imprint and enlist the translating and editorial services of the Merlin group. "He was eloquent, suave, compelling," Seaver recalled. The deal was struck and, given the cast of characters, somewhat surprisingly stuck. Beckett's *Watt,* the future Nobel Prize winner's first novel to appear in the English language, was published in Paris in July 1953.[4]

The Merlin group persuaded the reclusive author to meet Girodias on his sagging mattress in the back of the rue Jacob bookshop. It must have been an odd sight, the young, enthusiastic *Merlin* "juveniles" bobbing around the gaunt writer, the manuscript of *Watt* clutched to his chest. They advanced through the throng of curious customers in the bookshop to gather around Olympia's trestle table, which was already beginning to pile up with lesser if lustier literary endeavors. Girodias reported that Beckett did not utter a word during the meeting, not even a hello or a goodbye. "A strange bird—and a strange transaction" was the publisher's conclusion.[5]

That did not constrain Girodias from later characterizing the meeting as the literary equivalent of Stanley meeting Livingstone on the shores of Lake Tanganyika. Girodian hyperbole, to be sure, but the encounter did result in the successful publication of *Watt* and an agreement to publish three more of Beckett's novels (*Molloy, Malone Dies,* and *The Unnamable*) written in French. Patrick Bowles, a South African and another member of the Merlin group, translated the first in collaboration with the author, and Beckett rendered the other two himself. Girodias put them out as a trilogy in 1959.

Some admirers of Beckett have given Girodias little credit for his role. They point out that the master had refused a commission to translate De Sade for Jack Kahane's Obelisk Press in 1938 because he did not want his name associated with a press that primarily published erotica. They emphasize that Beckett neither liked nor trusted Girodias and that it was the Merlin group that, after all, discovered Beckett and brought him to Girodias.

It is true that the Merlinois were both the discoverers and the emissaries. But Girodias could have easily followed the example of the other English-language publishers who had already rejected *Watt.* Behind his reclusiveness, Beckett was keen to have the book published. Girodias correctly saw that *Watt* and the other novels, no matter how innovative and brilliant they were, had little chance of commercial success. It took five years to sell *Watt*'s first edition of two thousand copies. It was also a lengthy and arduous task preparing the other three novels for publication. But Girodias went on and published the trilogy and thus played an important part in bringing Beckett's novels to the English-speaking world.

I F THE Merlin group had one thing in common besides their devotion to Beckett and their determination to roll back the frontiers of literature, it was poverty. Paris was divinely cheap to live in at that time, but, even so, most of the group found it hard to make ends meet. So when their new benefactor suggested there might be ways of remedying the situation without moving too far from their literary pursuits, they did not hesitate.

Using the same persuasive charm that he had employed to cement the Collection Merlin–Olympia alliance, Girodias presented his plan. First, the market. In every far-flung corner of the still intact if tottering British empire, on every American warship sailing the seven seas, in military camps and bases the length and breadth of Europe existed a great, palpitating, unrequited yearning for *love*. Along with the yearning went regular pay packets and a shortage of the kind of reading material that might, albeit on a temporary basis, alleviate some of the agonizing symptoms of loneliness and all-male companionship. *Et voilà!*

The Merlinois were impressed. Now the scam. Girodias explained that the French publisher Gallimard had successfully launched a series of paperback detective stories, using a team of writers, called the Série Noire (The Black Series). Why not do the same with erotic novels? Why not employ the undoubted talents of the group, thereby easing their financial problems? Why not indeed, the young lions chorused.

Muffie Wainhouse recalls the heady atmosphere: "I remember one evening when Maurice packed Alex Trocchi, Jane Lougee, Dick Seaver, Pat Bowles, Christopher Logue, Austryn and me into his big Citroën and drove us to a restaurant. Here we all had our first *escargots,* then trout with Sancerre, *boeuf bourguignon* with Nuits St. Georges, cheese, Belles Hélènes and finally cognac. (At that time we were eating for about $1.50 a day; Christopher Logue for less.) Slightly avuncular, Maurice was a wonderful host and story teller. A convivial group; a merry evening. We also saw the possibilities of earning money.

"Afterward, we talked of little else in our café gatherings: the excitement, the danger, was it prostitution or not? There were enough members from McCarthyite America to be paranoid, and the British, with their tourist visas, were worried. Code words were needed, lest we be overheard by FBI spies or by the French secret police. The group around the table would throw out ideas: How about 'Gid' for Girodias and 'DB' for dirty book? It's hard to believe how clever we were. Or how young."[6]

Trocchi was the first to take the plunge. He and Girodias had hit it off immediately, sharing charm, a love of good food ("They were both foodies," says Logue), and a penchant for doing things the difficult way. Turning himself into a literary lady of easy virtue called "Frances Lengel," Trocchi swiftly wrote a modern version of *Fanny Hill* entitled *Helen and Desire*. Girodias was delighted. Soon, virtually every Merlinois was hard at work, tapping out sexual fantasies, and anything else that came readily to mind, on old upright typewriters in cheap, drafty hotel rooms, in friends' apartments, or in rented maids' rooms.

Christopher Logue knocked out what he admits was a pretty awful DB called *Lust* that Girodias later described as "a pre–James Bondian novel." As an inducement—or perhaps a reward—the publisher bestowed on Logue the sonorous pseudonym of "Count Palmiro Vicarion." Thus ennobled, the left-wing Logue produced collections of well-known bawdy songs and dirty limericks for which he wrote witty introductions.

John Coleman, in the guise of "Henry Jones," labored hard on *The Enormous Bed* and then, as "Stephen Hammer," on *The Itch*. Baird Bryant became "Willie Baron" and wrote *Play My Love*. John Stevenson, who was to be Olympia's most prolific pornographer, launched his career under the name of "Marcus van Heller" with *Rape,* followed quickly by *The Loins of Amon*. Austryn Wainhouse and Dick Seaver had already been drafted as translators, and, a little later, Muffie Wainhouse joined Girodias's growing empire as a secretary and editor.

Girodias named the series The Traveller's Companion and gave each book a plain yet distinctive design: a green cover with the title and author's name framed in a double border of black and white. Books were numbered and often carried advertisements for others at the back. Girodias usually printed five thousand copies of each title and paid a flat fee to the author that he admitted was modest but, nevertheless, "formed the substance of many an expatriate budget."[7]

When he ran out of money, new titles and blurbs for imaginary books would be invented, printed up in a brochure and dispatched around the world to the growing faithful clientele. Muffie Wainhouse remembers how a random group would be assembled for drinks "to work on the brochure." This gathering "turned hilarious as we invented titles and then the blurbs to describe them; brochures to sell unwritten books in order to pay the authors to write them."[8]

At this stage, Girodias realized that the mattress throne and the trestle table in the rue Jacob were no longer adequate for Olympia's expanding needs. He found more spacious if still spartan premises in the rue de Nesle, a cul-de-sac off the rue Dauphine not far from the Seine. This was the first real office occupied by the Olympia Press, and Girodias secured the whole of the second floor in a seventeenth-century building on the north side of the street. Jean-Jacques Pauvert, an avant-garde French publisher who had recently published *Story of O* by Pauline Réage while Girodias did the English version, rented a corner room between the toilet, staircase, and Olympia's files. The rest of the space was devoted to Girodias's multifarious activities.

Forming three sides of a large, central courtyard, the offices had fourteen-foot-high ceilings, wooden floors, and eight-foot-high windows that, when the weather was good, admitted a pale yellow light. Muffie Wainhouse, who came on board in January 1955, recalls the staffing arrangements:

"The skeleton crew included Lisa, the pretty German refugee, who was proficient in four languages. I was hired to handle English only because she had too much to do. She handled all foreign correspondence, the money, and bookkeeping. She was bright and rather inscrutable. [John Stevenson remembers Lisa as a beauty with sad eyes and enormous breasts. Miriam Worms, Muffie's successor, remembers her as a beauty with sad eyes and small breasts.]

"Lanine, a Russian sailor who had jumped ship when the Russian Revolution broke out and made his way to France, handled the storeroom and packaged all shipments. He also determined how book titles were pronounced. We all said *Vit Tigs* for *White Thighs*.

"Le Marin, another sailor but French, had left the sea under some cloud, which probably explained why his real name was never used. He handled all deliveries on a bicycle at first and later on a motorised 3-wheeler with trunk. His vehicle was kept in the vast cobbled courtyard that had been built to allow a coach and four to turn with ease.

"Independent and witty, Le Marin began our day when he whistled in to pick up his morning itinerary. Maurice, with a stack of assorted envelopes, would name a street as he handed them out: Montparnasse, Delambre, Vaneau, Varenne, Tournon. No need to write them down. Le Marin could translate: money to Bank A and Bank B, to Madame Girodias, to an artist, proofs to a reader, the printer, and so on. Le Marin took lunches long enough to include a siesta, possibly with *une petite amie*."[9]

Girodias remembered that Le Marin had a problem with a collapsed lung, and, rather than go into the hospital when it began to sag, he would insert his bicycle pump and reinflate it.[10]

Girodias's own office took up one entire wing and was a rather Zen affair with wall-to-wall carpeting in pale blue. The long table featured his art books, the shelf contained dictionaries and Olympia Press publications; there was usually nothing on his desk. The armchairs were pulled to the side because entry did not ensure an invitation to sit. The forced long walk from the door to his desk was dreaded, particularly by those who still had chapters to finish. The bench in the anteroom could accommodate four or five waiting supplicants.

Sometimes lawyers, impressive men with silvery hair, velvet collars, and oozing confidence, would visit. They would be closeted with Girodias for an hour or so before setting off for court in a jocular mood. In the mid-1950s Girodias was winning his lawsuits.

"Besides writers, there were walk-ins every day," Muffie says, "a lot of coming and goings and a lot of laughter. Four American soldiers stationed in Germany would somehow find their way to the rue de Nesle, probably hoping to meet 'Frances Lengel' (Alexander Trocchi) or 'Harriet Daimler' (Iris Owens). They had to make do with me and I like to sell things so I kept the latest books on my desk.

"Maurice hated this: 'Send them to the bookstore,' he would say. And, yes, we could take dollars. Lisa appreciated what all this did for the cash drawer and that she no longer had to fend off the Americans. There were also Dutch youths on bikes who would fill their knapsacks with books; and tourists of all kinds stocking up. But some people seemed to come on a simple pilgrimage. They just wanted to see the Olympia Press."

The office, however, took on a more somber aspect when bills were due. This generally occurred around 4:00 P.M. the day before deposits were to be made and check-writing done. Lisa typed the checks and prepared the envelopes. Bank A covered the bill paid by Bank B, and C covered A. Waking in the middle of the night, her recurring nightmare was wondering if she had covered C. Muffie says that she herself understood enough to appreciate that this was creative financing. "It occurred to me that it might work with no real money at all."[11]

Alone in his office, "Maurice might be calculating—in addition to book matters—the furnishing of a toy store for his recently widowed sister, or the opening of an art gallery that sold nothing but children's paintings. On little tablets sized $3'' \times 3''$, Maurice would expertly draw absolutely hideous faces. Purging himself of evil, he said. Lisa must have caught their meaning because she hated them and carefully threw them out each day. He also smoked, chain-style, 5 or 6 Gauloises, and then nothing for hours. He never tore the corner off the package but opened it entirely so that he could reach into his pocket and pull one out. If he offered you a cigarette, it was like helping yourself from a small bowl."[12]

With the move to the rue de Nesle came an expansion in production. New imprints, new authors, more manuscripts. Maintaining the initial letter "O" for uniformity and recognition, Girodias added the Ophelia Press, Ophir Books, and Othello Books to his fleet. These imprints were unequivocally down-market—designed specifically for the devotees of onanism—whereas Olympia's flagship, The Traveller's Companion Series, gradually acquired weightier armament.

The word was out on the Left Bank that quick money could be had for writing DBs. Norman Rubington, an American painter who had come to Europe on the GI Bill, was one of the earliest to visit number 8 rue de Nesle. Distinguished by his curly hair, bushy eyebrows, crackling laugh, and an imaginative, wacky view of humanity, Rubington was one of the wilder expatriates to settle in Paris. He married a Frenchwoman and had three children by her. But his life was beyond the family hearth, in the bars and restaurants, bookshops and art galleries, and in the apartments (and beds) of other women. Another Olympia writer summed up his lifestyle by calling him "a recluse about town."

He and Girodias met at the English Bookshop in the rue de Seine, the most popular haunt of English-speaking painters and writers at the time. The bookshop, which had an art gallery in the basement, was founded and run by Gaït Frogé, a young, well-educated woman from Brittany who was interested in avant-garde writing and painting. She and Norman had a long and tempestuous love affair, which eventually settled into a calmer friendship.

Girodias found in Rubington a kindred spirit, a combative social iconoclast with an original turn of mind. Rubington was soon at work writing *Who Pushed Paula?*, the first of several DBs. Later he blended his writing and artistic talents to produce a series of satirical collage books. His working relationship with Girodias, like his love life, had roller-coaster qualities but was sustained for many years in Paris and later in New York. As with other Olympia writers, induction meant a change of name. Norman Rubington, scion of Polish Jews, became "Akbar del Piombo."

Another prominent writer was Mason Hoffenberg, an American from a wealthy family who came to Paris to seek artistic inspiration and personal liberation. He also married a Frenchwoman, had a family, and wrote two DBs for the Olympia Press using different pen names, "Faustino Perez" and "Hamilton Drake." He was to go on to greater things, however, when he and Terry Southern teamed up to produce a sexual satire called *Candy*.

Olympia's women pornographers were led by Iris Owens, who soon introduced Marilyn Meeske to the joys of erotica. They had much in common. Both were American and had experienced one marriage apiece. They were young, pretty, sexy, witty, and hip. Miriam Worms remembered them coming into the Olympia offices together "like two Spanish widows, all dressed in black with kohl around their eyes. Marilyn would saunter up to Girodias and say: 'Any *mill* [*mille francs*], Maurice?' "[13]

Iris had lived in Greenwich Village, where she had begun to write. But she was twenty years old and decided it was time for a move. And where did aspiring writers and freethinkers go in the 1950s? Where else but to Paris. She had never read a pornographic book in her life, but this was no impediment, as her first book, *Darling*, a steamy concoction, revealed. Girodias was extremely pleased and turned her into "Harriet Daimler."

Marilyn Meeske came from the Midwest and was married to a sculptor when she arrived in Paris in the mid-1950s. Her marriage did not last long, and pressing financial need led her to the slopes of Mount Olympus. Iris Owens introduced her to Girodias, and together they wrote *The Pleasure Thieves*. When Marilyn sat down to write, she was in a state of literary virginity, also never having read a pornographic novel. Now launched, she selected her own pseudonym, "Henry Crannach," which was inspired by one of her favorite artists, Lucas Cranach, the fifteenth-century German painter. Inspired herself, she went on to write her own DB, its no-holds-barred content reflected in the title, *Flesh and Bone*.

Another woman who wrote erotica for Girodias was Denny Bryant, the young wife of Baird. Using the pen name "Winifred Drake," she let her imagination rip with an uninhibited novel called *Tender Was My Flesh*. The wife of Georges Bataille, Diane, apparently determined not to be outdone by her husband, wrote an erotic book with a sadomasochistic theme called *The Whip Angels*. Girodias published it using one of his shorter pseudonyms, "XXX."

And then there was the mysterious "Ataullah Mardaan," who wrote two DBs: *Kama Houri* and *Deva-Dasi*. Girodias says she was a young Pakistani woman who lived in Paris during the 1950s, Olympia's heyday. She was the daughter of a distinguished Pakistani psychiatrist, had been educated at Columbia University, and was married to a Dutch photographer. She wrote because, like everyone else, she needed the money.

"We enjoyed her irregular trips to our office when she would deliver her latest chapters for our approval," Girodias recalled. "She always wore flowing silk saris, her hair, thick and braided, had never been cut or coiffed, she was modest, beautiful, patient, polite and draped in veils as she handed us the not-so-innocent product of her cultivated mind. She was, in every way, what my father and I had dreamed a pornographer should be."[14]

I had always been skeptical of Girodias's "Ataullah Mardaan," suspecting the hydra-headed Trocchi, the inventive Rubington, or the prolific Stevenson to emerge at any moment from under the abundant hair and the swirling silk. The two books are standard pornographic fare with a Pakistani setting: action-packed, male-oriented, explicit in language and sexual activity.

Trocchi, the first suspect, was already dead, while Rubington and Stevenson denied any responsibility for the books. One of the early Olympia catalogues was decorated with photographs of the eyes of some of the authors. The doelike eyes of Ataullah feature on the same page as the fierce orbs and unmistakable eyebrows of Rubington. Nobody connected with Olympia in the 1950s could cast any light on the identity of "Ataullah," and even Patrick Kearney, the press's redoubtable bibliographer, admits defeat. So there it rests with the postscript that, having read a number of DBs by other women pornographers, I now think *Kama Houri* and *Deva-Dasi* could easily have been written by a woman.

Girodias continued to publish French writers. Books by De Sade, Apollinaire, and Bataille, which had helped launch Olympia, were followed by other works from that trio. De Sade's *120 Days of Sodom, Justine,* and *Juliette* were all translated by Austryn Wainhouse, the last two appearing in The Traveller's Companion Series. Alex Trocchi, using another pseudonym ("Oscar Mole"), translated Guillaume Apollinaire's *Les Onze Mille Verges,* converting the original English title, *The Eleven Thousand Rods,* into the infinitely more dashing *The*

Debauched Hospodar. The hardworking Austryn Wainhouse rendered Georges Bataille's *Madame Edwarda* into *The Naked Beast at Heaven's Gate.*

Girodias was particularly attracted by the work of Jean Genet, whom he applauded for confronting head-on the taboos and hypocrisy surrounding homosexuality in France. Genet's pugnacious attitude toward authority, and to those who upheld it, also appealed to Girodias. Girodias published English translations of *The Thief's Journal* and *Notre-Dame-des-Fleurs* (*Our Lady of the Flowers*) and reprinted *Querelle de Brest* (*Querelle Roman*) in its German version.

Girodias also published the eighteenth-century erotic classic *L'Anti-Justine, ou les Délices de l'Amour* by Restif de la Bretonne. This was translated by Austryn Wainhouse as *Pleasures and Follies of a Good-Natured Libertine.* Finally came *Le Livre Blanc* (*The White Paper*), a collection of nine erotic homosexual vignettes with illustrations. Jean Cocteau wrote a signed preface and did the illustrations; and although the text is anonymous, it is believed that Cocteau wrote it too. Girodias had the book translated and put it out in The Traveller's Companion Series.

Girodias made good use of family and friends. Brother Eric, who had become an expert and sensitive translator, was drafted for a number of books. Jacqueline Duhème, a professional book illustrator and longtime amour of Girodias, also lent a hand. Rubington illustrated his own collage books and other Olympia products, always in the guise of "Akbar del Piombo."

IF THESE PEOPLE were the stars in the Olympia firmament, they were accompanied by a number of smaller but constant celestial bodies, as well as by a few passing meteorites. There was Michel Gall, a French journalist and close friend of Girodias, who wrote a DB with a surprising theme that must have had Daniel Defoe spinning in his grave. This was *The Sexual Life of Robinson Crusoe.* Gall wrote it under the name "Humphrey Richardson" but became incorporated—as "Homer and Associates"—when he later put *A Bedside Odyssey* through the typewriter.

There was Sinclair Beiles, a self-exiled South African, who crossed apartheid's racial frontiers to become "Wu Wu Meng" in order to bring forth *Houses of Joy,* which, it transpired, was not all it seemed. Girodias tells the story: "In the case of Wu Wu Meng, we were duped. A young South African appeared one day in our office . . . a writer . . . of an extremely nervous and frantic nature. He explained to us, while clutching some pages in his hand, that he had been brought up in China, was the son of a missionary, read and wrote Chinese (it was in fact his first language), and was presently translating a rare Chinese novel, of a voluptuousness and sensuality that only the Chinese could achieve. For a price, he would continue the translation for Olympia Press, and . . . would bring us a new chapter every week. . . .

"The next week he returned with the second chapter and sat outside our office reading a Chinese newspaper. We asked him what was new in Peking, and he told us, talking rapidly and urgently. He took his money, left the second chapter and was gone. This arrangement continued until we had all of *Houses of Joy,* an extremely amusing and delicately indelicate book.

"Some months later we discovered that due to a lacuna in our knowledge of fifteenth-century Chinese literature, we had not been aware that we were buying a disguised and lascivious version of the Chinese classic, *Psi Men and His Many Wives,* which had in fact been translated by the distinguished Chinese scholar, A. C. Waite. But Sinclair Beiles had given us such a gorgeously doctored and original version of this work, that we cheerfully published the Beiles edition. We felt it was worth every yen we had paid him, and that publishers, like Prime Ministers, cannot be perfect."[15]

There was Alfred Chester, a serious and respected American writer of novels, short stories, and essays, who wrote a DB for Olympia using the pseudonym "Malcolm Nesbit." Entitled *The Chariot of Flesh,* the novel appeared originally in The Traveller's Companion Series and was reissued later under the downmarket Ophir imprint.

Chester lived in Tangier for many years, the home of another Olympia author, William Burroughs. Chester was a brilliant yet wayward character who was a homosexual, an alcoholic, and periodically addicted to drugs. A childhood disease had deprived him of all his hair, and for much of his life he wore a wig. Tangier, however, liberated him of many inhibitions, including the wig. David Herbert, a longtime Tangier resident, knew Chester well: "He was raving mad but very charming. He fell in love with a Moroccan fisherman and, overwhelmed by the experience, tossed his wig into a lake proclaiming that he wouldn't need it anymore."[16]

Paul Bowles, the American writer and literary doyen of Tangier, tells a story about Chester coming to visit him in Asilah, thirty miles south of the city. Bowles found him increasingly irrational and argumentative and, as a joke, sent a note to a friend in Tangier that said: "Alfred being impossible. Am arranging to have him rubbed out next week." Chester saw the note when he was back in Tangier, rushed over to the United States consul general, and demanded a detachment of U.S. Marines to protect him because his life was in danger. Bowles was called in by the puzzled diplomat, explained what had happened, and the matter was closed. Chester was eventually expelled from Morocco—quite a feat in those days—and went to Jerusalem, where he died of drugs and drink at the age of forty-two.[17]

One of Olympia's most successful authors was the immensely popular "Angela Pearson," who occasionally doubled as "Greta X." Angela catered to devotees of *le vice anglais,* who were, not surprisingly, mainly English. The titles of her books removed any doubts of their orientation: *The Whipping Club, The Whipping Post, Whips Incorporated* (all from the pen of "Angela Pearson"), *Whipsdom,* and the inspired *There's a Whip in My Valise* (both by "Greta X").

Marilyn Meeske remembered Angela well: "[She] was at the time the popular writer for Olympia. Her specialty was doing the sort of books about governesses who administer punishment. Fan mail . . . by the carload. . . . Letters began: 'Dear Angela: How did you ever realize my most intimate desire?' Lawyers, physicians, postal inspectors wished to meet her. They were convinced that she was the only one who truly understood them." But even Angela had to "crawl through the grey twilight for her pay. Would she be blue-eyed and demure? Would she wear jackboots and paint her lips blood red? Would she carry a personalized whip in a special attaché case? Nobody knew, because everything had been done through correspondence."

Finally, the moment of truth. "A great Englishman entered, with a florid complexion and Coldstream Guard moustache. He was ushered into Girodias's private office. Their conversation was brisk and filled with masculine tones. It was difficult to discern the subject. However, after a short period of time a rather disturbed but clear British voice boomed, 'Do you think my career would be ruined should I be discovered to be Angela Pearson?'"[18]

"Angela" did not have to worry, because Girodias kept the faith, as he did with all professional confidences between himself and his authors. While it was not a high priority in my research, I had hoped to take a peek under Angela's veil. I had almost given up when I came across an exchange of letters among Girodias's papers.

Olympia's most commercially successful writer in the 1950s was indeed an Englishman who has pursued an eminently respectable career. We entered into a correspondence, and at his request I have agreed to replace the veil to preserve his anonymity.

The first "Angela Pearson" book was written, he says, after "some experiences with two ladies of her persuasion." He sent the manuscript to the Olympia Press, and Girodias quickly replied, accepting it for publication. Later, author and publisher met in Paris and established a friendly and productive relationship that lasted about seven years. At the first meeting, Girodias said that he wanted more "Angela Pearson" books but later advised a change of name—though not of subject—and came up with "Greta X."[19]

The two men lost contact with each other for more than twenty years, when, out of the blue, the author wrote to Girodias expressing his willingness to saddle up and turn out some more "Angela Pearson" books. Girodias replied explaining the demise of the Olympia Press and the degradation of the genre. But he also came up with an idea. What about "a spoof on sado-masochism in the form of an amusing pseudo-autobiography, interspersed with excerpts from Angela Pearson books?" This would revive the market for the original books.

"There's a vast fortune to be made with such a book," he continued, "but it must be based on some human reality, the author's in the first place, and also the reader's . . . S & M was very big in the United States when I lived there, and still is, I'm sure; and as to England, WOW. . . ."

The author responded modestly by saying that he thought his experiences might be too dull. They mainly featured "the seduction of a number of likely girls by giving them one or more of the books to read, and then proceeding (or halting) according to their reactions." But another idea came to mind: "What about something dealing with the Pearson family—in particular Angelica, the daughter of Angela? The daughter *and* the pupil. Like mother like daughter. Something written autobiographically by Angelica: 'It was on the morning of my seventeenth birthday that my mother opened the door for me to a totally new sexual world.' Something like that. And then on with her experiences." Alas, nothing came of it. Girodias died eighteen months later, and Angela packed the whips away in her valise for good.[20]

Girodias leavened the regular diet of DBs with other, more respectable fiction. Chester Himes, the black American writer, was one contributor. Best known for his detective stories with Coffin Ed Johnson and Grave Digger Jones set in Harlem, Himes had his satirical novel *Pinktoes* published by Olympia.

Gregory Corso, the Beat poet, was also in Paris at that time, met

Girodias through William Burroughs, and contracted to write a book. Corso wrote it in a month and called it *The American Express,* a title that sent a flutter through the company's Paris office. Girodias threw a big party in a nightclub to launch the book and invited executives from the American Express office.

"A lawyer came along and wanted to stop the book from being published," Girodias said. "It would have been wonderful publicity if he had pressed charges but he chickened out."[21]

"They were worried," said Corso, "a dirty book with a big name. But they needn't have been because, although a lot of the action is in the basement of an American Express office, no one goes downstairs and fucks all the workers or has orgies or anything like that. It was all about revolutions. It was a joke. It wasn't erotic at all. In the whole book there was only one kiss. The book was total fantasy, total outsville, nothing to do with anything, right? I thought it was funny writing a book with one kiss in it for a dirty book company."[22]

Paul Ableman's experimental novel, *I Hear Voices,* a story of dreamlike adventures told by an imaginary schizophrenic, elicited an admiring review from the British critic Philip Toynbee. Congratulating the Olympia Press for offering its "generous services" by publishing this "brilliant and terrible little book," Toynbee bemoaned the fact that no British publisher had seized the opportunity to publish it.[23]

Some aspiring pornographers did not make the grade. One was George Plimpton, the veteran editor of *The Paris Review,* who wryly remembered his failure: "Girodias asked me to do a dirty book so I did a takeoff of Robert Louis Stevenson's *The Suicide Club,* a story about elderly gentlemen who have been on safaris and in wars. They are bored and play this complicated game of murder. I used the same venue, a castle, but all the crimes were sexual ones. I showed a chapter to the girl I was living with at the time and she burst into tears. Girodias was horrified—he was very prudish—and refused to publish it."[24]

Paul Bowles in Tangier might have turned his talents to pornography but only if the price had been right. He knew that Alfred Chester and William Burroughs had been signed up by Olympia and that they had received the customary one-time payment of considerably less than $1,000 a book. At that rate, he was never tempted to write a pornographic novel. "But if Girodias had offered me fifty thousand dollars, instead of the usual five hundred," he says, "I might have tried."[25]

. . .

GIRODIAS'S operational formula was simple. The normal five thousand print run of each DB was expected to sell within six to nine months. If demand continued, the book would be reprinted and the author was supposed to receive another payment. Agreement with the authors was usually verbal—written contracts were rare—and normal publishing formalities such as registering copyright were largely ignored.

Advances were paid in dribs and drabs, with Girodias doling out money like an African chief—to those who came when he happened to be flush, to those in great need, to those whose goodwill he wished to secure. Everyone would get something, but the handout would never be a lot, it would not be regular, and its extraction would demand constant supplication. Set against this was the reality that few other sources of income existed in Paris and that the $500 DB fee would sustain body and soul for several months.

John Stevenson remembered how it worked with him: "It was all very individual. I don't know how he paid Norman [Rubington], but I know how he paid Alex [Trocchi], and it was exactly the same for me. I would go in and say:

"'Maurice, I haven't got any money at all.'

"'Oh, my dear Steve,' he would begin, 'I've got the weekend to think of. . . .' Maurice had a weary charm that always seemed to work. But, as Alex would say, that guy has got fifty pounds in his pocket." Girodias, who never carried a wallet and kept his cash like his Gauloises—loose and accessible—"would pull out a modest cluster of francs and say:

"'Ah, let me see what I've got here. Will this be all right?'

"We gratefully took it."[26]

Books were usually about two hundred printed pages, and authors would come into the office clutching a dozen or so typewritten pages at a time. "Girodias would look through them," Christopher Logue remembered, "and then he would take a fold of 1,000 francs from his pocket, slip the notes from their metal clip, and hand them over his desk to you."[27]

Austryn Wainhouse recalled his own experience: "Girodias had an intense sense of family—wife, brother, children. We, the writers, were enlisted into the family. Sometimes we were fed instead of being paid—not a bad kind of patronage. But to get paid we would have to go to the office almost every day, sometimes three or four times a

day, and wait. As the money came in, he doled it out. He didn't keep
any records or pay any attention to contracts, agreements, et cetera."[28]

Muffie Wainhouse was not privy to any contractual arrangements
but knew that most of the deals with the writers were verbal. "No
one," she said, "was eager to have his signature on paper." One pat-
tern was a quarter of the total in advance, a quarter midway, and the
balance upon completion, this last half needing the most financial
encouragement to finish the job.

"Writers regularly drifted in enquiring what kind of mood Maurice
was in before asking him for a supplemental advance to repair a broken tooth, pay for an abortion, a trip to Belgium to have a passport
stamped, or to cover the rent. Even if Maurice were sympathetic or
generous, this rather paternalistic *modus operandi* fostered resentment.
It must have triggered memories of asking for one's allowance.

"Once, when the door was left open, I overheard the following
exchange with a young writer:

"MG: 'Well, no, this needs more work. There's no encounter before page 25.'

"YW: 'But, sir, if you'll look on page 10 I think you'll find . . .'

"MG: 'Yes, but we need more action, more fire. This is not up to
your . . .'

"YW: 'I'll try to do better, sir.'

"It was funny, yet rather horrible. Maybe there just wasn't any
money in Lisa's desk."[29]

ONE OVERSEAS-BASED AUTHOR, who had been published but
not paid, came to Paris seeking justice. He marched into Girodias's
office and challenged him to a duel, offering his publisher the choice
of weapons. Choosing discretion over valor, Girodias murmured that
such an action should not be necessary, reached into his pocket for a
much larger fistful of notes than was his wont, and paid up.

Girodias took all these interruptions in his stride. But Muffie Wainhouse remembers one occasion when his pace faltered. "The only
time I saw Maurice, the unflappable pornographer, flapped, even beet
red, was when a writer called to say that she would not be bringing
in her manuscript that day because of an injury. Her clitoris had been
bitten off during the night." Muffie, well versed in management and
the wiles of errant employees, puts this one at the top of her list of
calling-in-sick excuses. And no (alas), she does not remember who
made it.[30]

Girodias demonstrated a measure of genius in marketing and distribution. "He resolved problems which had paralyzed everyone in the trade heretofore," Austryn Wainhouse remarked. "In no time at all, he had a network of outlets, jobbers and depots stretching from Gibraltar to Macao. It was something to behold. Cartons, bales went out to booksellers in every conceivable latitude; whoever could read three words of English in Bombay, in Nairobi, in Barbados, there Girodias had a potential client. No American warship docked in a foreign port but the crew got down to buy objects which as reading matter may not always have contented them, but which as contraband smuggled in sea-bags fetched triple their price off Times Square. . . . Dirty book clubs mushroomed in London: you rented *The 120 Days of Sodom* for ten guineas a week. How well I recall Maurice's indignation when he learned of this."[31]

"Because he viewed his readers with a clinical eye and because he had no subjective interest in erotic literature, he best served his clients," Marilyn Meeske noted. "He knew what the market called for, necrophilia out, no money there; homosexual books do not really satisfy the boys in the service, the mountain climbers, the anchorites, the satiated marrieds, the orgiasts and the lone needies. For the most part it was a male audience, and they wanted good, old-fashioned, male-female sex with theme and variation."[32]

Olympia expanded in other ways into other countries. Branches were set up in Germany, the Netherlands, Italy, Denmark, and the U.K. Sales through the Paris bookshops, however, remained the bedrock of the operation. Gaït Frogé's English bookshop derived about half its income from Olympia's output. But the largest money spinner was Brentano's on the elegant avenue de l'Opéra. The bookshop dedicated a special, discreetly placed section to Olympia Press books. It was well known, and a steady stream of buyers would come in and head straight for it, make their purchases, and disappear.

As Olympia's list grew and its reputation spread, the French authorities began to show an interest. The heavy steps of the vice squad, delicately named La Brigade Mondaine (The Worldly Brigade), were heard on the stairs at the rue de Nesle. Books were taken away, banning orders issued, and lawsuits initiated and contested. Girodias adopted other tactics. Knowing that the worldliness of the police did not extend to an understanding of the English language, he played tricks with his books' titles. When the government put Trocchi's first DB, *Helen and Desire,* on its proscribed list, Girodias swiftly reissued it as *Desire and Helen.* The book successfully avoided detection—the vice squad was apparently moving alphabetically down Olympia's list—and sold briskly.

Miriam Worms, who became Girodias's assistant and editor in 1956, remembered the visits of the vice squad vividly. "The door would burst open and the room would be filled with dismal raincoats barking 'Girodias!' I would stall them—do you have an appointment? May I see your warrant?—until what they had come to seize was safely put away. They went into frenzies of hate and tried to intimidate me. Once I had arranged for *Time* magazine to send a photographer over, and he snapped the vice squad as if they were members of his family. They seized his camera. Maurice called his lawyer, they cut the line, Maurice called him back to say they had cut the line. It was quite hilarious."[33]

THE SUCCESS OF The Traveller's Companion Series kept the Merlin group and the other Olympia authors close to their typewriters. The most prolific were Alexander Trocchi, Norman Rubington, Iris Owens, and John Stevenson, but Christopher Logue, Marilyn Meeske, Mason Hoffenberg, and Austryn Wainhouse (as a translator) were not far behind.

Trocchi was indefatigable. During this period he operated under four different pseudonyms: "Frances Lengel," for straightforward DBs; "Oscar Mole," for translations; the glorious "Carmencita de las Lunas," one of Girodias's most inspired disguises, which Trocchi adopted to write *Thongs,* a book with a simple title on an unmistakable theme; and, in one impudent impersonation, a surprising transformation into "Frank Harris" to concoct a fifth volume of that great sexual athlete's memoirs.

Girodias had forfeited all Obelisk's rights to Harris's autobiography when he lost control of Éditions du Chêne. But he remembered that his father's original contract with Harris had mentioned a fifth volume. He contacted Nellie Harris, Frank's widow, who put him in touch with her lawyer, a man as ancient as herself with "discolored pupils, . . . shaky pince-nez and . . . old-celery skin."

A tortuous negotiation produced a deal: a million francs for the manuscript, sight unseen, and fifty thousand francs for *"le vieux salaud"* (the old bastard) of a lawyer. But when Girodias opened the slim envelope, all he found was a few drafts of articles and notes on politics, people, and literature. Not a single sexual adventure, not even an anecdote. This neither surprised nor worried Girodias because what he was really after was a contract that authenticated the existence of the fifth volume. "This would enable me to write a pastiche of Frank Harris whose legitimacy no one could question."

He took a taxi to *Merlin*'s offices in the rue du Sabot and told Trocchi about his plan. "He was delighted," Girodias reported, "because he adored Frank Harris—the inspired fabrications, his artless and lively style, his sexual excesses, *très fin-de-siècle,* with corseted ladies emitting little cries of pleasure." The two conspirators put their heads together and "rehearsed a few Harris idiosyncrasies: never to write, 'she said,' in a dialogue, but always, 'she cried,' etc." A fee was agreed on, and Trocchi promised to deliver "a masterpiece" in two months.

He was as good as his word. The book was published as Harris's fifth volume of his life and loves but with a subtitle: *An Irreverent Treatment.* (Girodias later reissued the book with the title *What Frank Harris Did Not Say* . . . and admitted to perpetrating "a feat of truancy dramatically opposed to publishing ethics.") Biographer Philippa Pullar praised the book for "omitting many of the repetitive portraits and stretching, with relish, the Oriental sexual fantasies, in a tone exactly Harris."[34] Some people think Trocchi wrote a better "autobiography" of Frank Harris than Harris himself. Girodias himself felt that the long-dead author would not have disowned this posthumous product, which "tingled with solid sex and fun."[35]

Trocchi was a talented writer whose creativity in the end failed to find a path through the minefield of his personality. After leaving France, he was to pursue a life of self-destruction and unrealized dreams and to produce one powerful, semiautobiographical work of prose, *Cain's Book.* But in Paris there was no hint of tragedy, just a virtuoso and uninhibited display of energy and charisma.

George Plimpton remembers him standing on a chair at the Café Bonaparte reading a chapter of his translation of Apollinaire's *Les Onze Mille Verges:* "He had a great brogue, and he looked like a fawn, an overgrown fawn. It was quite wonderful to listen to him."[36]

Austryn Wainhouse, who worked closely with Trocchi at *Merlin,* recalled their first encounter: "It was a great lean rascal in a raincoat, the collar pulled up, over its rim lay a long nose claiming all the space between two little eyes, deep-set, very blue, very winning, and manifestly not to be trusted. We got on wonderfully right away."[37]

Girodias saw Trocchi as "the big bad literary wolf of his time," as well as the first of Olympia's "all-out literary stallions. . . . Alex had a certain amount of electricity buzzing around his shaggy brow . . . [he] was always busy cultivating extreme attitudes, extravagant styles and wild dreams with great gusto and appetite. Sometimes he misunderstood his appetite for ambition, and launched into great projects, very few of which succeeded because there were too many other interests and also too many girls around."[38]

Not everyone liked him. Gregory Corso said that for him Trocchi was like "someone out of a swamp; somebody who was so chemically imbued that even with his great heavy coat you could see it all fuming in there. He didn't have what I like in people, something funny. He wasn't funny."[39]

The multitalented Norman Rubington shared Trocchi's ability to handle serious endeavors and more frivolous ones in tandem. While he was churning out pornography—after *Who Pushed Paula?* came *Skirts, Cosimo's Wife,* and *The Double-Bellied Companion*—he was also producing his satirical collage books. Rubington would make a collection of reproductions of old, mainly Victorian engravings, cut them up, and reassemble them. Sometimes he would add his own embellishments, and the collection would be pasted up in book form. The credit for that task would go to the artist, Norman Rubington. The writer, Akbar del Piombo, would then take over and weave a modern fable around Rubington's collages. Or perhaps it was the other way around. One never quite knew with a man who had so many names— "The Rube," "Norm," "The Eyebrows," "Akbar"—and so many separate lives.

But the result was dazzling: witty, original, surprising, and, above all, entertaining. The first book, *Fuzz Against Junk: The Saga of the Narcotics Brigade,* featured the heroic struggle of Sir Edwin Fuzz, Victorian Britain's "foremost narcotics expert and sleuth par excellence," against the drug gangs of New York. Two more collage books, *The Hero Maker* and *The Boiler Maker,* followed. Rubington also put together a hilarious illustrated history of the chastity belt, accompanied by a suitably tongue-in-cheek text by Marilyn Meeske. This appeared in *Olympia Review,* a literary magazine, published by Girodias, that made four erratic appearances in the early 1960s.

Rubington's collage books have become minor classics. They have had an influence on the use of collage and graphics in the visual arts, including the animated opening sequences of the "Monty Python" television series, as well as confusing critics over the identity of the two contributors. One review of Rubington's work in *The New York Times* contemptuously dismissed the notion that the writer, Akbar del Piombo, was none other than the American artist Norman Rubington.

Iris Owens was the lead mare of the Olympia stable, racking up four of her own erotic books and one with Marilyn Meeske. The ubiquitous Trocchi introduced her to Girodias after a disastrous trip to Spain that left her virtually penniless. The usual deal was made, and Iris returned to her "hotel hole" to write her first twenty-five trial pages. "I had never, in my girlish innocence and Americanization, read an erotic book," she later recalled, "but I sure had entertained some erotic thoughts."

She knocked out her pages and dropped them off the next morning. The good word came two days later: "Yes, I could write, he [Girodias] told me. Yes, he wanted the book, yes, he'd start giving me the two dollars a day for which we wrote, yes, yes, but, hesitantly, he suggested to me, gently, possibly, maybe I could tone down the book a bit. He explained that every single word I wrote did not have to be sexual! The book was just a little more than what his readers seemed to go for. So I tried hard to rein in my sexual fantasies. But, I was young and passionate and quite crazy, and the book went its merry course."[40]

Girodias called the book *Darling,* an off-the-wall title for an explicit fantasy about rape, and gave Iris the pen name of "Harriet Daimler," which she loved because she found it liberating. Three more books followed: *The Organization,* loosely based on De Sade's *Philosophie dans le Boudoir, Innocence,* and *The Woman Thing,* which bore more than a passing resemblance to her affair with Trocchi. Iris Owens shared with Norman Rubington and Marilyn Meeske the ability to infiltrate wit and humor into her DBs while ensuring that they were always "brutally frank." Girodias approved as long as the result did not turn into a parody that would have a detumescent effect upon an expectant one-fisted reader. An extract from *The Organization* shows her style:

"Madame de Saint Ange licked the pink stiff blood clotting the tips of Eugénie's teats, breathing, 'They're lovely . . . you need envy no woman. Ah, they're delicious,' . . . her mouth wandered the bosom, 'stiff and sweet in the mouth. I want to make them come,' she made kissing sounds on Eugénie's erect young nipples, 'to feel them flood my mouth and then soften. Ah, they stay stiff, valiant warriors, both of them. Let me bite. That doesn't hurt, my little libertine? Do you feel the heat going to your innocent belly? Tell me, does it travel down in a flush of pleasure? Do you feel that your body is going to open and let all the blood rush out?'

" 'Yes,' the girl giggled weakly. 'But that's not in the book.' "[41]

Girodias was clearly fascinated by Iris, not only by her beauty and her hip New York style but by the phenomenon of a powerful intellect wedded to a fertile sexual imagination. "She believes that she does not have a dirtier mind than other people," he wrote in *The Olympia Reader,* "though her facility and speed in writing out those extended sexual fantasies makes one wonder what she was really dreaming about while getting all the college degrees, marriages and divorces that are requisite in a normal American woman's life. . . . Harriet Daimler struggles against her impossible tendency to write more explicitly than the courts will tolerate."[42]

In the netherworld of erotica, the name "Marcus van Heller" approaches the stature of legend. Under that pseudonym, John Stevenson, who later became a British civil servant, churned out no fewer than twelve novels (ten in Paris and two in London).

Trocchi once again was the catalyst. One day in the *Merlin* office he turned to Stevenson and said: "Why don't you write a book for Girodias, Steve?" Stevenson was dubious but gave it a shot, and in no time he had been signed up. His specialty was historical DBs. He would choose a period of history, do some research, and write quickly and fluently. His first novel took about two months to finish, but after that he found he could produce a book in a fortnight. The research resulted in *The Loins of Amon* (ancient Egypt), *Roman Orgy* (Spartacus and the slave revolt), and *The House of Borgia* (Renaissance Italy), a subject that inspired Stevenson to stretch the fun and games to two volumes.

"I knew all about everyday life in ancient Rome," he says, "I could have told you exactly how they bathed and so on. I did some research on the Borgias, but I soon realized that the less you knew about them the better the book would be."[43]

Other writers later produced DBs in the United States using the Marcus van Heller name. Keen collectors of erotica, however, are not easily duped; they can tell a "real" Marcus van Heller from a fake one as quickly as a jeweler can distinguish a true diamond from one made of paste. Stevenson experienced the phenomenon himself. Sometime after he returned to London, he had to obtain two copies of the DBs he had written in England for a lawyer who was handling his affairs. Scouring Soho's dirty-book shops, he finally ran a small cluster of Marcus van Hellers to earth. "I took one look at them, and they were not mine," he remembers. "So, I took one to the guy behind the counter and said, 'look, this isn't an original van Heller.' 'Oh yes, it is,' he said, 'yes, it is.' I told him it wasn't, it wouldn't have this, and it wouldn't have that. I said, 'I know what I'm talking about. It's not an original.' He looked at me with one of those looks—I've got a right smart-aleck here—and he said: 'Listen, mate, if I 'ad an original van 'eller, you couldn't afford it!'"

At that point John Stevenson, loyal servant of the Crown, decided it would be prudent to maintain his cover. "I said, 'Yes, you're probably right,' and left."[44]

Unlike some of the other Olympia writers, Stevenson made up his own pseudonym, although Girodias claimed credit for it. "Absolutely wrong," Stevenson said. "My brother-in-law and I sat up in my *chambre de bonne* one night trying to work out a name, and I can actually remember part of the conversation. I said it would have to be a strong name, the first name has to be something like 'Mark,' and it has to be diabolical, so 'hell' came up. That got us to 'Marcus Heller,' and then we threw in a bit of the Flying Dutchman to produce the 'van,' and that was it."[45]

Stevenson liked Girodias but had trouble with him over his author's rights: "At one point Alex [Trocchi] and I found our books being pirated because they were appearing under the Ophelia imprint. We took them along to Girodias and said, 'God, Maurice, look what's happening!' 'Oh, the bastards,' he said, 'these pirates!' It was his own imprint. He had simply reprinted our stuff under the Ophelia name and didn't want to give us the money."[46]

Stevenson, like so many pornographers, began writing about his own sexual fantasies and getting turned on. Couquite Hoffenberg, Mason's wife, remembers him working in her house where the Stevensons stayed for a time until Mason threw them out. "Steve used to sing English songs as he sat typing his dirty books," she recalled. "He wrote easily, as if he were cooking."[47]

But overproduction, to change the metaphor, as with viniculture, produces thin wine. And exhaustion. Stevenson recalls, "It became boring trying to think of all the possible aspects of sex. You soon exhaust them, you can hardly write them down, and you wonder if you have said the same thing three pages back. Christopher Logue could have great fun doing his one book and being satirical. But I was doing them constantly and I couldn't put that much into it."[48]

When Logue agreed to write a dirty book for Girodias, he did indeed have something humorous in mind. "It was going to be called *The Abominable Circus*," he writes, "a story about a team of sexual exhibitionists on a world tour being chased, but also sought after, from country to country. Girodias rejected this. He did not think his books should mock their subject matter. So I settled for *Lust,* a dreadful concoction, telling myself it was the only 'left-wing DB' in the series. Of course it was nothing of the kind. A very poor book."[49]

Although Girodias demanded his pound of flesh, as it were, he gave due recognition to his author's efforts to produce a simple, uncomplicated dirty book that would satisfy the onanistic needs of Olympia's readers. In a "Publisher's Note" at the end of *Lust,* Girodias sympathetically registered "the cruel mental struggle sustained by the great Byzantine writer at the time of the composing of the present work of fiction. It nevertheless remains . . . a touching demonstration of his artistic integrity and of his deep knowledge of the human heart."[50]

But Logue had his day, after all. Turning from the labors of lust, he put together amusing collections of bawdy ballads and scatological limericks with delightful cover illustrations by the French artist Savignac. Each was put out under his pseudonym, Count Palmiro Vicarion. "I was rather taken with my name. In those days I was quite snobbish—in a left-wing way, of course."[51]

The book of bawdy ballads consisted of the kind of material that any rugby player would instantly recognize. It included such immortal verse as "The Good Ship Venus," which warns of the perils of sailing to China; "The Wheel," set to the tune of the hymn "O Master, Let Me Walk with Thee"; "The Hole in the Elephant's Bottom"; "Poor Little Angeline" ("Blacksmith, I love you—oh indeed I do. I can see by your trousers that you love me too!"); "Eskimo Nell" stripping off and taking on Dead-Eye Dick and Mexico Pete ("Have you seen the massive pistons on the giant CPR? With a punishing force of a thousand horse—you know what pistons are."); "The Ball of Kerrimuir"; "The Harlot of Jerusalem" with its rousing chorus; and "Abdul Abulbul Emir," who, it will be recalled, pitted his virility against the "long even stroke of Ivan Skavinsky Skivar."

In an introduction to *Count Palmiro Vicarion's Book of Bawdy Ballads,* Logue explained how the collection came into his possession. "Among my earliest memories is that of the house burning down. It was owned by my grandfather, Sforza Vicarion, [who] like all male children born in our family, had been educated in England . . . [where] he had acquired the nickname 'Puffer,' a certain skill in throwing darts, and a developed taste for obscene and witty ditties. . . . As we stood on the lawn watching the home of our ancestors blaze, he could not keep the pride out of his voice as, clapping the trembling housekeeper on the back, he boomed: 'Lord, girl, was there ever a finer show! Look at those flames!' . . . Then abruptly, as if lighted by a stray spark, Puffer struck his forehead and dashed into the flames. The housekeeper wept. The servants clustered around, warning me to keep a stiff upper lip. We grew silent. Suddenly, looking more like a cinder than a Duke, Puffer emerged from the flames bearing three large folios bound in leather, with brass hinges and toggle fastenings— asmoulder but intact. His eyes streamed, his tweeds were smoking, but he staggered towards me, saying, 'Here, my little bedwetter, I have saved them, the Songbooks . . . for you!' With that, he fell lifeless at my feet."[52]

Count Palmiro Vicarion's Book of Limericks also had an introduction, penned by the nobleman in Alma-Atta and dated January 1955: "Bowing before the insistence of several friends, I am finally surren- dering for publication some of my favourite limericks. Let me say at once that it has been no easy matter assembling these verses. For the limerick is usually found, or better still, *heard* in drawing rooms, sac- risties, bawdy-houses, all-night bars, Common Rooms, and at parties where the hostess loses control of the company; in short, in all the usual places were a sort of verbal tradition resides and a versifier may exist. Hence, a limerick, that very fugitive thing, has got to be mem- orised or hastily jotted on a bit of paper napkin, the back of a calling card, or even—as in the case of one of my best discoveries—on a square of toilet tissue. Either that, or it is lost."

Vicarion's selection ranges from the sweet:

> *Rosalina, a pretty young lass,*
> *Had a truly magnificent ass:*
> *Not rounded and pink*
> *As you possibly think—*
> *It was grey, had long ears, and ate grass;*

to the artistic:

> *When Titian was mixing rose madder,*
> *His model was poised on a ladder,*
> *"Your position," said Titian,*
> *"Inspires coition,"*
> *So he nipped up the ladder and 'ad 'er;*

to the scientific:

> *A mathematician named Hall*
> *Had a hexahedronical ball,*

> *And the cube of its weight*
> *Times his pecker, plus eight,*
> *Was four fifths of five eighths of fuck-all;*

to the poetic:

> *An avant-garde bard named McNamiter*
> *Had a tool of enormous diameter.*
> *But it wasn't the size*
> *Brought tears to her eyes,*
> *'Twas the rhythm—dactylic hexameter!*

to the limerick-plus or, in the Count's own words, "the extended witticism":

> *There was a young man named Skinner*
> *Who had a young lady to dinner.*
> *At half past nine*
> *They sat down to dine,*
> *And by quarter of ten it was in her.*
> *What, dinner?*
> *No, Skinner!*[53]

While Marilyn Meeske was not as prolific as Iris Owens in the production of DBs, she was an active and prominent member of the Olympia team. Apart from her solo flight with *Flesh and Bone,* she jointly wrote a DB with Iris (*The Pleasure Thieves*), edited *Olympia Review,* Girodias's literary review, and later worked as an editor for him in New York. While *Flesh and Bone* sprang from her own lively imagination (the title came from a poem by Dylan Thomas), *The Pleasure Thieves* started life as a screenplay about a jewel thief written by her and Terry Southern. The screenplay did not make it, so Marilyn and Iris got together, stirred in the requisite amount of sex, and another dirty book rolled off Olympia's production line.

"My trip was entering the man's world of sexual fantasy like a spy," she says. "What was Daddy thinking? The books were, after all, written for men."[54]

Marilyn had the knack of putting the unexpected and even some humor into what traditionally has been a predictable and humorless narrative form. In *Flesh and Bone,* she has a couple waking up in the morning after an athletic wedding night to find that a large birthmark on the face of the husband has appeared on the face of the wife. In *The Pleasure Thieves* she gives a starring role to a merkin, the eighteenth-century pubic hairpiece for women who had lost their foliage through diphtheria.

In common with most of the other DB writers, Marilyn Meeske had no illusions about what she was doing: "*Flesh and Bone* was written in random fashion, much in the way a shaggy-dog story is invented. It was a wordy sex-hash off the top of the head. I knew it wasn't literature; I understood the formula; I needed the money."[55]

Austryn Wainhouse turned out to be Olympia's translator equivalent of the writers Trocchi and Stevenson rolled into one. His list of credits included translations of two books by Georges Bataille, a novel by Restif de la Bretonne, several works by De Sade, and *Story of O* (a reworking of the first English translation done by Baird Bryant). He added, for good measure, an obscure, nonerotic novel of his own that comfortably secured the record for the longest title on the Olympia list. This was *Hedyphagetica. A Romantic Argument after certain Old Models, & Containing an Assortment of Heroes, Scenes of Anthropophagy & of Pathos, an Apology for Epicurism, & Many Objections raised against It, Together with Reflexions upon the Bodies politic & Individual, their Affections, Nourishments, &c.*

Wainhouse operated under two pseudonyms. The first was "Audiart," which he saw somewhere, possibly the name of a film actor. Girodias was not impressed and preferred the second: "Pieralessandro Casavini." Austryn produced this by alchemizing Wainhouse into "Winehouse," translating that into the Italian "Casavini," doing the same with the first names of a cousin called "Peter" and an uncle called "Alexander," and soldering them together. Wainhouse felt the effort he had expended on this task was adequately rewarded when an American critic, reviewing two of the books he had translated, referred to him authoritatively as the "Florentine polyglot, Casavini."[56]

Wainhouse remembers his first meeting with Girodias, orchestrated by the ubiquitous Trocchi. They met at the Deux Magots on the Boulevard Saint-Germain: "Monsieur Girodias came dressed in a dark suit. He shook hands with his left hand, for his right was in a bandage. He had the restrained, wooden motions of a very much depleted man. . . . I had to strain to catch what was emerging [from his lips] in a dim though not unmusical murmur.

"'Georges Bataille has spoken to me about you. I understand you have some texts.'

"'I have made a translation of his preface to *Justine*.'

"'And of *Justine* as well, I believe he said.'

"'And of *La Philosophie dans le Boudoir*.'

"He pursed his lips, looked upward at the ceiling for a moment, then redirected his somnolent brown gaze at me. 'I think I might be interested in seeing your work, if that were possible.'"[57]

With that the Olympia Press and Austryn Wainhouse were launched.

THE TRAVELLER'S COMPANION SERIES and other books published by Olympia circled the globe and often elicited reactions as bizarre as the publications themselves. Muffie Wainhouse kept a kind of "Lonely Hearts" file from Olympia's worldwide readership. She remembers some special contributors, the star being one Omar Benajee from Calcutta: "He was my first encounter with the Indian Mind. He typed on one of those little letter-envelopes that you open by tearing the perforations on three sides. Omar typed with no margins, so bits of words clung to the removed strip. He sent $7.33 in every letter. This was his lucky number? The amount he was allowed or simply able to send at a time? (It would purchase about one book plus a quarter of another one.) But what he wanted was a package of three books, so would I please hold his money until I had enough.

"Along with this banking, I began to cull other arresting letters. There were American soldiers, who had written nothing since the fourth grade, laboriously composing their book orders. One soldier who had not mastered currency exchange sent a $10 gold piece that his grandfather had given him. Desperate Italians wrote unimaginable English compositions. A German request came in for a book with lots of fuking [*sic*].

"But back to Omar. After his first shipment he sent a letter (and $7.33) describing the marvellous and holy gift he had received, the beauty of that most wonderful of human acts, the purity and truth of the writing, the wonder of such honesty, such unveiling of the human heart. No one ever matched Omar in length, style, or possibly, joy. But many wrote of beauty and truth and of how these were real books about real life. Some letters were almost unbearably poignant. Many spoke of their profound gratitude. Of course, I used the letters to entertain the authors who came in, but I shared the touching ones with Norman [Rubington]. Maurice thought all this rather silly."[58]

Miriam Worms recalled some other responses. "There was the Lebanese who suggested we sell inflated rubber women—a very good turnover, he said. And the English headmaster who caught one of his boys with a greenback and hoped the roof would fall on us and wipe us and our filth off the face of the earth. One day Norman Rubington was in the office when a letter arrived from an Indian who wanted us to send a runner to Orly airport, where he would be passing through in transit, with the latest Olympia list. Norman enacted the whole scene as the runner and had us all in stiches."[59]

John Stevenson got fan mail addressed to "Marcus van Heller": "One letter said I admire your books more than any of the others [in The Traveller's Companion Series] but I don't think you are always quite accurate. There was that bit in *The Loins of Amon* about the donkey and I remember when I was in Egypt I saw this exhibition and, you know, it wasn't like that."[60]

How did Olympia Inc. view its products and the role it was playing to a still repressed Anglo-Saxon world?

Muffie Wainhouse, Girodias's first editor, put it this way: "The dirty books were to make money, but even they had certain standards. Girodias did reject manuscripts. He appreciated books with wit— Norman Rubington's, for instance—but he was generally rather scornful of the genre and its readers. However, he became very protective against the censor because he considered the books innocuous."[61]

"Enough has been said about the influence of the printed word," Girodias wrote later, "but never enough about the liberating influence of the printed four-letter word." Referring to the greenbacks pouring off Olympia's presses, Girodias continued: "Those literary orgies, those torrents of systematic bad taste were quite certainly instrumental in clearing the air. . . . The imbecile belief that sex is sin, that physical pleasure is unclean, that erotic thoughts are immoral, that abstinence is the proper rule which may be broken at rare intervals, but merely for the sake of procreation—all those sick Judeo-Christian ideas were exposed for what they are. I insist that no little boys were ever corrupted by bad books of mine, and I do hope that they enjoyed them to the full, and gleaned at least a little useful knowledge therefrom; nobody seems to have died of shock, no reader was ever reported killed by a four-letter word."[62]

OLYMPIA'S ZENITH in the mid-1950s was also a high point in the young lives of most of its contributors. This was the shambling, pungent, easygoing Paris of the Fourth Republic, where every day seemed to bring something new in the cinema, in the art galleries, in the theater, on the bookstalls—not to mention a change of government. It was the Paris of the circular public pissoirs, where you could see the feet and the heads and hear the gush of the relieved as you strolled down the street. The Paris of the clanking Métro trains with their powerful mingled scents of yesterday's garlic, Gauloise Bleu cigarettes, and the smoking graphite from the brake drums.

It was the Paris of jazz, where self-exiled black American musicians played and lived, a city where drugs, especially hashish and heroin, flowed in from North Africa. The Paris where you could always find a cheap room, a cheap restaurant, a friendly café where you could sit and write or engage in brilliant, dizzying conversation with somebody interesting or simply dream of the infinite and intoxicating panorama that stretched out before you. It was the Paris of freedom and of experiment. You could say what you liked, write, paint, and act how you liked, drink and eat what took your fancy, smoke, sniff, snort, and shoot up what came your way, and penetrate—or be penetrated by—whoever turned you on. And all you needed were a couple of pounds or a few dollars in your pocket.

"Most of us romantic expatriates went to Paris to be free of the conventional horrors at home," Iris Owens said. "Maurice was my ticket to freedom. The payment for a book that took a maximum of two months to write, though meager, was sufficient back then for a six-month escape to Sicily or a winter in Hydra, a summer in Saint Tropez, where one was free to struggle with serious literary effort, the kind that didn't get published. We were natural DB writers. We were sexual revolutionaries with a need to shock, and our books were more exploratory than we thought at the time. There was a streak of anarchism in all of us. The reason why we broke new ground was that we were into sexual politics."[63]

"It was rebellious to be a pornographer," said Marilyn Meeske, "and publishing was a guerrilla operation."[64]

Girodias identified joyfully with the idea that there was a war on: "It was great fun. The Anglo-Saxon world was being attacked, invaded, infiltrated, out-flanked, and conquered by this erotic armada. The Dickensian schoolmasters of England were convulsed with helpless rage, the judges' hair was standing on end beneath their wigs, black market prices in New York and London for our green-backed products were soaring to fantastic heights."[65]

Terry Southern, who was not in Paris as long as the others, remembered it as a marvelous time: "It was an exciting literary scene, total freedom for writers, no editors suggesting changes, they just welcomed far-out expression. Great time for music. Charlie Parker, Miles Davis, Thelonious Monk, were there playing close up in small Paris clubs. It was extraordinary being that close to Charlie Parker. Drugs too. Not many people really into junk then. One of our main concerns was how to short-stop marijuana being turned into hashish, the Arabs' favorite. They were not interested in selling it to you in grass form because they didn't know how much to charge. We were trying to relive the 1920s era of Hemingway. Mason and I used to go to bullfights every year—Pamplona, San Sebastian, and then down to Madrid, Valencia, on to Seville. One year we had a 1935 Citroën, or we'd take the train. So, it was the drugs, the jazz, the great camaraderie."[66]

Most of the survivors of that period emphasize the sense of solidarity among the group. "There was no hero worship," says Iris Owens. "We all thought we were better than each other. Yet there was a group feeling, a sense of community. We were all fleeing from something. We were all sexual obsessives of one sort or another and we all identified ourselves as writers. Also, we were very young and romantic, filled with pain."

Christopher Logue's pain appeared to overcome him at one stage. He went off to the south of France to commit suicide. One account has him writing to Trocchi to inform him of his intention. Trocchi jumped on a train and found his friend sitting in a café near a pier where he had hired a rowboat. The plan was to row out to sea and slide gently over the side to oblivion. Logue says it wasn't quite like that. Trocchi did come after him but found him sitting on the beach, not in a café. There was no plan to go to sea, although Logue had acquired a tin of sleeping pills and had thought of using them or even throwing himself under a train. The story ended happily with the two young men returning to Paris together.

"Christopher told me his right to die was more important than his right to live," said Iris Owens.

For Baird Bryant, Paris was a wild time. "The rule was if you had any desire to do something, you did it. We had been living in an anachronism in the United States, like locking a child in a form-fitting cage and then growing up through the bars. We were searching for a change, getting loose and breaking our conditioning. We believed that the good came out in people when they were free. Break the conditioning and find your true nature. One of the most frustrating aspects of that conditioning was sexual. We regarded ourselves as part of the sexual revolution."

Bryant, like Corso and Hoffenberg, was drawn into the drug scene. "Paris became a surreal experience for me in the end," says Bryant. "Once I heard music coming out of a ten-inch loudspeaker over my head as I walked around the streets. Girodias seemed to understand more about this than me. He gave me the impression he was on another level. I wanted to be there too. I wanted to know what the fuck was going on. Burroughs was there, he knew what the fuck was going on."[67]

Corso didn't know what the fuck was going on either, but he did not lose too much sleep over it: "I got to Paris in 1957 when Mason and Terry were leaving. Norman was there, with Gaït—*Fuzz Against Junk* was big. . . . That's when I got beautifully into drugs. I'd just go and get the money, piecemeal, one thousand francs at a time [from Girodias] and then I'd go to Hadj and the Arabs and get the good dope and go back and write more of this stupid book. That was my routine. I thought, oh my god, what am I into here? I didn't know what the future would bring—I figured I could go through this. I can handle this, I can handle anything, I am a poet, right?

"I was crazy, I didn't know what was going on. Bill [Burroughs] knew what was going on. Allen [Ginsberg] knew what was going on. I didn't. But those were immortal times. Nobody died then, nobody I knew died in those days."[68]

The Olympia crowd not only wrote about sex but they did it, especially with each other. Alex Trocchi seduced Iris Owens; Austryn Wainhouse had an "episode" with Denny Bryant; Girodias had an affair with Muffie Wainhouse; Baird Bryant (after his divorce from Denny) married Trocchi's former girlfriend, Jane Lougee, but before doing that he was "embroiled" with Iris Owens; John Stevenson had an affair with Marilyn Meeske's sister; Eric Kahane says he had an affair with Marilyn; she says she didn't but she did have one with Mason Hoffenberg earlier in New York; Mason thought that his wife, Couquite, was having an affair with John Stevenson's wife, Mary, but she wasn't (she was having an affair with Norman Rubington). Marilyn had a brief encounter with Girodias in the French mime Marcel Marceau's apartment; Monique Sindler-Gonthier, a friend of Girodias, never had an affair with him—he didn't ask her—but she thinks she had one with his brother, Eric, who says, of course, she did. Everyone fell in love with Iris Owens, except Christopher Logue, who says he was terrified of her; after breaking up with Gaït Frogé, Norman Rubington had an affair with . . .

6

The
Wild Ginger Man

IN THE MID-1950s the Olympia Press received two unsolicited and unusual manuscripts. Girodias read them and felt he was moving "from wonder to wonder. . . . One was by a young unknown American writer living in England by the name of J. P. Donleavy, who had written a rather unruly but scintillating novel: *The Ginger Man*. The other by a Russian-born professor from Cornell University, Vladimir Nabokov: *Lolita*. . . .

"Donleavy accepted with good grace our remarks concerning the rambling, redundant form of his book and Austryn's wife, Muffie Wainhouse, did a great job editing it. Nabokov also complied—to a certain extent—with our suggestions that he suppress a number of French phrasings and locutions which endangered the delicate balance of his style. In both cases I think we acted efficiently and intelligently, as very few publishers would have done, and I was repaid in each instance by the blackest ingratitude."[1]

Thus began the interlinked sagas that led to the publication of two of the twentieth century's landmark novels, whose literary impact played a significant part in breaking down the walls of censorship in

Britain and the United States. The publication of *The Ginger Man* and *Lolita* brought their authors notoriety and fame, mental anguish and artistic salvation, and great wealth. The books lifted Girodias to the zenith of his publishing career, and *Lolita* produced his largest financial bonanza. But their appearance set in train two author-publisher vendettas that were unprecedented in the annals of publishing for their drama, personal venom, and sheer stamina.

"I SET OUT one June near the sea in County Wicklow, Ireland, to write a splendid book no one would forget," Donleavy wrote years later. "I knew then that the years would come and go and the book would live. It has taken more years than I ever could have imagined and more battles than I ever felt I'd have to fight but the fist I shook and the rage I spent has at last blossomed and before it should fade I'd like to say that I'm glad."[2]

Girodias first heard of the novel that was to become *The Ginger Man* when he received a letter from Donleavy in the autumn of 1954: "I thought there might well be a glimmer of something hiding there behind the diffident wording. Ten lines in all in a quaint abbreviated style, claiming the writer wished to submit a manuscript of about 125,000 words in English called *Sebastian Dangerfield,* previously rejected by Charles Scribner in America because of obscenity. 'The obscenity is very much part of this novel and its removal would detract from it,' Donleavy wrote. An engaging way of approaching the evil continental publisher, brass tacks from the word go."[3]

Girodias says he responded quickly and there ensued a rather "enigmatic correspondence." The manuscript was sent, held up by French Customs for "who knows what reasons," released, read, and found "potentially terrific but awfully over-blown, undisciplined, unmanageable." A letter was dispatched to Donleavy detailing the criticisms, pleading for extensive cuts throughout and shortening the interior monologues, and asking for a more effective title than *Sebastian Dangerfield.* Donleavy wrote back suggesting *The Ginger Man,* which was accepted.

Donleavy's novel recounts the exploits of Sebastian Dangerfield (the Ginger Man), an Irish-American student at Trinity College, Dublin, who has an upper-class English wife and baby daughter, a charming manner, and a competitively strong addiction to women and alcohol. Dependent on a wealthy but alienated father in the

United States, Dangerfield is usually broke, as are most of his friends. A charmer, a manipulator, and a lost soul, Donleavy's picaresque hero moves from one hilarious scrape to another, shadowed by a looming sense of disaster.

On the way, he jettisons his studies, is abandoned by his wife and child, says good-bye to his best friend, who returns to America, has several affairs, including one with a guilt-ridden, deeply religious lodger, and is pursued by creditors and the police. He ends up in London, where one of his Irish friends has struck gold. But it is too late. Dangerfield's momentum toward self-destruction is, it seems, irreversible.

Written in a staccato, sometimes contorted style, with constant switching from the first to the third person and great chunks of interior monologue, the book can be hard going. Nevertheless, it is a powerful, sweet-sour, funny-sad novel that manages to finesse its vices while strutting its virtues. Whether you are attracted to or repelled by him, the erratic passage of The Ginger Man is unforgettable.

By early 1955 "a slew of letters had been exchanged defining terms of contract." On February 11, 1955, Girodias wrote the following to Donleavy. "I would like to know whether you want the book to be published under your own name or under a pseudonym? Please think it over. Of course, my firm has a rather scandalous reputation and it might harm you in some way to publicly admit any connection with us. On the other hand we have published the works of quite a few genuine writers: so I will leave you free to choose your own solution. . . . Please let me know what you decide in that respect."[4]

Donleavy does not remember his exact response, but he specified that he wanted the book to appear under his own name. His impression was that Olympia had two divisions, one publishing reputable writers like Beckett and the other more "scandalous" ones. "I thought Girodias was just warning me about this other part of his firm," he said. Donleavy had heard of Merlin magazine and knew that a connection existed between the review and the Olympia Press. He assumed that The Ginger Man would be published in the same way as Beckett had been.[5]

Girodias did not agree with Donleavy's view that The Ginger Man's obscenity had prevented it from being published elsewhere: "It had been rejected by various publishers not because it was a DB but because it was beyond those people's grasp." Like Beckett, Girodias says, Donleavy was "too abstract and incomprehensible."[6]

Meanwhile, the editing process continued across the English Channel, from Donleavy's modest house in the back streets of Fulham to the busy offices of the Olympia Press in the rue de Nesle.

"He was cutting his manuscript into ribbons and mailing same to us in dribs and drabs," Girodias writes. "It was Muffie's task to unglue, decipher, correct, reconstruct and edit word by word that chaotic flow, since obviously Donleavy at his end, in a state alternately frantic and despondent, friendly and suspicious, was constantly losing track of what he was doing. Thus a second revision had to be accomplished at our end, or rather a painstaking reconstruction, a fact he preferred to ignore. I watched the process like a hen passing a particularly tricky egg, never sure whether it would not break into an untimely omelet before the delivery was completed."[7]

Muffie Wainhouse says the manuscript was "not a thing of beauty—indeed a rather sloppy, dog-eared affair. As I recall the editing, it was like orchestration—building crescendos, really. Chapters were in the wrong order. Within a chapter with four incidents, the climax might occur in the second. If Maurice OK'd these ideas they were written to Donleavy. For example, 'place pages 35 to 50 after page 68 and write a new transitional paragraph on page 34.' It was a lively correspondence, and pleasant. Donleavy usually agreed and would send new paragraphs, usually on stationery. Then I would go to work with scissors and paste."[8]

"We must assume that he did not make the changes on his copy and that is why the 'original' was eventually sought," she said. "But we did not tamper with the actual text; it was more a question of arrangement. And when I read his second book [A Singular Man] I thought, 'Oh dear, I wish I could have helped with this one, too.' The Ginger Man went to proof stages before he saw the whole thing. But he never objected; he was pleased with the book."[9]

Donleavy's memories of the publishing history of The Ginger Man, his first and best novel, are rather different. The manuscript had been read by many publishers in the United States and Britain. Scribners in New York had been impressed but eventually decided against publication. Donleavy did, however, manage to have a couple of extracts of the book printed in The Manchester Guardian. But a real breakthrough did not occur until Brendan Behan, a drinking and literary companion from their days together in Dublin, told him about the Olympia Press in Paris. "He mentioned it one night after we had had a fistfight outside a pub in Fleet Street."[10]

While agreeing to change the title, Donleavy said in 1992 that he still preferred the original "Sebastian Dangerfield." But he was emphatic that not a word was changed by Olympia in the editing process. "Every single word was specially put down—I still write that way today. . . . There isn't a single solitary word of that manuscript that *could* have been changed. It was *impossible,* even I couldn't change it. . . . It's all put in a rhythmic style so that it's readable."[11]

At a critical point in Donleavy's subsequent twenty-one-year-long struggle with his publisher, Girodias argued that the contents of *The Ginger Man* owed more to the Olympia Press than to its author. Donleavy, for his part, demanded the return of the original manuscript. But the original did not exist—much of it had gone into Muffie's wastebasket—and its disappearance seemed to bother no one at the time.

"We wanted to get to press, we wanted money, and success," Muffie says. "In those parties and luncheons when JPD [Donleavy] was in Paris we looked at sales and royalties. Did he ever ask for his manuscript then? Not to my knowledge. He bemoaned what those visits did for his liver. It's a wonder any of our livers still function. But they may have been impaired; how else do lawsuits grow from such blithe days?"[12]

Muffie Wainhouse says she loved the book and was a sympathetic and faithful editor, changing neither words nor meaning. Donleavy, however, relegates her role to copy editing: "By editorial work what she meant was that she corrected spellings and making sure what appeared in the manuscript actually got to the printer. I'm quoting her now telling me how hard she worked on it. But the fact of her doing any so-called editorial work is actually not the case. The book would have lost its whole character had an editor been fooling around with it," he says. "You couldn't fool around with *The Ginger Man.*"[13]

Nor, as events were to prove, with its author.

Establishing who did what in preparing *The Ginger Man* for its extraordinarily successful journey into publishing history is difficult forty years after the event. It is clear, however, that in the early stages Donleavy agreed with Girodias's suggestions to tighten and reduce the novel by about a fifth of its length.[14] The edited manuscript did disappear in the printing process, and the one Donleavy holds is a carbon copy of the original draft that he sent to the Olympia Press in 1954. On balance, it would seem that Muffie Wainhouse was a sympathetic and faithful editor who changed nothing of substance in the text. But it would also appear that a considerable amount of real editing—not simply copy editing—was done to put the novel into shape for publication. The main point, however, is that the collaboration worked and both author and publisher were happy with the result.

PAYMENT FOR THE BOOK, although unorthodox, caused fewer problems. It was agreed that Donleavy would receive £250 in cash from a bookseller in London called D. Cliff, a business friend of Girodias. "Mr. Cliff was a very respectable dealer in pornography," Girodias asserts, "whose speciality was bondage and flagellation." The publisher had befriended him "for the simple reason that he was a jolly good fellow notwithstanding his peculiar commerce."[15]

Donleavy remembers collecting his money: "I had to go down a basement in Soho, where a book dealer counted it out." The pound notes were handed over, and Donleavy made his retreat, fearing that someone would be following with a hammer to hit him over the head and steal his hard-earned quids. "Two hundred and fifty pounds was a lot of money in those days; you could practically live for a year in London on that." The payment was for the first print run of five thousand copies; it was agreed that more money would be forthcoming if the book was reprinted.[16]

The Ginger Man was published in Paris in June 1955. Sitting in his house in Fulham, Donleavy received two copies of his book. He tore open the package and looked at the front cover with its plain green, black-edged design. The book's title and author's name were fine, but he was surprised to see that the volume was "No. 7" in an unknown series called "The Traveller's Companion."

Surprise turned to shock and shock to fury when he turned to the end of the book. There he found a page devoted entirely to advertising a list of the other titles in the newly launched series. They included such delights as *Rape* and *The Loins of Amon* by Marcus van Heller, *School for Sin* by Frances Lengel, *The Libertine* by Robert Desmond, *Tender Was My Flesh* by Winifred Drake, *The Sexual Life of Robinson Crusoe* by Humphrey Richardson, and *The Whip Angels* by XXX. All of these, except *The Ginger Man,* were explicitly pornographic.

"When I saw that I realized it was total disaster," said Donleavy. "There were a few people of literary bent who had read the manuscript and were looking forward to writing reviews." But publication in a pornographic series, he said, condemned the book to oblivion. "It was a total and absolute disaster." What made the situation particularly galling was that when *Lolita* was published by the Olympia Press three months later, it appeared in an identical format but without any mention of The Traveller's Companion Series and no list of dirty books at the back.[17]

The blow was even harder to take because Donleavy says Scribners had been close to publishing *The Ginger Man* in the United States. In an interview in *The Paris Review* in 1975, Donleavy tells the story. He contacted John Hall Wheelock, an editor at Scribners, who agreed to read the novel. "After a few weeks Wheelock called me in. He said: 'We've all read the manuscript here. Three of our editors think it is one of the best manuscripts ever brought to this publishing house. The fourth thinks it's the best manuscript she's ever come across. But I don't think we can publish it.'

"This was because they had published *From Here to Eternity,* and it had brought them so much trouble and difficulty with its scatology they were not eager to go through it again. And, apparently, the young Mr. Scribner, who'd taken over the firm, was less liberal than the old man. So the editors were less likely to stick their necks out and to say, 'You must publish this book.'

"Well, when I got that reaction from Scribners—and this was the McCarthy era—I was aware that it was the end of the road. I realized that if I couldn't get it published with that kind of terrific reception, then it couldn't get published. Wheelock gave me the name of an agent who didn't believe that Wheelock had even *seen* me, and when he read a sample of the book thought it was most uninteresting and 'very unlikely anyone would publish it.' Random House also turned it down."

Later, Donleavy sent it to Little, Brown in Boston. "The editor called me around there on a hot, sweaty afternoon. He sat me a good distance away from his desk, and the manuscript was in a shadowy corner of the room. He leaned back in his chair very nervously and pointed at the manuscript, with his hand trembling, and said, 'There's obscene libel in that book!' So that was the end of Little, Brown."[18]

This was the background to Donleavy's apocalyptic reaction. He came to believe that Girodias had an ulterior motive in publishing *The Ginger Man* in The Traveller's Companion Series. This was to prove to the French authorities, who were threatening to close down the Olympia Press, that he was publishing books of literary merit. Muffie Wainhouse agrees but also believes that Donleavy, who had earlier asked for and received an Olympia Press catalogue, overstated his case: "When he later mentioned his disappointment at not being published like Beckett, I always thought that disingenuous," she says. "He did not seek out the Olympia Press because it printed Bibles."[19]

Girodias recalls the author's anger: "July 15, 1955: Donleavy acknowledges receipt of the first two copies of the book and expresses outrage and indignation at the fact that a list of Traveller's Companion titles is printed on the back page." But Girodias goes on to suggest that a rapprochement takes place. "Several more letters are exchanged to dispose of that incident until Donleavy's letter of July 28th in which he half apologises for his show of temper and offers his complete cooperation in the future. Peace is restored and our contract is confirmed."[20]

Donleavy does not remember it this way. He felt that any further involvement by Girodias in the destiny of *The Ginger Man* would be detrimental to the book. In October 1955 he decided to go over to Paris for his first face-to-face meeting with his publisher. His mission, he says, was clear: "I had to save my book."

"Hah!" commented Girodias. "At last we were going to meet and overcome all the unpleasantness and misunderstandings suffered in the course of the difficult parturition."[21]

SINCE THIS is the real beginning of their long struggle, I thought it useful to visit James Patrick Donleavy in his Irish retreat and to hear what he had to say almost forty years after the launching of hostilities.

It was a cold, windy December day with rain threatening; clouds chased each other over a sodden gray-green landscape. About two miles beyond Mullingar on the Sligo road, the gray bulk of Levington Park rose above winter-stripped trees. A study in architectural muscularity, Levington Park was built in the middle of the eighteenth century by a wealthy landowner who kept a mistress. Walls of stone, roof of slate, the house was unadorned apart from a square portico supported by two columns, a Georgian cornice, and six chimney stacks. Some two hundred acres of gently rolling farmland and half a mile of lakeshore enveloped it.

Donleavy's secretary opened the door and showed me into a large living room with dark green walls, white shutters and woodwork, outsize cushions scattered over the polished pine floors, and a grand piano in one corner. A peat fire burned in the grate. A photograph in the center of the marble mantelpiece showed Joe Louis, poised on his toes, gazing down at the fallen figure of Max Schmeling. The referee was pointing a decisive forefinger at the world heavyweight champion. Looking at the photograph, it is not difficult to think of another contest, this time with author and publisher squaring off.

The door opened, and Donleavy came in. In his mid-sixties, he was much as the photographers had him: medium-height, well built, with a boxer's sloping shoulders and long, loose-limbed arms; most of his hair and much of his beard were white; the aquiline nose, long face, and sad brown eyes resembled those of a sixteenth-century Spanish grandee rather than the features of his Celtic forebears. El Greco would have relished painting him. His predilection for tweeds was reflected in his jacket and waistcoat, although his trousers were cord. He wore heavy brown brogues and a blue open-necked shirt; a red silk handkerchief blossomed from his top pocket. His accent was more British than American: long a's in words like "can't" and "asked" and the soft-shoe shuffle in "schedule"; he was also fond of the British upper-class use—and misuse—of "one" instead of "I."

Tea was served by his secretary on a low trestle table supported by large flat stones in front of the hearth. It was an elegant spread crowned by a wickedly rich chocolate cake from Fortnum and Mason in London, the gift of a visiting friend.

"I was in Paris for one purpose only," he said, sipping his tea, "and that was for the book. When I first had dealings with the Olympia Press I was aware that they had published *Merlin,* a literary magazine; this was the only thing I could find in London at the time. So I was totally misled, although I had some idea that Girodias"—he pronounced it Girodia*ss*—"did publish pornographic books.

"But it never occurred to me that they would stick *The Ginger Man* in The Traveller's Companion Series, which was a deliberately pornographic series of works. What I expected was just the cover with *The Ginger Man* by J. P. Donleavy and the text. I couldn't have had any idea about The Traveller's Companion Series because it didn't exist until my book, along with the other first books in the series, was published. They all came out at once.

"So that caused the trouble. I didn't know anything until I received my first copy of *The Ginger Man.* And then"—he paused and laughed softly—"I swore *revenge.*

"But before I went over to Paris I had met an English poet and critic called Derek Stanford, whose girlfriend at the time was Muriel Spark, at a strange little place called the Renaissance Club. Stanford said he knew an English publisher who would be interested in publishing *The Ginger Man.* This was Neville Armstrong, who owned a publishing house called Neville Spearman. So I went to Paris armed with that information, and that is how I presented it to Girodias in order to save the book. It was essential that I should get it published in Britain. It was a serious work and had nothing to do with pornography or anything else."

The actual meeting in Paris, notwithstanding the fragmentary and often contradictory accounts of the principals and other participants, did not go at all badly. Girodias took Donleavy to coffee at the Old Navy Café in the Boulevard Saint-Germain and to lunch at a restaurant near the Odéon, where he appeared to have his own wines stored in the restaurant's cellar.

"I was impressed," said Donleavy. "Girodias was very cordial and hospitable. I formed a strong impression of him." Girodias, in his turn, also seemed impressed—especially with Donleavy's zoological knowledge, which he had acquired as a student at Trinity College, Dublin. Donleavy told him about the phenomenon of the sperm always seeking out the ovum. "Girodias turned to whoever was with us and said: 'Mr. Donleavy knows a great deal, you know.' "[22]

Muffie Wainhouse retains a brief but vivid impression of the first encounter. "We were all excited and pleased to meet each other when Donleavy arrived in Paris. I recall a jolly dinner with the three of us during which Donleavy, in heavy tweeds, confessed that he hated tweed and had his trousers lined with silk. Red silk. The only remembered confession of the evening."[23]

The chain of events and their meaning became more confused at the end of Donleavy's Paris visit. The social climax was a dinner and a party that Girodias laid on for his new author. It was held in Girodias's apartment over the La Bucherie restaurant, which was owned by "a jolly, round-faced, hard-drinking, rapier-tongued Russian lady."

"None of my guests at the Donleavy party," he wrote, "had yet read The Ginger Man. But everyone had heard glowing reports about it from Muffie and me. So, Donleavy was treated by all as one of the rising champions of the new literature." Girodias, the epicure, made sure that his guest would sample some of France's best wine. "It so happens that I was at the time in the throes of the supreme discovery—Burgundy wines—and the tables were loaded with the most magnificent samples of that unsurpassable wonder. Indeed, those were the days when the greatest vintage years, 1947 and 1949, had reached their full splendor, when a single sip of Clos-Vougeot or Romanée-Conti would turn you into a god, though certainly not a saint."[24]

Girodias went on to describe the party. "The night was warm and vibrant, a last burst of summer had come to us as a parting gift, no doubt to welcome our literary visitor. I turned away from the window and, among the male and female bodies sprawling on the couches and on the floor, some chanting, some snoring, I searched for my guest of honour. And there he was, propped up against the bathroom door, a slight man in a three-piece checkered suit; his sallow face looked like a cardboard mask with skimpy whiskers pasted on. My brother Eric was speaking to him urgently, straight into his left ear, with the obvious intent of keeping him awake. On his right, Michel Gall was crouching, describing to him with great convivial vehemence the theme of his book, *The Sexual Life of Robinson Crusoe*.

"Fortunately, Donleavy had chosen to stay at the hotel just round the corner, the Esmeralda, and I felt I had to take him home while he was still semi-conscious. But whatever consciousness he may have had, he promptly lost on the staircase. I had to support him and then carry him on my back down to the Esmeralda. Once we were there, after I had managed to prop him up against the desk in the lobby, he blinked at me and asked unexpectedly:

"'Are you Girodias's brother?'

"This left me nonplussed. So, he thought my brother was I? Ah well, another misunderstanding, we'll clear it up tomorrow, I told myself.

"But the next day, Donleavy, very groggy, had lunch with Muffie and left in the afternoon for London. We had exchanged not ten words during his short stay, and he had mistaken me for my kid brother. So be it."[25]

Terry Southern was in Paris at the time of Donleavy's visit and later described it in an article in *Grand Street,* a New York literary quarterly. From the outset he made it clear that he was convinced that Girodias was "trying to dupe J. P. Donleavy out of absolutely everything pertaining to *The Ginger Man*.

"'Donleavy is coming over from Dublin,' he told me. 'I'm hosting a *grande soirée* for him, and as part of his entertainment I'd like you to take him to that fancy bordello you and Plimpton go to. How much does it cost?' I told him I had no idea of the cost since I had been a guest. . . .

"The. *soirée* itself proved to be quite a gala affair—thanks mainly to the attendance of one particular acquaintance of Mason's and mine, Mohammed Hadj . . . proprietor of the Café Soleil du Maroc and ofttimes purveyor of what Girodias rather affectedly called 'the damnable wog-hemp.'

"On this occasion, however, Girodias's generally low opinion of Monsieur Hadj . . . seemed much ameliorated, perhaps because his M.O. for the evening, I soon began to discern, was to get Donleavy so totally blotto that he could have his way with him, in terms of contracts, royalties, or whatever else might relate to *The Ginger Man*. And in that regard it was apparent that a bit of hashish would be a welcome addition to his arsenal of derangements. 'Baudelaire,' I heard him confide to our hapless guest of honor, 'used to have it in his confiture.'"

Southern was then apparently sidetracked by Alex Trocchi and John Calder, the British publisher, "a deadly combo, derangement-wise." He thus failed to follow what he calls "the complete dismantling of J. P. Donleavy." His last sighting was of the new Olympia Press author "being bundled out of the door and into the Paris night by Gid [Girodias's nickname] and his brother Eric. I heard later that he returned to Dublin the very next day, back to the snug comfort of hearth and home."[26]

Donleavy's own memories differed. He remembered the party and meeting Eric Kahane, Girodias's brother. But he was emphatic he did not have too much to drink. "There was no question of my being incapable or drunk," he said. And since he weighed somewhere between twelve and a half and thirteen stone, "it would have been pretty impossible for Girodias [who was lightly built] to have carried me."

Gray areas occur in both Girodias's and Southern's accounts of the visit. Donleavy and Muffie Wainhouse attest to several meetings between the author and his publisher. Thus Girodias's statement about exchanging "not ten words" with Donleavy is odd. The business side of the visit, dealing mainly with the publication of *The Ginger Man* outside France and how proceeds from the sale of the foreign rights would be shared, was completed before the final party. Donleavy was not living in Dublin at this time, as Southern had him, but in London.

A Girodias-orchestrated conspiracy to render Donleavy incapable and somehow rob him of his rights in *The Ginger Man* seems far-fetched. Muffie makes the point that no other publisher was prepared to touch the book at this stage. While Neville Armstrong, the British publisher, was showing a strong interest in a U.K. publication, nothing had been decided. Furthermore, Donleavy had come to Paris not to give anything more away but rather to take something back. A wrong needed to be righted. He came to Paris in pursuit of a quest: to save the book. He was thus extremely unlikely, drunk or sober, to be susceptible to blandishments or pressure to make concessions.

"The agreement with Girodias as I recall it," Donleavy said, getting up to put some more peat sods on the fire, "was to split the American rights fifty-fifty with him. But, knowing that I could get a British publisher to bring the book out, I said I would have all the British rights but with the American and others, we would go half and half. In France I got my royalties, so there was no splitting there."

Donleavy has said elsewhere that Girodias agreed to this because they both realized that critical acclaim in Britain would increase the likelihood of profitable sales in the United States.[27] But the agreement was verbal; nothing was put in writing. "And that's how it was left," Donleavy said. "I returned to England thinking I had a deal."[28]

EARLY IN 1956, Donleavy worked out a contract with Neville Armstrong. He was given an advance and agreed to some cuts to avoid prosecution under Britain's draconian obscenity laws, the most restrictive in the Western world. The main deletion concerned a short episode in chapter ten when the hero, Sebastian Dangerfield, boards a suburban train in Dublin carrying a package of fresh liver. He is at first puzzled and then enraged when the people in the carriage react to him with a range of emotions running the gamut from embarrassment to coarse amusement to shock to outright hostility. It finally dawns on him that his fly is open. The chapter ends:

"What's he doing. Pointing into his lap. Me? Good Christ. It's out. Every inch of it.

"Leaping for the door. Get out. Fast. Behind him, a voice.

"'Haven't you forgotten something else?'

"Wheeling, wrenching the blood-stained parcel from the rack.

"Behind him.

"'You can't remember your meat at all today.'"[29]

Meanwhile, in Paris, Girodias seemed to be under the impression that relations between himself and Donleavy were on an even keel:

"I had not heard much from J. P. Donleavy since his tantrums of the year before apart from a few rather friendly letters. He had read both Beckett's *Molloy* and Nabokov's *Lolita,* for which he expressed his connoisseur's appreciation. . . . At least he could no longer accuse me of having his book used as a smokescreen to cover some shady pornographic operation when indeed the reverse was true. He seemed to understand that Olympia was in fact capitalising on erotic fantasy to earn the money needed to publish otherwise unpublishable authors such as Beckett, Nabokov, Miller or himself."[30]

Matters came to a head in the summer of 1956, not long before the expurgated version of *The Ginger Man* was due to be published by Neville Armstrong in Britain. Girodias had met Armstrong in Paris two years earlier. They had conducted some business, but there had later been a dispute over money so that when Armstrong's partner called on Girodias, he got a "chilly welcome":

"He hastened to express much contrition about that past incident, said that he had not been in the picture at the time and that things would have gone differently had he been personally involved in the deal. But now his immediate purpose was . . . to inquire about my willingness to license the British rights of *The Ginger Man* to his firm, possibly the only one liable to take such a risk; they would make a fortune for me. He added, with a little smile, that Donleavy had already given his agreement, as if I was then obliged to concur. I could only answer that if *The Ginger Man* were ever to be published in England, it would not be by his firm. Out."[31]

Girodias recalled that the same day a letter came from Donleavy announcing that he was coming to Paris to "discuss some plan with me." Girodias wrote back warning him about Armstrong's business methods, which he had experienced to his "detriment." Girodias ended his letter on a cheery note: "Well, toodle oo." Donleavy's response, Girodias said, alluded "to his visit to Paris the year before when, he claimed, 'you gave me the English rights. I hold you to this.'"

At this point, Girodias said, he experienced a sudden flash of enlightenment. "I felt that I had always known something like this would happen with him," he wrote. "Ah, that Donleavy! The danger in Dangerfield, a man of outsize ego who used art as an instrument of power, as a means to dominate other men. The hero of his [Donleavy's] book is not a simple cheater, he is a diabolical strategist who invokes love or friendship only in order to destroy his victims. It was therefore insufferable for Donleavy, the author, to see the fate of his book—symbol of his singularity, of his superiority—dependent on the goodwill of another man: 'the publisher.'"

Girodias said that in September he received another letter from Donleavy "claiming that during his visit to Paris last year I had agreed to let him sell the British rights of *The Ginger Man* in a cut version, on his own and for his sole benefit." Girodias commented: "If we had had such an exchange on that drunken occasion, I would have turned down his request with some vehemence. In any case, an alteration to our written agreement would necessarily [have] been confirmed in writing. It struck me that Donleavy's allegation (which went straight against his initial demand that the book should be published without any cuts whatsoever of the so-called obscene passages) was never even meant to be credible."[32]

Girodias was furious. "It was like a smack in the face, a broad lie meant to taunt me, and to fill me up to the brim with impotent rage."

Why impotence? Well, Girodias realized that he could only sue Donleavy in Britain, where his own notoriety as a purveyor of porn was already well established. "Would I ever dare take such a step since I was the devil incarnate for all British magistrates, policemen, aldermen, customs officers, and private councillors to the queen, as well as no doubt to the queen herself. Me, the puny, scandalous, lopsided, continental, depraved Girodias? Of course not? Well done, Donleavy!"[33]

By dropping the scene with Dangerfield exposing himself on the train, "that little insignificant four page chapter," Girodias concluded that Donleavy could legitimize his book in England. He could also "retain the whole profits from his treason for himself, and . . . make use of all the wonderful satanical publicity evoked by this exemplary conversion from pornography to literature. Never," Girodias sighs, "had the road to Damascus been paved with such saintly intentions."[34]

Girodias then played with the "silly thought of rushing to London to break the demon's neck." Given Donleavy's fighting prowess, tested in Dublin's bars and in the broad thoroughfare of Fleet Street, it was probably just as well Girodias did not succumb to this impulse. Instead, he did what he had done on countless occasions in the past and would do frequently in the future. He put on his coat and went to see his lawyer. His French attorney confirmed that nothing could be done in France and that "a legal action in London would probably be extremely chancy." However, he knew a British solicitor whom he considered "equal to the task." Enter Stanley Rubinstein, who, according to Girodias, was "feared by all, his very name [having] been known to put most adversaries to flight."[35]

Girodias wasted no time in firing his opening shot, a registered letter to Neville Armstrong in London informing him that he was going to apply for an injunction in the British courts to stop the publication of *The Ginger Man*. Armstrong returned fire with a defiant letter saying that Girodias did not own the British rights to the book and that he was shocked by Girodias's threats. Meanwhile, when he was not awakened in the middle of the night by bouts of rage and frustration, Girodias was dreaming about the mighty Stanley Rubinstein, "a little in the manner of the primitives who saw in their dreams the Almighty, his head in the clouds . . . Saint Stanley, deliver us from our enemies."[36]

While Girodias's case was handled by the well-known and powerful firm of Rubinstein, Nash & Co., publisher Armstrong and author Donleavy were represented by Gerald Samuels and Shine, then a lesser planet in the legal galaxy. In the splendor of Levington Park almost forty years later, Donleavy recalls the preparations for the battle:

"My publisher had no money to spend on lawyers; he was very much down-market and operated out of a side street in a back room. The law firm assigned a young man to the case. 'I'm just a lad from the East End,' he told me, 'but don't worry, we kick these public schoolboys around all the time in lawsuits.'" But Donleavy was worried. "The book could have been stopped in its tracks, right there and then and my career . . . might have been stymied for all time. So, it was a life and death matter. This was the crucial moment to stop the book."[37]

It was a race against time. The publication of *The Ginger Man* was imminent. Girodias was trying to get an injunction stopping the book from appearing while Donleavy's publisher, Neville Armstrong, was intent on keeping the legal field clear so that the book could be distributed.

Girodias provided an extended account of the preliminaries to the decisive meeting between the two sides that reveals much of his own ambivalent feelings about the law and the litigating process, a constant feature of his publishing life:

"I found myself one sombre November day (in the Inns of Court in London), looking through the high windows of the waiting-room at the tall trees and wintry lawns outside. The creaky steps, the musty odour, the clerk's tongue-in-cheek deference and the constant tea-brewing activities of the staff, all this was part of an age-old Dickensian strategy meant to soothe and mollify the client and prepare him in a subtle manner for the financial consequences of his visit.

"When you entered the Temple with your grudges and your folly you had already come a long way in your slow progress towards litigation, you had already exhausted treasures of patience and ingenuity to avoid the fatal issue. But now there was no other remedy, no turning back. It was simply a matter of kill or be killed.

"The solicitor would take you by the hand from now on, place a blindfold over your eyes, and guide you through the many corridors, waiting-rooms, chambers and courtrooms, all the way through an ordeal so long that, if it was ever concluded, you would be a different person, much older, scarred, wrinkled and wizened, and unable to remember why or even when it all started, a naked trembling victim like the anti-hero at the end of Kafka's *Trial*.

"As I stepped across the threshold of the august Stanley Rubinstein, I had already been conditioned to expect the worst. I was reassured, however, by the benign and friendly presence, the peasant-like savvy, the modesty of superior wisdom. A squat, elderly man with the trunk-like nose and small intelligent eyes of the stately elephant, he was surrounded by photographs from his college days, heavily emblazoned parchments, and all the paraphernalia you might expect. Next to him, a younger, smaller replica of himself was dutifully taking notes, his nephew Michael, who would one day succeed him and accede to the glory of the big crinkled leather chair.

"Mr R rubbed his hands, his nose, tried his very approximate French on me, gave up, and went on for a few minutes with those routines which gave him time to size me up. Telephone calls interrupted us, people carrying papers entered the room and left, we were served tea and crackers, so that time went by without any real exchange between us about the business at hand. Three days later I received a monumental letter from him confirming that Messrs. Rubinstein, Nash & Co. had agreed to represent my firm, and that they expected a provision from us much steeper than anything I had been led to expect. But still obeying my initial momentum, I paid the money and, after exchanges of letters with the solicitors of the defendants, Messrs. Gerald Samuels & Shine, papers were served, as they say, and the case was on."[38]

Donleavy, who seems to share his rival's love-hate relationship with the legal profession, took up the tale. "We had this big legal meeting . . . it's so fascinating in law how careful one has to be, even in the corridors of the law courts. When lawyers say don't open your mouth, don't say anything . . . it is always extremely good advice. . . . Neville Armstrong was asked how much money he thought he could make out of the book. That was a tense moment because Armstrong was reluctant to mention the bonanza he thought was ahead in the author's company. He said he thought he could make two hundred and fifty pounds out of it."

Terms of a settlement were discussed, and Armstrong's young East End lawyer said he had heard something in them that suggested it would be worth obtaining counsel's opinion. He said he had heard "words back there making me think we should." The words concerned the shape of the settlement between Donleavy and Girodias, the key phrase being "it will be spelt out."

"That was a crucial moment," said Donleavy. "Whatever it was it did not have to be spelled out at that point." But time was short, delays were inevitable while counsel's opinion was being sought, and the injunction still hung over the book like the proverbial sword of Damocles. Three days before publication of *The Ginger Man* was due, Donleavy decided to go to Paris to see if he could work out a deal with Girodias directly.

"I remember this was the lowest point in my entire life. There was this book waiting to come out in England and saving my whole future as an author. I don't think I could have stomached sitting down again with the energy and the drive to write. I was probably facing the end. How old was I? I couldn't have been more than twenty-four or twenty-five at the time. I don't remember whether I had two children then, certainly one. So I arrived in Paris in [a state] of some desperation. . . . It was like walking down to your execution, and I walked that road."[39]

Girodias took his arrival in Paris as a sign of weakness. Donleavy recalled, "I could tell by his attitude that he knew more than I did. I did not know, for example, that Neville Armstrong had sent someone to Paris earlier to do a deal with Girodias." But Donleavy says Girodias also misjudged him. "He assumed that my trip was one of weakness but instead he met with defiance." Their meeting went badly. Donleavy says that Girodias made it clear that he had to come to heel since he, Girodias, was in control of the situation. Donleavy decided that it was time to go. He stood up and said: "I'll see you in court."

He walked out of the rue de Nesle office aware, he says, not only that *The Ginger Man* might never appear in Britain, or anywhere else for that matter, but also that he could be faced with a massive legal case. "It was clear that no one was fooling. There was money around, and everyone was going to take the steps they were threatening to take."

On his way back to London, Donleavy was having a drink in the saloon of the Channel ferry when he noticed a striking woman, "the most attractive woman there," at the far side of the room. "She suddenly got up and came over, looking at me all the time. I thought, my God, what is this? Had I involuntarily offended her?" It turned out to be Miriam Worms, Muffie Wainhouse's successor at Olympia. The meeting, she recalled later, remained "curiously vivid—such an odd coincidence." They had a drink together and talked about Donleavy's difficulties. She pointed out that it was not customary practice for an author to sell a book to two publishers simultaneously and that he was bound to lose. "He was courteous without being friendly," she remembered, "exactly what the occasion required. I recall a pale face set in dark hair, a trim beard perhaps, a shade of Basil Rathbone? He was very sure of himself. He didn't give an inch."[40]

Back in London, Donleavy told Neville Armstrong the bad news. No deal. But Armstrong had news of his own. "I wouldn't like to be in Girodias's shoes," he said, "because he can't stop the book now." Counsel's opinion had come in, pointing out that the book's copyright had never been properly assigned to Girodias as far as British law was concerned. An exchange of letters was not enough; copyright could only be assigned by the author to someone else by completing an official form and signing it. It was a technicality, but it was sufficient to block Girodias's injunction. The next day, *The Ginger Man* went on sale all over Britain.

Girodias did not mention the copyright issue in his memoirs. Instead, he said that his lawyers received a letter from Gerald Samuels & Shine, Armstrong's lawyers. Its message was conciliatory: "our clients . . . ," it said, "have no desire to litigate on this matter, and if some sort of amicable arrangement can be come to between the parties, we would consider this possibility in the interests of all."

But this "peace offering," Girodias said, was addressed to his solicitors and not to himself. While Stanley Rubinstein made "an allusion" to it at the time, "it was in a deprecating manner meant to indicate that the defendants were seized by a case of cold feet," and that [judgment] only "reinforced my confidence in the issue." Girodias lamented wasting this "crucial chance" of "negotiating a separate settlement with Neville Armstrong, the villain, which would necessarily be at the expense of Donleavy, the arch-villain. Any coldblooded businessman would have seized the opportunity there and then, but, alas, I had put myself in the hands of the law: worse still, of the British law."[41]

With the publication of *The Ginger Man* in Britain, Donleavy had won a battle—but not the war. Girodias promptly sued him for breach of contract on two fronts, in Britain and in France, and later in the

United States. The struggle was to continue for another two decades, draining the energies of the combatants and enriching an army of British, French, and American lawyers.

Donleavy conceded that Girodias was "a brilliant litigant, but he should have wiped me out early on by pressing his actions. Instead, he allowed me not only to get more and more astute but to hire better and better lawyers until I finished up with Lord Goodman."

Donleavy's own tactics were to feign weakness, encourage Girodias to attack, and then, at the critical moment, "close my jaws on him." And, invariably, Girodias sprang to the attack. It was often thought that Donleavy was the aggressor, but it was always a case of Girodias suing the author and Donleavy aggressively counterattacking.[42]

In 1958 the expurgated version of *The Ginger Man* was published in the United States. But it was not until 1963 that the complete, unexpurgated book appeared in Britain, under the Corgi imprint. It took another two years for the full version to be published in the United States. Both Walter Minton of Putnam's and Barney Rosset of Grove liked the book but were scared off by the sulfurous Girodias-Donleavy feud. Finally, the book was published by Seymour Lawrence/Delacorte Press in 1965. It was a comment on the moral climate of the times that it took seven years in Britain and nine years in the United States to expose the reading public to Sebastian Dangerfield's own exposure on that Irish train.

The book was not a runaway success. However, it received marvelous reviews. The *New Yorker* writer Dorothy Parker reviewed it in *Esquire:* "I think it will be many a day before I come upon [a book] anywhere near as brilliant as *The Ginger Man.* [It] is the picaresque novel to stop them all, lusty, violent, wildly funny. It is a rigadoon of rascality, a bawled-out comic song of sex . . . as bawdy as they come . . . Mr. Donleavy, both in style and matter, need pull the forelock to nobody on earth but Mr. Donleavy."

Ian Hamilton, writing in *The Spectator,* had this to say: "It is a remarkable performance and Mr Donleavy is to be congratulated on the creative energy with which he inflates one low-life scene after another to the proportions of gargantuan comedy." Gene Baro, in *The New York Times,* said: "No one who encounters him will forget Sebastian Dangerfield. He is *The Ginger Man,* rogue fool, innocent, the hero of J. P. Donleavy's startling first novel; he is the hero at war with nothing less than life itself. . . . Perhaps Sebastian Dangerfield will prove to be the enduring prototype of the knavish charmer in our time."

Writing in *The Spectator* in 1964, V. S. Naipaul commented: "*The Ginger Man* has lasted for eight years, and its fame still grows. . . . It is one of those books which reveal their quality from the first line. . . . On every page there is that immediacy all good writing has. . . . *The Ginger Man* might well soon be seen as the most representative novel of the 1950s."[43]

I read the book shortly after it was first published, when I was in the Congo (now Zaire). Together with a group of friends, all of whom had read the book, we found ourselves talking like the characters and, after a few drinks, even playing their roles. One evening I would be Sebastian Dangerfield and a friend would respond as O'Keefe or Miss Frost, and so on; the next time we would swap parts. We were captivated by the characters, the language, the atmosphere—all in the heart of Africa, where a new nation struggled, amid mayhem and bloodshed, to be born. *The Ginger Man* became part of our youthful and somewhat chaotic lives. It remains embedded in my memory, more real in some ways than the epic crisis that churned around us.

During the 1960s *The Ginger Man* picked up momentum and became a bestseller. Its slow but steady ascent fueled the Girodias-Donleavy vendetta. On the one hand, the book's success made Girodias more determined to obtain what he thought was his legitimate share of the financial proceeds that were beginning to pile up. On the other, the flow of cash enabled Donleavy to lavish more and more money on his legal defenses. And the money was going in one direction only—straight into Donleavy's bank account. He got everything out of the British, American, and other foreign rights to *The Ginger Man*, although, not surprisingly, he never saw anything more from several reprintings of the book in Paris.

"Girodias was left to get whatever he could out of our [original] exchange of letters," Donleavy said. "But there wasn't anything spelled out—those words again—and so it all came to me."

For his part, Girodias admitted that he "was rather careless with contracts," never believing that one day those books would be worth millions. "In the case of *The Ginger Man*, I had a simple exchange of letters with Donleavy, but it was clear enough; the courts, later on, fully recognised that basic fact [that] I was entitled to one half of all subsidiary income, including from films and American republication. I must admit that this was too much of a share for my firm; I had merely followed the usual clause covering subsidiary rights in French contracts, unfair as it is.

"I made this known repeatedly to Donleavy by way of the lawyers for both sides, intimating that I was prepared to settle for a lesser percentage; and yet insisting at the same time that I would never give up my legitimate right to a decent share of the income since it was only thanks to me that *The Ginger Man* was turned from the mess it originally was into a real book, and subsequently into a bestseller.

"But this was precisely what Donleavy wanted so much to erase from the collective memory and also from his own. Success and money merely meant to him power over other men; and he was thus intent on destroying me not out of simple cupidity, but simply to show me how much better than me he was, and that, whatever I may have felt I had done for him, he had never had any need of my services to become the great writer he knew he was. All very childish, but there we are."[44]

"It was an impossible situation," said Donleavy, stirring the embers of the fire. "Girodias would never admit clearly that I was the owner of *The Ginger Man* and that he was a licensee of it. He had it in his head, as he did with the pornographic books, that he owned it, that it was his. It never occurred to him that I was the owner . . . having written it—that it existed—before he came on the scene."[45]

Donleavy's fear of failure in those days has the ring of anguish. He said that he had to force himself to go through "the terrible agony of being unknown and being able to face the world and the fact that it's a giant, vast place where nearly every man is saying: 'Dear God, hear my tiny voice.' Everyone wants to be heard." He was "desperate" to get himself recognized as an author. "It was essential, otherwise I would be dead. Quite literally."[46]

HOSTILITIES INTENSIFIED WHEN, in the mid-1960s, Hollywood became interested in filming *The Ginger Man* with someone offering $350,000 for the film rights.

"*The Ginger Man* and the pile that it began to represent was a great golden nugget," said Donleavy, "like the pot in a big poker game." Girodias, Donleavy is convinced, increasingly saw it as "a kind of solution to all his problems" and that he realized he was in a better legal position with Donleavy than he was with Nabokov, with whom he was also quarreling. "He wanted the film rights. But no one would touch them simply because I was the one signing contracts for the American and British publications and everyone knew that."

It has always been something of a mystery why *The Ginger Man,* which was turned into a play shortly after its publication, never made it to the screen. Donleavy explained that, although censorship would have been a problem in the early years, litigation with Girodias proved to be a major deterrent. "I suppose . . . I wouldn't do any deal that involved Girodias. That would have taken care of fifteen or twenty years." He said that a number of leading directors were interested in making the film, including John Huston, Mike Nichols, and, later, Robert Redford. He wrote a script for the film years ago and, more recently, helped his son put together a group to make the film.

The legal behemoth that had been set in motion consumed enormous amounts of time, nervous energy, and hard cash on the part of the two combatants. Donleavy admitted it "dogged" him all those years, although he appeared almost grateful for the legal education he obtained from it. At the time, however, the toll of the protracted litigation was severe and affected his work:

"It has influenced me more than almost anything else in my habits as an author. If you get a letter from a lawyer in the morning, it can ruin you for three days. So I had to devise a method during the long years of litigation so that I would never see mail. This was in London before I began *A Singular Man.* My mail was always delivered to an address which was known as my residence, but I never lived there. Mail was collected every three days at a strategic time of the day— 4:15 P.M.—so I would be able to calm down before I went to sleep that night and be able to write again the next morning. It worked extremely well. No one knew where I lived at all. I received no phone calls there, nothing. No one ever went there."[47]

He began to write *A Singular Man,* whose hero, George Smith, has endless legal problems, in the west of Ireland. "I remember the day when I started [the novel]. . . . I was in the middle of my litigations with the Olympia Press over *The Ginger Man* then, and I could see the mailman on his bicycle on the winding mountain road coming to me, four hours before he arrived; and I'd sit and wonder what bad news he had for me."[48]

The financial burden also left its mark. Donleavy obtained the best French lawyers through Lord Goodman, whose chief representative in Paris was a highly qualified French lawyer who had also been called to the bar in Britain. On one occasion Donleavy went over to Paris when Girodias had won a lower-court judgment. He was accompanied by Tessa Sayle, a literary agent, who was living with him at the time and spoke fluent French.

"We were in my Paris lawyer's very lavish apartment," Donleavy recalled. "It was a large room with a bar in the corner and pictures of the British royal family on the walls. About a dozen people were there having cocktails. I was sitting with Tessa, and I turned to her and said: 'Tessa, I believe I am employing everyone in this room. They're all speaking French, and I can't understand a thing that is going on, but I'm supporting them all!' "[49]

On his side, Girodias regarded Donleavy as his "persecutor" and accused him of pouring the bulk of his foreign royalties into the lawsuits. He also blamed his adversary for releasing hitherto hidden elements of paranoia in himself. "Donleavy's exceptional egomania had the effect of inducing a similar response in me," he wrote later. "For a quarter of a century our contest has dominated my life, professional and personal."

Girodias further believed that Donleavy's behavior influenced other Olympia authors: "One of its most disastrous effects was to set an example which was later followed by practically all of my authors. As book censorship started to crumble at last in America—following the successful publication of *Lolita* in New York in 1958—my major authors started one by one to sever their connection with me, whether contractural or just friendly, so as not to have to share with me the manna which they now felt to be within easy reach . . . like lemmings, all my fine champions were crossing the line—following the example set by J. P. Donleavy."[50]

The struggle moved into a new phase in the late 1960s. "It was a curious situation," said Donleavy. "We were fighting each other behind two companies acting as fronts." Girodias was represented by a Swiss company called Eratomique, and Donleavy had a company called The Little Someone working on his behalf. "Girodias's lawyers," said Donleavy, "used to get up and scream: 'We know who is behind The Little Someone Corporation—it is none other than J. P. Donleavy the author!' So the judge would say, 'That's fine, but produce the evidence.' If our names had been exposed we might have lost the action. But no evidence would emerge and the furor would die down—until the next time."

During this period, Donleavy had a lucky break. He was in New York one day, standing on the steps of a church on Fifth Avenue, when a stranger who was walking by suddenly stopped and came over to him. "Are you Mr. J. P. Donleavy?" he asked. He told Donleavy that his name was James Jurgens and that he had written a book for Girodias and lent him some money in a business transaction. When Girodias did not fulfill his side of the deal, the affair wound up in a New York court. Jurgens won the case, and Girodias was ordered to pay him $8,000, plus costs, but the money had never been paid.

Jurgens, a determined young man, pursued Girodias relentlessly and, through his lawyers, accumulated a mass of information about the publisher's activities in the United States and Europe. Jurgens offered to share his hoard with Donleavy and had his lawyers send copies of relevant documents to the author in Ireland. The most useful piece of information, Donleavy said, was documentary proof that Girodias and the Paris receiver of the bankrupt Olympia Press were behind the Eratomique Corporation, which was traced back to a nondescript side street in Antwerp in Belgium. "The next time the opposition's lawyers got up in court in Paris and said, 'We know who is behind The Little Someone Corporation,' and the judge said give me the proof, my lawyers jumped up and said, 'We know who is behind Eratomique. It is none other than Maurice Girodias, and here are the papers!' "[51]

THAT ROUND went to Donleavy, but the fight continued. Throughout the 1960s the legal struggle sputtered on in three countries and two continents, sometimes fizzling angrily when one side or the other appeared to gain a clear advantage, at other times almost forgotten. But, burning fast or slow, the contest remained a potentially lethal fuse for both men as they went about their daily lives. Their professional trajectories, however, were markedly different. Donleavy's star, as he acquired fame and fortune as a successful novelist and playwright, shone brightly in the literary heavens. Girodias's career, by contrast, had already peaked, and for him this was a period of struggle, disappointment, and growing oblivion.

BEFORE I LEFT Mullingar, Donleavy took me on a tour of his house and talked about *The Ginger Man* and his life as a writer. Lev-

ington Park has fifteen rooms, including nine bedrooms with bath-
rooms, a heated indoor swimming pool, a sauna, an exercise room,
an office for Donleavy's secretary, a large modernized country kitchen
designed by his former wife, Mary, and a magnificent formal dining
room with a black marble fireplace. There is central heating and peat-
burning fireplaces fired up with blackened, oven-baked orange skins
that serve as kindling and crackle and explode on ignition. Move away
from the sources of heat, however, and a damp Irish chill creeps into
the bones.

Donleavy has a formal study on the ground floor, where his own
books line the wall behind an expansive desk. He is not a collector—
or reader—of other people's work. "I never read other writers' novels," he said. Apart from many different editions of *The Ginger Man*
(he thinks there are eighty-five in all), there are framed posters of his
books that were turned into plays. Among them is the one that ad-
vertised the production of *The Ginger Man* at the Gaiety Theatre in
Dublin starring Richard Harris as Sebastian Dangerfield. The play was
closed down by the authorities after three nights. On the desk are
neat piles of all Donleavy's original manuscripts, meticulously annotated and folded, yellowing gently as they lie in wait for posterity.

Donleavy did not consider himself a success, although he has been
continuously published since the appearance of *The Ginger Man* and
has more than a dozen novels, plays, short stories, and nonfiction
books in print. "There is an indifferent academic regard for me as an
author," he said. "I never had any success, never had anything of any
kind that most authors dream about." When I mentioned the impressive pile we were sitting in and his habit of staying at Claridges
Hotel in London, he qualified his comment. "Maybe I am thinking
of this in the American terms of success . . . where you are, say, having
breakfast at the Plaza Hotel and you're waiting until eleven o'clock
to deal with the long-distance calls to California and someone is in
the Polo Lounge.

"That type of thing never came to me," he continued. "I was
secreted away in secret addresses, like Girodias probably, and lived
like Howard Hughes. Everything in my life was designed, everyone
turned into an enemy. . . . I had no friends of any description, either
in the literary world or any world. Most people forget that *The Ginger
Man* was excoriated and abused and condemned. There was very little
for me ever to feel positive or victorious about."

It is true that none of Donleavy's work has received the same critical acclaim that greeted *The Ginger Man* and neither he nor his writing attracts much attention in contemporary literary or academic circles. No biography has been written or is in progress. He seems to share with his old rival a persecution complex that could, on occasions, make him his own worst enemy. He said that endless litigation in his life had kept him working hard as an author and with that incubus it was important to keep oneself isolated. "You never go around to cocktail parties in case you might meet an enemy of some sort."

Donleavy, after two marriages, four children, and several other relationships, was living alone in Levington Park when I visited him. Although never poor—he grew up in a middle-class Irish-American family in New York—he knew hard times first as a student at Trinity College, Dublin, in the late 1940s and then as a struggling writer in London. He never finished his zoology degree at Trinity, but he led an active social life among a wide range of people that provided fertile material for *The Ginger Man*.

One of his friends was Gainor Stephen Crist, another American student, who became the model for Sebastian Dangerfield. In an autobiographical book on Ireland, Donleavy painted an amusing portrait of Crist, whose character and exploits foreshadow the wilder exploits of *The Ginger Man*. There are several photographs of Crist, a young man with a large head, small mustache, and a quizzical look in his eye. One shows him wearing a bow tie and an overcoat; in his hand, an electrical appliance.

Donleavy's caption reads: "Crist at the side gate of Trinity from which he is exiting to pawn an electric fire. This saintly expedient gentleman on this day had resolutely made the decision that money for a few pints and ball of malt in the pub would keep him as comfortably warm as any electric fire. And, as he said, the steam from his piss could prove it."[52]

Donleavy lost track of Crist in later years. Crist was twice married, returned to the United States for a time, came back to Europe, and then, pursuing an erratic path ("gargantuan horrors" always followed in his wake, Donleavy said), ended up in the Canary Islands, where he was suddenly taken ill and died at the age of forty-two.

As I was leaving, Donleavy noticed me looking at the Joe Louis–Max Schmeling photograph on the mantelpiece. The referee, Arthur Donovan, was also famous, he said, the best in the world at the time. The reason why the picture is there is that Donleavy's father hired Donovan to teach his young son to box. A last backward glance as I left produced a pang of sympathy for Girodias, the fallen fighter. The words of Seymour Lawrence, Donleavy's faithful American publisher, returned: "Litigation went on until Donleavy broke him."

A CURIOUS symbiotic relationship seemed to exist between Donleavy and Girodias. "The *Ginger Man* saga . . . in retrospect . . . appears as the *leitmotif,* or perhaps even the backbone of my publishing career," Girodias wrote near the end of his life. "Just as it turned out to play the central role in J. P. Donleavy's career as a writer."[53] Donleavy put it this way: "The Olympia Press was Girodias's life—he was to the Press as I was to *The Ginger Man.*"[54]

Muffie Wainhouse has a theory. "Basically, Maurice and Donleavy liked each other," she said, "and through the lawsuits that kept them together seems to run a thread of mutually unrequited love. Twenty-five years later, Donleavy is asking, 'What did he say about me?' "[55]

I put this to Donleavy. He looked surprised. "Good heavens! Gosh, I'm not sure of that. There may have been a strange element [in it], a self-perpetuating element." But his opinion of Girodias has not changed much after all these years. "Christopher Logue, who is a friend, used to say: 'Mike, you must treat him gently. Don't be too harsh on him.' [But] I regarded him as a bully, and this to me was unforgivable, this thing of attacking the weak—when he thought you were weak—and retreating from the strong. . . . I always regarded him with a certain degree of contempt for this reason. He treated his authors as kind of serfs, and he forgot that a man who signs his name to his own work is somebody who believes in this work. They were not people to be trifled with."[56]

Girodias believed that Donleavy's writing career was stunted by the years of litigation and that, in the end, he turned out a better litigator than writer. "He ruined his career as a writer pursuing me," Girodias said. "He hasn't done anything worthwhile since *The Ginger Man.*"[57] Donleavy, for his part, felt that Girodias was a better litigator than publisher. "He makes Howard Hughes look like a supermarket assistant," he said.[58]

IT WAS LATE when I left Levington Park. Rain was lashing across the forecourt, and a telephone pole had been blown down, blocking the road. Donleavy said he would show me another way to Mullingar, where I was spending the night. I put on my coat, but he came out with nothing over his tweed jacket. We drove down to the front lodge. He jumped out of the car to open the gates, rejecting the offer of an umbrella. The rain was coming down diagonally, thrashed by great gusts of wind. He sprinted for the gates. Bent to open them. Headlights framed him in the tormented night. White hair flying, body silhouetted, pinned for a fleeting moment against the iron grille.

God's mercy
On the wild
Ginger Man.

7

Light of My Life, Fire of My Loins: The <u>Lolita</u> Saga

IN THE SPRING OF 1955, Girodias had a telephone call from Denise Clarouin, a well-established literary agent in Paris who specialized in handling the French rights for English-language writers. She had been a friend of Jack Kahane, Girodias's father, and Girodias had met her on two or three occasions. But that had been many years earlier, and he was surprised to hear from her now. He was also intrigued. After a little chitchat and some complimentary remarks about the achievements of the fledgling Olympia Press, she said she would like him to meet her associate and friend, Doussia Ergaz. Madame Ergaz had something extremely interesting to discuss.

An appointment was made at Girodias's office in the rue de Nesle for the following day. Waiting for her to arrive, Girodias pondered what this Russian émigrée lady could be offering. "The memoirs of Prince Yossoupof or perhaps those of Rasputin himself?" Madame Ergaz duly arrived and created a good impression as a "lively, pleasant and intellectual Russian of the old school." She quickly made it clear that she was not peddling the memoirs of luminaries of Czarist Russia. Instead, she gave Girodias a brief biographical sketch of a Russian émigré friend, a writer, who had become an American citizen and was teaching at Cornell University. This man had already had several books published in the United States.

Sensing the direction of the conversation, Girodias warned her that his publishing house had a "specialist" character. Thus it might not be the right home for a work by her friend Professor Nabokov (of whom he had never heard), who seemed to be "frightfully respectable." Doussia Ergaz, Girodias recalled, was highly amused by his reaction.

"Oh, I understand your caution," she said. "But you surely are aware that almost all the great writers have written, sooner or later, a secret work. Take Pushkin, for example. But these books are usually discovered after the deaths of the authors and end up as curiosities without value. Vladimir Nabokov has not confined himself to a little stylish writing of the licentious kind, he has written a truly great novel, an exceptional book, quite remarkable—on the most shocking theme that can be imagined. He sent it to four American publishers, who know him well and have great respect for him, and all four were *horrified!*"

Girodias murmured that the book might have the same effect upon him.

"Oh, surely not!" she cried. "On the contrary, I am convinced that you will be enchanted. All that I know about you tells me that you will. You'll see."

Doussia Ergaz's enthusiasm knew no bounds. "It is called *Lolita,*" she went on, "that's the name of the heroine. A true seductress, you'll fall under her spell. I'll send it to you tomorrow but promise me that you will read it yourself, and as quickly as possible. . . . Ah, it's divine!"

With that, Madame Ergaz offered the back of her hand to Girodias's compliant lips and departed, leaving the publisher wondering whether he had just met the most "Romanesque of literary agents . . . or the cleverest?"[1]

The *Lolita* manuscript, in two professionally typed volumes, arrived at the Olympia Press's office the next morning. With The Traveller's Companion Series moving under a full head of steam, literature writ with a capital L was not the highest of Girodias's priorities. Nevertheless, Madame Ergaz's allusion to the book's theme, as well as her enthusiasm, had whetted his appetite. "I evacuated all the papers surrounding my swivel chair and . . . unplugged my telephone extension," he recalled. "I opened the first page. 'Lo-li-ta . . .' The charm worked immediately, the inner voice spoke up in clear, unmistakable tones: yes, this is *it*."[2]

THE EARLY GESTATION and struggle to find a publisher for *Lolita,* a novel dealing with the obsessive love of a middle-aged man for a precociously seductive twelve-year-old "nymphet," have been provided in meticulous fashion by Nabokov himself. His most detailed commentary on the book was written in November 1956 and accompanied the American debut of *Lolita* when it appeared in excerpted form in *The Anchor Review* the next summer. This essay, "On a Book Entitled Lolita," was later used as an afterword in many editions of the novel. The following is extracted from that commentary.

"The first little throb of *Lolita* went through me late in 1939 or early in 1940, in Paris, at a time when I was laid up with a severe attack of intercostal neuralgia. As far as I can recall, the initial shiver of inspiration was somehow prompted by a newspaper story about an ape in the Jardin des Plantes, who, after months of coaxing by a scientist, produced the first drawing ever charcoaled by an animal: this sketch showed the bars of the poor creature's cage.

"The impulse I record had no textual connection with the ensuing train of thought, which resulted, however, in a prototype of [*Lolita*], a short story some thirty pages long. I wrote it in Russian, the language in which I had been writing novels. . . . The man was a Central European, the anonymous nymphet was French, and the loci were Paris and Provence. I had him marry the little girl's sick mother who soon died, and after a thwarted attempt to take advantage of the orphan in a hotel room, Arthur (for that was his name) threw himself under the wheels of a truck. I read the story one blue-papered wartime night to a group of friends—Mark Aldanov, two social revolutionaries, and a woman doctor; but I was not pleased with the thing and destroyed it sometime after moving to America in 1940. [The manuscript survived and was translated into English by Dmitri Nabokov, the author's son, and published as *The Enchanter* after Nabokov's death.]

"Around 1949, in Ithaca, upstate New York, the throbbing, which had never quite ceased, began to plague me again. Combination joined inspiration with fresh zest and involved me in a new treatment of the theme, this time in English. . . . The book developed slowly, with many interruptions and asides. . . . Once or twice I was on the point of burning the unfinished draft and had carried my Juanita Dark as far as the shadow of the leaning incinerator on the innocent lawn, when I was stopped by the thought that the ghost of the destroyed book would haunt my files for the rest of my life."[3]

Nabokov worked hard on the book in the summers when he and his wife, Vera, were on butterfly-hunting holidays in various parts of the United States. He finished copying it out in longhand in the spring of 1954 and set about looking for a publisher, offering it, he says, to four different publishing houses in turn.

Nabokov records some of the publishers' reactions: "Certain techniques in the beginning of *Lolita* (Humbert's Journal, for example) misled some of my first readers into assuming that this was going to be a lewd book. They expected the rising succession of erotic scenes; when these stopped, the readers stopped, too, and felt bored and let down. This, I suspect, is one of the reasons why not all the four firms read the typescript to the end. Whether they found it pornographic or not did not interest me. Their refusal to buy the book was based not on my treatment of the theme but on the theme itself, for there are at least three themes which are utterly taboo as far as most American publishers are concerned. The two others are: a Negro-White marriage which is a complete and glorious success resulting in lots of children and grandchildren; and the total atheist who lives a happy and useful life, and dies in his sleep at the age of 106.

"Some of the reactions were very amusing: one reader suggested that his firm might consider publication if I turned my *Lolita* into a twelve-year-old lad and had him seduced by Humbert, a farmer, in a barn, amidst gaunt and arid surroundings, all this set forth in short, strong, 'realistic' sentences ('He acts crazy. We all act crazy, I guess. I guess God acts crazy.' Etc.). . . . an otherwise intelligent reader who flipped through the first part described *Lolita* as 'Old Europe debauching young America,' while another flipper saw in it 'Young America debauching old Europe.' Publisher X, whose advisers got so bored with Humbert that they never got beyond page 188, had the naïveté to write me that Part Two was too long. Publisher Y, on the other hand, regretted there were no good people in the book. Publisher Z said if he printed *Lolita,* he and I would go to jail.[4] Another wrote, 'It is overwhelmingly nauseating even to an enlightened Freudian. To the public it will be revolting. . . . I can see no possible cause that could be served by its publication. I recommend that it be buried under a stone for a thousand years.'"[5]

It seems that, with the advantage of hindsight, it was more complicated—and less one-sided—than Nabokov suggests. Since Nabo-

kov's death in 1977, a great deal of research on the birth pangs of
Lolita has been done. Publishers have reminisced, letters from Nabokov and his wife are in print, academics have combed through the
archives, and biographies have been written. It remains true that the
controversial nature of the novel itself proved to be the major obstacle
to publication. This was Senator McCarthy's America, where crossing
the frontiers of convention in any literary or artistic endeavor could
easily be equated with communist subversion and the practitioner
hounded into oblivion. Moreover, American publishing in the mid-
1950s was still in the dark ages, constrained by legal sanctions without
and self-censorship within. The writer Erica Jong recalled the effect
this had on a reader with a healthy curiosity:

"It was impossible to obtain a copy of John Cleland's *Memoirs of a
Woman of Pleasure* outside the rare-book room of a college library or
a private erotica dealer. (I tried.) Henry Miller's *Tropics* and D. H.
Lawrence's *Lady Chatterley's Lover* could not be purchased at your
local bookstore. The raciest sex manual available to the panting adolescent was *Love Without Fear* by Eustace Chesser, M.D. And *A Stone
for Danny Fisher* by Harold Robbins was as close as we got to a literary
sex education."[6]

But Nabokov's own actions played an important part in scuttling
Lolita's chances of finding an American publisher. First, his insistence
on using a pseudonym proved to be the ultimate deterrent with one
publisher. Second, his apparent distaste for another publisher, who
says he would have put out the novel, with or without a pseudonym,
closed off a second avenue for publication. All this led to *Lolita*'s
transatlantic passage to the unknown, untested Girodias and his publishing house of ill repute in Paris. It was a decision that Nabokov
regretted to the end of his life.

Nabokov was less than candid on the pseudonym issue. He glossed
over it in his principal essay on *Lolita* when he archly suggests that
using a pen name was not really his idea at all, that somehow he had
been cajoled into using it. "At first, on the advice of a wary old
friend," he wrote, "I was meek enough to stipulate that the book be
brought out anonymously. I doubt that I shall ever regret that soon
afterwards, realizing how likely a mask was to betray my own cause,
I decided to sign *Lolita*."[7]

While the friend's counsel may have reinforced the use of a pseudonym, it is abundantly clear from Nabokov's own instructions to
recipients of the *Lolita* manuscript, forcefully supported by his wife,

department of Romance literature at Cornell) who had helped him secure tenure at the university.[13]

This completed the round of four publishers that Nabokov mentions in his essay on *Lolita*. But the manuscript went on to a fifth, to Jason Epstein, a young rising star at Doubleday. Critic Edmund Wilson, a friend of the Nabokovs, sent it to Epstein, although he did not personally like the book, considering it "repulsive." (Wilson's wife, Elena, disagreed and thought it marvelous.) Nabokov made the same stipulations to Epstein as he had done to the other editors, that is, maximum security in handling the manuscript and the use of a pseudonym if the book was to be published.

Epstein was entranced with *Lolita* and, supported by his editor in chief, urged publication. But the head of the firm, which had recently fought a long and expensive battle in the courts over Wilson's own controversial novel, *Memoirs of Hecate County,* did not want another costly legal struggle and turned the book down. Epstein did, however, make an effort in late 1954 to have an excerpt from *Lolita* published in *Partisan Review,* edited by Philip Rahv, a friend of Epstein's and an admirer of Nabokov's.[14]

Nabokov, however, once again stipulated that a pen name should be used. This was unacceptable to Rahv, and he declined to publish the piece. Nine months later, while *Lolita* was being prepared for publication in Paris, Nabokov again offered *Partisan Review* excerpts from the novel, this time with permission to use his name. *Partisan Review* did not take him up on his offer.[15]

The nub was that Nabokov was afraid of losing his job at Cornell University. He was also concerned that the United States Post Office might seize the novel—or even the manuscript—if it knew about it. It was therefore clearly not "meekness" that lay behind Nabokov's decision to use a pseudonym. It was fear, albeit a perfectly understandable, thoroughly human fear of losing his livelihood in the United States, his third country of exile.

It seems curious that before he sent the manuscript to Paris, Nabokov did not follow the advice of Simon and Schuster's Wallace Brockway. Brockway had rejected the novel but recommended that the author should send it to Barney Rosset, the founder and head of Grove Press, who already had acquired a reputation as a courageous avant-garde publisher. I asked Rosset if he would have published *Lolita* with a pseudonym if the book had been presented to him.

"Sure, why not?" he replied. "Many famous books have been published that way. I found it unbelievable that Roger Straus wouldn't do it. In other words, he didn't really think that it was a good book, but if it had had Nabokov's name on it that would have made it okay. If you can't refer to an author's background, you have to judge it on the basis of the book. That was how we [Grove] defended *Lady Chatterley's Lover* and *Tropic of Cancer.* I argued that the author is irrelevant."[16]

Nabokov does not record why he chose not to follow Brockway's advice. Rosset believes it was because Nabokov was a snob who considered Grove too small and marginal to be the publisher of his novel. "He didn't quite know how he wrote that book. First, he tried to run away from it. . . . He certainly lacked courage. But beyond that he was arrogant and snobbish. That was more important than his lack of courage."[17]

Edward de Grazia, who has pieced together the publishing history of *Lolita* more thoroughly and convincingly than anyone else, believes that Nabokov increased the difficulty of finding a publisher in the United States by "insisting on secrecy and anonymity." Had that problem been resolved, De Grazia believes that Nabokov's *Lolita* "could have been successfully defended against charges of obscenity if a reputable publisher had brought it out in the mid-fifties."

But De Grazia points out that the prospect of a long and expensive legal battle to defend the novel was a major deterrent: "Only a large and stable house, or a bold one, could have expected to publish *Lolita* successfully at that time. Well into the sixties the likelihood of six-figure legal expenses was a powerful deterrent, and few American houses were willing to take such a risk, at least in the absence of strong prospects for a best-seller. Those who went ahead anyway gambled that the publicity sure to result from an attempt at governmental censorship would generate sales that would more than offset the legal costs."[18]

The turning point on the issue of a pseudonym came finally in the summer of 1955, fifteen months after Nabokov had begun his quest for a publisher. That was when Doussia Ergaz, Nabokov's agent in Paris, supported by Girodias, persuaded the author to abandon the idea of a nom de plume and sign the book.[19]

WHEN NABOKOV was having difficulties finding an American publisher for *Lolita,* he turned to Europe. "I wrote to Madame Ergaz [in August 1954] about my troubles. . . . I now asked her to find somebody in Europe who would publish *Lolita* in the original English.

She replied that she thought she could arrange it. A month later, however, upon my return to Ithaca . . . I wrote to her saying I had changed my mind. New hopes had arisen for publication in America. They petered out, and next spring I got in touch with Madame Ergaz again, writing her . . . that Sylvia Beach 'might perhaps be interested if she still publishes.' This was not followed up. By April 17 Madame Ergaz had received my typescript. On April 26, 1955, a fatidic date, she said she had found a possible publisher. On May 13 she named that person. It was thus that Maurice Girodias entered my files."[20]

It was thus, too, the beginning of a decade-long saga that was marked by initial friendliness, growing hostility, misunderstandings and contradictory memories, a spirited correspondence interspersed with occasional flashes of humor, and a single, bizarre personal encounter. One ingredient conspicuous by its absence on both sides was humility.

Nevertheless, the collaboration worked. *Lolita,* regarded by Nabokov—and many others—as his best book in English up to that time and perhaps his greatest novel, had been on no shelf but the author's own until Girodias came along. Nabokov was beginning to despair of ever having the book published. It was left to "the Prince of Porn," hacking away at the likes of *Flesh and Bone, The Whip Angels,* and *Lust,* to publish this passionate, anguished, and wonderfully written novel that was to shake the literary world and to undermine the foundations of censorship in the United States and Britain. It was also left to Girodias to fight the battles against censorship over *Lolita* with scant support from his illustrious author. Girodias did, however, share in the large financial rewards that *Lolita* eventually reaped, a bonanza that he chose, in his own curious fashion, to dissipate on the most unliterary of pursuits.

On receiving the manuscript, Girodias asked Muffie Wainhouse, his secretary-editor, and Eric, his brother, to read it. "My enthusiasm pleased him," Muffie recalled. "He seemed to be looking for corroboration."[21] Eric Kahane thought it was "a great book but a dangerous one for those days."[22]

Girodias later amplified his first reactions to *Lolita.* "I was struck with wonder, carried away by this unbelievable phenomenon: the apparently effortless transposition of the rich Russian literary tradition into modern English fiction. This was, in itself, an exercise in genius; but the story was a rather magical demonstration of something about which I had so often dreamed but never found: the treatment of one of the major forbidden human passions in a manner both completely sincere and absolutely legitimate. I sensed that *Lolita* would become the one great modern work of art to demonstrate once and for all the futility of moral censorship, and the indispensable role of passion in literature."[23]

Whether *Lolita*'s value as cannon fodder in Girodias's crusade against censorship was the result of hindsight is not clear. Girodias's "first" reactions to reading the book did not appear in print until more than five years after *Lolita* was published. By then the book's enormous impact on the debate over what was acceptable, what was obscene, what was literature, and so on, was evident. It is easier to believe, however, Girodias's statement that he "did not really believe in the commercial potentialities of the book, nor did he [Nabokov]" and that his decision to publish it was founded "exclusively on personal inclination."[24]

After testing *Lolita* on Eric and the faithful Muffie, Girodias telephoned Doussia Ergaz and declared his enthusiasm for the book with, he says, "a youthful imprudence," forgetting for the moment that the charming Russian was both a professional agent and a fervent admirer of the author. Madame Ergaz expressed herself delighted and then mentioned that Nabokov did not want the book to appear under his own name. If it were to, his job at Cornell University—"his only resource"—might be placed in jeopardy. He suggested a pseudonym that he had already used: "Sirin."[25] (Nabokov had used the pen name "Vladimir Sirin" on some of his earlier works written in Russian to distinguish himself from his father, also called Vladimir Nabokov.)

Two days later, Girodias and Doussia Ergaz met in Harry's Bar, the famous watering hole for Americans in Paris at 5 rue Daunou, or "Sank Roo Doonoo," as the advertisement in the *International Herald Tribune* used to put it. Negotiations proceeded, a deal was quickly struck, champagne drunk, hands shaken (and, no doubt, kissed), and *Lolita* was on its way from typescriptic dream to publishing reality. Girodias describes Doussia Ergaz's reaction: "After two glasses of champagne, cheeks a little flushed, she avowed, in her Russian accent, that the whole thing had been '*très mignonne*' [very charming]."[26]

The contract, signed in early June 1955, was relatively straightforward in the context of regular publishing practice. But that, ipso facto, meant it was unusual for the Olympia Press. Girodias complained, "I saw myself forced to sign an American-style contract with this author who took himself for an American." He said he acceded to Doussia Ergaz's demand for an advance of two million (old) French francs (about $5,000), whereas he had intended to pay only half a million.

He consoled himself with the thought that the long book could be put out in two volumes, and by assigning himself a generous 33 percent share of the worldwide English-language and translation rights. He ceded the film rights, thinking that *Lolita,* given the moral climate of the time, was unfilmable.

After the signing of the contract, two issues remained to be resolved: whether a pseudonym or Nabokov's own name should be used and what editing needed to be done. Girodias said that he argued strongly against the use of a pen name and that Doussia Ergaz "had to use all her influence to make him change his mind" before Nabokov finally complied. The author stipulated, however, that while it could be mentioned that "he taught literature at a large American university, its name should not be revealed."[27]

The editing of *Lolita* focused on Nabokov's use of a number of French phrases sprinkled throughout the text. Girodias sent Nabokov a deferential letter with a list of these words and expressions. Nabokov replied saying he had taken "into account what you say about the over-abundance of French phrases in the MS. Of your list of sixty I have cancelled or translated one third, but this is as far as I can go." He added: "I am delighted that you are doing LOLITA. Please rush the proofs and I shall rush them back."[28]

Later both men remembered the editing process somewhat differently. Girodias says he sent a list of "some 200" items, while Nabokov responded that "the only alterations Girodias very diffidently suggested concerned a few trivial French phrases in the English text, such as '*bon,*' '*c'est moi,*' '*mais comment,*' etc., which he thought might just as well be translated into English, and this I agreed to do."[29]

Girodias never claimed his editing went beyond this limited area. But an article on him and the Olympia Press that appeared later in *The New York Times Book Review* contained a reference to Nabokov doing "some rewriting [of *Lolita*] at Girodias' request." This brought a swift and trenchant protest from Nabokov, who wrote a letter to the editor of the *Review* correcting "this absurd misstatement."[30]

LOLITA WAS PUBLISHED in Paris in September 1955. It appeared in two volumes behind the increasingly familiar green covers of the Olympia Press. But, unlike Donleavy's *The Ginger Man,* it was not originally part of The Traveller's Companion Series, nor did it have a list of Girodias's titillating wares at the back.

The author, if not his publisher, had high hopes. "Dear Mr. Girodias," Nabokov wrote shortly before the novel was published: ". . . I am delighted that you have set such an early date for publication. I hope you have already started a publicity campaign. What are you doing about publicity in the U.S.?" He went on to recommend useful publications, friends, and admirers, including Edmund Wilson. He ended the letter: "You and I know that *Lolita* is a serious book with a serious purpose. I hope the public will accept it as such. A *succès de scandale* would distress me."[31]

The public was divided. Alfred Appel, a Nabokov specialist, described his first encounter with *Lolita* in an introduction he wrote for a later edition of the novel. "I was Nabokov's student at Cornell in 1953–1954, at a time when most undergraduates did not know he was a writer. Drafted into the army a year later, I was sent overseas to France. On my first pass to Paris I naturally went browsing in a Left Bank bookstore. An array of Olympia Press books, daringly displayed above the counter, seemed most inviting—and there, between copies of *Until She Screams* and *The Sexual Life of Robinson Crusoe,* I found *Lolita.*

"Although I thought I knew all of Nabokov's works in English (and had searched through out-of-print stores to buy each of them), this title was new to me; and its context and format were more than surprising, even if in those innocent pre–Grove Press days the semiliterate wags on fraternity row had dubbed Nabokov's Literature 311–312 course 'Dirty Lit' because of such readings as *Ulysses* and *Madame Bovary* (the keenest campus wits invariably dropped the B when mentioning the latter).

"I brought *Lolita* back to my base, which was situated out in the woods. Passes were hard to get and new Olympia titles were always in demand in the barracks. The appearance of a new girl in town thus caused a minor clamor. 'Hey, lemme read your dirty book, man!' insisted 'Stockade Clyde' Carr, who had justly earned his sobriquet, and to whose request I acceded at once. 'Read it aloud, Stockade,' someone called, and skipping the Foreword, Stockade Clyde began to make his remedial way through the opening paragraph. 'Lo . . . lita, light . . . of my life, fire of my . . . loins. My sin, my soul . . . Lo-lee-ta: The . . . tip of the . . . tongue . . . taking . . . a trip . . . Damn!' yelled Stockade, throwing the book against the wall. 'It's God-Damn Litachure!!' Thus the Instant Pornography Test, known in psychological-testing circles as the 'IPT.' Although infallible, it has never to my knowledge been used in any court case."[32]

While *Lolita* was not quite sinking without trace, it was not easy to descry bobbing around in the sea of new books that appeared during 1955. Girodias was disappointed. No reviews, no literary sightings, no excited readers' grapevine, no scandals. The only feedback he received was groans of dismay and irritable complaints from loyal readers and his dirty-book distributors in London. "Why are you publishing junk like that?" "Stick to the tried and true." "Trash like this is a sheer waste of time." And perhaps the best of all: "You're giving yourself a bad name."[33]

At that point, a curious thing happened. Graham Greene chose *Lolita* as one of his best three books of 1955 in a report that appeared in the *Sunday Times* on Christmas Day. (His other selections were rather different: *Boswell on the Grand Tour* and *The State of France*.) It was a unique act of unpremeditated publicity that brought Nabokov's unknown novel into the public eye and, more important, onto the desks of journalists, literati, and book reviewers. It also set in train the succès de scandale that Nabokov had always feared, as well as the accumulation of wealth—and the freedom it bestowed—that he had always desired.

Greene as protagonist was a good start, but what was needed was an equally prominent antagonist. One quickly emerged, and this brings James Patrick Donleavy back into the story. He was in the habit of going to Holland Park around this time with his son, who became friendly with another little boy. Donleavy and the boy's father got talking—Donleavy was correcting *The Ginger Man* proofs at the time—and struck up a friendship. The man was a journalist called Robert Pitman, who worked for the Labour Party newspaper, *Tribune,* and did some writing for *The Sunday Express*. Donleavy told him about his own book and had Girodias send him a copy. With it came *Lolita*.

When Graham Greene put his seal on the book, Donleavy says, few people knew why he had done so or what the book was about. "But Pitman knew, and he went up to John Gordon, the editor of *The Sunday Express,* and said: 'Hey, I know what *Lolita* is. Here's a copy, read this. It's published in Paris, and it's a dirty book about an old man having carnal knowledge with a nymphet.'"[34]

Gordon rose to the occasion. At the end of January 1956, he delivered a broadside against *Lolita* in his own newspaper:

"Without doubt it is the filthiest book I have ever read. Sheer unrestrained pornography.

"Its central character is a pervert with a passion for debauching what he calls 'nymphets.' These, he explains, are girls aged from 11 to 14.

"The entire book is devoted to an exhaustive, uninhibited, and utterly disgusting description of his pursuits and successes.

"It is published in France. Anyone who published or sold it here would certainly go to prison."[35]

Greene responded by setting up the "John Gordon Society," a group of censors who would examine and if necessary "condemn all offensive books, plays, paintings, sculptures and ceramics." The first meeting was attended by Christopher Isherwood, Angus Wilson, A. J. Ayer, and other literary figures, and several measures were adopted, including a campaign to keep Scrabble words clean and an invitation to publishers to print a book band with the legend "Banned by the John Gordon Society."[36]

Girodias kept a close eye on these events from Paris. "A very absurd and comical exchange followed," he noted, "including . . . a . . . drunken public debate—in which Graham Greene fought gallantly and cleverly for the book . . . the overall result of that commotion was to create a great deal of interest in *Lolita* among partisans and detractors, an infinitesimal number of whom had read the book."[37]

Nabokov himself recognized the miraculous impact of the Greene-Gordon debate. "Had not Graham Greene and John Gordon clashed in London in such a providential fashion, *Lolita* might have ended . . . in the common grave of Traveller's Favorites or whatever Olympia's little green books were called."[38]

Widespread interest in the novel arose on both sides of the Atlantic, whetting publishers' appetites while taxing their nervous systems. "The success of the Girodias publication must have stirred up some envy and regret among publishers in New York who had initially feared to take on *Lolita*," says De Grazia; "they and others began making inquiries of Nabokov about American publication rights, and of their lawyers about American free speech rights."[39]

Publishing interest in *Lolita* was not confined to Britain and the United States. The prestigious French publisher Gallimard, alerted by the controversy in Britain, signed a contract with the author in the spring of 1956 to publish the novel in French. Nabokov also sold a large extract to the *Nouvelle Revue Française,* France's leading literary journal, and Italian, Swedish, Danish, and German publishers began negotiations for translation rights.

Things moved slowly, however, and by the end of 1956 Nabokov

was again pessimistic about his favorite novel ever being taken seriously. "My poor *Lolita,*" he wrote, "is having a rough time. The pity
is that if I had made her a boy, or a cow, or a bicycle, Philistines
might never have flinched. On the other hand, Olympia Press informs
me that amateurs (amateurs!) are disappointed with the tame turn my
story takes in the second volume, and do not buy it."[40]

But just as *Lolita* was showing some signs of publishing respectability, if not yet of critical acclaim and commercial profitability, the
French government made an about-turn and banned the book. Girodias suddenly found himself fighting for the novel and for the survival of the Olympia Press.

"ONE DAY a police inspector of the Vice Squad . . . visited me,"
Girodias recalled. "He wanted some reading copies of a number of
books listed in our latest catalogue. I obliged. His allusions and general
attitude were rather disquieting, and I asked a friend of mine, who
knew the fellow well, to sound him out. The policeman made no
difficulty in explaining that the British government had requested
information about The Olympia Press, and that it was his job to build
up a file on us."[41]

For a few weeks nothing happened. Then, on December 20, 1956,
the twenty-five books the inspector had taken with him were banned
by an official decree signed by the Minister of the Interior. Among
them was *Lolita.* Girodias believes that British government pressure
on the French government, a constant if unrealized threat to the
Olympia Press's operations up to that point, intensified as the result
of the public dispute between Graham Greene and John Gordon over
Lolita. The vehicle for this pressure was a convention called the International Agreement for the Repression of Obscene Publications.

"In acceding to the request, the French government unwittingly
loosed a host of preposterous ironies," Brian Boyd, Nabokov's most
recent and most impressive biographer, points out. "Henry Miller and
Frank Harris, banned on the Olympia Press list, were already available
in France in French editions. J. P. Donleavy's *Ginger Man,* also
banned, was freely published in England. *Lolita,* now banned in its
English edition, was in the process of being translated quite legally
into French for France's most venerable publishing house. And since
Lolita could be legally brought into the United States once it was
smuggled out of France, France was proving itself more pudibund
than the Anglo-Saxon countries. Most absurd from a legal point of

view was that the ministerial decree against Olympia's books could only invoke a law restricting subversive *political* publications.''[42]

Girodias immediately counterattacked by suing the Ministry of the Interior, something that had never been done before in France. He also wrote to ask Nabokov for his help in defending his novel and contributing to the struggle against censorship. "When I decided to fight the *Lolita* ban, my first thought was to ask for Nabokov's help. I was rather surprised to receive a very adamant refusal to participate in what he called, with blithe unconcern, the 'lolitigation.' ''[43]

Girodias had written to Nabokov outlining his strategy, which included the publication of a pamphlet defending the novel. He also proposed that Nabokov should launch his own lawsuit against the French ban and make an appearance in Paris in defense of his work. Nabokov replied: "I very much regret that I lack the funds to attack the ban independently. . . . I simply do not make enough money with my books to permit such action, much as I would like to undertake it. Apart from this, I wish to give you every assistance in your campaign." He listed a number of items for publication in Girodias's pamphlet: his essay on *Lolita,* an article on the novel by a respected American academic, excerpts from the French translation of *Lolita,* his curriculum vitae, a list of published works, and some photographs.

"I would much prefer if you did not stress too much my being a professor at Cornell," Nabokov continued. "I am a writer primarily, and this is the important point. I do not mind being referred to as 'university professor teaching literature in a great American university.' But I would prefer you not to call Cornell by name." Nabokov ended by saying: "Wishing you success in this struggle for a just cause.''[44]

Eight days later Nabokov wrote to his American publisher friend Jason Epstein. "Would you be willing to advise me on a rather puzzling affair. Girodias (Olympia Press) wants me to sue the French government on account of LOLITA. He thinks it will help his own action if I join the fray. He rather bluntly states that matters would be helped by showing to the judges that 'the author of *Lolita* is an absolutely honorable and authentic writer' and by having 'respectability, responsibility and good manners' represented in the affair.

"I do not expect to win the 'heavy damages' he wants me to sue for. Neither can I lose (financially, that is) since Girodias offers to assume all expenses which will be reimbursable to him only in case I win.

"I am rather loath of exposing myself in the company of The

Olympia Press. But I am also rather at a loss to find a point of view from which to consider the whole thing.

"I have to take into account the fact that so far Cornell has been very tolerant. The matter simply has not been discussed, and no questions have been asked. But might not matters be made worse if I start a litigation, and possibly lose it?

"On the other hand, I wish to give every possible support to Olympia, though personally I do not care if the ban will be lifted or not, since Gallimard is going to publish the French translation anyway."[45]

By return mail Epstein advised Nabokov against initiating the suit. He urged him to remain aloof from the legal question until it clarified itself. Nabokov wrote to Girodias saying that he had been advised against conducting a separate lawsuit "mainly because of the distance, and because I could not possibly come to Paris in the near future. Perhaps even more important is the consideration that my university might not like the idea." Nabokov thanked Girodias for his "generous offer" to finance the litigation and sent him a distribution list of influential Americans for the brochure on Lolita.[46]

All this was entwined with the early stages of negotiations over finding an American publisher for Lolita, and a whiff of horse trading began to enter the correspondence. Girodias had already made it clear that, as the original publisher of Lolita, he expected a large share of an eventual American deal. To some American publishers his demands seemed naive; to others, plain greedy; and to all, highly unreasonable. The effect was to place another obstacle—in addition to the constant fear of prosecution—in the way of a successful launch of Lolita in the United States.

Thus, when Girodias wrote to Nabokov urging him to reconsider his role in defending Lolita in Paris, he received this reply:

"I have carefully read your letter of March 5, wherein you urge me to reconsider my decision in regard to lolitigation.

"You say that you fail to understand why Cornell might not like the idea of my intervention etc. To this I would like to say that the fact of my academic standing was introduced into the controversy was very embarrassing to me. I have an established literary reputation on both sides of the ocean, and I published this book as a writer, not as a university professor."

Nabokov went on to explain how he viewed the defense of Lolita: "My moral defense of the book is the book itself. I do not feel under any obligation to do more. However, I went further and wrote the essay on LOLITA, a copy of which is now in your hands. On the ethical plane, it is of supreme indifference to me what opinion French, British, or any other courts, magistrates, or philistine readers in general, may have of my book. However, I appreciate your difficulties."

As for changing his position on refusing any further involvement in "lolitigation," Nabokov said that if Girodias made it possible for him to sell the American and British rights of *Lolita,* "it might influence my decision considerably." Such a change, however, would require "a legal document exempting me from any financial responsibility whatever to lawyers and courts in France, even in case Olympia decided to go out of business or any other disaster occurred."[47]

Girodias made the argument that he and Nabokov shared identical interests. While it is true that they had a common cause over *Lolita,* Nabokov clearly had no interest in the other twenty-four books—most of them purely pornographic—that the French government had also banned. Nabokov wrote later: "He [Girodias] wanted me to defend *Lolita,* but I did not see how my book could be treated separately from his list of twenty or so lewd books. I did not want to defend even *Lolita.*" He added that he "certainly was justified" in acting as he did, "lest a shadow of responsibility fall on the university that had given me unbelievable freedom in conducting my courses . . . nor did I care to embarrass the close friend who had brought me there to enjoy that true academic freedom."[48]

Girodias did not give up trying to get Nabokov to come over to Paris and play a personal role in the defense of his novel. In addition to accepting all the financial risks of the legal costs, he offered to pay the author's travel expenses. Miriam Worms, who handled the correspondence and later met Nabokov, recalls the circumstances: "We wanted him to testify in person that *Lolita* was a serious literary work written by a serious author." Nabokov wrote back saying that Cornell would not like it.

"Nabokov was a coward," said Miriam Worms. "Although immensely grateful when Girodias first accepted *Lolita* for publication, Nabokov subsequently became resentful and ashamed of being published by someone he suddenly considered to be a scandalous publisher. Girodias was far too visible for Nabokov's taste, and he didn't have the courage to defend his own book."[49]

Eric Kahane, Girodias's brother and a Nabokov admirer, was working on the French translation of *Lolita* for Gallimard at the time. But he too felt Nabokov let his publisher down. "He didn't do a damn thing to help Girodias," he said. "What he really wanted to do was to get out of the contract with Olympia."[50]

Girodias pursued his case against the French government with vigor by marshaling support among French writers, publishers, and journalists. In April 1957 he published his pamphlet, which he called *L'Affaire Lolita: Défense de l'Écrivain*. It included all Nabokov's material; an extract from the novel in French; a spirited article by Girodias himself discussing the literary merit of *Lolita* and comparing it to *Ulysses,* the circumstances of the ban, and the "theory and practice of censorship"; and a number of supporting appendices. It was an impressive document published with great speed and in some style. But it was not only designed to save *Lolita*. The publication was part of Girodias's campaign to rescue all his banned goods (whether they were great books or just plain dirty books) and, ultimately, his entire publishing business.

While Nabokov stood aloof from the fray, Vera, his wife, began to see merit in Girodias actually losing the case. Writing to Putnam's president Walter Minton in January 1958, she noted that an "adverse decision" by the French courts regarding *Lolita* "might prove very much to my husband's advantage since there seems to be a provision in the French law releasing the author [from his contract] if the publisher cannot continue to publish the book."[51]

In early 1958, the Administrative Tribunal of Paris made a judgment in favor of Girodias's lawsuit, effectively removing the ban on *Lolita* and the other proscribed Olympia books. Gallimard, which had been holding back on publishing the book until the legal situation became clearer, announced that it would bring the novel out within a few months.

The tribunal's decision, however, turned out to be a pyrrhic victory for Girodias. In May the Fourth Republic fell and General de Gaulle took over. Confronted with a deteriorating war in Algeria and rebellion at home, the new government strengthened its security powers, including those of censorship. The Minister of the Interior appealed the Paris Tribunal's decision and won in the Conseil d'État, France's highest court. *Lolita* was once again beyond the pale.

But the ban only applied to the original English edition of the book. In April 1959, Gallimard finally brought out the French version, translated by Eric Kahane. Girodias says that he had asked Gallimard to mention in the preface to its publication the fact that *Lolita* had been first published by the Olympia Press. This was important, he pointed out, for his litigation with the French government, which had reached an impasse. He says, however, that Nabokov heard of his request and "opposed it violently."

"Gallimard's editor, Michel Mohrt, wrote me on February 27, 1959," Girodias reported. It was "a pathetically embarrassed letter in which he quoted Nabokov: 'You are mistaken in thinking that the French translation of *Lolita* has been made from the Olympia edition. This is not so. When last spring I prepared the Putnam edition I changed an entire paragraph in the Olympia edition and made several other corrections throughout the book.'" Gallimard apparently complied with Nabokov's wishes, and no mention of *Lolita*'s first publisher was made in the French edition.[52] Nabokov made no reference to this matter in later commentary on his relationship with his Paris publisher.

Girodias went back to war, but the problem was how to proceed. "There was no way of appealing against the final judgment of the Conseil d'État and of having the ban lifted on the English version by direct litigation," he wrote later. "In its verdict, the Conseil had stated that the Minister of the Interior's power not only to apply but even to *interpret* the law was absolute and could not be questioned even by the Conseil [itself]."

Girodias took advice, thought hard, and came up with a novel approach. "Since the French version of *Lolita* had been authorised while my own English edition was still under a ban, I had yet another way open to me: to sue the government for damages, under the pretext that an unjust application of the law had been made, and that the republican principle of equality between citizens had been violated. Surprisingly, that worked. I was called to the Ministry of the Interior, and a compromise was proposed to me: the Minister was willing to cancel the ban if I agreed to withdraw my request for damages. I agreed and the ban was finally abrogated on July 21, 1959, signed by [the Minister] himself."[53]

W HEN ERIC KAHANE was commissioned by Gallimard to do the French translation of *Lolita,* Nabokov must have felt that his precious girl had fallen into the clutches of a family business. Yet, after some initial doubts, he grew to like and respect the young translator and seemed pleased with the final result. Kahane was also satisfied. It was good for his professional reputation, and everybody made money out of it. But he says it was an experience he will never forget or ever want to repeat.

Starting in mid-1957, the task took him sixteen months of intense effort. Sometimes he could only manage ten lines of text a day. "It was like lace work," said Kahane, who ended up drained, exhausted, and in debt. Nabokov insisted on reading every word and conducted a huge correspondence, via Gallimard, with as many as four pages of a letter devoted to the meaning of a single word. At times this would verge on the ridiculous as, for instance, finding the best French phrase to describe the "peachy fuzz" on Lolita's arms. Kahane tried out *peau de pêche,* but Nabokov would not have it and came up with an archaic word meaning "wild gooseberry," which he said was in an 1895 edition of *Larousse.* "I don't remember who won that battle," said Kahane.

One of the most difficult problems was how to handle Nabokov's still numerous French phrases in the English version. How to translate, for example, Quilty's desire to have Lolita *souffler* him? A direct English translation or another French rendering (*faire le pompier, faire la pipe,* etc.) was too crude. One way out was to leave the original French phrases as they stood, but, in a *French* edition, that recourse risked damaging the novel's style.

Kahane scratched his head and came up with an idea. Since Humbert Humbert's father was a Swiss national, it seemed reasonable to look to Switzerland for a solution. Kahane knew a young German-Swiss couple and asked them how would they say "blowjob" in Switzerdeutsch. The girl blushed and was struck dumb. The boy said it didn't exist, people did not say things like that in German-speaking Switzerland. Refusing to accept defeat, Kahane invented a word: *Auspumpen.*

"Nabokov loved it," Kahane remembered with a laugh. " 'I salute you,' he said."[54]

" *LOLITA'S* FATE seems destined to have been colorful at every turn," writes Brian Boyd.[55] This was undoubtedly true as the long search for an American publisher entered its final stages. The path to that highly desirable event was paved with the promise of fame and riches, but it was also strewn with difficulties. And many of these were created by the two principals who had most to gain, namely Nabokov and Girodias.

While word of *Lolita* was spreading rapidly as the result of the Greene-Gordon debate in Britain, the ban in France and steady sales of the Olympia edition, the legal situation in the United States was undergoing a sea change. The critical development was a decision in the Supreme Court (*Roth* v. *United States*) in 1957 that decisively liberalized the environment in which controversial books could be published. In essence, the court found that books having literary, artistic, or other social importance came under the protection of the First Amendment of the Constitution, which guaranteed freedom of expression, and should no longer be regarded as "obscene." The judgment was written by Justice William J. Brennan, a liberal member of the court who went on to play a vanguard role in removing censorship of artistic—and, in the end, nonartistic—sexually explicit forms of expression in the United States.

Earlier that year in Paris, Maurice Girodias had made an important discovery. He had noticed that one or two copies of *Lolita,* which had been sent to people in the United States, had been confiscated by the U.S. Customs and then released a few weeks later without any explanation. "I decided to write to the New York Bureau of Customs to investigate," he recalled. He received "a rather miraculous letter signed by Mr. Irving Fishman, Deputy Collector for the Restricted Merchandise Division." The letter said: "You are advised that certain copies of this book have been before this Office for examination and that they have been released." This meant, Girodias continued, that "the U.S. Customs had had the remarkable mental—and may I say political—courage of finding *Lolita,* a book printed in Paris by my disreputable publishing firm, admissible in the United States. . . . That decision by one of the two Federal departments to exert moral censorship (the other being the Post Office) on literary material, was naturally of extreme importance: *Lolita* could now legitimately be published in America with practically no danger."[56]

It was not quite as simple as that. Customs rulings of that kind, especially informal ones, have "no precedental legal value," Edward de Grazia points out. Nevertheless, this development, "together with Nabokov's growing reputation and word of the book's virtues and popularity, led several American publishers to seek the right to publish *Lolita* in the States."[57]

In the summer of 1957 *Lolita* made her American debut when Jason Epstein published several large excerpts in *The Anchor Review,* a literary journal put out by Doubleday. The excerpts, amounting to almost a third of the book, appeared under Nabokov's name. The issue also included his essay "On a Book Entitled *Lolita*" and a long and favorable introductory article to the novel by the literary critic Fred Dupee. In a letter to Epstein, Nabokov said that he and his wife were "both delighted . . . the cover is splendid and most enticing. Your arrangement and selection of the *Lolita* excerpts is above all praise."[58]

Epstein had wanted to publish *Lolita* when he first read it in 1954 but had been overruled by Doubleday's president, who was so opposed that he refused to read the manuscript.[59] Epstein did not give up but thought a gradualist approach—like running extracts in *The Anchor Review*—was the best tactic. Nabokov trusted and respected Epstein more than any other American publisher and hoped that he would eventually succeed in publishing the whole book.

The growing interest shown by American and British publishers in *Lolita* served to highlight the nature of the obstacles that still hindered publication. Lingering legal and moral problems remained a serious deterrent. Even though the Supreme Court had swung in a liberal direction with the *Roth* case, it still took courage to put the new guidelines to the test, a test that could involve a considerable amount of money and time. In Britain, no publisher was ready to step forward until a new and more liberal definition of obscenity had been passed into law.

The largest hurdle, however, was bringing the Paris publisher and American author into line so that an agreement could be signed. Girodias on this occasion, as he was fond of pointing out, could not be bypassed as he had been over the British and American rights of *The Ginger Man*. "The rights had to be bought from me, not from Nabokov," he said.[60]

Relations between the two men were already poor when American and British publishers started to express a serious interest in *Lolita*. "I began to curse my association with Olympia Press," Nabokov later wrote, ". . . as early as 1955, that is from the very first year of my dealings with Mr. Girodias. From the very start I was confronted with the peculiar aura surrounding his business transactions with me, an aura of negligence, evasiveness, procrastination, and falsity. I complained of these peculiarities in most of my letters to my agent who faithfully transmitted my complaints to him but these he never explains in his account of our ten-year-long (1955–65) association."[61]

Nabokov's principal complaint, thoroughly justified, was that Girodias failed to send him royalty statements or indeed any financial information about the book's progress. In a lengthy rebuttal to Girodias's side of the story, published in *Evergreen Review,* Nabokov began by quoting the key clauses from his Olympia Press contract with Girodias. He put it in "strophic form" for the "reader's convenience":

8

In the event of the Publishers
Going bankrupt
Or failing to make accountings and payments
As herein specified,
Then in either event the present agreement
Becomes automatically null and void
And the rights herein granted
Revert to the Author.

9

The Publishers shall render statement
Of the number of copies sold
On the 30th June and 31st December
Of each year
Within one month from these dates
Respectively
And shall make payment to the Author
At the time of such rendering of account.

"The eighth stave, with that beautiful, eloquent, almost sapphically modulated last verse ('Revert to the Author'), is of great importance for understanding what Mr. Girodias calls 'our enigmatic conflict.' It will also be noted that while devoting a lot of space to the many 'disappointments' that my attitude toward him caused him, he never mentions in the course of his article the perfectly obvious reason for a writer's resenting his association with a publisher, namely, the fact of Mr. Girodias' failing repeatedly, with a kind of maniacal persistence, to live up to clause 9 of our agreement."[62]

Nabokov catalogues the financial breaches of his contract. The first half of his advance was paid a month late; the second half came three months after it was due, following considerable prodding. ("I write for my pleasure," Nabokov told him, "but publish for money.") From the time *Lolita* was published in September 1955 until March 1957, Nabokov says he did not receive a single royalty statement. Although entitled to annul his contract, Nabokov decided to "wait a little longer." The statement, when it came, was incomplete.

"The nuisance of non-statements did not fail to resume," Nabokov continued. "By the end of August, 1957, I had received none for the first semester of that year which was due on July 31. On September 2, Mr. Girodias asked for a postponement of two months, and I agreed towait till September 30, but nothing happened, and having had enough of that nonsense I advised him (October 5) that all rights reverted to me. He promptly paid up (44,220 anciens francs), and I relented."[63]

Girodias commented that "Nabokov's excuse for his action was futile and ineffective" and that their relationship was "irreparably damaged by it." But he failed to go into any details and, as Nabokov tellingly pointed out, he never addressed the critical questions of royalty and other financial statements in the *Evergreen* correspondence, or indeed anywhere else.[64] Paying his authors, as many Olympia Press writers have attested, was not Girodias's strong suit. Girodias found contracts boring, paperwork a burdensome chore, and the notion of regular accounting and payments an elusive ideal.

He was equally sloppy with copyright. Nabokov was aware that his copyright to *Lolita* had to be registered in the United States as soon as the book was published in Paris. For this he needed the exact date of publication and had some difficulty extracting it from Girodias. When Nabokov belatedly received his first copy of the book itself, he noticed that Girodias had added to the "Copyright 1955 by V. Nabokov" the words "and The Olympia Press."

"I learned from the Copyright Office in Washington that this matey formula (for which I had not given my permission) might cause trouble at re-publication in the U.S. which had to take place within five years. I was advised to get an 'assignment or quit-claim' from Mr. Girodias, and this I at once asked him to send me. I got no reply . . . , wrote to him again and again, but only . . . three months later got from him what I asked."[65]

Another "misdemeanor" recorded by Nabokov was Girodias's re-printing of *Lolita* in Paris "with his own introduction (in intolerably bad English) without my permission—which he knew I would never have given." Girodias's preface, which he called "Publisher's Digres-sion," with a note at the end accepting sole responsibility for it, was harmless enough. It traced some of the checkered publishing history of the novel, the Greene-Gordon fracas, the French ban, and Giro-dias's views on censorship. It was an interesting, straightforward if digressive account, written in Girodias's excellent and lively English. But, of course, he had not consulted his author before slipping it in.

Summing up his view of their relationship, Nabokov had this to say: "What always made me regret our association were not 'dreams of impending fortune,' not my 'hating' him 'for having stolen a portion of Nabokov's property' [as Girodias had claimed], but the obligation to endure the elusiveness, the evasiveness, the procrastination, the dodges, the duplicity, and the utter irresponsibility of the man."[66]

AFTER *LOLITA*'S DEBUT in *The Anchor Review* in June 1957, another year passed before an American publisher was finally found for the book. "Several publishers were interested in it [*Lolita*] but the difficulties Mr. Girodias created in our negotiations with American firms were another source of acute vexation on my part," Nabokov recalled later.[67]

Doubleday's Jason Epstein had never lost interest in publishing *Lolita* but was frustrated by Girodias's demands and remained cautious about the legal repercussions. In the spring, Nabokov had told him that McDowell Obolensky, a new publishing firm, wanted to publish the book. Nabokov was tempted to sign a deal. "What I would like best of all, would be to get an offer from you. Two or three weeks will certainly elapse before anything is signed and settled, but *Lolita* is young, and I am old."[68]

Epstein warned him against dealing with such a small and untried publishing house; *Lolita* needed the resources and reputation of a larger firm. The best strategy, Epstein said, was to wait until current Supreme Court obscenity cases were settled and to continue to surround *Lolita* "with academic praise and high critical authority, letting her peep out of the pages of *The Anchor Review* until eventually, little by little, the country gets used to her."[69]

Nabokov was deeply concerned about the danger of losing his American copyright to *Lolita*. Under the existing law, any work produced by an American citizen residing in the United States and published abroad could only be given a temporary copyright of five years. The law also stipulated that no more than 1,500 copies of the foreign edition could be imported. If either of these provisions were broken, the author would lose his copyright and the book would pass into the public domain, meaning that anyone could publish it and keep the proceeds.

Nabokov's temporary copyright was to expire in September 1960, and Girodias was threatening to advertise and distribute the book in the United States and even try to publish his own version there. Nabokov pointed out that if the U.S. copyright laws were broken, both he and Girodias would lose everything. The only answer was to find an American publisher as quickly as possible.

In the summer of 1957 Epstein made an offer for *Lolita* that Nabokov felt was reasonable but was reluctant to discuss with Girodias himself. "His last letter on the subject was curt—to put it mildly. He will certainly say no, if I submit your offer to him, and he may even choose not to answer at all." Nabokov also suggested the same approach to Ivan Obolensky, the son of a colorful Russian aristocrat who had been in the Czar's cavalry, who was doggedly pursuing a deal. "Mr. M. Girodias . . . is a difficult person. . . . I would be delighted if you could come to terms with the man." (Vera Nabokov was not so restrained; she later described Girodias as being of "a somewhat ogreish disposition.")[70]

A month later Obolensky flew to Paris to explore the possibilities of a deal. Girodias says that he was "spontaneously offered a 20 percent royalty" for the book by Obolensky, but the American publisher was apparently "frightened away by Nabokov's attitude when he met him later in New York."[71]

"One part of this passage is inaccurate," retorted Nabokov, "and the other [is] simply untrue. It was not I who dissuaded this particular publisher, but his partner. The account is inaccurate because Mr. Girodias does not say who was to get most of the 20 percent. 'I am prepared to accept this proposal,' wrote Mr. Girodias to me (apparently under the impression that he had got a definite offer which was not the case), 'if my share is assured at twelve and a half percent. The advance would be shared in the same proportion. Would you accept seven and a half percent as your share? I consider my claim justified and fair.' My agent wrote that she was *outrée de ces pretensions* ["incensed by these demands"].' "[72]

At this point a dark horse entered the race. This was Putnam's Walter Minton, who had somehow missed out on the expanding waves of "lolititillation" in the publishing world. At the end of August he wrote to Nabokov: "Being a rather backward example of that rather backward species, the American publisher, it was only recently that I began to hear about a book called LOLITA."[73]

I talked to Walter Minton, a fit-looking seventy-year-old, in his colonnaded colonial-style house—the house that *Lolita* built—among the pine and beech trees of Saddle River, New Jersey. "A man called Henry Exstein, who ran a remainder business, first recommended *Lolita* to me," he said. "He gave me one of the green Olympia Press copies, but I never did anything about it. A couple of weeks later, a young lady, Rosemary Ridgewell, a showgirl at the Copacabana in New York, sat me down one evening and said: 'You've got to read this.' I read it in her apartment that night in about three hours and knew that it was something extraordinary."[74]

Time magazine ran a racier description of Minton's literary scout. Rosemary Ridgewell, "a superannuated (27) nymphet," was "a tall (5 ft 8 in), slithery-blithery one time Latin Quarter showgirl." Girodias, who later got to know her in the same biblical sense as Minton, described her as "a very bright girl with a Dostoevskian nature." Her discovery had an ironic twist. She had first sighted *Lolita* not in its familiar green Olympia jacket but in Jason Epstein's *Anchor Review*. For her efforts, she received a finder's fee equivalent to 10 percent of the author's royalties for the first year, plus 10 percent of the publisher's share of the subsidiary rights for two years.[75]

In a raging snowstorm, Minton drove to Cornell University to make his pitch to the Nabokovs. "I told Vladimir that I could get him together with Girodias. Well, he didn't want to give anything to Girodias. He and Vera were absolutely convinced that they had been swindled. He said that he knew that at least three or four thousand copies of the Olympia *Lolita* had been sold in the United States whereas Girodias had only paid him royalties on a thousand or so. I said to him: 'Don't ever open your mouth about that to anybody because if it ever became established your copyright wouldn't be worth *beans*.' "[76]

Back from the snows of Ithaca, Minton went to work. The Nabokovs had given him their blessing to go to the mat with Girodias, but relations between author and publisher could not have been worse. Minton nevertheless managed to establish a working relationship with both sides, an achievement that was reflected in a modification of Girodias's demands for a higher royalty than *Lolita*'s author.

Nabokov noted the change: "On November 30, 1957, Mr. Girodias wrote in a mellow mood, 'I admit that I have been wrong on several occasions in the course of our dealings. . . .' He added that he no longer 'requested a larger share of the proceeds' of the American edition and that he was canceling his own 'alternative project' of bringing out his own 'American reprint'—a silly threat, the carrying out of which would have been his undoing."[77]

Minton was offering a top-of-the-market royalty of 15 percent to be shared by author and publisher. Nabokov, however, wanted 10 percent himself and would not agree to any deal that gave Girodias an equal share. Girodias would not accept 5 percent, so Minton added another 2.5 percent to his share, bringing the total royalty to 17.5 percent. While all this was going on, Barney Rosset of Grove Press came in with an offer of 7.5 percent to Nabokov and 5 percent to Girodias. But by this time, Minton had the game in hand, and an agreement was signed in March 1958.

Minton succeeded where other publishers had failed by moving quickly, convincing two extremely difficult people that their interests lay in a deal where each would have to compromise, and being ready if necessary to fight for the book in the courts. Putnam's published *Lolita* in August 1958, three years after its Paris debut and almost five years after Nabokov had begun his long search for an American publisher.

Within three weeks of publication, 100,000 copies of *Lolita* had been sold, the first book to achieve such a rapid rate of sales since the appearance of *Gone with the Wind*. By the end of September 1958 *Lolita* was at the top of the bestseller list and stayed there for seven weeks, to be finally bumped by the work of another Russian, Boris Pasternak's *Doctor Zhivago*. A dozen reviews accompanied *Lolita*'s appearance in the United States. "As with later reviews," Brian Boyd comments, "two-thirds were enthusiastic, a third puzzled, taxed, peeved, irked or outraged."

An interesting contrast appeared in the columns of the Sunday *New York Times*. Elizabeth Janeway, writing in the newspaper's *Book Review*, liked the novel. "The first time I read *Lolita* I thought it was one of the funniest books I'd ever come on. . . . The second time I read it, uncut, I thought it was one of the saddest. . . . Humbert is every man who is driven by desire, wanting his Lolita so badly that it never occurs to him to consider her as a human being, or as anything but a dream–figment made flesh. . . . As for pornographic content, I can think of few volumes more likely to quench the flames of lust than this exact and immediate description of its consequences."[78]

In the daily edition of the same newspaper, Orville Prescott took the opposite view: "*Lolita*, then, is undeniably news in the world of books. Unfortunately, it is bad news. There are two equally serious reasons why it isn't worth any adult reader's attention. The first is that it is dull, dull, dull in a pretentious, florid and archly fatuous fashion. The second is that it is repulsive . . . highbrow pornography."[79]

Nabokov seemed to be unaffected by the publicity that had suddenly lifted *Lolita* out of its long obscurity. Vera Nabokov noted in her diary during the first week following publication: "V. serenely indifferent—occupied with a new story, and with the spreading of some 2,000 butterflies." "The financial coup was a surprise and a comforting assurance for the future," Brian Boyd writes, "but he thought the critical acclaim merely his belated and inevitable due."[80] "All this ought to have happened thirty years ago" was Nabokov's laconic comment.

Nabokov was shocked later, however, when a girl of eight or nine years of age came to his door for candy on Halloween, dressed up by her parents as Lolita. "Before the novel's publication," Boyd notes, "he had insisted to Minton that there be no little girl on the book's cover, and now as a *Lolita* movie looked more and more possible, he warned Minton that he 'would veto the use of a real child. Let them find a dwarfess.' "[81]

Lolita was never prosecuted in the United States, but many libraries refused to stock it. Nabokov was invited to lecture at a number of universities and the Library of Congress. But "the Texas town of Lolita debated changing its name to Jackson," Boyd writes. "A city official in Los Angeles blew the whistle when he found the public library circulating the book—and Putnam's promptly received another large order from California. Nabokov found in his fan mail a potholder embroidered with the word *Lolita* and felt sure it had come from Edmund Wilson as a derisive tribute to a potboiler. 'Take me to your *Lolita*,' said one cartoon among many, and Groucho Marx announced, 'I've put off reading *Lolita* for 6 years, till she's 18.' "[82]

Girodias was to be proved wrong about the film possibilities of *Lolita*. The movie rights were sold to Harris-Kubrick Pictures for $150,000 plus 15 percent of the producers' profits in November, three months after the book had been published. Minton remembers Nabokov asking about the profits and the response of Irving ("Swifty") Lazar, the agent who handled the deal. "Walter, caravans have been lost in the desert off Palm Springs looking for the percentages of profits from films."[83]

James Harris and Stanley Kubrick were keen to have Nabokov write the script but wanted him to end the film with Lolita and Humbert married with an adult relative's blessing. Nabokov agreed to write his own version, for which he received sole credit and $75,000, but most of it was changed by Kubrick, who directed the movie. After seeing it, Nabokov's opinion was "that Kubrick was a great director, that his *Lolita* was a first-rate film with magnificent actors, and that only ragged odds and ends of my script had been used."[84]

Lolita, released in 1962, featured James Mason playing Humbert, Shelley Winters as Charlotte Haze, Peter Sellers as a marvelous Clare

Quilty, and Sue Lyon, an unknown actress who was anything but a "dwarfess," in the title role. She came across as a sturdy, sophisticated teenager rather than a petulant nymphet. The acting was superb, but the movie as a whole was strangely bloodless and completely non-erotic; the makers of *Lolita* did not permit themselves the luxury of a single embrace. "With Sue Lyon looking seventeen and Humbert's passion for nymphets entirely omitted," writes Brian Boyd, "the film lost all the tension and the horror of the novel."[85]

In Britain, Graham Greene's enthusiasm for *Lolita* encouraged the first tentative moves toward publication there. The Bodley Head, where Greene was both an author and a director, approached Nabokov in June 1957 and asked for a two- to three-year option to publish the novel, pending a change in the country's obscenity laws. Other publishers took a similar view, so *Lolita* had to wait another two years.

Nabokov had given Putnam's the right to choose a British publisher, and Minton selected Weidenfeld & Nicolson, a relatively new and aggressive firm. A deal was concluded that satisfied everyone, including Girodias, but actual publication remained difficult. George Weidenfeld, apologizing to Nabokov for the delay, explained the problem: "Under the present law the literary quality of the book in question is held to be entirely irrelevant and one is not allowed to call any witnesses to testify to the book's merits. Under the new bill [which became law as the Obscene Publications Act of 1959] not only will literary merit be taken into account in deciding the fate of the book but the defence will be able to call witnesses to testify to the book's literary merits."[86]

A campaign to prepare the way for the publication of *Lolita* was set in motion. In January 1959 Bernard Levin wrote an essay in *The Spectator* defending the book. A group of prominent writers, academics, publishers, and editors sent a letter to *The Times* supporting the publication of *Lolita* in Britain. The group included Isaiah Berlin, Maurice Bowra, Storm Jameson, Frank Kermode, Allen Lane, Compton Mackenzie, Iris Murdoch, V. S. Pritchett, Peter Quennell, Herbert Read, Stephen Spender, Philip Toynbee, and Angus Wilson.

They wrote: "We are disturbed by the suggestion that it may yet prove impossible to have an English edition of Vladimir Nabokov's *Lolita*. Our opinions of the merit of the work differ widely, but we think it would be deplorable, if a book of considerable literary interest, which has been favourably received by distinguished critics and widely praised in serious and respectable periodicals were to be denied an appearance in this country.

"Prosecutions of genuine works of literature bring governments into disrepute and do nothing to protect public morality. When today we read the proceedings against *Madame Bovary* or *Ulysses*—works genuinely found shocking by many of their contemporaries—it is Flaubert and Joyce whom we admire, not the Public Prosecutors of the time. Let good sense spare us another such case."[87]

Nigel Nicolson, George Weidenfeld's partner and a Conservative Member of Parliament at the time, was requested by Edward Heath, then chief whip, to drop publication because it could hurt the party, which was divided over the Obscene Publications Bill.[88] Nicolson refused. "The advice one often heard," he wrote in a letter to *The Times*, "was 'Publish and be damned,' but that was very bad advice. I did not want to be damned. I felt that this particular work was a work of such outstanding merit and so widely acclaimed that some publisher had to have the courage to make it available to British readers."

Lolita was finally published in Britain in 1959, but Nicolson paid a price for his principles. He lost his seat in the next election by a narrow margin, and his role in publishing *Lolita* was undoubtedly a contributing factor. Weidenfeld helped prepare the ground for the publication of *Lolita* and went on loyally to publish virtually all of Nabokov's works, whether they were profitable or not. (Minton, in contrast, was not unhappy to lose Nabokov after publishing six more of his books.) After the prepublication furor had abated, *Lolita* sailed serenely and unscathed into publishing history, generating literary praise, angry opposition, prurient interest, and sacks of cash.[89]

IN THE AUTUMN OF 1959, Nabokov and his wife visited Paris, the first time they had been to the city since they had fled the advancing German army in 1940 to seek refuge in the United States. Gallimard, *Lolita*'s French publisher, invited the couple to celebrate the publication of the book with a reception. Before he left America, Nabokov wrote to Doussia Ergaz, telling her that he did not wish "to make the acquaintance of Mr. Girodias" when he came to Paris.

Girodias picked up the story. "He wrote to my brother Eric that he was anxious to meet him to discuss the French translation of

Lolita. . . . I learned that a heated debate had taken place between the directors of the firm [Gallimard] when somebody had asked whether I should be invited or not. . . . Some argued that it would be unseemly to exclude me; and in the end caution prevailed, and it was decided to eliminate my name from the guest list. But Monique Grall, Gallimard's public relations lady, thought it would be amusing to transgress that decision, of which she had not been properly informed. She sent me an invitation."[90]

Girodias duly presented himself at Gallimard's "gilded salons" in the rue Sebastien-Bottin where, he said, he found Monique Grall in a corner "doubled over in helpless mirth . . . but the other Gallimard dignitaries . . . all rather pale." He immediately identified Nabokov, he says, "surrounded by a tight group of admirers; not too far away Madame Nabokov was impersonating dignity, destroying by her pale-fire presence the myth of her husband's entomological concern for the race of nymphets."

Looking around, he found, "hiding in a corner, my dear suffering, terrified friend Doussia Ergaz, choking on a macaroon. I asked her kindly to introduce me to the master, our master. . . . She at first protested, then complied. We made our way through the crowd. Nabokov was speaking to my brother in earnest, but he had very obviously recognised me. I was introduced, expecting at all moments a blow, a screech, a slap, anything—but not that vacuous grin, which is all the *paparazzi* were able to capture, much to their disappointment.

"As if he were seized by some sudden urge, Vladimir Nabokov pivoted on himself with the graceful ease of a circus seal, throwing a glance in the direction of his wife, and was immediately caught up in more ardent conversation by a Czech journalist." Girodias recorded that he was "both relieved and disappointed." He then downed a few glasses of champagne before plunging back into the crowd in the direction of Madame Nabokov.

"She was standing very quiet, very self-possessed. I introduced myself, but she did not acknowledge my presence even with the flicker of an eyelash. I did not exist: I was no more than an epistolary fiction, and I had no business wearing a body and disturbing people in a literary cocktail party given in honor of her husband, Vladimir Nabokov."[91]

And that was that—or so it seemed. The next day Doussia Ergaz called Girodias, "chuckling with delight and relief. She had had dinner with the Nabokovs after the party, and asked Vladimir what he thought of me. 'And do you know what he answered?' she added: 'He said: "Was he there? I didn't know."''[92]

Four years prior to writing this account in *Evergreen Review*, Girodias had written up the incident in *Playboy* magazine (April 1961). This version had a few embellishments that Nabokov zeroed in on with relish in his own account in *Evergreen Review*:

"The discrepancies between the two variants are typical of apocrypha. . . . In *Playboy,* he and I exchange a few 'not unfriendly' sentences. In *Evergreen,* the great meeting is wordless: I limit myself to a 'vacuous grin' and immediately turn away to talk 'ardently' to a 'Czech reporter' (an unexpected and rather sinister personage of whom I would like to hear more from our chronicler) . . . the passage in *Playboy* about the quaint way I 'plunged backwards and sideways with the easy grace of a dolphin' is now replaced by the 'graceful ease of a circus seal.'"

Nabokov went on to point out that "even *if* Mr. Girodias was introduced to me (which I doubt), I did not catch his name; but what especially invalidates the general veracity of his account is the little phrase he slips in about my having 'very obviously recognized' him as he was slowly swimming toward me amid the 'bodies.' Very obviously I could not have recognized somebody I had never seen in my life; nor can I insult his sanity by suggesting he assumed I had somehow obtained his picture . . . and had been cherishing it all those years.

"I am looking forward to Mr. Girodias's third version of our mythical meeting," Nabokov wrote. "Perhaps he will discover at last that he had crashed the wrong party and talked to a Slovak poet who was being feted next door."[93]

Girodias's third version took a little time, but, never one to disappoint, he finally obliged, in his memoirs, and with his customary verve. The preliminaries, with Monique Grall playing her subversive role inside Gallimard, remained the same. So did Girodias's dramatic entrance, when he was greeted by the appalled looks of the Gallimard hierarchy and the hovering paparazzi, who sensed "*le grand scoop de la saison.*" The embarrassed Doussia Ergaz was still choking on her macaroon, but, this time, Monique Grall was trying—without success— to hide herself behind a curtain.

Girodias advanced, "as if in a magnificent nightmare," into the salon. His brother, Eric, who was in a dense group around Nabokov, called him over. From afar, Girodias recalled, he and Nabokov exchanged looks. "It is clear that he recognises me at first glance, although he quickly turns away." Girodias approached, and Eric began to introduce him to the master. The paparazzi positioned themselves for the climactic moment. The group around Vladimir opened up involuntarily, "like a magic door in a fairy tale." At Nabokov's side was Madame Ergaz, wearing "the expression of the Virgin at Calvary." Girodias turned to her: "Ah, Doussia, at last you are going to introduce me." But, alas, it is not to be. Nabokov spun round "with the elegance of a performing seal" and sped off toward his wife, as if "responding to a telepathic message."[94]

Vera Nabokov's own version was brief and to the point: "Somebody had brought Girodias and his brother, the translator Kahane, to introduce them to me. Nabokov either was not in the vicinity, or walked away as they approached. I exchanged two or three words with Kahane (not with Girodias), and then left them. Girodias was *not* introduced to Nabokov."[95]

Miriam Worms was at the reception and remembers talking to Nabokov, who, she says, "cut Girodias dead." She was in a group of people around the author when someone "gushed over the French translation of *Lolita* and Nabokov said, 'It should be good—I worked on it.'" Miriam Worms found this shocking because Nabokov seemed to take credit for a remarkable translation that she knew Eric Kahane had done alone:

"Nabokov was contemptible. He couldn't accept that his best book was published by the Olympia Press, which he regarded as a scandalous outfit. He thought he was a genius and deserved recognition but hated the idea that it had happened through Girodias, although it might well not have happened without him."[96]

Eric Kahane remembers the party and Nabokov well. "We were talking. 'You're so young!' he said. He was very nice, very complimentary. Then there was a commotion at the door, and my brother entered. He came over to us, and as he was getting near, Nabokov veered away like an old warship not 'seeing him.' Gid was both upset and amused. Nabokov knew who he was but did not want to see him or shake hands. He did not want to admit that he had been published by a professional pornographer when here he was at Gallimard being hailed as a king."[97]

The symbolism of these events was more important than the elusive reality. It would be hard to invent a more appropriate cameo of the relationship between Nabokov and Girodias than the Gallimard party with the two men swooping around each other, diligently composing their detailed and conflicting postmortems on how they did—or did not—meet, and their refusal to let such an intrinsically unimportant event disappear into the oblivion it deserved.

NABOKOV'S PATENT DISLIKE of Girodias and his scorn for the Olympia Press did not prevent him from giving the publisher due recognition in writing—if not face-to-face—for having played the role of midwife to *Lolita*. "I often wonder what I would have done at the time of the initial negotiation with Olympia Press," he later wrote, "if I had learned then that alongside talented, albeit immodest, literary works, the publisher gained his main income from vulgar little books that he commissioned from meretricious nonentities, books of exactly the same nature as the pictures hawked on dark corners of a nun with a St. Bernard, or a sailor with a sailor."[98]

But having "pondered the painful question" of whether he would have agreed "so cheerfully" to Girodias publishing *Lolita* had he been aware in May 1955 of what formed the "supple backbone" of Olympia's production, he came to an inescapable conclusion. "Alas, I probably would, though less cheerfully."[99]

Nabokov wrote to Girodias in 1957 that he was positive that *Lolita* was his best book so far and that he would always be grateful to Girodias for having published it.[100] But he later pointed out that he thought Girodias was "not the right person to undertake the thing; he lacked the means to launch *Lolita* properly—a book that differed so utterly in vocabulary, structure, and purpose (or rather absence of purpose) from his other much simpler commercial ventures, such as *Debby's Bidet* or *Tender Thighs*."[101]

Like Donleavy, Nabokov appears to have been either naive or disingenuous about what he was getting into when he entrusted his masterwork to the Olympia Press. He always claimed that he knew nothing about Girodias except what he had heard from his agent, Doussia Ergaz. She reported that Girodias had published some good art books under the Éditions du Chêne imprint and that Olympia was putting out the English version of the critically acclaimed *Story of O*.

Yet when Nabokov first dispatched *Lolita* to Paris, he had joked to Edmund Wilson that he imagined the book would "finally be published by some shady firm with a Viennese-Dream name—e.g. 'Silo.'"[102] Also it seems hard to believe that Doussia Ergaz, in the thick of the Paris publishing scene, had no inkling of the thriving pornographic side to Girodias's operations or that, being aware, she did not pass on the intelligence to her client.

Nabokov also shared with Donleavy the ability to bear a grudge. But there was a difference. Donleavy had a hardheaded motive for continuing to fight his publisher to the bitter end because Girodias never gave up trying to obtain what he thought was due to him from *The Ginger Man*. Nabokov, however, signed a peace agreement, skillfully brokered by Walter Minton, that took care of the American and British rights of *Lolita* on the basis of a reasonable compromise. Nabokov got both the royalty that he asked for and a higher one than Girodias received. *Lolita* was successfully—and respectably—launched, everyone made money, and everyone should have been content.

Not the Nabokovs. "They never stopped trying to break the contract with Girodias," said Minton. "Time and again, 'You must stop paying him,' they would say. We had our lawyers look at it, and it was going to be a mess. Always at the back of my mind was the fact that at some point somebody would establish that their copyright was invalid because too many copies of the original Olympia edition had been imported. Nabokov had a good Russian ability to carry a grudge. He was a most amiable person, but when he didn't like someone it never vanished."[103]

As with all his books, Girodias adopted a proprietorial attitude to an author's work that could irritate the humblest of writers. Nabokov was far from humble, but such was Girodias's sense of ownership that it could be seen why, at a particularly exasperating moment in their correspondence, Nabokov said: "I would like to remind you, Mr. Girodias, that *I* wrote *Lolita*."[104]

In his relationship with Nabokov, Girodias imputed a sinister role to the writer's wife. "In the course of our exchanges the hand of his wife-secretary Vera had appeared several times, and I had a feeling then that, if there was to be trouble between us, that hand would deliver the blows."[105] Even when gratitude was being transmitted, Girodias saw the shadow of Vera. "'Without you,' he [Nabokov] wrote through the restive fingers of Vera, 'my book would never have seen the light of day.'"[106]

Looking back, long after Nabokov was dead, Girodias assessed the writer's attitude toward himself. "The humiliations of exile, his life as a nondescript professor, the difficulty of making himself known, and finally the rejection of the work of his life, *Lolita,* by American publishers, all that had imposed a crushing weight on his pride. To be forced, under these conditions, to be published by a Parisian pornographer undoubtedly represented the supreme insult."[107]

But, in the end, Girodias professed that he had no regrets. "Were it not for my firm, *Lolita* would still be a dusty manuscript in a nostalgic cupboard. . . . I do not regret having published this admirable book; in spite of many disappointments, it has proved to be a rather exhilarating experience."[108]

Lolita was pivotal in both men's lives. For Nabokov, the book gave him the long-sought literary recognition that he considered his due and the freedom to pursue his twin passions—writing and butterfly collecting—for the rest of his life. Girodias, once again, met his match jousting with an author. While Donleavy prevailed in the law courts and auction rooms, Nabokov proved to be astute and hardheaded in the realm of contracts and copyright. The difference was, this time, Girodias came away with kudos and money, though neither would last long.

With his earnings from *Lolita,* Nabokov gave up his tenured post at Cornell University. In 1961 he and Vera rented a suite in the Palace Hotel in Montreux, Switzerland, where they lived until he died in 1977. With his share, Girodias chose to indulge a passion, a fantasy that had nothing to do with publishing.

8

Good Grief, It's Candy!

ON A COLD winter's day in December 1956, Mason Hoffenberg, an American writer, poet, and talented coiner of the one-line riposte, paid a visit to the offices of the Olympia Press. Hoffenberg was no stranger at number 8 rue de Nesle. Donning the guise of "Faustino Perez," he had written *Until She Screams*, which had been published earlier in the year in The Traveller's Companion Series. Another book, *Sin for Breakfast*—this time from the fluent pen of "Hamilton Drake"—was in the works. His own serious, nonpornographic writing was, by contrast, in the doldrums. The problem was writer's block of massive proportions, usually striking after the opening paragraph or stanza, and quite often after the first line.

With Hoffenberg was his friend Terry Southern, another American writer, and the purpose of their visit was to present Girodias with an idea for a book that would be jointly written. Southern was then living in Geneva, where his wife, Carol, had a teaching job at the United Nations nursery school. Like Hoffenberg, he was a fledgling writer acutely short of money.

The meeting with Girodias went well. The book's plot was discussed, the authors' collaboration explained, and the delicate question of money broached. The two writers went their separate ways, Hoffenberg to his Paris apartment and Southern back to Geneva. Girodias noted that the project had got off to a good start and that the Hoffenberg-Southern collaboration seemed to be full of promise.[1]

Southern later described the genesis of the story that was to become *Candy,* a modern fable based loosely on Voltaire's *Candide:*

"I wrote a short story called 'Candy Christian,' about a fabulous, blue-eyed, pink-nippled, pert-derrièred darling who was compassion incarnate, living in the West Village, so filled with universal love that she gave herself—fully, joyfully—to Derek, a demented hunchback. Of course, that was merely the surface, the flimsy trappings, as it were; the meat and potatoes of the piece lay elsewhere. Suffice it to say I showed the story to [Alexander] Trocchi. He wanted to publish it in *Merlin*—for nil recompense. I told him no thanks; I had just had something published under a similar arrangement in an ultra-obscure mag called *The Paris News Post,* H. L. Humes editor in chief (before he met up with Plimpton, Peter Matthiessen, and *The Paris Review*).

"'Well, in any case,' said Trocchi, 'this spunky heroine of yours should have more adventures! I would like very much,' he went on, 'to see her involved with the Roman Catholic Church.'

"I asked him if he would like to write such an episode himself, since he had an absolutely Joycean love/hate in that regard. And he might have done so, had not another great friend of mine, Mason Hoffenberg, poet and hemp-maven extraordinaire, surfaced at almost the same moment and been doubly keen for the opportunity. Just as well, I decided, because Trocchi was now tokus-over-teakettle into the writing of *The Wisdom of the Lash* or some equally racy volume for Olympia's 'Traveller's Companion' series.

"'Alex tells me,' said Gid slyly over our next aperitif at the Flore, 'that you and your friend Mason have embarked on a rather picaresque saga. May I show a few pages to one of my senior editors?'

"The book we were writing—an extension of Candy's West Village adventure—was humorous, which could hardly be said of any of Olympia's books, with the notable exception of *Lolita.*

"'Not suitable for your list, I'm afraid,' was my reply.

"But he was determined to see it, and with characteristic gall and cunning he persuaded Trocchi to make a copy of our ms. and let him read it—or scan it. I don't think he was much into actual reading. In any case, he must have thought it suited his purpose, because he made us the grand-sounding offer of ten thousand francs a month, for four months or until we finished the book, whichever happened first. Grand-sounding, yes, unless one considered that the exchange rate then was one hundred francs to the dollar. I complained to Trocchi about it. But he was jubilant.

" 'That's four hundred dollars, man,' he exclaimed. 'Nabokov only got two-fifty. You're getting top dollar! Break out the bubbly! Light up the wog-hemp! Let's get on with a right rave-up!' "[2]

Girodias's version, unsurprisingly, is different. He first heard of *Candy*, he says, through Mason Hoffenberg. He does not mention when he first saw anything written, but it seems clear from later correspondence between Southern and Girodias that the deal was cut after the writer had returned to Switzerland. From staid Geneva, Southern quickly followed up the Paris meeting with a letter to Girodias. In it he outlined the novel's plot:

"The story . . . is in the tradition of *Candide,* with a contemporary setting, the protagonist an attractive American girl, Candy, an only child of a father of whose love she was never quite sure, a sensitive-progressive-school humanist who comes from Wisconsin to New York's Lower East Side to be an art student, social worker, etc. and to find (unlike her father) 'beauty in mean places.'

"She has an especially romantic idea about 'Minorities,' and, of course, gets raped by Negroes, robbed by Jews, knocked-up by Puerto Ricans, etc.—though her feeling of 'being needed' sustains her for quite a while, through a devouring gauntlet of freaks, faggots, psychiatrists, and aesthetic cults—until, wearied and misunderstood, she joins a religious order, where she finds fatherly rapport at last in the gentle priest, who, at the right moment of confidence is stricken with a severe chill, has Candy cover him for warmth with her body, and slips it to her.

"Almost disillusioned, she moves another step towards the mystical, to the Far East to become a Buddhist. Alone, in the ancient temple, before the great stone God, she begins to achieve the solace she seeks. In her hours of contemplation, she has found the point of fixation for her attention to be the nose of the Buddha—and there is emphasis given here to the almost incandescent beauty and redemptial qualities which that object (the Buddha's nose) takes on for her, as her spiritual self rises nearer nirvana. She senses, increasingly, and with increasing satisfaction, her great need of the Buddha, but this culminates in a transport of child-like Blakean joy with the ultimate realization that the Buddha, too, *needs her*—(something, you see, she had never been quite sure of with her father) and her state of pure grace is attained.

"The book ends, then, with an incident of war which destroys the temple, killing everyone, including Candy, on whom Buddha has toppled, its nose burying itself (ironically enough) in her vagina. It is not a sad ending, however, for there is, on the face of the prostrate girl, a smile of simple wonder, while below, from the lifted hem of her austere sack-cloth garment, her white, well-rounded legs arch out gracefully, raised ever so slightly, to facilitate this last great need and entry of her."

Southern cautioned that this description "does injustice to the story" but would serve to indicate that he had given "thought to the thing in its entirety." Entitled *Candy,* it would be "in a novella format (150 pages)" and he would use the pseudonym "Maxwell Kenton." He explained that while he was fully prepared to stand by the book, his literary agent in New York had advised him to use a pen name. She was trying to sell another novel of his and felt that "the explanation required would complicate things at this particular moment."

In a final comment, which is at odds with his later account of how much he was paid and the basis for such payment, Southern asks Girodias for an advance of Frs. 50,000 ($500). "I would," he says, "do it [the book] for 150,000 francs [$1,500] which, I believe, would be at the regular page-rate, if I could have a large amount now."[3]

Mail was fast in those days. Girodias received Southern's letter, dated December 10, 1956, the next day and replied immediately. Beginning "My Dear Southern," he went on to say how pleased he was to hear that *Candy* had not been abandoned but expressed concern about the book's proposed length. It would be too short, he explained, for The Traveller's Companion format. But, in the best tradition of creative publishing, he had a solution: "Is there no means of inflating the novella format to a full-size book, or adding to the story you want to write another shorter one?"

On the money issue, he wrote: "It is unfortunately a rather difficult period for me in that respect. If we could reach some understanding on the aforementioned problem [the length of the book], I could let you have the 50,000 you mention *in England.* Would that suit you?"[4]

Southern responded almost as quickly. "Dear Mr G: . . . the news that you could not use the format I had in mind gave me pause—to try to work it out in that new light (that is, 190–200 pages of 250 words) though now, having duly achieved the 'inflation' (being hardly, good sir, the kindest term, nor yet the most exact) I am prepared to do it."

Southern agreed that England would be fine as a destination for the advance of Frs. 50,000. "How could it be managed?"[5] There is no record of how the transaction was accomplished, but perhaps the services of Mr. Cliff, Girodias's friendly bondage and flagellation specialist in Soho, were again enlisted as they had been in channeling money to Donleavy for *The Ginger Man*. In any event, Southern received the money and the project began to take shape.

Thereafter the correspondence—and work on *Candy*—slowed down. Southern and Hoffenberg were writing separate chapters and sending them to each other for comments, suggestions, and editing. "When Mason first came in, he wrote a scene about Candy meeting a Jewish psychiatrist," said Southern. "That was great because he was very much into the Jewish ambience, and that's how that collaboration began. We'd do a chapter each, I'd do one and show it to him and he'd do one and show it to me—like two people telling each other jokes; each time you were motivated to surprise the other person. We had the same idea of where it was going. It was like *The Perils of Pauline*, putting the girl in different erotic situations."[6]

On Southern's side, part of the inspiration for the book came from the background of his wife, Carol, but not, she emphasizes, the physical attributes of the "fabulous, blue-eyed, pink-nippled, pert-derrièred" heroine. Sitting in her large Manhattan publisher's office where she runs the Carol Southern Books imprint of Random House, she remembers the fun of *Candy*'s early days. "Terry was excited at the beginning—the idea and the characters amused him."

Some of those characters were taken from Carol's American family and friends. Candy Christian's confused father, her lascivious Aunt Livia and more restrained Aunt Ida, and her room over the garage were loosely based on Carol's father, two of her aunts, and the family home in Maryland. "I was terrified my aunts, Agnes and Aster, would see the book," she says. The name of Derek, the demented hunchback ("'Your hump, your hump!' cried the girl. 'GIVE ME YOUR HUMP!'"), came from one of her former boyfriends.[7]

Did Girodias provide any guidance in the writing of *Candy*?

"Not really," Southern says. "But he'd sort of count the blowjobs, the sexual incidents, and evaluate them; a blowjob wasn't as important as a buck-in-the-ass. He never really appreciated any literary aspect of it or even the humor. This is odd from a publisher who had published Nabokov and Henry Miller."[8]

Girodias considered the geographic separation of his laboring authors a good thing. "They were obliged to write to each other—thus to write." If they had been together, he says, they would have wasted their creative energies in "futile games and jokes." Girodias thought the system of staggered payments best for this project because it was "necessary to control these artful rogues." From time to time, he says, he would receive a segment of the novel, "always destined to justify a pressing demand for money." Although the parturition of *Candy* was slow, Girodias was pleased that the collaboration worked and that this "heroine of the 20th century emerged conforming to the indivisible dream of her two daddies."[9]

At least one of the daddies, according to Girodias, had no trouble in believing in his nubile creation. Once when Southern was in Paris, Girodias invited him out to a restaurant. During the meal, Southern described *Candy* with "captivating gestures, tracing her haunches, moulding the fullness of her breasts." Southern confided to his publisher that whenever he thought of *Candy* he got an enormous erection [*des érections terrifiantes*]. "He did not know what to do," Girodias says. "He seriously wondered if his wife was going to leave him if he had to dedicate an entire book to this *Candy*."[10]

In his memoirs Girodias provides a pen portrait of *Candy*'s other daddy, Mason Hoffenberg, who had come to Paris on the GI Bill in the early 1950s. "He was a very amusing fellow . . . who was married to a small vivacious French lady, Couquite, with whom he had three children . . . and whom he strove to torture in every conceivable way." Couquite was the granddaughter of the noted French art historian Élie Faure. Her first child, Zéline, was from a previous marriage, but Mason adopted her.

Short in stature, with blond hair, Hoffenberg had large blue eyes that were "full of false innocence." He also had "the knack of coming up with the least expected and most unusual remarks . . . when people saw him they would start laughing convulsively without knowing why. . . . He became a master of the minimalist approach: it was enough to look at someone in a certain way, to stare at a girl's backside with a haggard grimace to suggest a whole story."[11]

Mason Hoffenberg came from a wealthy and staid American family. Gideon Cashman, who was later his New York lawyer, remembers meeting Mason's father. "He was a Hush Puppy distributor or salesman, a very straitlaced conservative fellow. He confided to me on one occasion that he regretted Mason did not turn out to be a square."[12]

From time to time Hoffenberg used to visit Deià, the Mallorcan village where this book was written, and it is there that I first met him. In addition to his humor, he had a formidable reputation for drug consumption that impressed even such veterans as William Burroughs. When Mason pronounced on the subject, as with his comment that Burroughs's *Naked Lunch* was the best book ever written on junk, you sat up and took notice. Unfortunately, his own fiction, beyond the joint effort with Southern on *Candy*, always seemed to stall in first gear.

But the café denizens of Robert Graves's adopted Spanish village did not abandon hope. One pleasant autumn day, Mason fans took new heart. He sat down at a table and announced that he had been working hard on a novel and was ready to share the opening chapter with his friends. "One day I was sitting in my office with my secretary," he began in his gruff, insinuating New York accent. "Suddenly, a klaxon sounded outside in the street. I jumped to my feet and said: 'What *is* a klaxon?' "[13]

CANDY HAD BEEN PLANNED to appear among Girodias's crop of spicy travelers' tales in the spring of 1957, but slow writing delayed it. "Terry got bored," says Carol Southern. "He was writing it in longhand, and I was typing it. He couldn't wait to get to the bottom of the page. 'Am I there yet?' he would ask. He was writing *The Magic Christian* at the time, so *Candy* was a sideline."[14] Other problems arose. Girodias did not seem to be certain about the title. Southern, however, penned him a spirited defense that seemed to settle the matter. "Candy is a very good title," he wrote in a letter that began "Dear Mr G: . . . for it has in English many sweet sexual sucking connotations, as well as brutally frank ones: 'as easy as taking candy from a baby,' being an old cliché, referring to seduction."[15]

The issue of whether or not to use a pseudonym for the authors was more troublesome and swelled the correspondence between Southern and Girodias. The publisher was keen to have Southern's name on the book. "It would substantiate our claim that most of our writers are genuine authentic legitimate authors," he wrote. "I swear that it would involve no actual legal risk for you, except in the worst of cases a slight fine (which I would be happy to pay). . . . Please think it over, because the problem is now of much greater importance to us than when we first discussed the book."[16]

The reason was that twenty-five Olympia books, including *Lolita*, had just been banned by the French government and Girodias was planning to mount a counterattack. Southern wrote back saying that while he sympathized with Girodias's problems, he had to abide by his agent's decision that he should not have his own name on Candy. Instead, he would use the pen name "Maxwell Kenton," which he had employed before on a detective story he had written with another writer. A pen name had been necessary, Southern says, because having two authors' names on a book was unknown at that time.[17] He assured Girodias that he would "readily acknowledge anything appearing under it as my own."[18]

Southern repeated earlier apologies for Candy's slow progress. "Working under deadline pressure is bad for me and I admit, with deepest apology, the mistake I made in contracting to do so." But he promised to move as fast as he could and ended his letter with the "blurb" that Girodias had requested for the new Olympia catalogue. This read as follows:

"Candy by Maxwell Kenton . . . the bitter-sweet story of a beautiful young girl's undoing . . . and of the men and boys who undo. Or perhaps it was the darling girl's own fault, for being . . . irresistible. You can decide, in nine exciting chapters: Candy and the Professor of Philosophy, Candy and the Italian Painter, Candy and the Jewish Writer, Candy and the Giant Negro, Candy and the Porto Rican Drug Fiend, Candy and the Mad Hunchback, Candy and Her Father's Twin, Candy and the Psychoanalyst, Candy and the Gentle Priest, Candy and . . . Buddha! A masterful satire, with something for every taste—except perhaps the prudish. Sure to be a Best Seller."[19]

Candy was eventually finished a year later, in the summer of 1958. Girodias was "pleasantly surprised" by the completed manuscript. "It was much better—and much funnier—than I had expected."[20] But he reminded himself that he was deceiving his braves clients about the nature of the product. "Candy," he said, "was more and better than an erotic novel."[21]

Girodias accepted the use of a pen name and, as the book was about to go to the printer, asked Southern for a blurb describing the pseudoymous "Maxwell Kenton." Southern promptly replied with the following:

"Maxwell Kenton is the pen-name of an American nuclear research physicist, formerly prominent in atomic research and development, who, in February 1957, resigned his post 'because I found the work becoming more and more philosophically untenable' and has since devoted himself fully to creative writing. 'Instead of bringing horror into a man's life,' he said, 'I would like to think of bringing some measure of entertainment and happy diversion to it.'"

"The author has chosen to use a pen-name because, in his own words again, 'I'm afraid my literary inclinations may prove in their present form, a bit too romantic . . . to the tastes of many old friends and colleagues.' . . . *Candy,* which aside from technical treatises, is Mr. Kenton's first published work, was seen by several English and American publishers, among whom it received wide private admiration, but ultimate rejection due to its highly 'Rabelaisian' wit and flavor. It is undoubtedly a work of very real merit—strikingly individualistic and most engagingly humorous. Perhaps it may be said that Mr. Kenton has brought to bear on his new vocation the same creative talent and originality which so distinguished him in the field he deserted. And surely here is an instance where Science's loss is Art's gain."[22]

The last phase involved Southern correcting the proofs, hunting for a quote from Voltaire, and recommending reviewers. "I'm going through a French *Candide,*" he wrote to Girodias, "with the idea of getting one of those nice 'prefatory quotes' to use at the beginning. This would, I believe, lend a further literary substance and aesthetic justification to the work, and give the critics something to get their teeth into right away." Southern came up with: "She did not know how innocent she was of the crime for which she reproached herself." ("Elle ne savait pas combien elle était vertueuse dans le crime qu'elle se reprochait.")[23]

For reviews, Southern suggested that Girodias should send the book to John Davenport of *The Observer,* Anthony West and Dwight Macdonald ("who prides himself on his unflinching appreciation of the off-beat and risqué") of *The New Yorker,* and Edmund Wilson. Southern added a final caveat. "On no account mention my name though."[24]

Candy was published in October 1958, number 64 in the burgeoning Traveller's Companion Series. Eager readers opening the book might have glanced with some surprise at the dedication. "To Hadj and Zoon," it read. Hadj was the Moroccan owner of the Café Soleil du Maroc in Paris and the source of large quantities of prohibited substances, purchased and absorbed by many of the expatriate artistic crowd at that time. Hadj and Hoffenberg were close, bound by good fellowship and regular transactions involving the best Moroccan kif and other more powerful consciousness-raising concoctions.

But Hadj was always cursing the Jews, Southern recalled, and once Mason said to him: "Don't you know that I am a Jew?" Hadj said that couldn't be so because all Jews' hands came down below their knees. He told Mason to stand up, examined him for a moment, and then declared triumphantly: "There you are! I knew you couldn't be Jewish. Your hands don't come down below your knees." When *Candy* was finished, Hoffenberg decided to bestow on Hadj a dubious kind of immortality by dedicating the book to him.

"Zoon" was Southern's choice. "He was really Mr. Soun," Southern remembered, "a grand old man with a snow-white beard that came down to the middle of his chest. He was from Mongolia, and one of his ID's said he was eighty-nine. His story was that he had walked to France. He had no abode and slept on benches. He'd go into a trance and get several hours' rest that way. He hung out on the boulevards and wore a loose-fitting cloak with big pockets full of books, booklets, and clippings. He'd come to the Soleil du Maroc, and when you mentioned something, he'd pull out the relevant document from his cloak. If he phoned you, he'd say: 'Ici *Zoon!*'"

On its publication, *Candy* immediately came under the scrutiny of the Brigade Mondaine, the Paris vice squad, forcing Girodias to take remedial action. He withdrew *Candy* and published in December what appeared to be a new book. Entitled *Lollipop*—the name came from Miriam Worms—it was *Candy* repackaged with a new title page and jacket. The deception seemed to work, and the book went on selling, albeit more slowly than other titles in The Traveller's Companion Series. "The book was much too hip to enjoy a normal sale as a regular 'd.b.,'" Girodias noted. "It took much more than the customary six to twelve months to dispose of the five thousand copies we had printed."[25]

Southern wrote to Girodias from New York in June 1959 to report that *Candy* was having "a small *succès d'estime* here in private circulation."[26] The book was being smuggled into the United States at a fairly brisk rate, and Southern said he and Hoffenberg and their friends from Paris used to bring copies in. They made themselves a little money by selling the books to the Gotham Book Mart in Manhattan, where the owner, Frances Steloff, was a *Candy* fan.[27]

WHILE *Candy* was pursuing what Girodias termed its "slow subterranean career," he received an offer from a publisher in Rome for the Italian rights to the novel. He wrote to the two authors offering them a proper contract to replace the simple work-for-hire arrangement, noting: "*Candy* was likely to enjoy quite a profitable career, and our earlier occult arrangement would be unfair to the authors."[28]

A formal agreement between Girodias and the two authors was

drawn up and signed in May 1961. It specified that the Olympia Press was the owner of all publication rights to *Candy* (also known as *Lollipop*). Proceeds from English-language reprint rights would be equally divided between the three of them. Money from translation rights and other subsidiary rights would be distributed on the basis of three-quarters for the authors and a quarter for the publisher. The authors were given the right to terminate the agreement if Girodias failed to make regular twice-yearly royalty payments to them.[29]

In early August 1962 Girodias received a letter from the Sterling Lord Agency in New York saying that it was representing Terry Southern over *Candy*. The letter ended: "Terry has never received any statement or payments for the period ending June 30, 1962, as promised in your contract. I wonder if you could please send that along to me."[30] Girodias promptly replied, saying there could be no such settlement for that period because the new edition of *Lollipop* (alias *Candy*) was just being released.

While the second edition of *Candy-Lollipop* was quietly selling in Paris, Walter Minton of Putnam's reappeared on the scene. One of his editors had spotted the book, and Minton decided to publish it. But this time he wanted to avoid dealing with Girodias by detaching the authors from their 1961 contract with the French publisher and then do a separate deal with them.

In September 1963, Mason Hoffenberg sat down in the house his wife had bought in the rue Daguerre in the fourteenth arrondissement to write to Girodias in his office in the rue Saint-Séverin in the fifth arrondissement. His first draft began:

Dear Gid,
The golden hues on the trees outside my window remind me of the rapid, relentless passage of time. It's autumn again, and this year, like those past, will soon be history. May I remind you . . .[31]

But, like many writers, he decided to have another stab at it, and the letter he actually sent went to the heart of the matter with fewer literary flourishes and in a less friendly tone:

Dear Girodias:
It's autumn again, and as 1963 draws to a close, Terry and I would like to remind you that the royalties due on *Candy*, on June 1st, 1963, are overdue—and that you still owe more than half the royalties called for in the statement you sent for the previous period.
Yours truly,
Mason Hoffenberg.[32]

Two months later, a letter arrived in the Olympia Press office from Terry Southern's New York lawyer, informing Girodias that the agreement between them had been terminated. "The reason . . . is your failure to render timely reports and remit the amount of royalties due the authors."[33]

Girodias immediately fired off an answer directly to Southern at his Connecticut home on the Blackberry River. He admitted that he had been at fault for "not having delivered statements and corresponding payments regularly." The reason was that he had been fighting against "nearly insurmountable difficulties in the past two or three years to keep my business on its feet. My publishing activities have been practically paralysed by the innumerable bans, fines and other niceties showered upon me."

In a passage that explains much about Girodias's unorthodox understanding of a publisher's contractual duties toward his authors, Girodias admits that he should have explained all this earlier. "But I was quite certain that you were being kept informed of my situation by Mason," he continued. "Frankly I did not see much point in sending whining, apologetic letters to you such as this one, as long as I was unable to pay what I owed you."

He goes on to stress—somewhat disingenuously—that he had given the two authors a regular contract only because he thought it was "fair," in view of the quality of *Candy,* but that "nothing forced him to do that." What he omitted to say was that he could not have sold the Italian rights of the book without first having a proper contract with the authors.

Girodias expressed pain at not hearing from Southern directly but through a lawyer. "It is both unfair and unfriendly. . . . I must say I am deeply surprised by your attitude in the matter. My God, I think I have been patient and friendly enough when you needed my help. Now that I am in a jam worse than anything you have ever known, I think you could try to be a little more generous—whatever my past and present faults may be." He ends with a plea: "Naturally, I will answer [Southern's lawyer's letter], but I would be sincerely relieved if you should step down from that legal pedestal of yours, and I promise that I will do my inhuman [*sic*] best to get some money for you as soon as I can."[34]

Girodias wrote to Southern's lawyer saying that he could not accept the termination of the contract and asked for the grounds for Southern's action. The lawyer replied, citing nonpayment of royalties, adding "nor has any attention been paid to the *prior notices of Mr. Hoffenberg given you on September 23, 1963* [author's italics]. This state of events could not be permitted to continue and, therefore, your rights were terminated." The lawyer made it clear that Southern and Hoffenberg were acting together and that if Girodias did not pay up, legal action would follow.[35]

Meanwhile, Minton was busy. He was stitching together his deal with Southern and Hoffenberg for the hardback and paperback rights to *Candy* in the United States, a deal in which Girodias was conspicuous by his absence. "Girodias didn't pay us for a long, long time," Southern said, "so we felt free to go to an American publisher."[36]

"The big problem was copyright," said Minton. "None of them had applied for a U.S. copyright, so the book was in the public domain. Since the book was out of copyright, Girodias had no rights in the United States. We signed a contract with normal royalties for the two authors and an advance of, I think, ten thousand dollars each. But we put a codicil in the contract saying that if anyone brought out a pirated edition of *Candy,* Putnam's would be relieved of the obligation to pay any further royalties to the authors."[37]

IN EARLY 1964, *Candy* made her American debut, tripping confidently from word of mouth succès d'estime to nationwide bestseller. Published in hardback by Putnam's, it was reviewed widely and sold rapidly. *Newsweek* called it the "most marvelous *dénouement* in modern letters"; the British critic Francis Wyndham thought it a wonderful novel, "a subtle and hilarious satire"; the *New Yorker* critic described it as the "funniest book" he had read for a long time; and Herbert Gold, the novelist, exclaimed: "Good grief, it's a very funny book."[38] *Candy* remained on the bestseller list for eleven weeks, was reprinted thirteen times before the year ended, and sold over a million copies. Paperback publishers and film producers began to position themselves to share in the *Candy* bonanza.

As *Candy* took off in the United States, Girodias with increasing desperation tried another appeal to his authors' better nature. In March 1964 he talked to Mason Hoffenberg in Paris and then wrote to Southern in Connecticut, copying the letter for Hoffenberg. He emphasized his "enormous difficulties" over the last two years that had "culminated last week in a one year jail sentence (not suspended this time) and a $20,000 fine." He went over the history of the book, reminding the authors of his role in creating it, the terms of the original deal, and the risks he had run in publishing *Candy.*

He then proposed a compromise: "I suggest that the validity of our contract be confirmed on both sides. I would then reduce my share of the US publication rights (only) to 25% of the income [down from 33.3 percent] and my share would be retained by you and Mason against the royalties I owe you, until our accounts are balanced."

Girodias ended with a plea based on past friendship: "Although you have good cause to be dissatisfied with my present financial dilemma, I still think that I have always acted in a loyal and friendly manner towards both Mason and you in all our previous dealings and I feel that this entitles me to being treated in a more understanding manner now that I am in a mess which defies description."[39]

Neither Southern nor Hoffenberg replied. Instead they were busy formalizing their professional relationship in anticipation of a film contract. The impetus had come from a move by United Artists to take an option on *Candy*. Terry Southern was already established as a Hollywood scriptwriter, and it was widely assumed that *Candy* would soon be on the screen.

In a one-page document, the two authors confirmed their verbal arrangement "to split 50-50 all benefits, direct or indirect, flowing from our book, CANDY, its publication and exploitation anywhere in the world." The rest of the short agreement dealt with the sale of film rights and the making of a movie. The language suggested concern on the part of Hoffenberg that he might be squeezed out of a film deal because, unlike Southern, he had no Hollywood scriptwriting experience. All money received from the production of a film of *Candy,* the document said, would be divided equally, "inclusive of all profits which may be derived by Terry Southern as a producer, except such earned salaries as may be earned by Terry Southern as a director, associate director or film editor."

One sentence suggested that Mason already harbored suspicions that Terry might act on his own. "No agreements to pay Terry Southern any sums of money for any of the foregoing personal services have been entered into as of the date of this agreement." The document ended: "During the period in which the screenplay is being written Mason Hoffenberg will consult with Terry Southern on the screenplay. Failure by Mason Hoffenberg to consult with Terry Southern will not, however, affect either of the foregoing sharing arrangements."[40]

Meanwhile, Southern was handling the minor dramas of *Candy*'s publishing career in the United States and Hoffenberg was engrossed in the major dramas of his personal life. *Candy* was excerpted in several magazines, and Southern found himself defending the novel's pristine integrity on more than one occasion. When *Nugget* magazine bought serial rights and sent Southern the proofs before publication, he felt constrained to write sternly back to the editor, Seymour Krim.

> Dear Seymour:
> I am very sorry to have to say so, but in my view the selections you propose to publish contain omissions so extensive, and alterations so radical, as to seriously misrepresent the actual and distinctive character of the novel itself. . . .
>
> Now, Seymour (I mean, really!) I can understand your position in regard to wanting to avoid the use of the more dramatic of the so-called four-letter-words; and, out of my friendly feelings for you, and with a nightmare grimace of hilarity frozen across my heartbreak, I cheerfully went along with *all* of those deletions. Other deletions, however—such as "damp," "jelly-box"—are just too highly (and senselessly) crippling in terms of style and tone, and have got to be restored, or corrected. . . .
>
> I certainly cannot go along with such changes as Aunt Livia's "hot greaser cock" to "hot greaser stuff." The word "stuff" has vague and amorphous connotations, where it is well known that Livia required an organ of stout and smart definition, and it does, I must say, reflect editorial shoddiness of a very shocking order indeed. I'm not insisting on the word "cock". . . . "Hot greaser joint" is acceptable, as is "bit," "wood," "rod," "dip-stick," "shaft," "staff," and "jelly-roll" (or "jumbo," *or* the very contemporary "zoomba"!). So here's a nice optional layout for you, Sy, (with a little Rorshack-test [*sic*] thrown in, eh? Hee-hee). Anyway, just to make sure you don't use "stuff" (mah people don talk dat way).
>
> You'll be hearing from my powerful solicitor who is charged to oversee these instructions.[41]

Over in Paris, Mason Hoffenberg was in the thrall of drugs, and his marriage to the vivacious Couquite was breaking down. The couple had separated, but Mason used to come and take the young children (Juliette was about five years old and Daniel around two) out to the park from time to time. One summer's day he said he was taking them to the Luxembourg Gardens, and Couquite remembers him asking for the children's coats, which she thought strange but let it pass. That was the last she was to see of her children for several weeks. Mason took them first to Italy by train and then caught a plane to New York.

"When I heard they had been kidnapped and were in New York, I jumped on a plane and flew over there," Couquite said. "I took my aunt, a fierce lady, with me, and we found the children with Mason's mother. I had to get lawyers involved, and my aunt said she would sit in the parlor of Mason's mother's house until the children were handed back to me." The children were eventually returned, and Couquite took them back to Paris.[42]

Mason had started drugs in the 1950s and became progressively more erratic and paranoid. "I didn't notice it to begin with," said Couquite. "It started in Saint Tropez with Chet Baker, the jazz trumpeter, and others. Mason would get clean, detoxicated, and then have the pleasure of starting all over again."[43] (William Burroughs called him "a kicking junkie.")

In July 1964, Terry Southern's lawyers made good their threat by starting a legal action against Girodias in Paris. The suit was aimed at annulling the 1961 Southern-Hoffenberg-Girodias contract, securing royalties due to the two authors from the second printing of *Candy,* and obtaining a comprehensive report on any other publishing deals that Girodias had made behind the authors' backs. Girodias responded with alacrity, charging his own lawyers to fight the suit with everything at their command. Meanwhile, he was deep into negotiations for the sale of the British rights of *Candy*.

In the United States, something infinitely more dangerous than Derek the hunchback's confusion was threatening *Candy*'s triumphant progress. The phenomenal success of the hardback version of *Candy* had not only attracted considerable interest among paperback publishers, it had drawn their attention to the novel's copyright.

Walter Minton had arranged to do the paperback version through Dell Distributing Company but was held up releasing it because the hardback was selling so well. Then he heard that Lancer Books, a rival firm, had printed up half a million paperback copies of *Candy* and was preparing to "drop them on the street." He gave the signal to Dell, and the *Candy* paperback war was on.[44]

While Putnam's version appeared under the real names of the authors, the Lancer paperback retained the pseudonymous "Maxwell

Maurice Girodias, in the garden of the Grande Séverine in Paris, at the height of his twin careers as publisher and impresario

Jack Kahane, founder of the Obelisk Press, with his wife, Marcelle
Girodias, and the future Frog Prince, Maurice

Henry Miller, whose novel *Tropic of Cancer* was first published by the Obelisk Press

The original cover of *Tropic of Cancer,* designed by fifteen-year-old Maurice Girodias

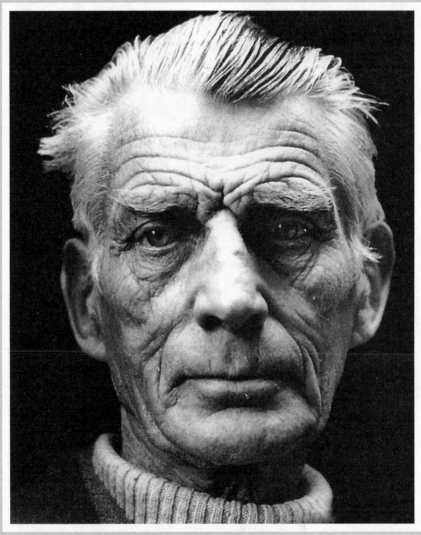

Samuel Beckett, whose novels *Watt, Molloy, Malone Dies,* and *The Unnamable* were first published by the Olympia Press in Paris

Olympia's ace translator Austryn
Wainhouse ("Pieralessandro Casavini,
the Florentine polyglot")

Muffie Wainhouse, Girodias's first
editor-assistant in the early days
of the Olympia Press

Three of the Merlin group—Patrick Bowles, Jane Lougee, and
Christopher Logue ("Count Palmiro Vicarion")—with George Plimpton
of *The Paris Review* in the background

TERRY STEVENSON

The Olympia Press's leading
female pornographer, Iris Owens
("Harriet Daimler")

FRANK MONACO

Norman Rubington ("Akbar del Piombo"), the painter,
pornographer, and collage-book magician whose line
illustrations appear in this book

Another of Olympia's
pornographers, Baird
Bryant ("Willie Baron")

Olympia's most prolific pornographer, John Stevenson
("Marcus van Heller")

James Patrick Donleavy in Fulham, London, where he received his first copy of *The Ginger Man* and swore revenge

Vladimir Nabokov, with Eric Kahane, at the Gallimard reception for the French publication of *Lolita*

The coauthor of *Candy,*
Terry Southern,
in New York

Candy's other parent, Mason Hoffenberg

Dominique Aury in
the 1950s, around the time
she wrote *Story of O*

Dominique Aury
in 1994

Richard Seaver, suspected of being "Sabine d'Estrée," American translator of *O*

Jean Paulhan, whose relationship with Dominique Aury inspired *Story of O*

The first American publisher of *O*, Barney Rosset of the Grove Press

The Beats: (left to right) Gregory Corso, Allen Ginsberg, and
William Burroughs

Tangier days: (left to right) Peter Orlovsky, William Burroughs,
Allen Ginsberg, Alan Ansen, Paul Bowles (seated), Gregory Corso, and
Ian Sommerville

The successful purchaser
of the Olympia Press,
Mary Guinness

The veteran Olympia editor and loyal patron of the
Grande Séverine, Miriam Worms

Girodias's assistant in Olympia's
dying days, Holly Hutchins
("Miss Olivia Pringle")

Marilyn Meeske ("Henry Crannach"), who wrote
Flesh and Bone, edited the *Olympia Review,* and
wondered, as she wrote, "What was Daddy thinking?"

Maurice Girodias, Paris, 1990

Kenton" on the cover, embellished by the blurb "Not One Word Changed! This is the ORIGINAL, UNCUT AND UNEXPUR-GATED edition as first published in Paris." The price of the Lancer book undercut the Putnam edition by twenty cents (seventy-five cents as opposed to ninety-five cents).

"Dell did a remarkable job in getting the book out in a week," Minton remembered. "Lancer got out first, but we caught them up on the West Coast. In the end we sold between two and two and a half million copies and Lancer sold about a million."[45]

Lawyers for the two publishers marched briskly into the fray. Putnam's asserted that it held the United States copyright to *Candy* and therefore had exclusive rights to publish the book. Lancer's legal counsel did not dispute Putnam's right to publish but defended its own right to do the same by arguing that the original Olympia edition of the book was not protected by copyright. Meanwhile, Minton invoked the codicil in Putnam's contract with Southern and Hoffenberg and stopped paying them royalties.

Terry Southern believed that Girodias was working hand in glove with Lancer. "The cruel irony," he says, "was that the book was not copyrighted, and so Girodias went to Walter Zacharias of Lancer and did a deal. It was a pretty rotten thing to do."[46]

"I never heard that Girodias had anything to do with getting Zacharias to do the book," said Minton. "But if he talked to Zacharias about it, that's all he needed to do. I doubt very much if Zacharias paid Girodias anything. I never heard of Walter Zacharias paying anybody anything unless you put a gun to his head, and you'd probably have to shoot him halfway to prove that the gun was loaded."[47]

Girodias revealed later that he had once offered Zacharias a thirty-day option on *Candy* for the U.S. paperback rights. Walter Zacharias said that he paid Girodias for the rights, in cash. There was no official deal because there was no copyright. As for Minton's comments, Zacharias shrugged and said: "Walter is a very bitter man. He panicked and sold his company for practically nothing. The difference between us was that he was the son of a rich father and I was the son of a poor father."[48]

In October 1965, Girodias had a meeting with Terry Southern's agent in New York about settling the dispute. First, he went over familiar ground by stating that *Candy* would never have been written if it had not been for his own role. Second, nothing had forced him to sign the 1961 contract with Southern and Hoffenberg, "it was simply because I never considered taking advantage of them." In a typically Girodian flourish, he summed up: "So much for the ethical aspect of the problem."

Girodias's view of the copyright problem was that neither Putnam's nor the authors were "in a position to claim ownership of the copyright," whereas the Olympia Press had "a very good chance of obtaining confirmation of its ownership." He made it clear that he was going to sue all American publishers of *Candy*, "with or without the authors' approval or participation."

Turning to the authors' contract with Putnam's, Girodias considered that they had been forced to accept very hard terms from their American publishers and that they were reaping the bitter harvest. Also, a film deal was "a dead loss" in the absence of a settlement. The only way out would be to renegotiate Putnam's agreement with Olympia, as likely owner of *Candy*'s U.S. copyright.[49]

At the Frankfurt Book Fair in mid-October, Girodias talked to Walter Minton and later noted that he thought a compromise could be worked out with the head of Putnam's, "but only if we would settle our differences with the authors first." Back in Paris, Girodias took the view that the sheer length of the French litigation worked in his favor since it weakened the authors' bargaining position elsewhere and generally muddied the waters.[50]

Toward the end of October, Girodias wrote to the Copyright Office of the Library of Congress in Washington, D.C., explaining the genesis of *Candy* and the conflict that had developed around the book. Would it be possible, he asked, for the Olympia Press to secure a U.S. copyright for the first edition of *Candy*, "notwithstanding the American nationality of the two authors"?[51]

In November the indefatigable Girodias had two long meetings in New York with Putnam's lawyer. He followed this up with a letter to Mason Hoffenberg containing the details of a proposed settlement. In essence, the agreement exchanged Girodias's validation of the authors' contract with Putnam's for their revalidation of their 1961 agreement with Olympia. Each side would pay what it owed to the other, and Putnam's would cough up $100,000, to be divided equally between the three of them. Olympia would join forces with Putnam's and the authors to fight the American paperback pirates; legal expenses, royalties, and damages would be shared. Film rights would be sold jointly by Olympia and the authors.

Girodias added that he was not sure that Minton would go along with his proposal "as it is." But even something "not quite as satisfactory" would still be worthwhile, and, Girodias wrote, "I am convinced that we should take it—and forget about that stupid, suicidal feud." It was time for both the authors to act, and Girodias ended the letter with a threat. He told Mason that he had applied for the U.S. copyright of *Candy* and were he to obtain it "within the next few days or weeks, I would not necessarily consider myself bound by the above proposal if you do not decide to accept it now."[52]

THIS WAS the first serious move toward a general settlement. But it would take another fifteen months before an acceptable compromise could be reached that had the support of all parties. At this stage it seemed that everyone was playing cat and mouse, with each player casting his opponent (or opponents) in the role of mouse. Southern and Hoffenberg were waiting, with some optimism—for so their lawyers led them to believe—for a favorable verdict in the Paris litigation. And if that did not happen, or took too long to happen, there was always the possibility that Girodias's "unbelievable difficulties" would multiply even further and drive him out of business, or mad, or both. They were also waiting for the lucrative film deal to materialize while casting sidelong glances at each other. And they were waiting for the blocked money from Putnam's hardback edition of *Candy,* as well as revenue from the company's booming paperback sales.

Walter Minton was waiting for a crack at the pirate publishers who were undercutting Putnam's sales and making him look foolish. He was also waiting, less unhappily, to pay the authors what had accrued to them from the hardback and paperback sales. The pirate publishers—by now at least three were selling the book—were waiting for the statute of limitations to expire so that they could no longer be prosecuted. The film producers, eager to put the nubile *Candy* on the screen, were waiting for the god-awful mess to be cleaned up so that they could get their hands on the rights.

Over in Paris, Girodias was waiting for the Library of Congress to grant him the U.S. copyright to the book, for the Paris lawsuit to go in his favor—or, second best, to go on forever—and for a miracle to bail him out of the financial crevasse into which he had pitched himself. (He was, by now, bankrupt, and Olympia was up for auction.) All in all, it was a scenario that might have held appeal for another of Girodias's Olympia authors, with the promise of an even more minimalist title: "Waiting for . . ."

In December Girodias received his eagerly awaited response from the Copyright Office. After outlining the legal framework, the Copyright Office addressed the "crucial question" of who was the author of *Candy*. If the novel had been a "commissioned work," then Southern and Hoffenberg could claim authorship. But if it had been "a work made for hire," Girodias, as publisher (i.e., employer), could be considered the author. However, the evidence submitted by Girodias left "considerable doubt" over the issue, and the Copyright Office declined to pass judgment: "It is our policy that under ordinary circumstances it is up to the applicant rather than the Copyright Office to determine whether a work was 'made for hire' . . . you will probably wish to explore it thoroughly with your attorney."

The reason for the Copyright Office's caution became apparent at the end of its assessment. *Candy* was already the subject of two still unresolved court cases concerning copyright. One was Putnam's versus Lancer Books; the other was Hoffenberg against the Copyright Office itself, seeking (with Putnam's help) to establish his own rights to the novel.[53]

This carefully calibrated response was almost two months in the making. One can easily imagine the discussions that went on around a table littered with coffee cups in an overheated Washington office:

"This *Candy* thing is a can of worms, and Girodias is probably the biggest worm of them all."

"But we've gotta come up with something, right?"

"Right. How about this? Let's kick off with the letter of the law, followed by something on how confused current practice is, then a bit of policy fluff, and finally toss him back to the lawyers. Oh, and better mention that our asses are being whipped in the courts, too. How about that?"

9

Good Grief,
It's <u>Still</u> Candy!

WHEN GIRODIAS received the Copyright Office's letter, he did not have a lawyer in New York. But he quickly took the proffered advice and found one. This was Leon Friedman, a lively, astute, and enormously patient attorney, who became a close friend of Girodias.

Girodias first heard of Friedman through Marilyn Meeske, whose sister Patricia ("Patti"), also a writer, was married to the lawyer. In January 1966 Girodias and Friedman signed a contingency agreement over *Candy* in which the lawyer was to get 15 percent of the proceeds of a settlement, with a maximum of 30 percent if the matter went to trial.[1]

In his first long communication with Friedman, in February 1966, Girodias told him that his friend Christian Marquand, "a one-time successful French movie actor turned would-be director," was interested in getting everyone together to produce a settlement so that a *Candy* film deal could be made. Girodias would be cut in, selling his share in the property "for nominally $5,000, plus a personal nontaxable payment to me of $30,000." The only problem was that "we cannot make a deal for the movie rights and not settle the rest of the conflict with the authors."

On the French litigation, Girodias reported that the case would take a minimum of two years to reach a final judgment and that he and his French lawyer were confident they would win. The lawyers representing Southern and Hoffenberg were equally confident, but the American lawyer was "totally ignorant of French law" and the French lawyer was "getting practically no money . . . for his work—so he's not working." He paused to vent his exasperation. "Lawyers!"

Girodias went on to tell Friedman (a lawyer, no less) about a long talk he had had with Walter Minton on the telephone before he left New York. "Minton's position is quite simple, in a way, healthy. If no copyright can be established on the book, then he has no reason to pay royalties to the authors. But he would be willing to settle the roughly $68,000 he has offered to pay them if the authors and myself acting jointly were able to give him a regular copyright . . . which he would use to win a victory against Lancer and the other pirate publishers."

Girodias ended his report with a round of grapeshot for every participant in the *Candy* tragicomedy. One was "a psychopath alcoholic," another an "addict," a third "an outsize crook," and at least two were "totally insane." This was followed by a rooster's crow for himself. "Why, I feel like the noblest, gentlest, purest and sanest little guy compared to that menagerie," he exclaimed. "Leon, if you ever do anything with that business, God bless You!"[2]

Leon Friedman, in his first major intervention in what was to be a yearlong, cliff-hanging negotiation, started by talking to Walter Minton, Gideon Cashman (Hoffenberg's lawyer), Seymour ("Cy," "Sy," or "Si") Litvinoff (Southern's lawyer), and Claire ("Cindy") Degener, who worked for the agent Sterling Lord, who represented the authors, and was Lord's wife at the time. In February 1966, he reported back to Girodias in a persuasively argued five-page letter. Its essence was:

· Girodias might be able to obtain $100,000 out of a settlement and would be advised to take it.
· This would break down as follows: $25,000 from the paperback sales of *Candy* (estimated at about 1.4 million), $17,000 from a successful action against the pirates, $25,000 for his share in the event of a film sale, $25,000 to $30,000 from future foreign publication rights.
· Minton's position was that he was not prepared to pay anything unless the Copyright Office issued a certificate to Girodias or the

authors. "Walter Minton wants your participation in the case against the pirates," Friedman wrote, "but he has already instituted an action in Washington [to obtain copyright for the authors] which, if successful, would deprive you of your only asset vis-à-vis Putnam."

· There was "absolutely no possibility of getting any money from the authors for the hardcover sales" of Candy. But Girodias would not have to pay them anything for past sales of the Olympia edition of the book.

· Southern and Hoffenberg were keen to make their movie deal, "but they can await the outcome of their Paris action if they cannot come to terms with you. . . . the hearing scheduled for March 4 [in Paris] is crucial."

· Girodias would have to pay them their share of any money he had received from the foreign sales he had made, including Britain, where he had been busy selling the rights, unknown to the authors. Friedman sounded a note of warning here: "If Terry and Mason discover that you have any dealings with any London publisher, I believe they would be extremely disturbed."

· After delving into the arcane world of copyright law, Friedman concluded that he was doubtful that a court would decide that "a valid employer-employee relationship" existed between Girodias and the two authors. "The Copyright Office may be more lenient in awarding a certificate if there were no pending controversy, but they would do it now only if Mason withdrew his action in Washington and supported us. . . . Bureaucrats do not take independent action when their position is under attack in the courts. . . . I think in an adversary situation with Terry and Mason hollering the other way, our legal position would be very tenuous."

Friedman ended with firm advice: "I would be lax in my duty to you, Maurice, if I did not give you my honest appraisal of how the situation stands after talking to the various parties and analyzing the law and your assets in this matter. You do have some bargaining position, but as of now it is certainly not worth more than $100,000."[3]

Girodias, who seemed capable of writing letters in his sleep, responded immediately with his own five-pager. He first raised the film deal that he had been discussing with Christian Marquand. "Of course Cy Litvinoff does not know the details of my negotiation with (or through) Marquand: the official sum I am supposed to have agreed to is $5,000. Nobody is to know the real figure (the remaining $30,000 . . . to be paid in Switzerland, tax-free). It is essential that the secret be restricted to you, Marquand and me. Naturally, the idea was to show Mason and Terry how willing I was to reach a general compromise, by accepting a ridiculously low figure for my share of the film rights. Naturally, I am well aware of the possibility that Marquand may have secretly offered more to Mason and Terry than the $10,000 or $15,000 they are supposed to get. . . . Everyone is lying to everyone else, but isn't that better if it is done sincerely? The big thing now is to save everyone's face."

Having established the Machiavellian nature of his own negotiations, Girodias moved on to lambaste the gutter morality of his opponents, notably the pirate publishers. "Lancer are a bunch of odious boors . . . and they have behaved in a way so low and treacherous with me . . . that they deserve a lesson, and should be made to pay punitive damages . . . But Greenleaf! [another pirate publisher] . . . they are the most cold-blooded, malevolent trio I ever met. If Lancer deserves some punishment, the Greenleaf people must take a beating such that they will at least stop stealing my property."

GIRODIAS then threw a new ingredient into the stew. This concerned the British rights to *Candy,* where, he reported with gusto, "we now have a superlative imbroglio to disentangle." He said the British rights were the only thing he sold on his own. "I have sold the rights to Tandem, or rather to a substitute company acting for them, with a £5,000 advance which has been received by me. . . .

"But the secret about the Tandem deal was not kept very carefully by them, and I myself deliberately told Mason Hoffenberg a few weeks ago that I had sold the British rights for a good deal of money, without saying how much or to whom. My motives in doing that were to show how absurd the feud between us was, etc. But that piece of news did create something of a commotion. Yesterday in London I saw Stokes, the Tandem man, who seemed a little nervous. I knew that he had not been able to get the money to pay me the £5,000 advance and to print the book from Tandem's respectable backer, but from a syndicate of dirty book dealers—although I did not know that at the time of signing."

On the Paris litigation, Girodias remained optimistic and was keen to know if Friedman could find out exactly when Southern and Hoffenberg first sold the film rights of *Candy.* He hoped it could be established that they did so *before* they canceled their 1961 agreement with himself, thus making them guilty of the first breach of contract.

Girodias's view was that it was too early to settle. "It is perfectly all right for you to let the other parties know that we are not going to resume the talks until after the French hearing. Let them fume and rave about the British situation. Time is on our side: they want the film to materialise, they want to avoid tying down the British edition with a number of local lawsuits as they have done in America, and they are increasingly aware of the fact that I am no longer bankrupt, that my position is being fast consolidated. . . . Let's be foxy."[4]

On Valentine's Day 1966, Friedman wrote back to Girodias with firm but friendly advice. On the film deal, he reported that Southern's lawyer had told him that he did not care if Christian Marquand gave Girodias "half of Paris" for his rights as long as the authors got what they considered a fair deal. "You must have no illusions about pretending you are only getting $5,000 from Marquand," Friedman went on. "Everyone here knows there is more coming and I doubt whether you can get any negotiating value from the fact that on paper you are getting only $5,000."

The case against the pirate publishers would hinge on the ownership of the copyright to *Candy* and whether or not they had made any effort to establish who owned it. Moving on to the Paris litigation, Friedman said that it looked as if the authors had first sold the film rights *after Candy* was published in the United States. This, if true, would not help Girodias's case in the French courts since it had occurred after he himself had failed to abide by the terms of the 1961 contract.

Friedman sounded a warning note over Girodias's British capers: "I am not as sanguine as you are about the effect of the British imbroglio. This will prove to Terry that you are dealing behind his back." His lawyer's eye had detected a handwritten clause in Girodias's deal with Tandem that was important. It meant, he said, that "if we cannot settle with Terry and Mason in the near future and they enjoin [stop by injunction] Tandem's publication of the book, you must repay the £5,000. I realize that Tandem is obligated to publish an edition within six months . . . or they will forfeit the £5,000. You have a horse race here to see whether Terry will enjoin Tandem before April 22 or whether you can get past that date and keep the money. Bedlam was never as hectic as this.

"Time may be on your side with Terry and Mason," Friedman conceded, but not with Minton. "At some point he is just going to decide to proceed on his own and not pay you anything at all— including the $30,000 which is now in the bank on the soft cover sales. If we can settle with Minton, this would put great pressure on Terry and Mason also. . . . Maurice, I wish you could get a million out of this but $100,000 is not a bad figure. I don't mean to sound pessimistic but your optimism in this situation strikes me as unrealistic. . . . There is always the possibility you will end up with nothing . . . if we go on too long without settling."[5]

In March Friedman wrote to the Copyright Office to make a formal application for Olympia's ownership of the *Candy* copyright. He supported the claim with an impressive array of case law. Around this time Friedman and Girodias obtained a copy of the original Putnam's contract between Minton and the two authors. When he noticed the date on it, Girodias became incensed because he remembered an incident in Paris when Mason had come up to him in a bar and asked to borrow his pen. The pen was never returned, and Girodias was convinced that Mason had stolen it to sign the contract with Putnam's.

Friedman and Girodias also unearthed details of a separate deal that Minton had later cut with Mason Hoffenberg. Putnam's needed the signature of at least one of the authors to begin legal proceedings against Zacharias of Lancer and the other pirates, which involved, among other actions, suing the Copyright Office for the book's copyright. Southern refused to sign, but Mason agreed to if Minton would pay him an advance, there and then, on his share of the paperback royalties. Minton agreed and handed over $10,000. "I don't know why Terry didn't do it," said Minton. "I guessed he was pissed about the fact that [after the pirates published *Candy*] we stopped paying him royalties."[6]

While waiting for a decision from the French courts, Friedman drew up a draft settlement between all the parties. He was by then the only person talking to everyone involved since Litvinoff and Cindy Degener were not talking to Minton and the authors were not talking to Girodias.

In London, Michael Rubinstein, the nephew of Stanley Rubinstein, who had handled *The Ginger Man* litigation for Girodias, had become involved in the *Candy* negotiations, although he admitted he did not know "nearly enough of the background." Writing to Girodias in April 1966, he described a meeting he had had with Seymour Litvinoff and Cindy Degener in London. During it he heard an alarming piece of news. Southern and Hoffenberg had apparently obtained a loan of $130,000 from United Artists under "a joint venture agreement" and had to repay it by the end of June, a little over two months hence. If they failed to do so, United Artists "might be entitled to seize all proceeds due to them on U.S. book publications . . . so that there might well be no proceeds from such publications to share with Olympia Press under the terms of this draft agreement."[7]

Girodias zeroed in on this deal in his next letter to Friedman. (During the month of April, Girodias wrote no fewer than six letters to his American lawyer.) "It is a very important factor, as it means that the authors have one more pressing reason to settle their quarrel with me." He told Friedman he thought it vital to have "a precise and *verifiable* breakdown of the $130,000. . . . I am sure that we will find a lot of interesting things when we get those figures." The authors, he reckoned, were engaged in a game of "pure bluff, childish bluff, just like their assumed confidence in the outcome of the French trial."[8]

As SPRING ADVANCED, the transatlantic game of cat and mouse became more fraught. A decision in the much-delayed French lawsuit was expected daily. A response from the Copyright Office on the key issue of who owned *Candy* in the United States was overdue. Time was running out for the authors to repay the $130,000 they owed United Artists. And Girodias was walking on dangerous ground in London with his wheeling and dealing over the British rights to *Candy*.

In May 1966, the French court decided unequivocally that Southern and Hoffenberg had the right to break their 1961 contract with the Olympia Press and ordered Girodias to pay them the royalties he owed them, as well as the authors' legal costs. Concealing his disappointment, Girodias immediately appealed the verdict.

Then came the good news. The Copyright Office had made its decision: The Olympia Press was the rightful owner of the U.S. copyright to *Candy*. This put the score at one-all and refueled Girodias's combative spirit. A week later Friedman reported that negotiations over a final settlement of the *Candy* dispute were "proceeding apace. . . . Gideon Cashman has been brought into the picture and has no objections to the way we are proceeding. You will be promptly informed of what finally transpires. After things are settled with the authors, we will go immediately to Walter Minton."[9]

Girodias replied: "Your letter . . . comes like a breath of fresh air after a long anxious wait. . . . I think we are entitled to a reward, i.e. money. Immediate money."[10] Girodias had already given Friedman his power of attorney to act for him in business transactions and litigation, and in July he heard from the lawyer that all the details of the *Candy* agreement had been settled. Girodias would be getting a copy as soon as it had been typed, as well as an explanation of "various changes." Friedman added: "I hope to see Walter Minton this week about getting some of that immediate money."[11]

At the beginning of August, Friedman sent Girodias the draft settlement with details of a number of trade-offs that had become necessary. "All in all," he concluded, "I think the contract is a fair one and, more important, should start yielding you money very quickly."[12]

Two days later, Girodias wrote back. "Thanks for . . . the long-awaited contract; may I say that reading it gave me a shock equivalent to the one I received when I learned that we had lost the case in Paris? That is probably very unkind to you as you have been devoting so much work and know-how to this negotiation." Girodias followed with a barrage of arguments, comparative figures, complaints, and breast-beating—all designed to demonstrate what a raw deal he was receiving. "Really, Leon, is there any way for me to walk out of that agreement without doing anything illegal? I expected something pretty disappointing, but what I got is something like complete lunacy. . . . can we get out of it?"[13]

Friedman, apparently oblivious to this outburst, began validating the agreement by sending it to all the principals for signature. He also sent three copies to Girodias in Paris for him to sign with the comment: "Walter Minton is acting in a peculiar fashion, as usual, and does not want to start talking to us until all the parties, including you, have executed the agreement, so please rush the attached back as soon as possible."[14]

About to leave for "a well-earned week's holiday" in Ibiza, Girodias scribbled a hurried note to Friedman, worried that he had not heard anything from New York since his outburst.

By mid-August Friedman had secured all the signatures, except those of Girodias and Hoffenberg. Meanwhile, the British publishing firm that had put up the money for Tandem to buy the U.K. rights to *Candy* from Girodias a year earlier was pressing him to repay the £5,000 because Girodias was planning to sell the rights to another publisher. Friedman wrote to the firm with the news of the overall settlement that gave the authors exclusive control over the U.K. rights to the book. The money Girodias owed would therefore be paid by the authors' literary agent, Sterling Lord.

Then, on August 22, 1966, Girodias pulled the trip wire. Friedman received a telegram from Paris: VERY SORRY MUST IRREVOCABLY REFUSE EXECUTE CANDY CONTRACT AS BEING AGAINST MY IN-TERESTS AND ALL PREVIOUS UNDERSTANDINGS AS EXPLAINED IN MY UNANSWERED LETTER AUGUST 4TH STOP . . . PLEASE NOTIFY IMMEDIATELY OTHER PARTIES MY POSITION STOP . . . REGARDS MAURICE GIRODIAS.[15]

Friedman replied the same day. "I received your cable today and was absolutely floored. I never received any letter dated August 4th relating to your thoughts about the *Candy* contract. All I received was a copy of a letter dated August 8th to Michael Rubinstein in which you acknowledge that you have 'at last completed our settle-ment with the authors of *Candy*.' (I think it very strange that of all the letters you have sent me over the past months, this is the only one never received.)"

He then read Girodias the riot act. "I must tell you that unless you sign the agreement as I sent it to you, I can no longer represent you in any matters whatsoever. I feel my professional integrity is at stake here. You represented to me and to other parties that I had full au-thority to negotiate and execute the settlement agreement. I cannot allow myself to be used in the way you have done, Maurice, any further. I put hundreds of hours into the settlement and I think did far better than anyone could have done. It is only because the other side trusted me that I was able to get what concessions I did."

Friedman went on to tell Girodias that he was legally bound to the agreement, that the authors would not accept any other proposals, and that Minton's willingness to cooperate, combined with the pros-pect of a lucrative film contract with Columbia Pictures, promised "substantial income."

"I am sorry that everything had to end this way," Friedman con-cluded, "but you must understand my sense of frustration. I believe I have helped straighten out a number of your affairs very advanta-geously and that my skills could be very useful to you in the future, but I cannot let the rug be pulled from under me the way you have done."[16]

A furious spate of letters followed from Paris. Girodias could not understand how his letter of August 4 had failed to reach Friedman. But nothing had changed: The proposed settlement remained "a di-saster," and he confirmed his total opposition to it.[17] Girodias flew to London in a hurry and wrote again after he returned to Paris. "I have just returned from London where the worst is happening. . . . I am now in the hands of [a publisher], who are themselves in the hands of another group. . . .

"I am trying to find a way out, and the only one would imply my own company becoming the co-publisher of the British edition of *Candy*. . . . At this point, there is absolutely no need to argue who is right or who is wrong of you and me. I am in an absolutely hopeless situation right now and all that matters is to get out of it."

Unable to accept the settlement that Friedman had crafted, Girodias attached his terms and asked Friedman if he would submit "this last offer of mine" to the other parties.[18]

Friedman replied immediately. Girodias's errant letter of August 4 had finally arrived marked "*Affranchissement Insuffisant*" ["Insufficient Postage"]. "My guess," wrote Friedman, "is that since you had no return address, they sent it on to me by ship rather than air so it arrived in three weeks rather than two days. . . . But no matter. Too much has happened in the interim. I cannot help but feel that you simply changed your mind about the settlement, decided you wished to continue your vendetta with the authors and therefore deliberately misread the contract and looked for an excuse to repudiate it."

Friedman concluded: "I would have had no problem if you had simply said 'no deal' when you were in New York. But when you tell me to go ahead and complete everything . . . and then you change your mind again, I cannot go on any more. . . . I realize your emotional reaction to the way the authors betrayed you. But that cannot guide your actions forever. I believe now you just want to deprive them of any return from *Candy* no matter what it costs you. I am not going to be a party to that kind of revenge. I don't know what they are planning to do now. They have the option of enforcing the contract which is most certainly legally binding on you. . . . I have no choice but to acknowledge I had the authority you represented I had and I will sign affidavits if necessary."

Friedman ended more in sorrow than anger. "I still consider you a friend, Maurice, but I feel your method of doing business is foreign to me. I can be as aggressive as necessary when the occasion demands . . . but I demand some kind of honor from those I work with."[19]

Girodias fired back, unrepentant and under pressure. "What an exceptional muddle. . . . My August 4 letter travelling the slow way. . . . And my daughter Juliette barging in at this point! It would be comical if so many other uncomical things were not involved." He then sharpened his criticism of Friedman, accusing him of negotiating new terms with the authors without telling him and signing the agreement without consulting him. But he changed his tone in closing: "May I say, after what precedes, how grateful I am for your hospitality to my daughter. I had a note from her saying how sweet and good you had been, which naturally enhances the atmosphere of high paradoxical madness and general schizophrenia. I do hope that we will find ourselves soon in a reciprocal situation where the good, enlightened and constructive things take precedence."[20]

Girodias then sent off letters to Southern and Hoffenberg declaring the Friedman-orchestrated settlement of July to be null and void. Seymour Litvinoff wasted no time in sending a tart reply: "I am sure that your long and distinguished career in publishing has familiarized you with the meaning of . . . a Power of Attorney. I enclose herein a copy for your perusal, should you have forgotten the document you signed. . . . If it is your great desire to spend more time in the French Courts, you have certainly chosen the direct path. We at this end will hold you to your Contract, and will, of necessity, have some more lawsuits to bring against you."[21]

WITH LITVINOFF'S intervention, the haggling widened and, as the melodrama moved into its final phase, Cindy Degener of the Sterling Lord Agency reappeared as a key player. It seems that Girodias's problems in London were far worse than his letters suggested. The people he was dealing with had found out that he did not have the rights to *Candy,* and all their efforts to get him to repay their £5,000 fee had failed.

Friedman recalled Girodias telephoning him in the Hamptons from Paris during the Labor Day holiday weekend. "He was desperate and contrite. He said if he didn't get the British rights, he'd be in serious trouble—not just money trouble. 'My life is being threatened, Leon,' he said. I called Cindy and said we've got to redo the deal. Maurice is in physical danger. He must have the British rights and can have less elsewhere."[22]

Cindy Degener remembered the people Girodias was dealing with in London. "I was physically afraid of them. They were serious about breaking legs. Maurice said he had promised them something and then he didn't deliver. I knew he shouldn't have lied to them, but he did."[23]

Girodias followed up Friedman's plea with a letter to her explaining his position and enlisting her help with a settlement. He enclosed a copy of his terms and a sweetener in the form of a 5 percent royalty for the authors from an eventual British paperback edition of *Candy*. He mentioned the Litvinoff letter, "the purpose of which seems obscure, but which contains an assortment of threats and derogatory appreciations." He also expressed concern about Friedman. "I am deeply chagrined by the disagreements which have arisen between Leon and myself in the last unfortunate chapter of our story." He ended the letter on a personal note: "I am glad that you liked my kid brother, who seems to have reciprocated the feelings. And may I immodestly add that I am quite likable myself, if seen in my proper light and perspective?"[24]

Michael Rubinstein, Girodias's British lawyer, also came back into the picture. "It seems that the *Candy* affair generates the most extraordinary confusions!" he wrote to Friedman. "The situation . . . appears to have reached a point of maximum confusion, and it certainly presents major dangers for my client." He explained that technically the people who had bought the U.K. rights to *Candy* from Girodias had no obligation to return them since Girodias had failed to come up with the money on time. But Rubinstein added that this group had lost most of their "freedom of movement" in the negotiations because they had "given guarantees to a third party on whose financial help they are dependent."[25]

While Friedman made it clear to Girodias that he did not officially represent him anymore, he nevertheless kept him abreast of what was happening in New York and continued to advise him to settle before it was too late. "How long can this continue?" he pleaded. "Surely your energies should be devoted to some other project." He also reminded Girodias of his bill. "I do not want to press you when I know you are in a difficult financial position but I am out-of-pocket $90 already ($20 which I loaned you when you were here and $70 for one of our long-distance phone calls in which I could not reverse the charges). Since I, too, am very hard-pressed for cash, I think it only fair that I receive at least a small down payment for my work for you. I would like at least an additional $300 and some acknowledgement that I will receive what is owed to me in the future."[26]

In early October Terry Southern signed the new draft settlement. Leon Friedman noted that he did not expect any difficulty in getting Mason Hoffenberg to sign too. He did, however, check with Cindy Degener to see if any disagreement between the two authors would cause difficulties. The answer was satisfactory. He reported to Girodias that one author's signature on the document was "sufficient to convey any and all rights to license or publish *Candy*."[27]

But further objections from Paris checked the momentum of the negotiations. "Alas, once again I will appear unreasonable," Girodias wrote to Friedman. "And yet, in this instance as well as in previous ones, if anyone is being difficult and unreasonably demanding, it certainly is not me, but whoever has dreamed up that new clause Three [the size of the authors' royalty from the British rights to *Candy*]. Sheer madness. . . . Some diabolical personage is always ruining our chances at the last minute; and of course it is not hard to guess that Mr Litvinoff has been at work in this occasion as in previous ones.

"However, I am writing to old Cindy to state my case—once more. At least she will not be able later to complain that she was taken by surprise."

Girodias went on to ask Friedman to resume as Olympia's official representative in the negotiations and offered him an additional $3,000 for his pains in the event of a successful outcome. "I will send you $300 as soon as humanly possible to take care of odds and ends." The Mr. Micawber of publishing ended appropriately: "I plan to arrive in New York on the 17th for the KILL. (A fascinating deal with New American Library is on the way.)"[28]

CINDY DEGENER responded favorably to Girodias's objections, Friedman drew up the final agreement, and all seemed set for a successful outcome when Mason Hoffenberg, a shadowy figure throughout much of the negotiations, refused to sign. A flurry of telegrams kept the French and American cable companies busy. Friedman cabled Girodias: MASON INSISTING KEEPING FIRST MONIES PROMISED BY MINTON WHICH CAN BE RECOUPED LATER DEGENER OBJECTING STOP SINCE MINTON PROBABLY NOT PAY ANYHOW WILL TRY TO PERSUADE DEGENER ACCEPT TERMS.[29]

Girodias needed a speedy conclusion desperately. Not only were his kneecaps—or worse—in danger from the people in London but a new and lucrative deal with the New English Library (NEL) for the British rights to *Candy* and other Olympia titles was in jeopardy. NEL refused to sign until Hoffenberg had added his signature to the American settlement. It seemed that Girodias had jumped the gun by promising *Candy*'s rights to NEL before the American agreement was completed.

"On the strength of his [Southern's] signature of the contract and of the changes agreed by Cindy, I . . . made irrevocable commitments to third parties," Girodias admitted.[30] NEL voiced the suspicion that perhaps Hoffenberg had already sold the British rights without telling any of the parties involved. The British publisher was therefore in a strong position, Girodias reported.

"They know that I am quite desperate for money and they are making use of that situation to try to impose all kinds of new clauses— under the pretext that the American contract is not properly exe- cuted. . . . I can hardly tell you how tense the situation is," Girodias wrote to Friedman in early November. The crisis did not, however, entirely obscure other targets of opportunity. An article in an issue of the *Los Angeles Times* had contained some questionable remarks about Girodias and the Olympia Press. He raised them at the end of his letter: "I'd very much like to know what you think. It seems to me there's a one million dollar libel suit in that."[31]

While the main plot proceeded apace, another scenario was playing itself out. This was an increasingly acrimonious dialogue between the two authors. Southern wrote to Hoffenberg around this time:

Dear Mason:

I think I understand your attitude and feelings about *Candy* and related matters. I don't believe, however, that you understand mine. Since I have found it somehow impossible to communicate them to you in conversation, I want to set them down, as follows:

1. The reason our royalties were withheld, and the reason there has been no movie deal to date, was the appearance of the pirated editions. Girodias instigated the pirated editions because we cut him out of the Putnam deal. You will remember that it was your idea and at your insistence that we *did* cut him out. Admittedly I was at fault to go along with this, but I was not in favor of it. So that in my mind, the whole fiasco is basically your responsibility.

2. We had a very firm contract with Putnam in *one respect,* i.e. that they could not issue a paperback edition before *one full year* of hard-cover distribution. You sold out (for $10,000) this one piece of negotiating leverage we had with them by signing the waiver allowing them to publish it in advance of the contractual period.

3. After all this time and a great deal of work by a lot of people to negotiate a settlement with Gid, which would clear the title for a movie sale and get us our royalties from both Putnam and the pirate, your obstreperousness in not signing is incomprehensible— except as some absurd form of blackmail.

4. If you accept another 10 (or 11) from Putnam, you will have received 20 (or 21) to my zero. The only money I've received

directly or indirectly from *Candy* was the screenplay money—of which you got half.

5. In fact, the only money I have made from writing has been through screenplay work, and had nothing whatever to do with *Candy* but stemmed directly from my work on *Dr. Strangelove*. Kubrick hired me to work on *Dr. Strangelove* because of *The Magic Christian*. *Candy* had not then been published in America, and Kubrick had not read it. . . .

6. Finally, but without, I assure you, wishing in any way to underestimate the value of your contribution to the work in question, I feel I must remind you that of the total 224 pages (Putnam edition) you wrote 64 and a half pages (i.e. pages 64–121 and a half and pages 123–130) which constitutes little more that one third of the whole, and which, you may recall, I rewrote.

In view of all this you can surely understand how I find it difficult to agree that you should realize more from the project than I. Right? T.[32]

MEANWHILE, Girodias was busy in London. Frustrated by NEL's caution, he offered the British rights of *Candy* to Mayflower Books for £20,000. In a letter to the firm, Girodias outlined the terms of his contract: "I have already warned NEL that I did not consider myself bound by our negotiations." The new deal was based on an American settlement that was not yet a settlement. Girodias airily stated the basis of Olympia's ownership of *Candy:* "Our ownership derives from a contract with the authors; our New York attorney can supply all the necessary information in that respect."[33]

But it seemed that neither NEL nor indeed any British publisher would close a deal with Girodias over *Candy* until both authors had first signed the American agreement. Girodias knew this and, while thanking Cindy Degener for her efforts, tried to speed things up with a threat: "If the contract is not duly executed by Terry and Mason by the end of this week I will have no option but to start another legal action."[34]

In the middle of all this, Friedman separated his shoulder playing touch football and finished up in the hospital. And Mason Hoffenberg vanished. By the end of November, Friedman had recovered sufficiently to resume his quest for a settlement. He caught up with Mason Hoffenberg in the West Hollywood Hotel on Santa Monica Boulevard in Los Angeles. "Mason was, as usual, fairly incoherent when I talked to him," Friedman reported to Girodias. "It turns out that his real concern was not with Walter Minton at all. He wants to be guaranteed that if Terry is signed to do the screenplay on *Candy* he will also participate. In other words, he wants to be treated the same way that Terry is down the line with respect to the movie.

"I told him that I didn't represent Terry and could make no commitments for him. Obviously, I said, Terry is in a different bargaining position than he is. Mason insisted that he did not want to be 'done in' by some surreptitious movie deal whereby the rights would go for a very small amount and Terry would reap the benefits of a good price for the script. I told him no one had any intention of doing that and that he should talk to Cindy about it. When I told him that unless we acted quickly the statute of limitations would expire against the pirate publishers, he got very disturbed and said he would be back in New York by the end of the week."

Friedman felt confident that he could wrap things up if he could sit down with Hoffenberg and Cindy Degener. He ended on a stern note about money: "I must remind you about the question of my fee. I have to pay certain long distance phone calls to you and see no reason why I should be out of pocket such amounts. You said that I should be getting some money shortly and I would appreciate your expediting payment."[35]

Girodias's response was a one-line cable from Paris: IF NO SATIS-FACTORY DEVELOPMENTS MUST IMMEDIATELY START ACTION.[36]

In early December Walter Minton, who had been keeping a low profile, wrote a revealing letter to Girodias saying that he would like to see the *Candy* affair settled. "But you must understand that I am in a very difficult position," he said. "When we began action against the pirates we had to have the signature of one of the authors on the complaint—that's under our strange copyright regulations. Southern would not do it. Mason did—on the condition that we came to an agreement with him about royalties on the paper edition. . . .

"So we have a perfectly valid contract with Mason that has nothing to do with the copyright situation or anything else. It is why . . . it was necessary that Mason saw more in the agreement with you and Terry than he would lose by settling for one-third of a 25% share rather than the one-half that he had by agreement. I postponed making the accounting to him that was due—on the grounds that there was a possible settlement with you and Terry in the air. But when he showed up in New York and demanded money, there was nothing I could do. Except pay him. . . .

"God knows I'd like to see this matter settled. And believe me, my position is that the money is there and it makes absolutely no difference to us whether it goes to Mason, to Mason and Terry, or to Mason, Terry and you—aside from the fact that I would like to see you get some reward for your efforts. Is that clear?"[37]

JUST AS Minton was stepping on board, Hoffenberg was jumping off. "We are coming to the end of the road with Mason," Friedman wrote despairingly to Girodias. "Cindy is so disgusted that she has given me virtual carte blanche to arrange a deal with Mason. Gideon Cashman is so disgusted with Mason that he is thinking of dropping out altogether. Mason is coming to see him Tuesday [the following day]. He will again tell him that he must sign at this point or forever give up any possibility of getting money from *Candy*.

"Mason may just be playing some elaborate game to get everyone's attention at this point. . . . [His] travels around the country and his refusal to talk sense make it impossible to move any quicker than we have been. I will cable you as soon as anything significant happens."[38]

Two days later Girodias telegraphed Friedman that he was trying to enlist the help of Hoffenberg's family.[39] MASON IN NEW YORK HIDING WITH CASHMAN AND SOUTHERN STOP INTERVENTION ON YOUR PART UNDESIRABLE UNTIL SITUATION CLEARS, Friedman cabled back.[40] Girodias followed up with a letter saying that he had cabled Mason in New York—OLYMPIA HAS IRREVOCABLY [one of Girodias's favorite words] ASSIGNED CANDY COPYRIGHT TO SOUTHERN STOP YOUR CHANCE COLLECT SHARE DEPENDS ON YOUR WILLINGNESS SETTLE . . . PLEASE UNDERSTAND YOU WILL BE EXCLUDED VERY SUBSTANTIAL MONEY UNLESS SETTLEMENT IMMEDIATELY EXECUTED . . . HOPE YOU UNDERSTAND YOUR RESPONSIBILITIES.[41]

Girodias also orchestrated a letter from Hoffenberg's wife to his mother in New York and wrote Friedman that "she says that she is quite certain the mother will do her best to influence Mason in the right direction . . . up to now, the mother probably did not realize what the situation really was—all she knew was her son's version of the story; and God knows what that is." Girodias fervently expressed the hope that "with all the Hoffenberg females on our side we will finally overcome our last difficulty."[42]

The next day Girodias dispatched another letter to Friedman looking for a way around Hoffenberg's refusal to sign the agreement. "But perhaps by the time you get this everything will be in order? All my letters seem to end on that optimistic note!" And then a postscript: "Just had a call from Mason's wife, who says she had a call from him yesterday. She feels that Mason is going to keep going just in order to show everyone how important and desirable he is. That we already knew. The only way to convince Mason is to show that we don't need him. . . . This is not a situation where logic will prevail, but only childish bluff."[43]

The following day Friedman wrote to Girodias. "Mason is back in town and everyone is treating him as if he had the plague. He is still determined to get equal screen play credit with Terry Southern for any movie made of *Candy*." Friedman said that he was arranging a round-table conference, "which everyone will attend and straighten the whole matter out once and for all. . . . I wish I could push everything along quicker but there is no way to do it. Terry will not even countersign the changes [on the agreement] until we have settled with Mason one way or another."[44]

A CONFERENCE took place at Gideon Cashman's Park Avenue office on Thursday afternoon, December 15, 1966. The group—Cashman, Friedman, Degener, Southern, and Hoffenberg—went over the details of the settlement. Cashman remembers being relieved that his client turned up. "Mason frequently disappeared," he said, "then he'd come back out of the blue. The discipline of appointments was not part of his personality."[45]

Friedman remembered trying to persuade Southern to be nice to Hoffenberg to get him to agree. It was hard work, and the result was unclear when the meeting broke up. The next day Friedman followed up with a letter to Cashman recalling that the current version of the settlement recognized the various interests of the parties. It was vital to move on in order to obtain the authors' royalties from Walter Minton, to arrange for a movie sale, and to take action against the pirate publishers.

Friedman stressed that the agreement must be signed by Hoffenberg within a week and that, if he failed to do so, "we will have to withdraw the proposed settlement and Terry and the Olympia Press will take whatever steps they deem desirable without Mason's participation."[46]

After the meeting Friedman called Girodias in Paris with the news that final agreement was close. The next day Girodias wrote back expressing his joy at the outcome: "Great! What relief! My first comfortable night in many months. . . . What's more we got refunded quite unexpectedly of an overpayment by the tax people this morning, which explains the enclosed $100 (which makes $200 in all as we sent you another $100 money order last Tuesday: did you get it?). . . . What next! . . . Leon, again thank you for everything. Without you that gory business would never have been resolved. Let's hope that things will take a turn for the better and that we will all be millionaires soon. That would be a nice change, wouldn't it?"[47]

But once again Girodias's euphoria was premature. A week of ominous silence in New York elicited an anguished handwritten letter to Friedman. Friedman's response was to send out the agreement, which Hoffenberg continued to refuse to sign, to NEL's lawyer in New York and to Girodias's lawyer in London.[48] In a telegram to Girodias on December 29, 1966, Friedman explained what he was doing: SOUTHERN AGREEABLE ACTING JOINTLY WITH YOU ON BASIS OF LATEST REVISED AGREEMENT WITH HOFFENBERG SHARE SPLIT EQUALLY AND HELD IN ESCROW.[49]

As the new year began, Friedman had to return to the hospital for treatment. Before going in, he wrote to Girodias with bad news. "The last contact I had with Mason was to give him a flat ultimatum that he must sign the contract by December 30. He said he was not going to, and I said Terry and I would go it alone. There is no other way to deal with that man. He may wake up in about two weeks and decide to sign; but cajoling him was finally self-defeating: he thought it just showed weakness, and was trying to hold out for more money."

Friedman reported that Southern was ready to go it alone. "Terry is so angry at Mason that he is very anxious to sign a deal with us and proceed to exploit *Candy* between the two of us. I am preparing some papers along those lines, and I am sure I can get Terry to sign them very shortly."

Turning to Girodias's recent suggestion of working a side deal with Hoffenberg, Friedman thought it dangerous but offered an idea of his own: "To try to bribe Mason at this point would jeopardize a continuing relation with Terry. For that reason, I would not like to approach him. However, there is no reason why you could not do so on your own (without my knowledge, of course). If it ever came to the surface, I could probably smooth over any difficulties with Terry."

He warned Girodias to be careful with Hoffenberg. "Mason has shown a fantastic stubbornness . . . and certainly has not shown any good will to you. He is convinced that you will not pay any of the royalties on the British deal. It may be that approaching Mason now will stiffen his resistance to signing the general agreement. Any approach that you make to him should be designed to induce him in the first instance to settle everything (which would, of course, be the best solution for NEL)."

The level of frustration had reached such a point that Friedman showed he was not above a bit of intrigue himself: "Terry is now very much with us and may be very co-operative on the English deal. . . . Approaching Mason may destroy Terry's good will. I would strongly recommend that you act in a conspiratorial tone with Mason, telling him to tell no one else about it. You should destroy this letter immediately after reading it."[50]

In reply, Girodias's fertile mind came up with another ploy. He suggested that Southern should take action against Hoffenberg in Paris because, under French law, any disagreement between coauthors must be submitted to the courts. He added that the logic of the new tactics should exclude Hoffenberg from any recovery money from the pirate publishers. Walter Minton should also be cut out because his help would not be needed and because "he had made that traitorous side-agreement with Mason."

Fired up, Girodias continued: "Now that Mason is out of it for all practical purposes, we have regained our freedom to get decent royalties from him [Minton], not peanuts (the $100,000 he offers is half of what he should pay on 150,000 hard cover and a million and a half paperback copies)." A new and separate agreement, between Southern and himself, splitting all the profits and expenses from legal action against the pirates, would be necessary. "What do you say?"[51]

Shortly after he received Girodias's letter, a copy of a letter from Gideon Cashman to Cindy Degener was delivered to Friedman's bedside. He breathed a huge sigh of relief. Suddenly, there was no need to say anything, anymore, about the *Candy* affair. The miracle had occurred, and the wheeling and dealing, the maneuvering, the second-guessing, the double-crossing, the endless letters, the heated telephone conversations, the frenetic cable traffic all, as if by a prearranged signal, stopped. It was a little like Armistice Day in 1918 when the guns finally fell silent. Cashman's letter began:

Dear Cindy:
After many a swallow, comes the spring. Similarly, after many a delay, comes Mason Hoffenberg. Yesterday, Mason was in my office and signed the documents which I am enclosing herewith.[52]

· · ·

THE FINAL AGREEMENT, which had taken so long to put together, was a relatively simple affair. Dated January 10, 1967, its main
provisions were:

· All money received by Southern and Hoffenberg from *Candy* was
to be divided three ways: 40 percent for each author and 20 percent
for Olympia.
· Hoffenberg was to keep the $11,000 he had received in his side
deal with Minton but it would be considered as an advance payment
and be deducted from future income from the book.
· Olympia was granted exclusive publication rights to *Candy* in Britain and would pay the authors a 5 percent royalty on any hardback
and paperback editions. The authors would receive a £2,500 advance,
shared equally, on the sale of the British rights.
· Money already received by Southern and Hoffenberg from the
U.S. rights and from past film deals, and money received by Olympia
from its past editions of *Candy,* was to be retained, and no accounting
was required.
· All rights to *Candy,* except in Britain, were to be held by the
authors. Copyright would be in their names.
· Olympia and the authors would act together against the pirate publishers and share legal expenses and any money recovered. Any other
party joining them, e.g., Putnam's, would also share in legal expenses
and recovery money; the amount would be mutually agreed.
· The authors were to account for previous film deals, and any
money left after obligatory repayments would be divided between
them and Olympia.
· The legal action in France would be terminated.[53]

After the document was signed, Friedman turned to Walter Minton, who had agreed to release $100,000 owed to the authors for the
hardback and paperback sales of *Candy* in the United States. This was
divided on the agreed basis after legal and other costs had been deducted. While everyone received some money, no one got rich on
the book—except the pirates. The marathon struggle over *Candy*
proved to be fatal since it muddied the copyright issue and gave the
unauthorized publishers time to sell the book hand over fist when
Candy was hot (as it were). "The pirates killed us," said Walter
Minton.

Putnam's had little success in the courts. The copyright bid, using Mason Hoffenberg, was turned down. Putnam's appealed and lost again. "Our lawyer asked me if I would like to take it to the Supreme Court," Minton said, "and I said, no, I would not. He said, would I mind if he did? I said as long as I don't have to pay the fees, absolutely. So, he did and lost again."[54]

Putnam's also lost its case against Lancer, the judgment coming before Olympia was awarded the *Candy* copyright. (Girodias and Friedman won a small settlement out of court from Lancer in a later case.) Ironically, the case that Putnam's did win was the case that Minton wanted to lose. "We had a censorship action in New Jersey, and I hired a local lawyer. I wanted *Candy* to be banned, to put the thing on hold and allow time for our copyright action in Washington to succeed. But the judge threw the prosecutor out of court and said the book was not obscene. My lawyer said, 'That's great!' I said, 'Son of a bitch!' "[55]

"Securing the copyright of *Candy* for Olympia came too late to curb the pirates," said Friedman. "Lancer's huge print run was decisive. But the copyright was crucial for the overall settlement, the movie deal, and future litigation to protect the book, its authors, and its publishers. Putnam's and the authors made a big mistake cutting out Girodias in the first place. Maurice was right when he said they hurt themselves in order to hurt him. If we had done at the beginning what we did at the end, we would all have made an enormous amount of money."[56]

In Britain the story had a happy ending for Girodias. He bought off the London heavies by paying what he owed them, and he clinched his deal with the New English Library, receiving £50,000 in exchange for the rights to *Candy* and other Olympia titles.

The agreement also paved the way for a film of *Candy*. Christian Marquand was the prime mover, but things were delayed as he tried, with the help of Marlon Brando, to put together a suitably star-studded cast. Cindy Degener represented both the authors and Girodias and played an important role in handling the movie rights. The flavor of that process—and the frustration that derived from the long quest to reach a settlement—appeared in a memorandum she wrote in February 1967 for the "Candy Committee":

"For the next few days I will be at the Connaught in London. I want you to know that in spite of all the columns in the less toney papers, we have not sold *Candy* to the movies. We are awaiting the success or failure of Marquand in signing [Elizabeth] Taylor and

[Richard] Burton. . . . all the brain work and expenses for attempting to retain Taylor, Burton, [Ringo] Starr, and [Peter] Sellers is being paid for by Brando on behalf of his friend Marquand. . . .

"All the majors have been informed by me that the copyright matter is cleared worldwide. I assume that with patience and tenacity I can finally get the price that we must have which is $200,000 cash in hand with no fancy payment schedules, etc. We have suffered so that nothing but cash in the front will salve me."[57]

The deal was eventually put together, and everything seemed to be going well when history repeated itself. Mason Hoffenberg refused to sign. Gideon Cashman was still his lawyer and recollects vividly what happened next: "The producers asked me to go to Paris to persuade Mason to sign the contract. I arrived on a night flight and to my surprise was met by Mason himself in a Citroën 2CV. He took me to my hotel and told me to meet him at the Coupole at midnight. I went along, but he wasn't there. I waited until about two A.M., but he didn't show up.

"The next day he telephoned me to apologize and set up another meeting. Same time, same place—midnight at La Coupole. Same result. Mason didn't turn up. He called again the next day and set up the same arrangement once again: midnight at La Coupole. Well, when he didn't show this time I tracked down his fleabag hotel at one-thirty in the morning, found his room, and knocked on the door. I heard a groan, opened the door, and there was my client facedown and spread-eagled on the bed. He muttered that he would meet me at a nearby pizza place at four A.M. I went there, and he turned up in surprisingly good shape. We discussed the movie contract, and, as dawn was breaking over Paris, he signed it and I caught the next plane back to New York."[58]

Terry Southern remembered the film with mixed feelings. "When Christian Marquand, a friend, begged for a short option, I persuaded Mason that he should have it. Marquand, through Brando, signed up Richard Burton and got financing. I had already written a script, and they said it needed some rewrites. But then Marquand went and got a Swedish girl, Ewa Aulin, to be Candy. I couldn't believe it, the girl had *got* to be American. But he insisted. He said: 'I want to give the film a universal quality.' She couldn't speak any English and had to be looped and dubbed in.

"At that point I withdrew. Both Mason and I got some money from the film. They changed the script and . . . Richard Burton was a kind of Dylan Thomas poet who had a wind machine sweeping up his scarf. Brando was some kind of holy man. Charles Aznavour played a Richard III figure who was supposed to represent the hunchback. No, he didn't sing. It was nothing like the book, but, due to its all-star cast, it did make money."[59]

Star-studded it was. In addition to Burton, Brando, Aznavour, and James Coburn, it featured Walter Matthau (General Smight), John Huston (Dr. Dunlap), Ringo Starr (Emmanuel, the Mexican gardener), and Sugar Ray Robinson (with the gloves off as Zero). But nothing could save the film from its makers. The British Film Institute's review was representative and not unfair. It described the movie as a "frenzied, formless and almost entirely witless adaptation of the enchanting Southern-Hoffenberg pornographic parable. No longer does Candy blithely chirrup 'Good Grief!' at each new sexual calamity, while welcoming the opportunity to give herself to alleviate sex-suffering humanity. Instead she defends her modesty with some vigour—her falls from grace being obscured by bowdlerisation as well as censor cuts—thus robbing the book of its point as well as its charm."[60]

LOOKING BACK, the principals had different views on the *Candy* saga. I used to see Mason occasionally in New York in the mid-1980s, looking small and vulnerable and either just getting into a scrape or just coming out of one. When I called him once, I had already heard the bad news on the Greenwich Village grapevine.

"How are you, Mason?"

A pause.

"You know I've got lung cancer?"

"Yes."

"Well, apart from that, I'm fine."

Like some of the other American writers who had spent time in Paris, Mason seemed to have brought something of the city with him. His sparsely furnished Upper East Side apartment, with its stripped wooden floors, simple kitchen, and worn burgundy leather chair where he always sat, could have been anywhere in the Latin Quarter.

After tulip tea and pound cake, Mason lit up a cigarette. "Why not?" He shrugged.

"Girodias made young, unknown writers feel good because he paid them chapter by chapter," he said. "Writing dirty books was a good way of making money to pay for the typewriter and to learn how to use a thesaurus."

But, in the final analysis, Girodias was "a cheap crook." Mason reckoned that Girodias wanted to sound like the Douglas Fairbanks of the publishing world, "but no one liked him." The publisher put out Mason's two pornographic books in America under the author's own name without his permission. "I could have thumped him," Mason said with a sudden bitterness. Girodias's business dictum, he added, was "Don't pay the writers."[61]

On my last visit, Mason was not well. He moved stiffly in and out of the old leather chair. Two walking sticks were propped up against the wall. He was going to the Veterans Association hospital once a week for painkilling drugs but not having treatment. He was still capable of a deadpan joke, a derogatory comment about his erstwhile publisher, and he still enjoyed a lungful of smoke. Not long afterward, he died at the age of sixty-three, leaving many of us wondering about that klaxon and other unfinished Hoffenbergiana.

In order to see *Candy*'s coauthor, I drove up the winding Housatonic Valley to Terry Southern's home in Canaan, Connecticut. It was a peerless fall day, the hillsides rippling with color and gold and russet leaves blowing across the road. I passed through hamlets of white clapboard houses with gigantic pumpkins on their stoops. Antique stores multiplied, signaling gentrification and weekend tourism. Yet a local diner, where families ate early and together and the waitresses called you "Hon," had a friendly atmosphere.

Southern was sitting in the living room of his "pre-Rev" farmhouse built on the Blackberry River in the middle of the eighteenth century and set in twenty-five acres of water meadows and woodland. It was a comfortable, rambling house with sloping floors, worn rugs, peeling paint, afternoon light picking up dusty shelves of books, the smell of woodsmoke, and a patina of loving neglect. A tall, lumbering, unkempt figure, Southern was then in his late sixties. On the coffee table was a liter bottle of red wine, two-thirds empty. He lived with Gail, his second wife, who ran a dance studio in town. He had one son, Nile (by Carol), a writer and filmmaker.

After *Candy,* Southern went on to became a top-rank Hollywood screenwriter. During the 1960s, he cowrote scripts for *Dr. Strangelove, Easy Rider, The Loved One, Barbarella,* and *The Cincinnati Kid.* His novels from that period include *The Magic Christian* and *Blue Movie.* Then nothing for twenty years. In 1992 a new novel, *Texas Summer,* was published by Richard Seaver, a fellow "Olympian." The novel appeared without fanfare, and disappeared. Southern taught film writing once a week at the Columbia School of Journalism and wrote the occasional article. Money was tight.[62] His literary output, like much of his conversation, was punctuated by long silences.

Carol Southern blamed the corrupting impact of Tinsel Town: "I think Hollywood had a terrible influence on him. He was a very disciplined writer, worked every single day, was wonderful company, did not drink to excess. Then Hollywood gave him permission to act out the dark side that all of us have. It's an old story. Few people have the character to withstand that kind of immediate fame, and he was such a star."[63]

Southern wielded a rapier pen for choice targets. In 1991 he wrote "Flashing on Gid," a hard-hitting article about Girodias in *Grand Street*. Southern depicted Girodias as a pretentious snob, a stuck-up phony who had no interest in literature or in the merits of the better books he was publishing and who was sly, duplicitous, and venal in his business dealings. The article contained many funny stories, told with verve and apparent total recall, but was marred by factual errors. "Flashing on Gid" caused a stir among the Olympia cognoscenti, many of whom thought it threw more light on the character of the author than on the man he was profiling.

Southern was kinder to Girodias during lunch in a heavily beamed dining room: "He was a charming roué. I always had a good time with him. He was never in a position to cheat me, although he used to hang us on our ten-thousand-franc payments while we were writing *Candy*. He'd lie about checks in the mail. When you met him again, you'd feel like punching him out, but then he'd be so charming and offer you a fine old brandy or something."

An epitaph? "I'd have to think about that, but I'd be more inclined towards praise than damnation because he was, no matter how you slice it, associated with dandy literary events."[64] Terry Southern died in October 1995.

Leon Friedman reflected on the *Candy* saga in his comfortable town-house office in New York: "It was such a mess dealing with those prima donnas, but in the end things worked out. The film was made, the lawsuits against Lancer were settled, and Girodias made a lot of money out of his British deal."

The telephone on the leather-topped desk rang. "Jean Harris on one," said Friedman's secretary. A brief conversation took place. "If Clinton wins," Friedman told the murderer of Herman Tarnower, creator of the Scarsdale Diet, "it will be good for you."

Returning to the past, Friedman talked about Girodias. "He was infuriating much of the time. There are three things a lawyer wants out of a client: You want him to tell you what he is doing, you want him to follow your advice, and you want him to pay you. Maurice did none of the above. But something always redeemed him. Although he treated me badly, I had a real human attachment to Maurice. I miss him."[65]

10

Une Lettre d'Amour:
The True Story of
Story of O

> "Who am I finally," said Pauline Réage, "if not the long silent part of someone,
> the secret and nocturnal part which has never betrayed itself in public
> by any thought, word, or deed, but communicates through subterranean
> depths of the imaginary with dreams as old as the world itself?"[1]

FOUR YEARS before he published *Candy,* Girodias had put the Olympia imprint on an equally controversial but quite different book. This was *Story of O* by Pauline Réage. It relates the experiences of a young Parisian fashion photographer, a woman called O, who is taken to a château in Roissy, a Paris suburb, by René, her lover. During her stay she is systematically turned into a slave through regular whippings, sexual assault by a number of men, long hours chained up in dungeonlike rooms, and the insertion of progressively larger ebonite shafts into her anus to accommodate better the predatory phalluses of her masters. All this is done with her consent, for her love of René.

After a time, René hands O over to a family friend, a cold, gray-eyed Englishman called Sir Stephen. The saga of brutality, humiliation, and submission intensifies. O is branded on her buttocks, and rings, bearing her name and Sir Stephen's, are fitted through her labia. O also indulges her taste for women, both enjoying the act of seduction and working as an accomplice of René and Sir Stephen to provide new recruits for the château.

The final humiliation comes at a party when an owl mask is put over O's head and a chain is attached to one of the rings in her labia. She becomes a human cipher at the disposal of any man—or woman—who desires her. Yet, paradoxically, she has never been calmer and happier in her life. She is on the brink of the ultimate self-sacrifice, and she experiences a feeling of total absolution.

The novel, elegantly written in a cool, matter-of-fact style, lingers over O's inner feelings, her clothes and toilet, the architecture and interior decoration of the places where she stays, and the sensual details of her couplings with other women. Religious references abound, and the story is permeated with mystical and sacrificial imagery. These provide an unsettling counterpoint to the clinical description of O's remorseless degradation.

STORY OF O FIRST APPEARED, simultaneously in French (as *Histoire d'O*) and English, in June 1954.* It was initially overshadowed by Françoise Sagan's much more innocent tale of sexual love, *Bonjour Tristesse,* which won the triple crown of publishing that summer: critical acclaim, scandalous reputation, and huge sales. Gradually, however, *Story of O* began to emerge as an intriguing mixture of succès d'estime and succès de scandale. Quite apart from its explicit sexual content and the quality of the writing, *Story of O* was distinguished by a laudatory preface written and signed by Jean Paulhan, one of France's most respected literary figures, and the mystery that shrouded its author, the pseudonymous Pauline Réage.

During the last four decades, *Story of O* has never been out of print. For a period in the 1960s, it was the bestselling and most widely read contemporary French novel outside France. It has been translated into two dozen languages, has sold millions of copies, and has been turned more than once into a film. Moreover, the book has established itself as a literary landmark—a seminal work of erotica that expanded public acceptance of what could be published and that hoisted a beacon for

---

*Maurice Girodias erroneously added the definite article to *Story of O* when he published the novel, rendering it *The Story of O*. He made the same mistake with William Burroughs's *Naked Lunch*.

a new genre. *Story of O* has also been attacked by feminists, who have viewed it as an act of treachery by a woman writer pandering to male fantasies; at various times, copies of the book have been publicly burned. These critics decry, among other things, the passages that deal with O's acquiescence in physical violence. At one point, Sir Stephen says, "I am going to put a gag in your mouth, O, because I'd like to whip you till I draw blood. Do I have your permission?"

" 'I'm yours,' O said.

" 'Excuse me, O,' he murmured . . . then he let her go, and struck."

In contrast to the high visibility of the book, its author retreated into the shadows, venturing forth to be interviewed in print when the book was first turned into a film, but always hidden behind the mask of "Pauline Réage." For forty years speculation surrounded Pauline Réage's identity and centered mostly on male candidates, among them André Malraux, Henry de Montherlant, André Pieyre de Mandiargues, Raymond Queneau, Jean Paulhan himself, and even an American, George Plimpton. ("It wasn't me," Plimpton admitted with a laugh, "but it's a rumour I prefer not to scotch.")[2]

In Paris and among international bibliophiles, there was informed speculation, but conclusive proof was lacking, doubts remained. A few knowledgeable people believed that there was probably more than one author, and Paulhan, as the writer of the novel's preface, was always a prime suspect.

A small inner circle, including family members and the Paris publishers of the book, knew the identity of the author all along, but its members proved remarkably loyal over the years in refusing to reveal it. It is noteworthy that Paulhan never divulged the truth publicly, for he was, in fact, the central cause of the mystery: *Story of O* was expressly written for him by a woman who feared that he might end their long affair. It was a book he described as "the most ardent love letter any man has ever received."

THE AUTHOR OF *Story of O* sat opposite me, a small, neat woman with gray hair and gray-blue eyes. She was wearing a navy blue dress with a matching cardigan and a blue cravat that had a discreet red stripe running through it. She wore no makeup, and her only jewelry was a heavy gold ring in the shape of a scarab on her wedding finger. Smooth, firm hands and open sandals enhanced a suggestion of youth, yet she was approaching her eighty-sixth birthday.

Forty years ago she wrote *Story of O,* not as a novel to seek pub-

lishing fame and fortune, but as a letter to her lover, Jean Paulhan. It
was, she said, *une entreprise de séduction.* "I wasn't young, I wasn't pretty
. . . it was necessary to find other weapons. The physical side wasn't
enough. The weapons, alas, were in the head.

"'I'm sure you can't do that sort of thing,' he said.

"'You think so?' I said. 'Well, I can try.'"[3]

This French Scheherazade is Dominique Aury, journalist, editor,
and translator, Chevalier de la Légion d'Honneur, a highly skilled and
respected woman of letters. Jean Paulhan, who died in 1968, was a
writer, critic, and editor, one of France's intellectual "immortals,"
confirmed by his membership in the Académie Française. Paulhan's
preeminence in France as a literary critic was akin to that of such
contemporaries as Edmund Wilson in the United States and Cyril
Connolly in Britain. He was also a philanderer. Their love affair
spanned three decades, during war and peace, occupation and liberation, and through Paulhan's long second marriage, and it produced
a strange progeny: the first explicitly erotic novel to be written by a
woman and published in the modern era.

Aury wrote *Story of O* when she was in her mid-forties and felt
Paulhan, almost seventy, was going to abandon her. It was designed
to *ensnare* (her word) a sophisticated man. "What could I do?" she
said. "I couldn't paint, I couldn't write poetry. What could I do to
make him sit up?" She had no thoughts—or intention—of publication. She had written nothing like it before, nor has she since.[4]

O had the desired effect. Paulhan loved it from the opening sentence and urged her on. He wrote his flattering preface to the book,
arranged for its publication, and took the heat when the French authorities moved against the novel and its author. The French publisher, Jean-Jacques Pauvert, who brought the book to Olympia, and
Girodias himself were also subjected to threats and harassment by the
government.

DOMINIQUE AURY'S family was originally from Brittany. Her paternal grandfather fought in the Franco-Prussian War and then, with
his wife, sister, and brother-in-law, went to England, where the family
worked in French restaurants. Her father was born in London and
spent the first fifteen years of his life in the cosmopolitan Soho district.
He was bilingual and had dual nationality, and when the family finally
returned to France in the early years of this century, he became an
English teacher.

He married and Dominique, his only child, was born in 1907. Her mother decided she did not want to bring her up and passed the newborn infant to her mother-in-law. Dominique grew up as a solitary child in her grandmother's house in the country and developed a passion for books, which she read equally well in French and English. She obtained a diploma to teach English but never used it. Instead, she went into journalism and began translating English works into French. She worked for literary magazines during the war and joined Gallimard, the French publisher, in 1950. She has remained with Gallimard ever since and still comes in from her home, in the suburbs, three times a week, driving fast through the Paris traffic in her car, an old Peugeot. Besides translating, she sits on a readers' committee that chooses new titles to be published and copyedits manuscripts.

Aury first met Jean Paulhan in the early part of the war. It was, appropriately, a love of literature that brought them together. She was in her early thirties, single and unknown, working as a journalist and helping distribute a clandestine newspaper called *Lettres Françaises,* a title that does not bear a literal English translation. Paulhan was in his fifties. His first marriage, which produced two sons, had ended in divorce a decade earlier, and he was married to a woman called Germaine Dauptain, who had a daughter and a son by a previous marriage. Already well established as one of France's leading intellectuals, Paulhan was an important editor at Gallimard and had been editor of the *Nouvelle Revue Française,* the country's most distinguished literary magazine, from 1925 until the German invasion of France temporarily stopped its publication.

Aury had been working on a collection of French religious poetry from the late sixteenth century and early seventeenth century, having come across an untapped, unpublished collection in the Bibliothèque de l'Arsenal in Paris. Her father knew Paulhan and said he would introduce her to him. Paulhan had a reputation for encouraging new writers and for being approachable. She met him in the Gallimard building, which was then, as it still is, at number 5 rue Sébastien-Bottin, on the Left Bank. Paulhan liked the poetry, and he persuaded Gaston Gallimard, the head of the firm, to publish the collection.

Her first impression of Paulhan was of a big man with broad shoulders and slim hips who was "very nice, very charming, and had a sense of humor." During the editing process, she came to know him better, but on one occasion she covered herself with confusion. "I made myself quite ridiculous," she said. "I took him, with great care, a copy of *Lettres Françaises* and told him, 'Put this in your pocket and don't show it to anybody.' He looked at it and smiled because he was its editor and publisher—something I had no idea of at the time." Their work in the French Resistance drew them closer. "He asked me once if I could conceal people, but I was living with friends and had no room," she said. Paulhan's coeditor of *Lettres Françaises,* Jacques Decour, was arrested by the Germans and shot. Paulhan was also arrested, but he was released upon the intervention of the new editor of the *Nouvelle Revue Française,* who was a collaborator.

Did she fall in love at first sight? "No, no," she said. "It was slow, but it went very—efficiently. I didn't realize what was going on at first. It wasn't the first time that someone had taken an interest in me, and I was just a bit intrigued. At first, I thought it was a caprice. But, no, it was better than that. He was a wonderful person." During the bleak days of the German occupation, they became lovers, adding another element of clandestinity to the one they shared in the Resistance.

After the war, Aury worked with André Gide on a magazine called *L'Arche* and, when that collapsed, joined Paulhan on a new literary review that Gallimard supported. By this time she was widely recognized as his mistress. "If we had been in China," she said, "I would have been his second wife." But they were not in China, and she was a single woman, now living with her parents. He had a family and was married to a woman who was already suffering from an incapacitating and incurable disease. Aury loved Paulhan more than ever and he seemed to love her, but fidelity was not his strong suit; he had a roving eye, and there were other women in his life.

In the early 1950s, the fear that constantly stalks a great passion grew and threatened to overwhelm her. She felt desperate and began to look for a way to express her love, a way to seduce him anew—a way that would appeal to an intellectual, a man of letters who was still attractive to younger women. She knew he was an admirer of the Marquis de Sade and had written a learned introduction to his works. She also knew, only too well, the nature of her own sexual fantasies, which had begun in her lonely adolescence.

The conjoining of his tastes and her fantasies gave her an idea. She mentioned it to Paulhan, but he was skeptical. She said she would try anyway. Almost twenty years later, in a pseudonymous account, Aury described in the third person what happened next. The author, she wrote, had started writing *Story of O* at night, "lying on her left side with her feet tucked up under her, a soft black pencil in her right hand. . . . The girl was writing the way you speak in the dark to the person you love when you've held back the words of love too long and they flow at last. For the first time in her life she was writing without hesitation, without stopping, rewriting or discarding, she was writing the way one breathes, the way one dreams.

"The constant hum of the cars grew fainter, one no longer heard the banging of doors. Paris was slipping into silence. She was still writing when the street cleaners came by, at the first touch of dawn. The first night entirely spent the way sleepwalkers doubtless spend theirs, wrested from herself or, who knows, returned to herself."[5]

Night after night, Aury continued writing until the early hours of the morning, writing to save her life. There was no question about it. Her love *was* her life.

"The first sixty pages flowed out of me," she said, "They wrote themselves. . . . Why was it like that? I don't know, probably because I had been dreaming—not dreaming exactly but thinking about it, I suppose."

Full of trepidation, she showed what she had written to Paulhan. "What if the fantasies that it revealed were to outrage her love, or worse, bore him or, worse yet, strike him as being ridiculous? Not for what they were, of course, but because they emanated from her, and because one rarely forgives in those one loves the vagaries or excesses one readily forgives in others."[6]

Her fears proved groundless. Paulhan read avidly and became her first and most passionate literary admirer. "Have you got any more?" he would ask. "Do you have the next chapter? Keep at it."

After the explosive beginning, the writing slowed not because she found it difficult but because she tried to give the story more of a structure. She wrote on, sometimes in pencil, sometimes in ink, usually in the same small school-exercise books. When she left Paris during the summer, she sent the manuscript, chapter by chapter, to Paulhan by post. She kept nothing—no first draft, no carbon copies. On her return, she continued writing, and during their assignations Paulhan would sometimes ask her to read sections of the story aloud to him.

"In the dark car, in the middle of an afternoon or some bleak but busy street . . . where you have the feeling you're transported back to the last years of the previous century . . . the girl who was reading had to stop, break off, once or more than once, because it is possible silently to imagine the worst, the most burning detail, but not read out loud what was dreamt in the course of interminable nights."[7]

What fascinated and excited Paulhan, she said, was the relationship of the story to her own life. As she wrote in her pseudonymous account, "I saw, between what I thought myself to be and what I was relating and thought I was making up, both a distance so radical and a kinship so profound that I was incapable of recognising myself in it. I no doubt accepted my life with such patience (or passivity, or weakness) only because I was so certain of being able to find whenever I wanted that other, obscure life that is life's consolation, that other life unacknowledged and unshared. Then, all of a sudden, thanks to the man I loved, I did acknowledge it, and henceforth would share it with any and all, as perfectly prostituted in the anonymity of a book as, in the book, that faceless, ageless, nameless (even first-nameless) girl."[8]

She wrote that she frequently wondered about the origins of her "oft-repeated reveries, those slow musings just before falling asleep, in which the purest and wildest love always sanctioned, or rather always demanded, the most frightful surrender, in which childish images of chains and whips added to constraint the symbols of constraint. All I know is that they were beneficent and protected me mysteriously."[9]

Many scenes in the book may strike readers as neither beneficent nor protective. One scene, for instance, describes O thus:

"They made her kneel . . . with her bust on the ottoman, her hands still tied behind her, with her hips higher than her torso. Then one of the men, holding her with both hands on her hips, plunged into her belly. He yielded to a second. The third wanted to force the narrower passage and, driving hard, made her scream. When he let her go, sobbing and befouled by tears beneath her blindfold, she slipped to the floor, only to feel someone's knees against her face, and she realized that her mouth was not to be spared."[10]

Weren't these male fantasies? "That's what everybody says," Aury replied. "I've always been reproached for that. All I know is that they were honest fantasies—whether they were male or female, I couldn't say. There is no reality here. Nobody could stand being treated like that. It's entirely fantastic."[11]

An often neglected aspect of *Story of O* concerns the heroine's relationships with other women, which reveal a different side of O's character: manipulative, playful, and ruthless in her quest for physical pleasure and psychological control.

"What O missed was not, properly speaking, Jacqueline, but the use of the girl's body, with no restrictions attached. If Natalie had not been declared off-limits to her, she would have taken Natalie, and the only reason she had not violated the restriction was her certainty that Natalie would be give to her at Roissy in a few weeks' time, and that, some time previously, Natalie would be handed over in her presence, by her, and thanks to her."[12]

Aury emphasized that she saw an important distinction between the fantasy of her fable and the authenticity of its material details. She researched the history of clothes, studying a collection in the Louvre, and became fascinated with the eroticism of eighteenth-century female dress. A mask that O is compelled to wear was based on a painting by the artist Léonor Fini, whom Aury admires. (A beautifully produced collector's version of the book with illustrations by Fini was later issued.) Roissy, where O's initiation and degradation take place, is north of Paris and has become familiar through the octopuslike Charles de Gaulle airport that now sprawls across its chalky fields.

And the characters? O began as Odile, based on a great friend of that name. "She was one of the North African group that came to Paris after the Liberation and was very much in love with Albert Camus at one time," said Aury. "We worked together, and she later married a Royal Air Force pilot and went to England. She knew all about the name and was enchanted. But after a few pages I decided that I couldn't do all those things to poor Odile, so I just kept the first letter. It has nothing to do with erotic symbolism or the shape of the female sex."[13]

The other main characters had a slightly more substantial basis. René was the "vestige of an adolescent love, rather the hope of a love that never happened." He never had the "slightest suspicion that I might be capable of loving him." Jacqueline, the model whom O invites to live with her and then seduces, is the character most nearly like someone in the author's own life. Aury said that her first love was a girl of that name who was at her school. "Jacqueline was a big, blond, and beautiful girl. We were both fifteen, and we were in love with each other."

Did they have an affair? "Of course, why not? It was quite common in France, that sort of thing. It never hurt anyone. But her parents did not like it, and took her away from the lycée." She said that Jacqueline had also loved René and had been the first to break her heart. With a stroke of her pen, Aury finally got her revenge by shipping the lovely and unsuspecting Jacqueline off to Roissy. Sir Stephen came out of the blue, based on a man she had glimpsed at a bar, "half-seated on a stool, silent, self-composed with that air of some grey-eyed prince that fascinates both men and women."[14]

After writing for about three months, Aury found that she could not go on. Paulhan said it was all right. "You can stop now," he said.

Later she read De Sade's works for the first time. She thought that the first fifty pages of *120 Days of Sodom* were a masterpiece. "Unfortunately, the rest is no good," she said. "It's unreadable."[15] The content did not surprise her, but De Sade made her understand that "we are all jailers, and all in prison, in that there is always someone within us whom we enchain, whom we imprison, whom we silence."[16]

Meanwhile, Paulhan was more enthusiastic than ever about the book and began looking for a publisher. He had his secretary type the manuscript and wrote his comments in the margin. Aury is emphatic that he made no further contribution other than challenging her in the first place, encouraging her to go on, and changing one word in the text. "He took out *one* adjective," she said with a smile. "*Sacrificiel.* 'Oh no, oh no!' he exclaimed. So I said, all right, cross it out. He changed nothing else—not a single comma."[17]

P AULHAN took the manuscript to his friend Gaston Gallimard, but Gallimard turned the book down. (A readers' committee voted four to one against it). Aury said that Gaston Gallimard was a libertarian, open to new ideas, but he respected contemporary conventions and did not want to be involved in a sexual scandal. The manuscript was then passed on to André Defez of Les Deux Rives [The Two Shores], who was more daring, having published exposés of the Freemasons and France's involvement in Indochina. He accepted *Story of O* and paid the author an advance. But the Indochina book had provoked a court case, which was draining his financial resources, and he eventually decided not to take the risk of further prosecutions. He reluctantly returned the manuscript.

Finally, Paulhan went to Jean-Jacques Pauvert, who, at the age of twenty-seven, had already made his mark as an innovative and fearless publisher. His most striking achievement had been publishing the entire works of the Marquis de Sade, an act that led to a series of court cases that were to last for eight years.

Pauvert said Paulhan brought him the manuscript of *O* at the end of 1953. He read the book overnight and thought it a masterpiece. Was he surprised at its provenance? "Not at all," he said. "I knew

Paulhan was interested in erotic literature at that time. I already knew Dominique Aury as a journalist, writer, and translator, and I found the writing to be of the same superb quality as her other work."[18]

Pauvert decided to make a special effort to produce a memorable book. The first edition of *Story of O* was printed on fine paper and had a handsome yellow cover with the title in black and a title page in two colors; in some copies the title page was embellished with a small medallion-sized lithograph by Hans Bellmer, a Surrealist painter. Paulhan contributed his preface, entitled "Happiness in Slavery," praising the book and calling it both "dangerous" and "decent." Pauvert inserted his four-page prospectus in every copy, describing the novel as an important work in the history of literature. He printed six hundred copies, all numbered, of which one hundred were destined for the friends of the author and the publisher. "It was a very beautiful, unusual book," Pauvert said. "Everything was done with great care."

All the negotiations and the business side of the venture were handled by Paulhan and Pauvert, and the copyright was registered in the name of "Editions Jean-Jacques Pauvert." It was agreed that the novel and its preface would be treated as an entity, with the two works always published together. The author would receive a royalty of 12 percent and Paulhan 3 percent.[19]

O BEGAN its English-language career when Pauvert mentioned it to Girodias, with whom he was sharing the rue de Nesle offices at the time. "Girodias and I had talked about joint projects, and he had told me about his erotic books that were sold to sailors," Pauvert recalled. "I passed him the manuscript of O, and he said he would like to do an English version." Girodias claimed that Pauvert hesitated to publish the book. "I gave him encouragement," Girodias said, "and when . . . I told him I would publish the book in English at the same time he would release it in French, he finally made up his mind."[20]

Leaning back in his chair in his Paris office, Pauvert exploded with laughter. "It was Girodias who asked me, and I said, fine, no problem. But it was then that the trouble started. He did a very, very quick translation in two or three weeks, and his English version came out almost the same time as mine. I imagine that Dominique Aury has told you—it was a terrible translation."[21]

Pauvert said that Girodias told him the translation was done by his brother, Eric Kahane. "But his brother is an excellent translator," he continued, "and I wonder if it was really his brother who did it. They were both a little puritan. That corresponds a bit with what I know of Eric. Perhaps he found the book disgusting and rejected it because it is unthinkable that he would have done such a bad translation. Dominique Aury was furious, Paulhan was beside himself, and then, on top of that, Girodias did not pay us. He didn't pay anyone."[22]

There was no contract for the English-language rights between Pauvert and Girodias. "We didn't have one," said Pauvert, "because I was wary of Girodias. Dominique Aury was also wary of him, especially after she—as a translator herself—saw what he had done with the English version of the book. Dominique Aury showed me things like when a person called 'Madeleine' was mentioned, it was translated as 'cake.' She wrote a letter to me around this time complaining about Girodias and the English edition. She said we must stop all this."[23]

Girodias did not impress her, Aury confirmed, either as a publisher or as an individual. She did not remember much about the first translation, and her attitude was that it was better not to be involved. "This is because I am a translator myself," she said, "and I get into a rage when I find something is wrong. Since I could not do a thing about it, it was better not to see it."[24]

Pauvert was right. The first English translation of *Story of O* was done not by Eric Kahane but by Baird Bryant. Austryn Wainhouse, Patrick Bowles, and Alex Trocchi—Girodias's *traducteurs de choc,* as he called them—were all busy at the time. Baird and Denny Bryant had just arrived in Paris and were available, so Girodias hired Bryant to do a crash translation because he wanted to bring the English version of the book out with the French edition. Bryant complied and was, he remembered, paid the then princely sum of $600 for the task. This led to assignments for Bryant and his wife, and they were soon at their typewriters hammering out DBs for The Traveller's Companion Series.

STORY OF O MADE A relatively sedate transition from private love letter to public erotica. But it began to circulate, be talked about, and read by intellectuals, by the fashionable, and by reviewers. Most of the reviews were favorable, and writers such as Georges Bataille and André Pieyre de Mandiargues praised it highly.

Then, in February 1955, less than a year after its first appearance, it won a small literary prize. This was the Prix des Deux Magots, which was generally awarded to new and unconventional books; past winners have included some well-known and respected novelists, notably Raymond Queneau and Antoine Blondin.

The prize was a mixed blessing. While it confirmed the novel's literary quality and daring, it also attracted the attention of the French government. Pauvert and Girodias were summoned by the police and grilled about the book, the identity of the author, and Paulhan's role in it. Neither of them cooperated, refusing to reveal the author's name or her whereabouts.

The police found her anyway. "They came to my house, where I was living with my mother," Aury recalled. "They said they had come to talk to me about the book. My mother kept out of the way, and after they had gone I told her that it had been a mistake. They had been looking for someone else, I said. My mother seemed to accept the explanation."[25]

Legal action by the government against the book was set in motion. Jean Paulhan's lawyer was engaged to defend the book and protect its author. ("We must not bore her with this" was the lawyer's opinion.) Paulhan found himself a target too, notably when he became a candidate for selection to the Académie Française, France's most prestigious organization of the arts and sciences. Aury confirmed the story, long current but often thought apocryphal, that on the day of decision about Paulhan's suitability for membership of this august body, his opponents had a copy of *Story of O* placed on every chair in the gold-encrusted chamber. "This tactic didn't impress anybody," she said. "He was elected, and we made a good sale—forty books!"[26]

Fan and hate mail arrived. One particularly offensive letter cursed her mother's womb that had produced her. "My poor mother!" Aury exclaimed. Did her mother know? "A friend once mentioned to me, in the presence of my mother, that he thought I was the author. After he left, I thought there would be a showdown with her. But she just turned to me and said: 'Would you like another cup of tea?' "[27]

Aury never mentioned the book to her father, whose secret collection of erotic books she had discovered in her midteens. Did he have any idea that she had written it? "Probably, but he never said anything. He was very English in that respect, although he did not have a drop of English blood. He was quite capable of not saying anything when he wanted."

She decided to remain anonymous to protect her family, but she also admitted to a taste for clandestinity, which she had acquired during the German occupation of France. She had not intended the book for publication, and she had no interest in the public attention that successful and controversial authors often find to be their lot. Colleagues at work who knew were discreet, and she developed a standard reaction for the curious and the bold. Whenever she was asked if she had written *Story of O,* she would politely reply that it was a question to which she never responded.

The French government's actions against *Story of O* ended suddenly and strangely. Aury explained: "A friend of mine, a medical doctor who had been my gynecologist for years, was living with a man who had just become the Minister of Justice. Paulhan said, 'You must ask her to arrange a meeting.' So I went to her and told her I would like to see the Minister. Three days later I received an invitation to lunch at Croissy, a suburb southwest of Paris.

"The house was old with a small garden. At the end of the garden was a ruined chapel where Napoleon and Josephine had been married. We sat down to lunch, I beside the Governor of the Bank of France with the Minister of Justice and my friend opposite. Lunch was served, and I remember we had chicken with courgettes. It was quite rare to have chicken and courgettes together, but it was very good. Then we got up and went to the salon for coffee.

"Some of the other guests left, and I got up to leave as well. I said: 'Monsieur le Ministre, je vous remercie.' He said he would see me to my car. I said good-bye, and he kissed my hand: 'Madame,' he said, 'I was very pleased to meet you.' That's all. The next day he issued a decree ending all the proceedings against *Story of O.* Under French law, when a minister does that, no one can ever resume legal action. That was the end of it."[28]

While the French version sailed clear, Girodias's English edition ran into foul weather. The Brigade Mondaine made one of its increasingly frequent visits to the rue de Nesle. Girodias's relations with Pauvert had worsened, and he claimed the French publisher instigated the raid. Pauvert exploded again, this time with derision, and denied the charge. "He was completely crazy, the poor fellow, he was drinking far too much at that time."[29]

Taking defensive action, Girodias changed the title of *O* to *The Wisdom of the Lash.* But before reprinting the book, he had a new translation done, this time by Austryn Wainhouse. Wainhouse says that Girodias realized the first translation was bad. "It would have sold perfectly well to the sailors, he told me. But he thought it was a very fine book and needed a better translation. . . . I can see the book almost page by page, episode by episode. I probably simply fixed it, you know, repaired the previous one."

Wainhouse tried to find out who the author was and tested his theories on Girodias. "But he didn't say one thing or another." What did Wainhouse think of the book as he worked on it? "It was a very striking and unpleasant book, the sort of book one reads with conflicting feelings—it left one divided and upset. It seemed to me to be marvelously written with incredible evenness and control. But, at the end, a very disturbing book."[30]

Pauvert pointed out that Girodias had the rights to publish only a single English edition. "His printer told me that instead of publishing two thousand copies, which was the arrangement, he had five thousand printed," Pauvert said. "Girodias certainly did not have the right to retranslate the book and print it again, but he did it anyway. And this time he suppressed Paulhan's essay. Paulhan and Dominique Aury were not pleased."[31]

No one gave Girodias the right, either, to change the title from its original to the inventive but definitely down-market *The Wisdom of the Lash*. The omission of Paulhan's essay, however, was probably not a deliberate act of sabotage. Girodias put it down to a mistake by the printer, who, he claimed, was drunk at the time and simply overlooked the future Academician's carefully wrought prose when the book went to press.

The vice squad ordered the seizure of a number of copies of the English edition of *Story of O*. But the book was never officially banned, and the police eventually turned their attentions elsewhere. During the late 1950s and early 1960s, the book continued to be reprinted and to sell steadily in both its English and French versions. It is still selling in the 1990s.

O REMAINED A Parisian phenomenon until 1963, when Pauvert sold the American rights to Barney Rosset of Grove Press. Rosset did a straightforward deal with Pauvert, who legally controlled all the foreign rights to the book and who stipulated that a completely new translation should be made. Copies of the book sent by Pauvert to Rosset were seized by U.S. Customs in New York but, on appeal, were released by none other than Irving Fishman, Deputy Collector, Restricted Merchandise Division, the same offical who had given the green light to *Lolita* five years earlier.

When Girodias found out what was going on, he claimed that he was the owner of the English-language rights. He asserted that the Grove translation was done solely to get around his copyright to Olympia's English version and thus spirit the book out of his hands. In a letter to his American lawyer, he complained: "My two excellent friends Barney Rosset and Jean-Jacques Pauvert get together, and there goes, under my nose, another book for which I have fought like the devil. Of course, Jean-Jacques needed the couple of thousand dollars Barney presumably paid for the contract, and he just dismissed me as a negligible quantity (Jean-Jacques is like that)."

Girodias admitted that he had no written contract with Pauvert; their arrangement had been a simple verbal one. But that meant, he argued with a splendid flourish of Girodian logic, that Pauvert could not "prove that he is right any more than I can."[32]

"That's a funny way of looking at it," said Barney Rosset with a laugh. "Pauvert had not sold him the rights, therefore, he had no contract showing that he *didn't* sell them to him." Rosset liked the book enormously. "It was a great book with great sexuality," he said. "We did a new translation simply because we did not like the previous one."[33]

The new version of *Story of O,* complete with Paulhan's original essay and a commentary by André Pieyre de Mandiargues, made its debut in the United States in 1965. The book received a generally laudatory reception among reviewers. "An ironic fable of unfreedom, a mystic document that transcends the pornographic and even the erotic," wrote *Newsweek. The New York Times Book Review* saw Pauline Réage as a more dangerous writer than the Marquis de Sade since "art is more persuasive than propaganda. . . . Aiming only to reveal, to clarify, to make real to the reader those dark and repulsive practices and emotions that this better self rejects as improbable or evil, Pauline Réage succeeds in drawing us irresistibly into her perverse world through the magnetism of her own selfless absorption in it."[34]

In another *New York Times* piece, Edwin A. Roberts, Jr., questioned the book's literary merit but underlined Paulhan's point about the work's essential "decency." "Chains and crops notwithstanding . . . what is ultimately extraordinary about *Story of O* is that in summary it isn't really very 'dirty'. . . . It is completely matter-of-fact: the author's style is so evenhanded, so crisp, so unemotional that one might think she learned her trade at the Associated Press."[35]

The new translation—the third English rendering of the French text—was completed by one "Sabine d'Estrée," introducing another pseudonym, another mystery. The identity of the euphonious Sabine d'Estrée has remained a secret for almost as long as the author of the work she translated. Once again people in the know have been extraordinarily loyal and discreet. But while Dominique Aury at least provided some clues through her own writing and the occasional interview, her American translator was less forthcoming. Where one might have expected enlightenment—in a "Translator's Note" that Grove included in the book—one finds instead a tantalizing mixture of fact, conjecture, coyness, literary one-upmanship, and disinformation.

"I have never met Pauline Réage," the fair Sabine writes, "although, through questions of the translation, I have been in indirect communication (via the French publisher, Jean-Jacques Pauvert), and received the author's comments. I trust I am not betraying a confidence, or appearing immodest, when I say that the author has gone out of her way to say how pleased she is with those portions of the translation she had read.

"As one who had read the work in French when it first appeared, and admired not only its contents but the extreme felicity of its style, what troubled me most about the earlier English version was its seeming disdain for this obvious style. Subsequently, I learned this translator was a man, and it seemed to me that this fact alone sufficed to explain both the embarrassment—*male* embarrassment—manifest in his version, and also why Pauline Réage had gone out of her way to comment favorably on mine.

"*Story of O,* written by a woman, demands a woman translator, one who will humble herself before the work and be satisfied simply to render it, as faithfully as possible, without interpretation or unwanted elaboration. Faced with a work such as *O,* male pride, male superiority—however liberal the male, however much he may try to suppress them—will, I am certain, somehow intrude."[36]

Dear Sabine. Sexual identity has become more confused since that was written. Perhaps the translator has undergone a sexual mutation in the interim, or was not what "she" seemed to be in the first place. Perhaps *Story of O,* after the mangling it had received from the pens of male translators, did indeed "demand" a female translator. But, alas, it never got one because "Sabine d'Estrée" is, almost certainly, the unmistakably masculine figure of Richard Seaver.

Seaver returned to the United States in 1954 and a few years later joined Rosset at Grove. Since Seaver was a skilled translator who had lived in France for many years, it was not surprising that Rosset would turn to him when he needed a new and polished translation of O. Aury said she remembered seeing the American translation of the book and that it "seemed to be all right." But she had no recollection of being in communication, indirectly or otherwise, with the translator. After leaving Grove, Seaver worked for other publishers before acquiring his own firm, Arcade Publishing, which he runs from the Flatiron district in Manhattan. His wife, Jeannette, is French, and her middle name is Sabine.

STORY OF O HAS A STRANGE ENDING. On the last page of the book there are two short paragraphs that read:

"In a final chapter, which has been suppressed, O returned to Roissy, where she was abandoned by Sir Stephen.

"There exists a second ending to the story of O, according to which O, seeing that Sir Stephen was about to leave her, said she would prefer to die. Sir Stephen gave her his consent."

When I asked Aury about these alternative endings, she shrugged. "I didn't know how to end it, so I left it open. Why not? I am not a novelist, you know."

She had more to say about the novel's "final chapter," which was written at the same time as the original story but not published with it. "It was extremely bad, abominable. It was a mistake . . . it was the other side to the dream . . . it was a degradation into reality . . . prostitution, money, force, etc. . . . . *Story of O* was pure dream, pure fantasy. *Return to the Château* was reality with all its banality, harshness, and sordidness. It was '*une mauvaise fabrication,*' as we say. It should have been suppressed."[37]

It *was* suppressed, for fifteen years, and the members of the O trio—Aury, Paulhan, and Pauvert—appear to have disagreed over who did the suppressing. What is clear is that in 1968 Pauvert, who was having financial problems, was prompted by the commercial success of *Story of O* to approach Aury with an idea for a new book. The result of their discussions was a two-part sequel to the novel.

The main section was the suppressed chapter. It retained its original title, *Retour à Roissy* (*Return to the Château* in the English translation), which was used as the book's overall title. In the terse disclaimer, signed "P.R.," that precedes this section, Aury wrote: "The pages that follow are a sequel to *Story of O*. They deliberately suggest the degradation of that work, and cannot under any circumstances be integrated into it."

The second part, smaller but more interesting, was the prefatory essay in which Aury described, largely in the third person, how she came to write *Story of O*. She entitled the essay "Une Fille Amoureuse" ("A Girl in Love") and signed it "Pauline Réage." The book was published in Paris in 1969.

The account in "A Girl in Love," Aury said, is accurate. It is a moving piece of writing describing the clandestine love affair between a single woman living with her mother and a married man living with his family. Aury began writing it in the spring of 1968, in a hospital room where Jean Paulhan lay dying. Paris was in the throes of revolution as the students fought the police from barricade to barricade. President de Gaulle's government appeared to have lost its nerve, and the threat of civil war seemed frighteningly real. Paulhan was in a clinic in the Paris suburb of Neuilly, and Aury slept on a cot in his room. For months she worked at Gallimard south of the Seine by day and drove north through the tear gas and littered streets to Neuilly to be at Paulhan's side at night.

She had not asked permission to stay in the clinic. During one of her early visits, she had noticed a fold-up iron bed in his room—"an abominable bed with lots of bumps in it"—and simply decided to make use of it. "The staff of the clinic were horrid at the beginning. They looked at me as if I were the devil incarnate, but they didn't dare put me out. After the first few weeks, they showed more respect. I slept there for four months."[38]

While she was there, members of the Paulhan family would come and go—all except Germaine, who was confined to her bed at home. The relationship between the two enduring women in Paulhan's life was a curious one. In earlier days, they had met socially, and Aury had occasionally been invited to lunch or dinner at the Paulhan home. Germaine knew about the affair but, according to Aury, never accepted it. The rest of the Paulhan family seemed to have adopted a more philosophical attitude.

Aury said that she kept her distance, but Paulhan was not particularly discreet and often asked her to pick him up at his house in her car. On one occasion when she came to fetch him, she recalled, the woman who was looking after Germaine came out into the street and said to Paulhan, in her hearing: "You should tell that girl not to come and stop in front of the door, because when Madame hears the car she weeps." Aury said she made a scene. " 'Jean, you might have told me,' I said. 'It was stupid of me, but it was much more stupid of you.' It was horrible, and I never went near the house again."[39]

Some aspects of the affair were conducted relatively openly. The couple went away on foreign trips—to Venice on one occasion, to Naples on another, and once to Guinea, where Aury had a friend. It was there that Paulhan bought her the heavy gold scarab ring that still encircles her wedding finger.

Several years before Paulhan died, he told Aury that he would like to give her a present. What did she want? "He said he had quite a lot of valuable paintings and could sell one or two. Or I could travel." 'Or,' he said, 'do you want a house?' I said I'd rather have a house." A house was bought, in the countryside not far from Paris, and from time to time Paulhan would come and stay with her.[40]

During the latter part of Paulhan's life, an incident occurred that still puzzled her; she called it "a stupefying encounter." One day, after Germaine had become bedridden, Aury received a telephone call from Germaine's daughter, whom she knew, asking if she might come and see her. "'All right,' I said. 'Come over to my place.' I thought that she was going to tell me, 'That's enough of that,' and that I should be more serious. But not at all. She said her mother was not very well looked after. She asked me, without mentioning anything to her mother, to come and take care of the household—the kitchen, the servants—and help look after Germaine herself. I told her that it was impossible, not for me—I would do it willingly—but for Germaine. It would kill her." Aury's voice rose as she told this story with great animation. "It would *kill* her."[41]

Jean Paulhan died in October 1968, at the age of eighty-three, and Dominique Aury's nightly vigil in the Neuilly clinic ended. Earlier that year, one of her best friends and her beloved father had died within days of each other. In 1970, her mother died. Germaine Paulhan lingered on for two more years. "During the last fourteen years, she had been increasingly paralyzed," Aury said. "It was horrible. Poor Germaine."

RETURN TO THE CHÂTEAU did not initially do well. *Elle* magazine considered publishing an extract but finally decided against it. A new wave of puritanism was sweeping France, and sales were disappointing. Grove picked up the American rights, once again harnessing the translating talents of Sabine d'Estrée, and published the book in 1971. Girodias, who had gone bankrupt, was out of the loop and increasingly frustrated. He was busy suing the French publisher at the time on the grounds that "Pauvert's treason, aided and abetted by that other scmuck [sic] Mr Rosset himself, was really too insolent and infamous to go unpunished."⁴²

While the commercial fortunes of the sequel may have been disappointing, a remarkable revival of the original took place a few years later. In 1974 a French film was made of O and a sudden burst of publicity sent public interest—and sales—soaring. The script, says Dominique Aury, was well done, but the direction and acting were terrible. The result was "*abominable*." Pauvert agrees: "It was a stupid film."

L'Express, France's leading weekly newsmagazine, did a cover story on the film and ran three consecutive extracts from the book. O took on a new lease of life by going into paperback for the first time and appearing in a book club edition. "We never sold so many copies," said Pauvert. "Nineteen seventy-four was the year of *Story of O.*"

O's revival generated a new interest in the book's author, and Aury was persuaded to come out of the shadows on two separate occasions. Her only condition was that her anonymity as "Pauline Réage" should be respected. The first interview, conducted by Jacqueline Demornex, ran in *Elle* in September 1974. The second was the result of an initiative by Jean-Jacques Servan-Schreiber, the founder, owner, and editor of *L'Express.* He suggested to Pauvert that an interview with the author of O should be done. Pauvert agreed and nominated his girlfriend, Régine Deforges, who was then an unknown journalist. She later became a prominent feminist, a writer of erotica and other fiction, and a publisher. Pauvert introduced Deforges to Aury, and the two women hit it off immediately.

The Demornex interview in *Elle* was as short as the Deforges discussion was long. In both, the author was remarkably candid and revealing. But after they were done, she retreated again, wrapping herself in a cocoon of silence for another twenty years.

Jacqueline Demornex, describing her first encounter with "Pauline Réage," said that she felt that she was in the presence of a nun. In the interview, the author elaborated on the difference between O and its sequel, *Return to the Château.* "I wanted to break [O's] world of fantasy, to see what was happening, to see if the story was becoming real. . . . It was a good way to show that the realization of a fantasy can only be disappointing."

Asked about her feelings of having produced a book that had had such an impact, she said that she believed all books of that kind—whatever their quality—provided a catharsis or purge for the reader.

Reading a fantasy such as O removed the need to live it. If the book was troubling to readers, if it produced an echo, it was because it had captured something that haunted them in their own psyches. "An author only transcribes what is already there," she said.

She said she fully approved of "free love." "Making love, in passing as it were, is fine. You cannot condemn that liberty. The men who despise women with whom they have slept are contemptible. The physical encounter between two human beings who desire each other is perhaps one of the rare things that makes life worth living. Life is . . . abominable. One goes from deception to deception, and when something good happens it invariably ends badly."

Her pessimism, she said, was based on her experience of treachery. She was not a jealous person, she stressed, but being betrayed by someone in whom you had total confidence was a terrible experience. This happened to her when she was very young and very much in love. "After that, nothing is the same," she said. "You do not say to yourself: 'The man in question did not love me,' but: 'Is *that* what love is all about?'"

Aury told Demornex that she had been truly in love three times in her life. There was a parallel between being in love and surviving a war. Time assumed a different quality; it was stolen time, a reprieve. And one's life was at risk. Echoing the fate of O, she said: "What is the end of love, if it is not death? To be no longer loved without reason . . . is the worst of punishments. Death is preferable."

Challenged on how many women found O's submission revolting, Aury defended herself by pointing out that O is always free to refuse such treatment. "I think that in all true passion, there is a quest for the absolute that can only be attained through a feeling of abandon, of a total dispossession of self. . . . Passion is a serious matter."[43]

The second interview, with Régine Deforges, produced a fascinating, freewheeling account that Pauvert published as a paperback, entitled *O m'a Dit* [*O Told Me*], in 1975. This was later published in the United States as *Confessions of O*. Once again, the author of O retained her anonymity as "Pauline Réage," saying that it was too late to reveal herself. "The images, the dreams have left me," she told Deforges. "I wrote for a man who is dead, and I will be dead soon."

Aury recalled reading classic works of erotica that she came across in her father's library when she was fourteen or fifteen years of age. She read *The Decameron, The Letters of a Portuguese Nun, Les Liaisons*

Dangereuses (her favorite), and other books. When her father found out, instead of punishing her, he explained the facts of life to her with elaborate diagrams. An older girlfriend then proposed a meeting with a male cousin who would give her a more practical demonstration. (Aury suspected her father was behind this proposal.) The cousin promised to show her everything but not to deflower her. A rendezvous was arranged and the encounter took place. The first sight of the young man's erect penis was a little frightening, she remembered, but that was offset by his inordinate pride in the instrument, which she thought rather comical. "As for all the fluids, sweat and mingled saliva, I did not find them very pleasant. Fortunately, there were towels, hot water, and eau-de-Cologne."[44]

As a young woman, she would walk along the Champs Elysées and sometimes flirt with a man if he took her fancy. On one occasion she actually picked up a good-looking man, and they starting seeing each other, meeting for a drink from time to time. At the third or fourth rendezvous, he suggested they should go to "a quiet little bar," which turned out to be a small hotel. They went to a room, and he embraced her and put his hand on her knee. At that moment he switched from addressing her with the formal *vous* to the more intimate *tu*. "I stood up, slapped his face, and left," she said. "I was indignant because he addressed me as *tu*."[45]

This reaction, she believed, proved to her that while she was capable of imagining virtually any scenario between a man and a woman, she was not able to put them into practice herself. The distinction between her dream world and the real one was clearly defined. She did not consider this either a logical or courageous situation, and it troubled her. But she learned to accept it.

Returning to the theme of O, she believed that many women have dreamed of being free to sleep with whomever they choose with the full approval of their partners, receiving total absolution. "In love, can liberty be anything else?" she asked. "He whom you love becomes your accomplice and you his. Faithfulness of the heart and freedom of the body, a miracle, the reconciliation of opposites. What a dream! I have always believed it is possible."[46]

O HAS BEEN much written and talked about since it first appeared. Peter Fryer, who wrote an excellent book on the British Museum's collection of erotica in the mid-1960s, placed O in its historical context: "Fifty years ago, *Histoire d'O* would have been relegated to the domain of sexual pathology. Today we can look more honestly into the human heart, for we know there are tendencies towards, and fantasies of, both cruelty and submission in 'normal' people. To read *Histoire d'O* is to become more understanding about some of the bypaths that love may legitimately take. Even for readers who have already come to terms with these aspects of themselves, it has an hallucinatory effect. At one level it is an erotic daydream transfigured by literary skill—notably by obsessive detail, Henry James's 'solidity of specification'—into something approaching genius. At a deeper level it is an allegory, chilling in its implications, of the human alienation to which we cling."[47]

Odile Hellier, not the model for O but the founder and owner of the Village Voice Bookshop in Paris, provides a feminist and personal view of *Story of O:* "I read the book in the 1960s between the sexual (the Pill) and the feminist revolutions. Today with 'political correctness,' the novel is viewed by hard-core feminists as a work of female masochism verging on pornography. At the time, however, I and my women friends saw the book differently.

"What impressed us was that the heroine, O, was not a passive lover or a victim. In traditional works of erotica, women performed acts imagined by their male lovers. But here O was the initiator, the one who controlled the imagination, enacting her *own* fantasies. She was daring and took responsibility for her perversity. The sacrificial aspects of her passion gave the story a sort of religious, mystical dimension that reminded me of other similar stories from the past, particularly those of religious mystics tortured by masochistic passions.

"Another element that we admired in *Story of O* was the style, the beautiful, composed, elegant sentences that raised the book to the level of true literature. What remains in my memory is a mysterious, mystical mood and a character who was ready to sacrifice herself out of a great passion.

"It is more difficult to see O's magic now because there is so much trash around. Everything was behind curtains then. Your imagination could roam. Now everything is open and the mind is tainted.

"I have not reread the novel and do not intend to. Of course, were I to read it now, I might see it differently. But I believe that when I first read the book my critical senses were freer, more open than they might be today. American feminism has left its mark on us, and it is difficult now to view erotica without the feminist spy in us passing judgment. But, in any case, literature is *not* real life, and I would rather preserve my first impressions."[48]

• • •

IN THE LATE 1980s Dominique Aury found herself short of money. She contacted Pauvert, who said he would try to sell the manuscript of *Story of O* for her. He, in turn, contacted a wealthy Swiss collector, who was interested in rare and unusual erotica. He had recently acquired De Sade's *120 Days of Sodom* and was reputed to have the best collection of unusual and high-quality erotica in Europe.

The collector wanted Aury's original handwritten manuscript, the typescript with Paulhan's editing suggestions and comments, some correspondence between the author and Paulhan concerning the book's publication, a letter from Pauvert explaining his role in the affair, and a letter from the author herself describing the background to the book. "We sold it all for quite a bit," Aury said, "for several hundred thousand francs."

"The total figure was well under one hundred thousand dollars," said Pauvert, who added that he had never seen the original handwritten manuscript of *O* before. "It was in Paulhan's possession until he died, and then, under his will, it was returned to Aury. It was, as she says in 'Une Fille Amoureuse,' written in school exercise books in pencil, a pile this high." He indicated with his hand. "A dozen or so, not very large—that's *Histoire d'O*."

Aury said the collector offered her an additional payment of thirty thousand francs [about $6,000] for her letter, which he said could be a single page. "I had never been paid so much in my whole life and never will again," she said with a laugh. "And since he was paying so much I wrote him three pages instead of one—ten thousand francs a page!" Not long after buying the manuscript, the collector died suddenly of what Pauvert called a "brutal, stupid illness." He was in his late fifties.[49]

NEITHER Dominique Aury nor Jean Paulhan was young when their love affair produced *Story of O*. Their common passions were books and passion itself. Their relationship underscored the centrality of love to life, the creative and destructive forces that passion can unleash, and the ease with which the human heart can be broken. Aury would never have written *O* if it had not been for her love of Paulhan. She had no pretensions to writing fiction, no feminist drive to break the mold. She was—and remains—an intensely private person.

Looking back, what does Dominique Aury think of the book she

wrote in another age? "C'était une lettre d'amour," she said forcefully. "Nothing else." And the scandalous side of O? "Much ado
about nothing," she said.

The dreams and the fantasies abandoned her long ago. The man
she wrote for has been dead for a quarter of a century. All that remains
of a great love, a driving passion, and the terrible fear of loss are words
on a printed page. The integrity of the book—Dominique Aury's
story indissolubly linked with Jean Paulhan's essay—has been respected, as was the integrity of their love affair, with her at his side as
he lay dying. The years pass, and Dominique Aury has no regrets as
her days and nights gather speed, taking her toward what she calls "a
great silence."

So, THAT IS the story of *Story of O.*

Or is it?

Is there, like the book itself, a second ending, another mystery?
After I had written this chapter, I tested it on a few knowledgeable
people. Most of them thought it had the ring of authenticity. But not
all. The doubters detected a wrong note, glass instead of crystal. I
thought I had come to the end of the trail, but their questions suggested that further investigation was necessary.

First, however, a point of clarification. The person I believed—and
still believe—is the author of O wears two masks. "Pauline Réage"
is one; "Dominique Aury" is the other. The calm, gray-eyed woman
who related her tale of passion and desperation has yet another persona, her true identity. She asked me not to reveal it, or the details
of her family, and this I agreed to do.

One of the earliest and most scholarly doubters of Dominique Aury's authorship of O was Dr. Eric John Dingwall. For many years
Dingwall was honorary curator of the Private Case, the British Museum's huge and once zealously guarded collection of erotica. From
the day that O was published to the day that he died over thirty years
later, Dingwall believed that the novel had been written by a man.

His most erudite challenge came from another Englishman, Owen
Holloway, who adored the book, researched its origins, and eventually met and became a friend of Aury, whom he was convinced was
the author. In a long and lively correspondence, Dingwall and Holloway fought the good academic fight, and, in my view, Holloway
emerged the victor. On one occasion Holloway, accompanied by his
wife, went on vacation with Dominique Aury in France, and she gave

him a signed copy of the original French edition of O, specially bound in red moroccan leather. This book is now in the British Library.

One of Holloway's most cogent arguments was an analysis of Dominique Aury's writing style, which he found to be quite distinctive in all her work, whether criticism, essays, or, in the case of O, fiction.[50] In contrast, the style of Jean Paulhan, who many people still think may have been the author or coauthor of O, is markedly different from that of the novel itself.

The other doubters fall into two categories. First, there are the people like Richard Seaver who were in Paris at the time of the book's appearance and, in one way or another, were closely connected to its publishing history. Second, there are the bibliophiles, collectors, dealers, and scholars who, although more distant, nevertheless have strong and informed opinions about the novel's origins.

The two schools are united by their rejection of conventional wisdom and by the nature of their apostasy. Neither group denies that Dominique Aury had a hand in writing O, particularly the early sequences. But they believe that she was not responsible for the whole of it and that the book was the work of at least two—possibly several—writers.

Richard Seaver read my draft carefully and commented: "Look, it's more complicated, more mysterious than you think. You have to ask yourself: 'Is Dominique Aury telling you the whole truth?' Her account of the book in 'A Girl in Love' is an idealized one; there is no reference, for example, to Paulhan's philandering. The origins of her pen name, Pauline Réage, are not as simple as she suggests. Was her handwritten manuscript—the one that her own publisher, Pauvert, had not seen until she sold it—written before or *after* the typescript that he published the book from in 1954?"

I asked Seaver if he could be more specific. He said he could not because he was "sworn to secrecy more than thirty years ago." He would need to talk to someone in Paris, "the person to whom I gave my word," before he could tell me more. "But Paulhan being dead," he added, "that makes it easier." (A clue or a snare?) I asked him about "Sabine d'Estrée," who I think is none other than himself. He smiled. "Sabine d'Estrée and the author are linked," he said. "Someone else, apart from Dominique Aury, was involved in writing *Story of O*."[51]

The second group of doubters is well represented by Clifford Scheiner of C. J. Scheiner Books in New York. Scheiner is in his early forties and has two lives. One is working as a physician in the emergency department of Kings County Medical Center, Brooklyn, which serves one of New York's worst combat zones. The other is nurturing his vast collection of "erotica, sexology and curiosa" as his weekly advertisement in *The New York Times Book Review* puts it.

Scheiner brings a scholarly interest to his book business, an approach that sometimes makes it hard for him to decide whether he is a collector or a dealer. He reads all his books, writes reviews, goes to auctions, and meets authors, publishers, and collectors. He once sold a rare and famous erotic work by an Italian Renaissance writer to the buyer of the O manuscript. Scheiner holds strong views on the novel's authorship:

"I believe that Dominique Aury wrote some of it, but that it was essentially a group effort with probably several people involved." He also believes that the novel was in part a roman à clef, that is, a story based on real people and real events. He theorizes, for example, that the artist Léonor Fini, whose masks Dominique Aury admired enough to place over O's head, and even Maurice Girodias, were models for various visitors to the "château in Roissy."

Scheiner said that several erotic works had been produced by a group of people who practiced what they wrote about. One example was Anaïs Nin, Henry Miller, and friends, who wrote erotica for hire as well as being regular practitioners. Another was the novel *L'Image* by the pseudonymous Jean de Berg, which was published in Paris shortly after *Story of O* and dealt with the same subject. The book was dedicated to "P.R." and contained a preface signed with the same set of initials.

Scheiner said Alain Robbe-Grillet, the French novelist and filmmaker, admitted to a mutual friend that his wife, Catherine, wrote *L'Image*. When I asked Dominique Aury about the preface, which most people assumed had been written by her, she laughed and said that Robbe-Grillet had written it himself and then signed it "P.R." as a joke. ("Jean de Berg" published another novel in the 1980s, and a female figure, dressed completely in black, with her face swathed in a black veil, was interviewed on French television as the author. This, once again, was Catherine Robbe-Grillet.)

I suggested to Scheiner that Dominique Aury's account of how and why she wrote O had been remarkably consistent over the years. He said he was not surprised. "Her story is consistent because it is the official line, and the more she repeats it the more consistent it becomes." Scheiner believes the group that put the book together, including Paulhan and Pauvert, agreed that Dominique Aury should be recognized as the sole author, thus allowing the other participants to fade into the background.[52]

W HOM TO BELIEVE? Was Dominique Aury telling the whole truth? Or has she been covering up for others all these years? Was Jean Paulhan more involved than he admitted? Does Jean-Jacques Pauvert, original publisher and guardian of the copyright, know more than he is telling? Were the events at the château infinitely more real than the dreams and fantasies of a single woman? Who is the mysterious "Sabine d'Estrée"?

I started with Sabine. Although originally a peripheral character in the story, she now seemed to hold the key to the mystery, assuming that Seaver was right. But if she were not Seaver himself, then who was she? Was she even a "she"? Was "Sabine" a pen name or a real one? How was she connected with Dominique Aury, who had said she knew nothing about the American translation of O or the identity of the translator?

The first step was some basic historical research. The most memorable d'Estrée in French history was Gabrielle d'Estrée, the beautiful mistress of Henri IV, who died in childbirth at the age of twenty-six. A famous painting of Gabrielle and her sister, seated in a bathtub, with Gabrielle tweaking her sibling's nipple, hangs in the Louvre. This picture is a favorite illustration among the compilers of anthologies of erotica. As for the first name, Sabine, it is unusual in any language but again evokes a well-known painting, *The Rape of the Sabine Women*. It also happens, as I had discovered, to be Jeannette Seaver's second name.

A helpful librarian culled every document in the Grove Press archives in the Special Collections Library of Syracuse University, New York, that had any connection between Grove and *Story of O*. He sent me a series of meaty packages, and in the first lay a small bombshell—a letter dated October 27, 1964, that began:

Dear Mr. Seaver:
    Thank you for the most pleasant lunch yesterday which I enjoyed more than I can say.
    I am also pleased to learn that you are happy with the translation of O, and I have been going through it since our conversation bearing in mind the suggestions you made. . . .

The letter went on to discuss the technical points of the translation, ending with "I agree with the *spirit* of simplicity which you emphasized, and hope I have attained it throughout." Then a paragraph about how all payments for the translation should be made—"sent to me c/o Mr. Seymour Litvinoff" (the same name and address on the letterhead) and made out to "*Seymour Litvinoff, as attorney.*" This point was stressed: "They should not merely be sent to him and made out to me, but actually made out to him as attorney." The letter ended:

> Please keep me apprised of publication plans, and let me know when
> I may expect to read galleys. Again, many thanks for your help.

The letter was signed: "Sabine," and typed underneath: "Sabine Destré."

A week later Seaver sent a Grove office memorandum to Judith Schmidt asking her to draw up a letter of agreement "between Grove and Sabine Destré" for the translation of *Story of O*. "Advance and all monies accruing should be sent to S.D. c/o Seymour Litvinoff, Esq." Sabine Destré wrote back to Judith Schmidt on December 9, 1964, saying that Seymour Litvinoff had instructed her to return one copy of the agreement "covering your use of my translation of *Story of O*." She asked to be kept informed about publication plans, saying that she understood the book would be published in the coming spring.

Was there a real Sabine after all? Why was her last name spelled differently? What was our old friend Si Litvinoff of *Candy* fame doing in this theater?

Sabine made a few more indirect appearances in the Grove material. To the question "Who is Sabine Destré?" from someone who was commissioned to write an introduction to the Grove edition of *O*, Seaver had replied: "Sabine Destré is the pseudonym of a young lady-translator whose translation, Pauvert has told us, the author particularly liked."[53]

When James Price of Secker & Warburg in London wrote to Seaver inquiring about the British rights to *O*, he requested information about the author. "Is she real?" he asked. Seaver responded obliquely: "As for the translator, she appears to be a friend of the author's (who herself remains unidentified, although rumors are rife)."[54]

After Grove published the novel, royalties began to flow in increasingly large amounts. At first Sabine's checks went to Seymour Litvinoff, but in 1967—two years after the book appeared—they were switched to Ronald S. Konecky, another Manhattan attorney. Between January 1967 and December 1969, Sabine received over $11,000, an unusually large sum of money for a translator in those days.

The professional relationship between Sabine Destré and Dick Seaver was a loyal and lengthy one that extended for at least fifteen years beyond the translation of *Story of O.* When Grove published the sequel, *Return to the Château,* in 1971, Sabine translated it. She also translated at least two other erotic works from the French originals. When Dominique Aury's conversations with Régine Deforges (*O m'a Dit*) appeared in an American version as *Confessions of O* in 1979, they were published as "A Seaver Book" by Viking Press and translated by Sabine d'Estrée. In other words, when Seaver moved publishing house, so did Sabine. There is no trace of Sabine doing translations for anyone but Seaver.

The two previous translators of *O,* Baird Bryant and Austryn Wainhouse, said they had no idea who had done the Grove version. Letters to the British and American translators' organizations drew blanks. A letter to Owen Holloway in London brought a reply from his wife with the news that he had suffered a stroke a year ago and was unable to "enter in any correspondence or help in any way."[55]

A meeting and correspondence with the Scottish writer and critic James Campbell, who covered similar ground in a book on expatriate writers in Paris in the 1950s, was helpful. He had interviewed the Seavers jointly in New York and discovered Jeannette's second name was Sabine. He suggested getting in touch with Patsy Southgate, a translator for Grove and the former wife of Peter Matthiessen, the American writer. Campbell said he had been told on "reliable authority" that Patsy Southgate was "Sabine d'Estrée." He also thought the style of the translator's introduction to *O* was "un-Seaverlike."[56]

I called Patsy at her home in the Hamptons, Long Island. "No, I did not translate *O,*" she said. "It was before my time, and I don't know who did it." She did, however, translate *L'Image* by Jean de Berg, which she thinks was written by Alain Robbe-Grillet and his wife, writing in tandem about their favorite subject.[57]

On to Los Angeles, where Seymour Litvinoff, former New York attorney and Terry Southern's one-time business manager, is a film producer. We talked a bit about Southern, and then I broached the subject of Grove, *O,* and Sabine. "I was Dick Seaver's lawyer in the 1960s, and a friend," he said, "and I set up the system of payments from Grove to Sabine Destré. The checks came to me. But I cannot say who Sabine is. I don't know who she is." Back to New York and on to Ronald S. Konecky, Esq., who declined to talk to me directly. "No, I am afraid that Mr. Konecky does not know where Sabine Destré is," his secretary said. "He suggests that you call Seymour Litvinoff in Los Angeles."[58]

Dominique Aury had mentioned that all she knew about the identity of the American translator of O was that it might have been the same person who had translated Charles de Gaulle's memoirs, an idea that both flattered and amused her. Richard Howard, award-winning American poet, translator, and teacher, translated many of De Gaulle's writings, and he discussed the matter on the telephone from Texas.

"I reviewed O for *Evergreen Review*," he said, "but I did not translate it. I don't know who Sabine is. It's a composite name most likely, and the translation was probably done by the Seaver crowd. Not Patsy Southgate? She did *L'Image*, which was definitely written by Alain Robbe-Grillet's wife."[59]

Back to Paris. I meet Dominique Aury at Gallimard's office, and we go around the corner to the Montalembert Café, which claims it dispenses "*charme et caractère*" with its refreshments; Dizzy Gillespie playing "My Heart Belongs to Daddy" on the sound system competes with what I hope will be new revelations about the mystery of O. We go over the now familiar ground, and I tell her about Seaver's reservations, that the story of the book is more complicated, more mysterious than it appears.

"It's nice of him to think so," she says with a smile, "but it's not. No one else was involved. Absolutely no one. Those small pages about how the book was written ["A Girl in Love"] are the pure truth. It's very amusing when you write the plain truth; people never believe it."

When I mention Seaver's doubts about the pseudonym Pauline Réage, Dominique Aury says she went to the *mairie* [town hall] in the small town where her father had a house in the countryside and looked at a map. There she found a place called "le Grand Réage," "a place of woods, meadows, and cultivated land." "Pauline," she insists, derived from two famous women—Pauline Borghese, Napoléon's beautiful and wayward sister, and Pauline Roland, a celebrated socialist and champion of women's rights in late-nineteenth-century France.

As for Sabine d'Estrée, she reiterates that she does not know who she is. The rumor about De Gaulle's translator rendering O into English appears to be just a rumor after all. "People will say anything," she comments, "as long as they find it funny or amusing or scandalous."

I pass on Scheiner's suggestion that she might have done the translation herself. "I'm a well-known translator, but no, I did not do my own book. Of course not. I translate English into French, but I don't translate French into English. It doesn't work both ways, it works just one way." When I press her for any other ideas, she says: "I thought that Sabine d'Estrée was Alain Robbe-Grillet's wife. That's what I thought, but I'm not sure. She was a lovely creature, Nabokov fell in love with her." Was she a translator? "Apparently. I heard it said, but I don't know. Alain wouldn't say anything, of course."

I tell her about crossing the path of Owen Holloway, his impassioned defense of her, and the leather-bound signed copy of O lying in state in the British Library's Private Case. She smiles again and produces a strange coda to a strange story. "By a curious coincidence," she says, "I knew his first wife—she was an Armenian woman who lived in Paris—long before I met him."[60]

I move on to Jean-Jacques Pauvert's subterranean office beneath the Librairie Palatine and opposite the massive pile of Saint Sulpice church. The French publisher is scornful of the doubters. "Seaver n'est évidemment au courant de rien [he is completely out of touch], and Scheiner is a mythomane [a mythmaker]. There is no question of there being more than one author of Story of O. As for Sabine d'Estrée, she had absolutely no contact with Dominique Aury, who does not know her. Nobody has ever seen her."

And Catherine Robbe-Grillet? "A good example!" Pauvert says dismissively. "O gave her the idea of writing an erotic book, but L'Image has none of the weight or quality of O. It had a false preface signed by Pauline Réage. I called the publisher of L'Image to protest. Robbe-Grillet did it. It shows you the climate of the time. . . . It would be quite normal for Seaver to be drawn into this.

"It is important to understand that Story of O was kept in a very small circle," Pauvert continues. "It was Dominique Aury, Jean Paulhan, and myself. The three of us had talked about the book for some time before it was published. It was a secret between us, and I had known Dominique Aury since 1942, twelve years before the book appeared. I recognized her style immediately when I first saw the manuscript. She is a great writer and absolutely uncopyable. . . . Paulhan said he could not write like that . . . his own style was quite different, very dry, ironic, he could not change it."

Pauvert stresses that it was equally important to understand the atmosphere of the times. "It was quite extraordinary and funny. When the book first appeared there was a scandal, but no one wanted to talk about it and we didn't sell many copies. After it won the Deux Magots prize, the word began to circulate among journalists and in literary circles but not, unfortunately for me, among the bookshops. There was much speculation about the author—that she was the celebrated Madame Louise de Vilmorin or none other than the wife of Edgar Faure, a government minister. But the secret was kept.

"As the atmosphere changed, people took a delight in claiming they had written O. One day in 1957 or 1958 my wife and I went on holiday and stopped in Chartres for dinner at a nice restaurant. At a table behind us there were five or six people, well dressed, in their late forties or early fifties, probably notables of the town, quite cultivated people, talking about books. Suddenly one of the men said: 'You must understand that since Paulette wrote *Histoire d'O* she has had a very difficult time, isn't that right, Paulette?' His wife, a good-looking woman, about forty-five years old, wearing a fine pearl necklace, replied: 'Yes, you know, it's been terrible for me because if I had known, what with my husband's position, it's absolutely terrible.' This seemed to be going on all over France. There were literally hundreds of people claiming to be the author of O."

Pauvert says it is quite possible that Seaver met someone in Paris's literary salons who told him that he or she was the author or coauthor of the book or that four or five people had written it. "But it wasn't us," he says. "There was one author—Dominique Aury—Paulhan, and me. That's all. I had never heard of Dick Seaver or Barney Rosset at that time, nor had Aury or Paulhan. I didn't meet them until the early 1960s, almost ten years after O was published. Even Girodias was not fully in the know. He knew Paulhan and thought the author was Dominique Aury, but that's all. Girodias's circle included Seaver and people like Austryn Wainhouse, but none of them knew who was the author of O."

Pauvert says it is quite normal for a publisher not to see the original manuscript of a book because he would expect to work from a clean typescript, which is what he did with O. When he finally saw the original, was he convinced it was genuine? "Ah yes, you would be convinced, too, if you saw it. It was on small square exercise books from that period, written in pencil, as she has said." He points out that Dominique Aury has a distinctive handwriting. "It would require an extraordinary forger to falsify that," he says with a laugh. "No, that's her manuscript. That's certain."

What, then, is the explanation? "I think it is probable from what I know of Dick Seaver that he is honest, believed something he heard, and gave his word in good faith," Pauvert concludes. And Scheiner's doubts? "That's Scheiner, he always thinks there are secret societies, groups of people doing things, and so on."[61]

LATER, in New York, I talked with Judith Schmidt (now Judith Douw), who had worked with Rosset and Seaver at Grove Press. She said her "gut reaction" was that Sabine d'Estrée was Seaver but that she could not be absolutely sure. Georges Borchardt, a veteran New York literary agent who represented the author and the French publisher of O for thirty years, was more emphatic. "Sabine d'Estrée," he said, "is Dick Seaver."[62]

When I reported back to Seaver, he said that he had been in touch with Sabine d'Estrée, who "lives in France," but she had not released him from his vow of silence. She was "a very shy, secretive person," he explained. She had, however, agreed to write me a letter establishing her identity. I am still waiting for the letter.

AFTER THAT the trail goes cold, unless Dick Seaver or someone else warms it up again. Does the story of Story of O have a second ending after all? I think not. I believe that Dominique Aury was the sole author and the novel was conceived, born, nurtured, and took its place in literary history the way she and her publisher have described.

That leaves the elegant little mystery of "Sabine d'Estrée." If money were to be wagered, I would place mine unequivocally on the Seavers, even if it means accepting that Dick took himself—or Jeannette—out to lunch in the autumn of 1964, wrote a "thank-you letter" the following day, and laid an elaborate paper trail to confuse aspiring literary sleuths.

11

What William Burroughs Saw on the End of His Fork

IN JANUARY 1958 a tall, spectral figure dressed in a gray suit and a gray hat checked into a seedy hotel without a name in rue Gît-le-Coeur, not far from the offices of the Olympia Press in the Latin Quarter. The hotel in this dank, narrow street, which runs down to the quai des Grands Augustins on the Seine from the rue Saint André des Arts, was owned and run by a minute but redoubtable lady called Madame Rachou.

She rented out rooms, often in an arbitrary fashion (not every applicant would be accepted), to a colorful collection of painters and prostitutes, jazz musicians and petty criminals, poets and hustlers, writers and junkies. The building creaked with age. Sparsely furnished rooms shared their secrets through thin walls, the smell of cooking and toilets (the Turkish hole-in-the-ground squat that France has never entirely abandoned) impregnated the fabric of the building, and the plumbing had a life of its own. From its clientele the establishment had acquired a reputation as a cheap, convenient, and tolerant flophouse, and a name—The Beat Hotel.

The stranger liked the place. "The room smelled of dust and Gauloise cigarettes, and you could do pretty much what you wanted, nobody bothered you," one of his biographers later wrote. "Nobody came bursting in *pour faire la chambre;* they didn't care whether they made the chamber or not. You could paint on the walls and bring your own furniture in, and in the bar, a glass of wine was cheaper than a cup of coffee." Madame Rachou dispensed both from the zinc-topped counter, standing on an overturned wine crate.[1]

The thin, ghostly figure was William Burroughs, scion of the American adding machine family, drug addict and experimenter extraordinary, homosexual, and writer-in-the-making. Although he had not yet met Girodias, his *Naked Lunch* manuscript had already been seen—and rejected—by the publisher. A year earlier, while Burroughs was still living in Tangier, Allen Ginsberg, his friend, literary mentor, and reluctant lover, had taken it to Girodias. This was the first step toward the publication of what is probably the best novel ever to be written about drug addiction and the launching of Burroughs as one of the most original and innovative writers of the second half of the twentieth century.

Girodias recalled his first sight of the manuscript that Gregory Corso had suggested Ginsberg try out on the publisher.

"One rainy day—in the spring of 1957, I believe—Allen Ginsberg brought in a rather bulky, pasted-up manuscript and declared that it was a work of genius such as I could never hope to find again in my publisher's life. William Burroughs, the author, was then living in Tangiers and this first full-length book of his was made of jigsaw illuminations harvested in the course of fifteen years of drug addiction.

"It was a brilliant, completely iconoclastic work, but I gave it back to Allen after a few days of reflection with the philistine remark that the material was wonderful but it would be inaccessible to the lay reader due to the deliberate lack of any rule whatsoever in the organization of the text."[2]

"That manuscript didn't make much sense, it was in such a state of disrepair, eaten away by the rats, it was completely dilapidated . . . unreadable, collages, bits and snatches, and any publisher has a tendency to reject a manuscript which looks that way, because it indicates all kinds of perverse instability—you can smell trouble. . . . there's a lack of discipline—I saw some brilliant pieces, but it didn't look like a book, so I asked Allen if he could help Burroughs put it into shape. I said I would be glad to read it again.

"That took a long time and finally he came back with a tidy manuscript which I read and it was unquestionably a work of genius, and

I thought it should be published right away. Then it happened very fast because I work very fast, always trying to stay one step ahead of the censors—publish fast and sell fast."[3]

Terry Southern had a much racier version of how *Naked Lunch* came to be published. One day, he says, Corso came up to Mason Hoffenberg and himself as they were having their morning cup of coffee at the Café Saint Germain des Prés. Corso "plopped a manuscript down and said in his usual gross manner, 'Now dig this.'

"It turned out that the ms was, of all things, *Naked Lunch*. It seems that Burroughs had given it to Allen Ginsberg and he had given it to Gregory. Mason and I set out to convince Gid that it was worthy of his distinguished imprimatur.

"His [Girodias's] first response was to leaf through it impatiently. 'There's no fucking in the book,' he said. 'No sex at all in the book.'

"We pointed out something on page seventeen.

"'Ah, yes!' he said triumphantly. 'All the way to page seventeen! And still it's only a blow job!'"

Girodias, said Southern, then showed them some letters from Olympia Press loyalists pleading for books that were "brutally frank" or "frankly explicit."

"'Can we truly recommend such a work as this to these readers? And the title is no good. What does it mean, this *Naked Lunch*?'

"I told him that Jack Kerouac had suggested the title, hoping that might impress him. But Mason had the right idea: he said that it was American slang for sex in the afternoon.

"Gid brightened somewhat. 'Ah, *comme notre cinq-à-sept!*' he declared, referring to the cherished French tradition of having sex (with a mistress, of course) every day from five to seven P.M.

"'No, this is more like an orgy,' he was told.

"And eventually he came around.

"I have read, God (certainly) knows, other accounts of how this great milestone book came into print, but the actual facts are those above. The scary thing about it is that Girodias could have as easily remained adamant."[4]

What did Gregory Corso think? "No way! It was me and Ginsberg—it's all bullshit, they had nothing to do with *Naked Lunch*. Ask Allen, he'll tell you. Allen knows, Allen doesn't bullshit. . . . To me that was Girodias's big number because nobody would publish that book. It's amazing when you look at it today and you wonder why not? I mean what's so outrageous about the son of a bitch?"[5]

Each account contains omissions, inaccuracies, and embellishments, as well as truth. Ginsberg took the manuscript to Girodias in the autumn—not the spring—of 1957 and had it rejected for several reasons. Girodias clearly did not see any commercial possibilities for the book. The sexual content, as Southern pointed out, was sparse. It was also largely homosexual, which was not Girodias's stock in trade, although he did have some homosexual books on his list, most notably those of Jean Genet. And even the homosexual passages were not particularly arousing. "It was emetic rather than erotic," Burroughs biographer Ted Morgan notes.[6]

Naked Lunch was—and remains—a difficult book to read. Burroughs's erratic, plotless, flow-of-consciousness technique was one thing. But Girodias also had to contend with a bedraggled typescript that had spent a rough summer in Ginsberg's rucksack while he was traveling in Spain and Italy, and that still needed considerable editing. Moreover, Ginsberg's boundless enthusiasm for the work was probably counterproductive. By the late 1950s Girodias was well known as a receptive avant-garde publisher and was used to hearing extravagant claims about new writers, whose manuscripts piled up in the offices of the Olympia Press.

With the advantage of hindsight, it is easy to blame Girodias for being insensitive and rejecting a work of talent. But it would have been an unusually brave and perceptive publisher to take on *Naked Lunch* in those repressive days. Ginsberg knew that no one else was interested in publishing the book. Hence his disappointment when Girodias, his last hope, turned it down.

After Girodias's rejection, the manuscript languished for a while. Then, in April 1958, Ginsberg sent it to Lawrence Ferlinghetti's City Lights Books in San Francisco, but it was again rejected, reportedly because it was "disgusting."[7] Ginsberg turned to Irving Rosenthal, the editor of *The Chicago Review,* and sent him eighty pages of the book. Rosenthal wanted to publish it, but the University of Chicago authorities objected.

"Rosenthal . . . was really the only editor who understood what I was doing," Burroughs recalled. "And then *The Chicago Review* folded out from under him, and me. . . . About the same time I was announced in the *Nation* as an international homo and all-round sex fiend. . . . I wrote to Paul Bowles [in Tangier]: 'It looks like *Naked Lunch* is finished. I have no idea if it will ever be published in a complete form. Complications and the manuscript scattered all over Europe.'"[8]

Rosenthal responded to the ban on Burroughs and others in the pages of *The Chicago Review* by resigning and launching a new magazine called *Big Table,* again a name suggested by Jack Kerouac, who had a knack for titles. The first issue appeared in March 1959 with ten episodes from Burroughs's book, a piece by Kerouac, three of Gregory Corso's poems, and much of the other material that had been planned for *The Chicago Review*. An American flag adorned the cover.

Big Table might have slipped quietly into the overcrowded graveyard of little magazine history if it had not been for two events, one planned, the other serendipitous. The Shaw Society of Chicago sponsored a poetry reading to raise money for the new magazine and invited Ginsberg and Corso to read their poems. On arrival, the poets were surprised to see that the Chicago press was running stories about the beatniks invading the city. *Time* magazine also ran a story on the "invasion." "We'd done readings before," Ginsberg remembered, "but this was the biggest reading I ever had. Oh, and also a heroic reading. . . . It was a classic reading, exalted."[9]

The second event was the seizure of several hundred copies of the first issue by the Chicago postal authorities. The rest of the ten thousand copies were sent by road to New York and San Francisco, where, due to the publicity generated by the poetry reading and the impounding, they rapidly sold out. "Thanks to the stir, Burroughs found a following, and *Naked Lunch* became a desirable literary property," writes Ted Morgan.

But not desirable enough to seduce publishers in the United States or Britain. Once again it was the well-dressed, urbane Monsieur Girodias who stuck his neck out and made a firm decision. Intrigued by the impact of this "new literary phenomenon" in *Big Table,* Girodias asked Ginsberg to resubmit the manuscript, which had been added to, edited, and made more presentable. "I had been ready to run away . . . ," Girodias wrote later, "but on re-reading the definitive version of his book, I had become a fan, a convert. And, once again, a committed publisher."[10]

Ginsberg took Burroughs to see his new publisher in the rue Saint-Séverin office. Girodias remembered it being "a spring day with people already in shirt-sleeves, even shorts. Burroughs appeared dressed in a kind of old gaberdine the colour of a wall, a frigid air, his head covered with an ageless felt hat, everything rotted by the rigours of the weather. He looked like an American gentleman of good family who had fallen on hard times.

"But, behind this crumbling rampart, there is the world of the *Naked Lunch,* the last frontier, the horrible quintessence of our universe . . . the drug of drugs. . . . It is the *Chanson de Roland* of the 20th century, the cry of the hero who is prepared to die in full ecstasy!"[11]

Girodias paid Burroughs a flat fee of $800 for the book, the standard rate for DBs in the late 1950s, and ordered the usual print run of five thousand copies. *Naked Lunch* duly appeared in July 1959 as Number 76 of Olympia's Traveller's Companion Series. The book was to prove to be a watershed in Burroughs's life and a literary beacon in the landscape of fiction. For the time being, however, the forty-four-year-old author's life remained in its well-worn groove. As *Naked Lunch* was about to appear, Burroughs was busted.

"Eight am. tap, tap, tap. They had an order for my arrest issued April 9th. I wonder who grassed? Spent a horrible junk-sick day in vast Kafkian building while they typed out forms and took my picture, and when they went off to develop the picture there was nothing on the plate. . . . Not for nothing am I known as 'The Invisible Man.' Three tries and two hours before they got a picture. The machine was broken or something. Twelve hours in the fucking joint. . . . All they were looking for was pot. Didn't even mention the word junk."[12]

FOR A MAN who was later to earn the nickname "El Hombre Invisible," William Seward Burroughs II had remarkably solid beginnings. He was born in 1914 in St. Louis, Missouri, and his paternal grandfather was the inventor of the adding machine. Burroughs's mother, who came from a Southern family, was a cold, distant woman who had a Victorian distaste for any manifestation of the bodily functions. Burroughs's father was warmer and possessed a mordant sense of humor, which the boy inherited. The couple got on well apparently, and William and his older brother, Mortimer, led a conventional, well-to-do American childhood in the country's heartland.

But Burroughs did not fit in. He says he was "shy and awkward and at the same time furtive and purposeful." Others recognized the outsider quality. A St. Louis patriarch said he did not want the young Burroughs in his house again because he looked like "a sheep-killing dog," and a matron from the same elite described him as "a walking corpse." Burroughs also says he knew from an early age that he was homosexual.[13]

The conventional path led Burroughs through Harvard and Columbia universities, but there it ended. Henceforth, he would pursue his own strange destiny. The new road would take him through drug

addiction, marriage, fatherhood, an accidental killing, countless foreign places, and a long, painful apprenticeship as a writer. William
Burroughs's final destination, ironically, would be the American
plains, where his journey had begun. But he would return as a different man, *un hombre transformado,* a legendary veteran of the Beat
Generation, a famous writer, and a mythic cult figure who had also
been elected to the American Academy and Institute of Arts and Letters. In the small college town of Lawrence in Kansas, William Burroughs would rest the body, the mind, and the spirit that had been
the collective object of a lifetime's experiment. That experiment had,
in turn, expressed itself in a unique corpus of writing.

Two stops along the way held a special significance. The first was
Tangier, where *Naked Lunch* slowly took shape, and the second was
Paris, where the novel was published. When Burroughs arrived in the
North African city in January 1954, he was leaving behind his Beat
friends Allen Ginsberg, Jack Kerouac, Neal Cassady, Gregory Corso,
and many others. He also left behind his wife, Joan Vollmer. He had
shot and accidentally killed her in Mexico City, when, in a drunken
game of William Tell, he fired a fraction lower than he should have
done and fatally missed the glass balanced on her head.

He left behind his young son, Billy, addicted from birth. Billy was
destined to live erratically and to die tragically at the age of thirty-
three, drunk in a ditch, his transplanted liver soused in alcohol. Burroughs also left behind his first published novel, *Junkie: Confessions of
an Unredeemed Drug Addict,* an account of his addiction in the United
States and Mexico, written in a laconic, deadpan style.

When Burroughs stepped ashore in Tangier, he brought with him
a heavy drug habit, a consuming passion for boys, a $200 monthly
allowance paid by his parents, and an unruly collection of notes, letters, short stories, and other fragments of fiction.

Tangier stands on low hills on the northwestern tip of the African
continent, overlooking both the Mediterranean Sea and the Atlantic
Ocean. When Burroughs arrived, the city was still under the international control of eight European nations and the United States. It
had three official languages (French, Spanish, and Arabic), two cur-
rencies (French franc and Spanish peseta), and no taxes or customs
duties of any kind. It was a city of gleaming white houses, mosques
and minarets, dusty palm trees, pungent souks, and open-air cafés.
Tangier's climate, moderated by the two seas, was pleasant, its cosmopolitan inhabitants tolerant, and the cost of living seductively low.

Tangier suited Burroughs well. "He caught at once the special character of the city, its quality of exemption," Ted Morgan writes. "It was exempt from every interference. There was no pressure of any sort to curtail private behavior. Hard drugs were routinely sold over the counter. Kif and hashish were openly smoked in little clay pipes with wood stems. Boys were so plentiful you had to fight them off. Here at last was the sanctuary of complete noninterference he had sought in his wanderings. The cop stood there with his hands behind his back, a benign and unthreatening presence. In Morocco, no stigma was attached to homosexuality. . . . Tangier was also a place where magic was part of daily life, where sorcerers mixed love potions and poisons, where members of secret brotherhoods went into trances and cast spells."[14]

Burroughs rented a room and gravitated to Tangier's abundant and colorful lowlife. He was not invited to Barbara Hutton's casbah castle nor was he inducted into the social whirl presided over by David Herbert (self-exiled second son of the Earl of Pembroke and Tangier's self-styled "queen mother"), who lived in the pretty bougainvillea-clad village of Djamaa el Mokra that looks down over the city. And he did not get to know, as soon as he would have wished, the man and writer he most admired in Tangier: Paul Bowles.

Burroughs was taken to see Bowles shortly after he arrived in the city, but the meeting did not go well. To Bowles, the newcomer seemed "rather grey and insubstantial, as though flickering in and out of focus," Ted Morgan relates. "He looked furtive, like someone being questioned at a police station. Perhaps it was the drugs he was taking." Burroughs, for his part, felt snubbed. He wrote to Ginsberg describing Bowles as "a shameless faker." And to Kerouac he reported: "The one time I met Paul Bowles he evinced no cordiality. Since then he has made no effort to follow up the acquaintance. . . . He invites the dreariest queens in Tangier to tea but has never invited me, which, seeing how small the town is, amounts to a deliberate affront."[15]

An old friend, Gavin Young, invited me to come to Tangier, and he took me round to the undistinguished modern apartment building where Bowles had lived for twenty-five years. A maid opened the door and showed us into a shadowy, airless interior. The hall was full of trunks and old leather suitcases, lined up as if ready for a long voyage, waiting for the driver to take them down to the car. We went through the living room into a small bedroom that had the cluttered appearance of a secondhand bookshop.

Bowles was recovering from a long bout of sciatica. He was silver-haired, frail, and tired-looking and lay propped up on pillows on a narrow bed. The curtain was drawn across the only window in the room. Light came from a single source: a clip-on, angle-poise lamp fastened onto the bedside table and turned to shine on the wall behind the bed. The wind roared and rattled outside, where, we knew, the sun was shining with an early autumn brilliance. But Paul Bowles's bedroom could have been in midwinter Lapland or the gloom of the Amazon rain forest. Or anywhere.

Gavin Young, who had known Bowles for some time, made the introductions, handed him a box of his favorite corn flakes, and left. We shook hands. Bowles wore a large signet ring on the little finger of his right hand, enhancing the impression of a streak of traditionalism in this rather patrician-looking man who had led anything but a conventional life.

"Few people wanted to meet Burroughs when he first came to Tangier," Bowles said. "My wife, Jane, called him 'Morphine Minnie.' She didn't like him and thought the police were after him and that he spelt trouble. But she grew to accept him. Brion Gysin, the painter, did not want to meet him either, but I thought they would hit it off, and, when I got them together, they did."

Bowles got to know and like Burroughs. He particularly liked his directness and humor. "Bill could be very funny," Bowles said, adjusting his pillows. "Once he came to dinner with us and had just been to the funeral of the owner of a popular bar—the Parade—who had dropped dead in his own bar. Burroughs, who always looked like an undertaker anyway, put down his furled umbrella, took off his gloves, and said in his Midwestern drawl: 'Well, Paul, you've just missed a very good funeral.'"[16]

The humor helped cement the friendship. Burroughs himself mentioned one incident that moved things along. "I am having tea with Paul Bowles and he is entertaining this grim, rich American woman. So I was talking about Yage [a South American plant with hallucinogenic properties], knocked out on gage and lush, and she says, 'How long does it take to rot you?' and I said: 'Lady, you should live so long,' and she left the room. So I thought that finishes me with Bowles, but nothing of the sort. He had been amused apparently. And I have seen him twice since, and dig him like I never dig [*sic*] anyone that quick before. Our minds similar, telepathy flows like water. I mean there is something portentously familiar about him, like a revelation."[17]

As Burroughs's friendship with Bowles slowly strengthened, most of his time was occupied with sex and drugs and, when he had the time and energy, writing. He had a regular boyfriend, a Spanish youth of eighteen named Kiki, and he had found a new drug, a German-made synthetic morphine called Eukodol, which he could buy with his parents' allowance over the counter.

"[It was] the best junk he had ever had," writes Ted Morgan. "The manufacturer, having discovered that it had a side effect of euphoria, stopped making it, but there was still a supply in Tangier, which Burroughs proceeded to exhaust. At first, he shot Eukodol every four hours, then he narrowed it down to two. Between shots, he felt the gravity pull of junk in his cells. When he looked at himself in the mirror, he seemed almost transparent, his body pared down to bone and muscle. He looked down at his dirty trousers which he had not changed in weeks. His life had but a single purpose: Eukodol."[18]

Burroughs himself described the daily routine and the difficulty of getting down to work. "All day I had been finding pretexts to avoid work, reading magazines, making fudge, cleaning my shotgun, washing the dishes, going to bed with Kiki, tying the garbage up in neat parcels and putting it out for the collector . . . buying food for dinner, picking up a junk script. So finally I say: 'Now you must work . . .' and smoke some tea and sit down and out it comes all in one piece like a glob of spit. . . . Sometimes I'd try to write sitting at a café and it would turn out like this: 'Sitting in front of the Café Central in the Spring like, rainy sunshine. Sick. Waiting for my Eukodol. A boy walks by and I turn my head, following his loins like a lizard turns its head to follow the course of an ant.'"[19]

Yet, somehow, Burroughs managed to write. He went on and off drugs; kept up a regular correspondence, especially with Ginsberg; paid a visit to the United States, where Ginsberg, Kerouac, and other friends read his material and encouraged him to keep going; he went to Venice to see friend and fellow writer Alan Ansen, who was to prove to be an invaluable editor and critic; and took the cure in London, where he was treated with apomorphine, a morphine derivative, that was to keep him off drugs for a time. It was on one of his trips to London that he was interrogated by suspicious immigration officials at the airport.

"And why have you come to England, Mr. Burroughs?" he was asked.

"For the food and the weather," Burroughs drawled without missing a beat.

During his worst addiction, Bowles paid Burroughs a visit. "He was living down in the medina, in a brothel. He lay in bed all day, shot heroin, and practised sharpshooting with a pistol against the wall of his room. I saw the wall, all pockmarked with bullet holes. I said to him, 'Why are you shooting your wall, Bill?' He said, 'It's good practice.'"[20]

By 1957 Burroughs had something resembling a manuscript, and Paul Bowles remembers visiting him again in a small hotel called the Villa Muniria. "It was the dirtiest place I had ever seen," said Bowles. "'What's all this paper on the floor, Bill?' I asked. 'It's my new work,' he said. He told me it was all right to leave it there. There were hundreds of pages of yellow foolscap all over the floor covered with footprints, bits of old cheese sandwiches, rat droppings—it was filthy. When he finished a page he'd just throw it on the floor. He had no copies and when I asked him why didn't he pick it up, he said it was OK, it would get picked up one day."[21]

The day came in the spring of 1957 when the Beats, en masse, arrived in Tangier, drawn there apparently by osmosis rather than invitation. Kerouac was the first on the scene, followed by Ginsberg and his new lover, Peter Orlovsky, and finally Alan Ansen came over from Venice to join what Ted Morgan calls "this writers' equivalent of a quilting bee." Slowly and laboriously they plowed through three years of Burroughs's work. Ansen, who had performed a similar task with W. H. Auden's writings, worked "like a great professional pedantic scholar with an unruly library full of dignified ancient manuscripts," according to Ginsberg. Two months later they had produced their quilt, a typed manuscript two hundred pages long.[22]

The main problem, Ginsberg said, was whether to give the book, which had no plot, a linear shape or try to blend all the separate incidents together. "I couldn't solve that problem nor did Kerouac try, and Burroughs didn't seem to have the inclination to judge that kind of stuff—he was producing more all the time." It was a problem that would remain unsolved until the manuscript's second submission to Girodias. Burroughs then voluntarily shifted some of the material around, and the French printers, who did not understand English, involuntarily shifted quite a lot more. This curious process seemed to

work and gave the novel what Ginsberg calls "a very beautiful structure . . . with a beginning and an end that act like a parenthesis enclosing the chameleon-like changes in the middle."[23]

Burroughs kept on writing during the summer of 1957, the words
pumping out of him whether he was in Copenhagen, in France, in
Spain, in Tangier, or somewhere in between. He continued to write
to Ginsberg, discussing the problems of the novel and asking his advice. In September he wrote about the book's central theme: "I am
working on Benway and Scandinavia angles, also developing a theory
of morphine addiction. . . . Incidentally, this theory resulted from the
necessities of the novel. That is, scientific theories and the novel are
inseparable. What I am evolving is a general theory of addiction which
expands into a world picture with concepts of good and evil."

He also passed on some tragic news about his Spanish boyfriend,
Kiki, who had taken up with the male leader of an all-female Cuban
orchestra. "Poor Kiki was murdered last week in Madrid by that shit
of a Cuban singer. Seems the frantic old fruit found Kiki [in bed] with
a girl and stabbed him in the heart with a kitchen knife. Then he
attacked the girl but the nabors rushed in and the Cuban took off,
but was shortly afterwards detained by the Civil Guard."[24]

A month later Burroughs wrote again to Ginsberg with more news
of the novel but also a curious personal revelation that had sprung
from the writing. "I feel myself closer and closer to resolution of my
queerness which would involve a solution of that illness. For such it
is, a horrible sickness. At least in my case. I have just experienced
emergence of my non-queer persona as a separate personality. This
started in London where in dream I came into room to see myself
not a child but adolescent, looking at me with hate. So I said, 'I don't
seem to be exactly welcome,' and he say: 'Not welcome!!! I hate you!'

"And with good reason too. Suppose you had kept a non-queer
boy in a strait-jacket of flesh twenty-five years subject to continual
queer acts and talk? Would he love you? I think not. Anyhoo, I'm
getting to know the kid, and we get on better. I tell him he can take
over anytime, but there is somebody else in this deal not yet fully
accounted for and the kid's not up to deal with him, so I hafta stay
around for the present. Actually, of course the kid and all the rest of
us have to arrange *a merger. A ver.*"

Burroughs ended with a postscript. "Did I tell you about the rat
who was conditioned to be queer by the shock and cold water treatment every time he makes a move at a female? He says: 'Mine is the
love that dare not squeak its name.'"[25]

A brief note followed near the end of the work on the novel and Burroughs's time in Tangier. "I do nothing but work. . . . Given up liquor entirely. Writing the narrative now, which comes in great hunks faster than I can get it down. Changes in my psyche are profound and basic. I feel myself not the same person. I am about ready to leave Tangier. I really can't seem to interest myself in boys any more. Love to all."[26]

THE PUBLICATION OF *Naked Lunch* by the Olympia Press in 1959 lifted Burroughs out of obscurity. He joined his Beat Generation friends Ginsberg, whose poem *Howl* had been published in 1956, and Kerouac, whose novel *On the Road* appeared in 1957, in the public limelight, where the trio were hailed as the new heroes of the literary underground. Burroughs, however, was too much of an outsider to join his friends on the highly exposed Beat trail and instead concentrated on his writing.

In any case, fame and its twin, notoriety, did not come immediately. Olympia Press books were rarely reviewed, and Burroughs had to wait for almost three years for serious and widespread critical attention. Girodias sold the American rights of *Naked Lunch* to Barney Rosset of Grove Press in November 1959, not long after the novel's Paris debut. But Rosset did not publish it until 1962 because he had his back up against the wall defending *Tropic of Cancer* in lawsuits all over the United States.

After Rosset bought *Naked Lunch,* he had ten thousand copies printed, but they sat in a warehouse as the lawyers wrangled over Miller's book, which Girodias's father had first published in Paris almost thirty years earlier. Anticipating substantial American royalties from *Naked Lunch,* Girodias urged Rosset to publish the novel and complained bitterly over the delays. The irony was that, at Rosset's behest, Girodias had been instrumental in persuading Miller to let Grove publish *Tropic of Cancer* in the United States, and now the success of his efforts seemed to be working against him. But Rosset was adamant. He could not afford to fight on two fronts at once. And if he lost with Miller, who was well known and had plenty of support, he would undoubtedly go down with the unknown Burroughs.

Rosset said he loved Burroughs's novel and was eager to publish it: "I think *Naked Lunch* is one of the great books of the twentieth century. Dr. Benway, for instance, the madness of that character, he is one of the unforgettable characters of modern literature. I think the novel has changed the language, the way of writing, and the way of looking at things."

And the author? "Burroughs is a very dry, very withdrawn person. Unfriendly on the surface, he is extremely intelligent and sharp and witty. He wasn't a [rodent] exterminator for nothing, and now he shoots holes in his paintings."[27]

While *Naked Lunch* languished in an American warehouse, its author received valuable exposure in a most unlikely place: Scotland. John Calder, the British publisher, invited Burroughs to join a group of American writers consisting of Mary McCarthy, Henry Miller, and Norman Mailer to the Edinburgh Festival of 1962. Among the other writers was another Olympia author and drug experimenter, Alexander Trocchi, who abandoned his many aliases and appeared as his combative and charming self. The gathering gave Burroughs an unprecedented platform for his ideas and work. It also evoked praise for *Naked Lunch*—still unknown to most people—from Mary McCarthy, who liked the novel.

After the Edinburgh Festival, Rosset decided to release *Naked Lunch* from captivity and distribute it. *Tropic of Cancer* was still in the courts, but the publicity from Edinburgh and assurances from Rosset's lawyer, Edward de Grazia, convinced the publisher that the time had come. The book sold quickly and was extensively reviewed. But in January 1963, three months after it appeared in the bookshops, it ran afoul of the law in Boston. The novel was judged obscene, and another long legal battle began. The following year Grove won the case for *Tropic of Cancer* in the United States Supreme Court but lost the obscenity prosecution over *Naked Lunch* in Massachusetts in 1965. De Grazia, however, took the case to the state's highest court and won it with a definitive ruling in 1966 that effectively ended literary censorship in the United States.

In Britain John Calder took the lead in 1963 by publishing a compendium of some of Burroughs's work that included material from *Naked Lunch* and was called *Dead Fingers Talk*. A lively literary debate ensued but the book was not prosecuted, so, having successfully tested the waters, Calder went ahead and published *Naked Lunch* in 1964.

The legal problems in the United States did not impede the book's literary trajectory. The quality of the reviews and the literary weight of the people who wrote them rapidly confirmed the book's status. Mary McCarthy's long review, perfectly timed in the inaugural issue of *The New York Review of Books* three months after *Naked Lunch* first appeared, fueled the novel's liftoff more powerfully than any other.

While noting a parallel between Burroughs and Jonathan Swift, Mary McCarthy stressed the book's originality, although she accepted that parts of the novel could bore and disgust the reader. "The literary notion of time as simultaneous, a montage, is not original with Burroughs; what is original is the scientific bent he gives it and a view of the world that combines biochemistry, anthropology, and politics. . . . This must be the first space novel, the first serious piece of science fiction—the others are entertainment." She also praised Burroughs's humor as being "peculiarly American, at once broad and sly."[28]

Newsweek wrote that *Naked Lunch* was "indeed a masterpiece, but a totally insane and anarchic one."[29] Novelist Herbert Gold felt that Burroughs's literary technique would remind readers of "Villon and Corbière, the gasping, torrid Celine and the furious Swift, Alfred Jarry and Jean Genet. . . . At best, this book, which is not a novel but a booty brought back from a nightmare, takes a coldly implacable look at the dark side of our nature."[30] Paul Bowles liked it, read it three times, and commented that he thought Burroughs was the greatest American humorist.[31]

At the Massachusetts obscenity trial, the novel's social importance was also expounded. Dr. Paul Hollander, a Harvard sociologist, testified that *Naked Lunch* "confronts the reader with the reality and consequences of drug addiction . . . without trivializing or softening them. . . . The book is important not only because drug addiction is sociologically important but because Burroughs succeeds in demonstrating the impoverished social relationships of the addict as well as the interconnections between addiction and other deviant behaviour, especially homosexuality. Burroughs' observations and information about drug addiction correspond to the scientific data on the subject."[32]

But for every favorable review came a hostile one. Critic George Steiner called the novel "a strident bore, illiterate and self-satisfied right to its heart of pulp."[33] The most extreme and damaging attack was a blast of vitriol from *Time* magazine that took aim at Burroughs himself: "He is not only an ex-junky but an ex-con and a killer. In Mexico, having acquired a wife, he shot her between the eyes playing William Tell with a revolver. . . . He has even been in the army but not for long; he reacted to being drafted by cutting off a finger joint, and was discharged." Ted Morgan, who notes that Burroughs had cut off his finger joint "under entirely different circumstances," records the writer's reaction. "The review brought him to boiling point. He sued for libel in London, where he was then living, and won. But the damages he collected, which the court deemed to be just compensation for the damage to his reputation, amounted to five pounds."[34] The true story of the finger joint was that Burroughs, driven to distraction by the infidelity of a male lover in New York, had bought a pair of poultry scissors and used them to cut off the top joint of his little finger. The incident had nothing to do with the draft.[35]

Girodias considered that Mary McCarthy's support was decisive in launching Burroughs and his work: "She did a really wonderful job in a very spontaneous manner. She had such a strong position and people were surprised that she would endorse such a crazy outsider. I don't think his public image would have evolved without her. . . . There was something in her that was close to his puritanism and intense respectability. Bill had a bizarre reputation coming from Tangier . . . but they shared a strait-laced attitude."[36]

AFTER *Naked Lunch* appeared in Paris, Burroughs stayed on in the Beat Hotel, writing, mixing with the other expatriates, and sliding back into drugs. He had found paregoric, a camphorated elixir of opium, often used to treat diarrhea, that could be bought over the counter, but he remained catholic in his tastes. Baird Bryant remembered going over to the Beat Hotel with laudanum, which Burroughs would cook up in his room and then they would shoot up together. "It helps to be high when you are reading his stuff," said Bryant, whose junk-lined veins knew what they were singing about in those days. Bryant once took a double-exposed photograph of Burroughs when they were high. A ghostly picture emerged of Burroughs wearing what looked like a general's uniform with skull and crossbones on the lapels. El hombre invisible chuckled: "The general of death," he said.[37]

On one occasion, Burroughs and Beckett were brought together over dinner. Beckett asked Burroughs to explain his "cut-up" method. The American writer obliged, and Beckett said: "That's not writing, that's plumbing." The two men relapsed into silence, but not sobriety, for the rest of the evening. Beckett made amends later when he was asked about Burroughs and said he was "a writer," a description that Burroughs took as a great compliment.[38]

Drunk or sober, high or low, Burroughs never stopped writing. Girodias published two more of his books, *The Soft Machine*—the first of the "cut-up" books—in 1961 and *The Ticket That Exploded* in 1962.

But problems arose between publisher and author when Burroughs discovered that Girodias had not paid him his share of the Grove Press proceeds from *Naked Lunch*. The arrangement had been that the American royalties would be divided on the basis of two-thirds for Burroughs and one-third for Girodias and Burroughs would receive his share via Girodias, not directly from New York.

Rosset paid the royalties on time, but Burroughs received nothing until he protested. The system was later changed to direct payments, but by then Burroughs had lost several thousand dollars, swallowed up by Girodias's "cancerous restaurant," as Burroughs called it, and other activities of the spendthrift publisher.

Burroughs was particularly hard up at the time. He had finally told his parents that he would not need an allowance anymore because he thought he would be able to live independently on his royalties. When Burroughs confronted his publisher in Paris in early 1964, Girodias confessed and said the money was gone. Burroughs wrote to Alan Ansen about it: "Some people are self-destructive and want to lose money. . . . What a stupid bastard he is."[39]

If Burroughs had been a Donleavy or a Nabokov or even a composite Southern-Hoffenberg, the trumpets would have rung out and serried ranks of lawyers would have marched into battle. But Bill Burroughs was a more forgiving man who could show sympathy for Girodias's troubles. He never forgot that Girodias had published *Naked Lunch* when no one else would touch it. He also remembered how the publisher had helped him in other ways. One day, after he had been arrested and held by the French police for drugs, he went to tell Girodias what had happened. He had found his publisher practicing the tango with Judith Schmidt, Rosset's assistant. Girodias had broken off in mid-pirouette and contacted a lawyer, who handled the case and got Burroughs off with a small fine.[40]

Girodias recalled that he and Burroughs were never close friends. "It was difficult to talk to him because he never spoke. He was ghostly and silent, passing through walls, looking frail and terminal. It was an effort for him to go on living and carrying suitcases from hotel to hotel. Once I saw him in the street with this big suitcase and I picked it up because I was slightly younger and healthier and he got very offended and grabbed it back.

"He was a strange presence in my life. I was not Alfred Knopf, of course, but I was on top of a small business and I never had the time to go out to Bill and get him to speak out. And later [when] I was out in the street, [there were] some authors I was unable to pay, and

Bill was one of them. Paul Bowles wrote to me to express his disgust that I had not paid Bill. Bill was wonderful about it. He never complained."[41]

Allen Ginsberg confirmed that Burroughs and Girodias remained on friendly terms despite the publisher's fraudulent behavior. "It was only money they were arguing about. Burroughs felt that Girodias had done him a favor at the beginning, and that is always important. One way or another, I think that Burroughs always felt that there was a debt of honor to Girodias."[42]

NAKED LUNCH has stood the test of time. During its thirty-five years of published life, it has never been out of print and it has established itself as a major literary work and cultural icon. Burroughs went on to produce a huge body of work—novels, short stories, essays, and memoirs. He has written film scripts and acted in movies. He is also a painter who exhibits from time to time. But *Naked Lunch* remains his most personal, most innovative, most passionate book, and it is the work for which he is best known.

Over eighty years old in 1995, Burroughs rarely moves these days from Lawrence, Kansas. He has survived a triple bypass heart operation and a broken hip. He paints a little, writes a little, fishes, shoots, and drinks vodka and Coca-Cola in moderation. His passion is no longer boys but cats—he has six of them. His faithful and protective secretary, James Grauerholz, who has done much to give order, shape, and coherence to Burroughs's work, filters visitors to the writer, and organizes his public life.

One of the greatest ironies of Burroughs's strange career is that he might never have become a writer if he had not accidentally killed his wife. He could easily have finished up as so many other talented junkies have done: spiraling downward with nothing in their heads except their next score, their next fix. A few friends and acquaintances would have remembered him as a dry, intelligent, offbeat, gay guy who looked like death even on a good day.

But Burroughs bucked the stereotype, went to hell, returned, and reported. More than thirty years after shooting his wife, he wrote: "I am forced to the appalling conclusion that I would never have become a writer but for Joan's death, and to a realization of the extent to which this event has motivated and formulated my writing. I live with the constant threat of possession, and a constant need to escape from possession, from Control. So the death of Joan brought me in contact with the invader, the Ugly Spirit and maneuvered me into a lifelong struggle, in which I have had no choice except to write my way out."[43]

In 1992 *Naked Lunch* appeared on the silver screen. The director, David Cronenberg, who made *The Fly* and *Dead Ringers,* wisely decided to craft the film as a fictionalized biography of Burroughs rather than attempt to transpose the novel. The result is a superbly acted nightmare with Peter Weller as the deadpan William Lee/William Burroughs central character, Judy Davis as Joan, and later as Jane Bowles in Tangier, and a marvelous if too brief appearance by Roy Scheider as Dr. Benway. Filled with spooky insects, giant bugs, and other high-tech horror gadgetry, the film of *Naked Lunch* captures the book's hallucinatory qualities without losing either its humor or its somber message.

Naked Lunch, nevertheless, remains a remarkably difficult, at times inaccessible book. It probably qualifies for that growing pile of great, unread classics, widely bought, knowledgeably talked about, and little read. How should it be judged? Barry Miles, who wrote an excellent appreciation of Burroughs, his "favourite writer," sets the novel in its context:

"Some readers, confused by the chance order of the chapters, the lack of obvious narrative and the multiple viewpoints of the characters, wonder what *The Naked Lunch* is ultimately about and why it is so highly regarded. It was written for the most part in the pre–rock-and-roll, straitlaced Doris Day–Debbie Reynolds era, when the USA had the world's highest standard of living but a very low quality of life. . . . *The Naked Lunch* confronted the paranoid Red-baiting anti-communism of McCarthy, and the cynical detachment of the creators of the atomic bomb. It drew attention to Anslinger and Hoover for their ugly drug laws which treated addicts as criminals, hounding and persecuting them instead of going after organised crime. . . . It was an attack on the snoopy, interfering puritan ideology which caused Prohibition and persecuted homosexuality. It revealed the anaesthetised language and hypocrisy which permitted segregation and attacked the bureaucrats who maintained their positions of power with hanging, the electric chair and the cyanide gas chamber of Californian justice. It was an American confessional: exposing everything from the mundane life of the fifties American housewife to the full horror of capital punishment."[44]

Naked Lunch is also a seminal novel about drug addiction, a chilling tale that somehow manages to compound description, condemnation, and prescription. As for the title that puzzled Girodias and so many others then and since, Burroughs said it means exactly what the words say: "NAKED Lunch—a frozen moment when everyone sees what is on the end of every fork."

"I awoke from the Sickness at the age of forty-five," Burroughs reported, "calm and sane, and in reasonably good health except for a weakened liver and the look of borrowed flesh common to all who survive the Sickness.

"The Sickness is drug addiction and I was an addict for fifteen years. When I say addict I mean an addict to junk (generic term for opium and/or derivatives including all synthetics from demerol to palfium). I have used junk in many forms: morphine, heroin, dilaudid, eukodol, pantopon, diocodid, diosane, opium, demerol, dolophine, palfium. I have smoked junk, eaten it, sniffed it, injected it in vein-skin-muscle, inserted it in rectal suppositories. The needle is not important. Whether you sniff it smoke it eat it or shove it up your ass the result is the same: addiction."[45]

Burroughs was cured of his addiction, but, being an honest man, he believed that he had to treat this "health problem" head-on, which meant depicting the Sickness for what it is: "brutal, obscene and disgusting." Fortunately, a powerful writing talent and a driven personality were coupled with the honesty. Thus endowed, William Seward Burroughs II was able to describe, in an unforgettable book, what he had seen on the end of *his* fork.

12

Glorious Nights, Weary Days

DURING THE SPRING OF 1959, residents of the Latin Quarter who lived close to the ancient church of Saint-Séverin were intrigued by the activity at number 7 in the street named after the church. Builders, plumbers, architects, carpenters, electricians, decorators, government inspectors, and caterers were constantly going in and out. The four-story building, which had been almost derelict, was rapidly being transformed. But into what?

The Olympia Press had moved to 7 rue Saint-Séverin from the rue de Nesle the previous summer because both Girodias and his co-tenant, Jean-Jacques Pauvert, needed more room. The bustle, however, had nothing to do with Olympia, which occupied a single floor in the building. It was something completely new, Girodias told inquirers, nothing fancy though, just a modest bistro that would use up some of the vacant space in the building. It was to be called Chez Lolita, but threats of legal action from across the Atlantic had put paid to that; instead, the new venture was baptized La Grande Séverine.

It was well named. From the seed of a cozy neighborhood café, a large and extremely grand entertainment complex sprang up and, for a time, flourished. Thomas Quinn Curtiss, journalist, writer, and regular patron, reported on its evolution:

"La Grande Séverine opened modestly as a bistro, but quickly grew into something more bizarre. Today [August 1960] it boasts of seven rooms on two levels. On the ground floor there is a 'turn-of-the-century' bar with a 1900 tiled floor; a red room inspired by Chinese and Japanese examples; a blue room, Le Salon Cagliostro, so called because of the old Spanish tarot cards painted on its mirrors; a very green and refreshing winter garden with bird cages of the rococo school; while downstairs there are three rooms: a bar, a dining room and a central room with a dance floor."[1]

From 1959 until 1964, La Grande Séverine saw come and go almost a dozen different places of entertainment that, in addition to those noted by Curtiss, included the Salle du Grand Siècle, a sophisticated, candlelit restaurant where a chamber orchestra played nightly; La Salle Suèdoise, a very clean restaurant specializing in lighter dishes; Chez Vodka, a Russian-style cabaret room—Girodias's favorite—with a balalaika orchestra and a kitchen run by a ninety-two-year-old chef from pre-Revolutionary Russia; the Batucada, a Brazilian-style club for Latin American music; the Club de Jazz, with top American musicians; and a theater in the vaulted, medieval basement.

Girodias, who loved entertaining and feeding people, had always dreamed of opening a restaurant. (Miriam Worms's theory is that he started it because he had nowhere to go in the evenings.) His chance came when *Lolita* sailed to the top of the American bestseller list and stayed there long enough to fill his pockets as they had never been filled before. What possessed Girodias to run such a huge establishment is unclear. He said the whole thing became "a devouring passion," which seems true. Once launched, he could not stop, not even after a damaging fire sent him a signal he should have heeded.

He regretted it later. "For five years La Grande Séverine absorbed all my energies, my time, my imagination. She was the fatal mistress who kept me away from my duties and . . . instead of becoming a grandiloquent and catastrophic nightclub owner, I should have fled the ugly police-infested Paris scene, and followed my authors and my books to America. It was so clear, so evident. What awful blindness."[2]

But in 1959 he saw it differently, and the result of his labors was a unique creation that reflected good taste, elegance, style, and panache—all in a city not short of those qualities. The glory nights of La Grande Séverine coincided with the publication of Girodias's most famous books—*The Ginger Man, Lolita, Candy, Story of O, Naked Lunch*—and were the high-water mark of his career. This was the moment when *The Economist* called him "the most celebrated avant-garde editor of his time." The Séverine was a strange crown for a publisher, but then Maurice Girodias was a strange publisher. The dream did not last, and, as it faded, Girodias's life took a downward turn.

A central figure in the Grande Séverine adventure was Michèle Forgeois, who was living with Girodias at the time. She helped with the overall design, the decor, and the furnishings. She proved to be a talented scavenger in flea markets and demolition sites, and among her many discoveries were a magnificent teak bar and some exquisite ceramic tiles, dating from around 1900, that served as Le Bar's centerpiece. When the Séverine opened, she and Girodias's youngest sister, Sylvie, ran it as co-managers.

The builders, who were Spaniards, were led by an exiled communist called Marcos. A skilled craftsman and hard worker, little surprised him, and his "can-do" attitude appealed to Girodias. But even he was taken aback when the patron decided to excavate the ancient cellars beneath the building and the workmen's shovels began to toss up skulls and skeletons. As they crossed themselves, Marcos and his team realized they had uncovered part of the medieval burial grounds of the neighboring Saint-Séverin church. Gregory Corso remembers attending the opening night of the Séverine and being greeted by his host with a drink in one hand and a skull in the other.

At its height, the Séverine employed sixty-five people, including a number of well-known singers and musicians. Jazz musicians Kenny Clarke and Chet Baker, Memphis Slim, the blues singer, Marpessa Dawn of *Black Orpheus* fame, and Mae Mercer, another black American singer, all performed there. Mae Mercer, a large, powerfully built woman, had a tempestuous affair with Girodias that was marked by noisy rows and physical combat, with Girodias invariably on the receiving end.

The staff were always a problem, partly because they were paid erratically and partly because of a lack of control. Michèle Forgeois said that when she was in charge, they would be searched after work, but the checkups stopped after she had gone. The musicians ate caviar and smoked salmon and quenched their perpetual thirst with the best champagne. Tantrums, walkouts, and internecine feuds were common. One night the chef and his entire kitchen staff marched out, the chef spitting on Girodias's steak as a parting gesture. William Burroughs dropped by one morning to find the place stripped as if an invading army had swept through it. "Even the lemons had gone."

Customers were a problem too. There were not many of them, although Girodias and his staff, family, and friends made herculean efforts to promote La Grande Séverine. Miriam Worms, who was working upstairs in the Olympia office, recalls the countless occasions when she and her husband put on their evening clothes to "act as props" or to be photographed for publicity handouts. "We were the most photographed people in Paris," she said, "and the Séverine certainly had a regular clientele. Us."[3]

Once someone came round to the Olympia office peddling advertising space in the *Police Gazette* and Girodias promptly bought a half-page advertisement for La Grande Séverine. This lit up the Brigade Mondaine, whose sights were already trained on the Salle des Fumeurs d'Opium, the misleading name of Girodias's Chinese restaurant, and on the dubious theatrical happenings being staged in the Séverine's basement.

Girodias invited all his friends but treated them as if they were in his home rather than in a place of business. Juliette Kahane, his youngest daughter and now a writer and editor, recalled La Grande Séverine. She was taken there by her father when she was a fourteen-year-old schoolgirl, and patrons thought she was a nymphet. She was particularly impressed by Marpessa Dawn's not wearing a brassiere, a sight that shocked her straitlaced cousins. The Séverine was popular with Paris's artistic crowd—people from the cinema and theater, publishers, writers, and painters. But they also tended to use it as a private club or residence where food, drink, and entertainment were on the house.

Girodias's numerous creditors were the most faithful customers of all. Monique Sindler-Gonthier, a friend of Girodias, remembered her husband taking her there and saying, "We can eat and drink as much as we like because Girodias owes me money." A Belgian publisher, who was in a similar position, regularly used to round up as many friends as he could and take them over to the Séverine for a free feast.

When people failed to come in the dog days of winter after Christmas and the New Year, Girodias would tell Michèle Forgeois to change the decor. They were bored with the old decor, he said, that's why they were not coming. He could not accept that it was a normal seasonal slump caused by cold weather and depleted budgets. "Maurice adored spending money even though he burned himself badly," said Michèle Forgeois. Why? *"Pour s'amuser."*[4]

And then came another kind of burning. Early one summer's morning, Girodias and Michèle Forgeois received a telephone call from Sylvie. "Come quickly," she said, "La Grande Séverine is on fire!" Girodias pulled on some clothes, jumped into a taxi, and went over to view the smoldering and thoroughly drenched remains of his dream. The ground floor and most of Olympia's offices on the floor above were in ruins. Coco, the parrot, and his harem of female parrots were carbonized in their cage. Miraculously, the ceramic tiles and teak bar—the glorious centerpiece of Le Bar—survived intact.

Miriam Worms and her husband, Jean-Pierre, were there. She had no difficulty in recalling the drama. "Sylvie called me at six A.M. with the glad tidings and asked me to come at once. *'Tant mieux,'* I remember saying in a daze. 'Maurice wants you to come straight away.' I rushed over, and there was Girodias in the middle of the charred destruction with a serene smile on his face.

"It was the only time I saw him other than perfectly dressed. I was struck by two extremities—the smile and no socks. A smoked salmon had been resmoked, and we found it a bit salty. We went up to the first floor. The smoke had made a very pretty pink and gray effect on my office walls. *'Regarde, comme c'est joli,'* Girodias said in a state of beatitude.

"We wondered whether he considered the fire to be suitable punishment for whatever sins he attributed to himself. The beatitude soon gave way to action, and he declared the restaurant would be open within three weeks. Everybody thought Girodias had lit the match himself for the insurance. Only we knew that he wasn't properly covered."[5]

With Marcos and his team working overtime, the Séverine rose from the ashes and, in doing so, grew larger with the expansion of the theater through further subterranean excavations. Girodias reopened with a charming and well-produced review called *Les Playgirls,* which received good notices. This was followed by a stage adaptation of Norman Rubington's *Fuzz Against Junk,* translated by Eric Kahane. But Girodias's star production was De Sade's *La Philosophie dans le Boudoir,* which his brother also adapted for the stage.

Monique Sindler-Gonthier remembered the opening night: "It was a gala affair. A girlfriend and myself went dressed up in Saint Vincent de Paul nuns' habits, the ones with the winged hats, which we had rented. The place was packed, there were probably about a hundred and fifty in the theater." Victoria Reiter, who was working for Girodias at the time, also had clear memories of that evening. "*Le tout Paris* was there, including the head of the Paris police or the Brigade Mondaine, I don't remember which. The play was like the Comédie Française crossed with Brecht. Guys didn't take off their pants. You saw copulatory movements but not—to quote *Hustler* magazine— pink. It was on the very far edge of contemporary acceptability, and the whole thing was very funny. The avant-garde audience loved it."[6]

Eric Kahane did not remember seeing the vice squad chief, but he confirmed that everyone was there. "*Philosophie* was rather well done but very tame. No boobies and things—all very sedate, eighteenth-century sort of thing. But the whole attitude towards de Sade in France at that time made it appear sulfurous."[7]

It was perhaps fitting that La Grande Séverine should go down with the helping hand of the divine Marquis. The vice squad raided the theater not long after the opening night and closed it down. But Girodias defied the ban. Insisting that the show must go on, he climbed onto the stage the following night and read the text of the decree to an attentive audience before the actors came on. The police, surprisingly, took no action. They were probably influenced by the presence of President de Gaulle's former education minister, Edgar Faure, and other luminaries whom Girodias had specially invited, such as the novelist-diplomat Romain Gary and his wife, actress Jean Seberg, and filmmaker Roger Vadim, who was accompanied by actress Catherine Deneuve. The next day, however, the vice squad moved decisively, and the theater never opened again.

Girodias finally ran out of money, credit, and credibility. The restaurants closed their kitchens, the bars stopped serving drinks, the musicians put away their instruments and moved on, and Girodias's creditors returned to their drawing boards to devise new tactics for settling their debts. Number 7 rue Saint-Séverin went back to being just another shabby, unremarkable building in a shabby medieval Parisian street.

LOLITA's triumph in 1959, when it was at the top of the bestseller list in the United States, was the peak of Girodias's publishing career and gave him heroic status at the Frankfurt Book Fair that year. There were parties in castles and celebratory dinners with Barney Rosset, George Weidenfeld, Walter Minton, and others. Publishers from all over the world clustered around the Olympia stand, eager to find out what might next be cantering out of the Saint-Séverin stable. Miriam Worms remembered being offered bribes for good tips.

The hothouse growth of La Grande Séverine had pushed the Olympia Press office higher and higher up to the roof of the building. Starting on the first floor, the office finished on the fourth, just under the attic. The enterprise also consumed much of Girodias's time and energy, but he did not stop publishing. Instead, he stopped sleeping, spending most of his days at the office and a good part of his nights at the Séverine. "At dawn, I would finally stagger to bed," he said, "my brain drowned in liquor and sick optimism, and I would catch two hours of sleep before resuming my daylight activities: my publishing career. . . . Consider the inhuman plight of the born optimist."[8]

But somehow he managed to continue to publish notable, if not bestselling books. One was *Zazie dans le Métro* by Raymond Queneau, a prolific novelist, essayist, a director of Gallimard, and a member of the Goncourt Academy, which awards France's most prestigious literary prizes. He was a former teacher and old friend of Girodias, so Olympia was a natural outlet for the English version of *Zazie*. Eric Kahane and Norman Rubington translated the book into English, and Jacqueline Duhème, a book illustrator and one of Girodias's most enduring girlfriends, did the illustrations. The book was later adapted for the stage and turned into a film.

Zazie was a bestseller in France when it first appeared and won a prize for black humor. The novel's impudent, profane, adolescent heroine with her rebellious attitude toward anyone in authority made Zazie a popular fictional figure of the day. A review in the *New York Herald Tribune* described the book as a "wacky little *chef d'oeuvre* . . . odd and frequently hilarious . . . a plotless wordtwister that defies description. . . . try to imagine *Alice in Wonderland* rewritten by Henry Miller and James Joyce, with Lolita in the title role."[9]

In one of Girodias's punchy little introductions to his best-known authors in *The Olympia Reader,* he describes Queneau thus: "Born in the port of Le Havre in 1903, [he] was a brilliant student of philosophy, later a student of every café, street corner, billiard hall in Paris. . . . his works are illuminated by a sense of the comic ordered by a sense of the coherent. . . . [he] writes to make people laugh, and, of course, in the best Gallic tradition, to think. The reader catches the contagious, horsey, sonorous laugh of Queneau, which is nowhere more clearly or perfectly sounded than in *Zazie*."[10]

Another novel published by Olympia around this time was *Steiner's Tour* by Philip O'Connor, a writer who had attracted critical attention with his first book, *Memoirs of a Public Baby*. The British critic Philip Toynbee described that novel as "a true and moving book," and Dorothy Parker wrote that O'Connor being "always outside society, saw into it with blinding clearness. As to his writing, I think there can be no calmer word than 'superb.'"[11] *Steiner's Tour* had been rejected by several publishers before Girodias agreed to do it on the condition that the author made some revisions, which he did. The book was not as successful as O'Connor's first novel, but it was a worthy addition to the Olympia list.

Continuing in the vein of more serious books, Girodias published a war novel set in Korea called *Night* by Francis Pollini. Next in Olympia's expanding catalogue came an investigative account about a famous British murder case. This was *Murder vs. Murder: The English Legal System and the A-6 Murder Case* by Jean Justice, a crusading investigation of an alleged miscarriage of justice in Britain. Girodias also reissued two of the better-known Obelisk books: *The Young and the Evil* by Charles Henri Ford and Parker Tyler, and *The Black Book* by Lawrence Durrell, with a new preface by the author describing how he felt about his first serious novel thirty years after he had written it.

One of Girodias's most intriguing books in this period was a complete departure from any of his previous publications. Entitled *The Black Diaries of Roger Casement,* it was largely put together by the publisher himself. Although much had been written about Casement, *The Black Diaries* gave a new twist to a familiar story. The book also provided an unusual insight into Girodias's own complex character, which bore some similarities to Casement's.

Roger Casement was born in Northern Ireland in 1864 and educated there and in England. His first job was with a Liverpool trading firm that sent him to West Africa. He later entered the British Civil Service and returned to Africa, serving as a consul in various parts of the continent. He achieved world renown for exposing, with irrefutable evidence, the appalling labor conditions in the plantations and mines of the then Congo Free State—run as the Belgian king's private fief—and the rubber-growing regions of Peru. For these and other services to the British Crown, Casement received a knighthood.

With the outbreak of World War I, Casement threw in his lot with the militant Irish nationalist movement. He made his way to Germany and, openly defying Britain, attempted to recruit an "Irish Brigade" among captured Irish prisoners of war. In April 1916, just before the disastrous Easter Rising in Dublin, Casement landed from a German U-boat on the Irish coast and was caught and taken to London. In a famous trial, he was convicted of high treason.

A campaign to save Casement from the gallows was launched in Britain, Ireland, and the United States. During its course, extracts from Casement's private diaries, which contained explicit descriptions of homosexual activity and fantasies, were circulated, almost certainly by British officials. Many people thought the British government had fabricated the diaries; others were convinced they were genuine. In any case, the diaries had a negative and decisive impact on the appeal, which was rejected. Casement was stripped of his knighthood and hanged in Pentonville Prison on a summer's morning in 1916.

Girodias's interest in Casement's story began when a man called Peter Singleton-Gates walked into his office one day with a copy of the diaries under his arm. "He was a little British journalist out of a 1940s film," said Miriam Worms. "I don't remember where he had got them from but they were still under a British government ban. It was the time of the Suez crisis [1956], and the British were putting pressure on their allies, the French, to close down the Olympia Press. Girodias hated the British because of that, and this motivated him to do the book on Casement."[12]

But it was more than that. Girodias seemed to find in Casement a kindred spirit, an imperfect yet human individual who had risen above his imperfections in pursuit of his ideals and had, in the end, triumphed, even though he paid for that triumph with his life. "To me, indeed, Casement is a hero," Girodias wrote later. "He was politically confused, emotionally unbalanced, maudlin when depressed and absurdly naive when in his best form; but he was exceptionally generous, he had extraordinary courage and a simple human wisdom which sprang from his natural goodness. He was a knot of confusions, religious, sexual, political, and professional, but that did not prevent him from sacrificing everything to the causes in which he believed."[13]

Peter Singleton-Gates had obtained copies of the complete diaries in 1922. He believed them to be genuine, revealing "the gross side of this otherwise generous and noble character," and he decided to write a book about Casement and the diaries. But the heavy hand of the British government, flourishing the Official Secrets Act, stopped him in 1925 after he had spent two years on the project. Then came "a fortuitous turn." The head of Scotland Yard, who was well disposed to Singleton-Gates, allowed him to compare his copy of the diaries with the originals, which had been taken from Casement's

London lodgings at the time of his arrest. "I had prints of the hand-writing of Casement. I had further armed myself with the typed copies of several erotic entries . . . and I compared them. To me there can hardly be any doubt that the diaries found in Casement's lodgings in Ebury Street were his true diaries, in his own handwriting, containing erotic experiences of his own."[14]

Putting the book together raised difficulties. Miriam Worms said Girodias could not find anyone else to write the necessary biographical and contextual background material, so he did it himself and she did the editing. Girodias became obsessed with the project, which took about six months, and the two of them finished up on such bad terms that they were no longer talking to each other. Instead, they would communicate through editorial notes, especially when Girodias's English went astray. "He would write something like 'Casement was one of Ireland's greatest *deads,*' and I would have to correct him."[15]

Singleton-Gates was pleased that someone was prepared to put out the book he had wanted to publish so long ago. The collaborative effort resulted in a splendid volume that not only contains the actual diaries but more of Casement's writings and speeches, including his final address to the jury at his trial, and other relevant background material. The book is over five hundred pages long and has more than eighty duotone illustrations and endpaper maps of central Dublin at the time of the Easter Uprising.

The Black Diaries of Roger Casement was published simultaneously in Paris, London, and New York in 1959, thirty-four years after Singleton-Gates had been stopped by the British government and thirty-five years before the diaries themselves were finally made available to the public in 1994. The fear of censorship, however, continued to cast a shadow over the book. Only the Olympia edition in Paris carried all the diaries. The British and American versions dropped the one for 1911, which, according to Girodias, was the "coarsest but not the most explosive." He also claimed that the authenticity of the diaries was further established by Casement's heirs accepting royalties from the sales of the book.[16] (Olympia authors may raise a collective eyebrow here at the notion of Girodias sending royalties to anybody.)

The book, Girodias reported, was never reviewed, but "its effect was immediate: The British Home Secretary admitted that Casement's diaries were still in existence, and they were publicly displayed. A very limited number of self-appointed experts, both British and Irish, were authorized to study them; the former declared they were convinced that the diaries were authentic and the latter that they were gross forgeries. Thus the balance of confusion was neatly preserved."[17]

"The book is the key to Maurice's personality," said Barney Rosset, who published the American edition. "Casement was an outsider, a flawed hero—just like Maurice. It was all about identity. There was Maurice, half Jewish, half French, a renegade in a certain sense but still thinking of himself as a principled person.

"Casement was perfect: He was an Englishman who swore that he was Irish, who was gay, which got him into terrible trouble, and he wrote these so-called reprehensible diaries which the British used to destroy him and which the Irish say were frauds. But they weren't frauds and they weren't reprehensible, and he was gay and he was a great pioneer of human rights and a great person to uncover. So it fit Maurice, and it fit me too. I loved the book, and I thought it was the best expression of himself that Maurice ever achieved."[18]

OLYMPIA'S DECLINE did not deter Girodias from trying new ventures. In 1961 he launched *The Olympia Review,* "an illustrated, urbane, vociferous literary monthly." The first three adjectives sailed close to the truth, but "monthly" the new journal was not. Only four issues were published, the last one appearing in 1963, but the magazine was still a worthy accompaniment to Girodias's other publishing activities. Edited by Marilyn Meeske, *The Olympia Review* was a lively collection of fiction and nonfiction, photographs and drawings, with a regular column by Terry Southern called "The Spy's Corner." Olympia authors and their friends were featured heavily, but there was an effort to look beyond the Left Bank for new talent. Material included extracts from the Olympia Press's forthcoming novels by William Burroughs, Henry Miller, and Paul Ableman; new poems by Lawrence Durrell and Gregory Corso; and a miscellany of articles, such as a debate in Britain in the House of Lords about *Lady Chatterley's Lover;* a pictorial study of Paris *clochards,* "alleged to be the wittiest tramps in the world," and the hilarious illustrated history of the chastity belt, served up by historian "Henry Crannach" and artist "Akbar del Piombo."

But by the mid-1960s, even Olympia's Mr. Micawber could no longer keep up the game. As he admitted later, "My publishing career, at that point, had nothing much to do any longer with publishing books. . . . It had to do with desperately trying to hold together the last shreds of the business, to fight tedious lawsuits, to literally invent money where none could be found, to supplement reality with alibis, syllogistic exercises, absurd dreams and bad checks."[19]

Girodias was then in his mid-forties, and Miriam Worms, who worked closely with him during the height of Olympia's success, described his appearance at this time: "He looked like a tallish undertaker, always dressed in a dark suit, an almost prim-looking gentleman. He had flat feet and moved as if he were sliding along, arms slightly away from the body, a specter, a ghostlike figure. He had translucent skin and impeccable hands, always clean. He was always washing his hands—the Macbeth syndrome, will they never be clean? He didn't fit into journalists' preconceived notions of a porn publisher at all. But what a contrast between appearance and behavior!"[20]

To make matters worse, just as the barriers of censorship were coming down in the Anglo-Saxon world, they were going up in Gallic France. This penalized Girodias while benefiting his closest counterparts, Barney Rosset in the United States and John Calder in Britain. In France the change began with Charles de Gaulle's return to power in 1958. It was a slow process that did not seriously affect Girodias's publishing freedom until the early 1960s. But the timing was disastrous because, as censorship tightened in France, the Olympia Press moved closer to join La Grande Séverine in the knacker's yard of bankruptcy. The hostile publishing climate, particularly for Olympia's specialist wares, made a comeback that much more difficult.

The most worrying aspect was the increasing number of bans on Olympia books already in print and the seemingly endless legal processes that accompanied the bans. The government had reactivated an old law that had been little used in the twentieth century. This was *outrage aux bonnes moeurs par la voie du livre,* "O.B.M" for short among the lawyers. Girodias said he was prosecuted not only for existing Olympia titles but for several that were out of print and even for two or three books that he had not published at all. By the mid-1960s he had collected four to six years in suspended prison sentences, $80,000 in fines, and an eighty-year ban on all publishing activity.

Girodias did not make things easier for himself by his irreverent attitude toward the courts and judges. Once, when he had been sentenced to a three-month suspended sentence for publishing an obscene book, he muttered under his breath, "Kafka." The elderly judge, who was a little deaf, heard "*caca.*" "Nine months!" he barked.

France was changing in many directions. It was becoming more organized, more technologically advanced, less *laissez-faire,* more serious and modern, and much more expensive. "All the fun and gaiety have left this nation," Girodias lamented. "The Algerian war chased the last colonies of young artists and loafers away from Paris; in this hygienic-looking city, whitewashed by government decree, the spirit is dead, the secular feast ended."[21]

Meanwhile, over in Ireland, a bearded, sad-looking man, with the face of a sixteenth-century Spanish grandee, was watching and waiting.

Time to say adieu. Time to cross the ocean.

13

Olympia USA

WITH La Grande Séverine bankrupt and the legal wrangle with Donleavy still unresolved, Girodias decided to move his operations to New York. His first priority was to find a partner, and the obvious candidate was Barney Rosset's Grove Press, which had been established in the early 1950s and had published a number of Olympia titles. Rosset was the rebellious son of a wealthy Chicago family, and he shared Girodias's taste for challenging the establishment and pushing forward the boundaries of acceptability for the written word. He published a wide range of avant-garde books in the 1950s and 1960s that brought him the same mixture of fame, notoriety, and occasional financial windfall that had been Girodias's lot in Paris. Leon Friedman, Girodias's New York lawyer, began putting together a deal.

After intensive negotiations, Friedman produced a draft contract that he thought was fair to both sides. Both parties agreed to the terms, but at the last minute Girodias, according to Friedman, "changed the numbers" and the deal fell through. "It was a good contract," Friedman said, "and Maurice would have made good money out of it. But his attitude was if the other guy wants to sign a contract, it can't be a good deal."[1] Girodias saw it differently. After it was all over, he wrote to Friedman: "It's all like a bad dream, concocted by the Superman of sadism, Barney Rosset."[2] "It's just as well we didn't get together," said Rosset, who laughed when he heard the Superman epithet again. "It wouldn't have worked."[3]

Girodias continued a fruitless search for an established publishing partner and ended up with a business manager who invested some money in the venture. An office was found, staff hired, authors commissioned, and the new vessel, Olympia USA, unfurled its sails.

Back on the other side of the Atlantic, Paris Olympia maintained a fragile presence, although teetering on the edge of bankruptcy. A new assistant had taken over in 1965. She was Claudia ("Holly") Hutchins, a young American who had lived in Paris for most of her life and had answered an advertisement that Girodias had put in the *Herald Tribune*. She noted in her application that reading was one of her "great pleasures." Dirty books, however, had escaped her attention. As she climbed the stairs of number 7 rue Saint-Séverin, she was under the impression that she was about to meet the publisher of *Ulysses*. On the top floor of the building, she found "a dusty office full of papers, books, and a rather gentle man behind a huge desk."[4]

The "gentle man" hired her, and Holly Hutchins was to spend the next three years of her young life helping him stop the Paris Olympia Press from foundering while Olympia USA struggled to leave port. "You felt like you were working for someone who was trying to survive," she said. Her job description expanded quickly to embrace secretary, office manager, and reader of manuscripts. Paris Olympia published only one new book during this period, although manuscripts continued to flow in, many of them by women. Holly spent a great deal of her time typing refusal notes amid the dust, letters that would begin: "Dear _____: Thank you for your letter of 3 April enquiring about your manuscript, *The Snake Pit* [or *Gin and Lime* or *Palace of Ignominy*], but I regret to say . . ."

She also ran the mail-order business under the name of "Miss Olivia Pringle," a fig leaf for the Olympia Press. "I would send DB's in small brown packages to distant countries where such lore was banned. . . . And sometimes to outwit the censors I would cut up books such as *The Whipping Club* into several parts and mail it in different envelopes over a period of time." She would receive personal as well as professional letters: "Dear Olivia, I would very much like to meet you . . ." One man came into the office and showed her pictures of himself in the nude; another marched up to her and said: "Take me to *The Whipping Club*."

The daily rhythm of the Olympia office had not changed much from its early, high-flying days. Regular visitors still included Girodias's lawyer, Laurette Kahane and her daughters, the vice squad, other publishers, Olympia authors, and a lot of women friends. Holly remembers people constantly coming in to be paid—authors, printers, and an entire Russian dance group that had worked at La Grande Séverine. After some writers had been in, she would find syringes in the toilet.[5]

Another key figure in this transition period was Victoria Reiter, then known as Vicky Morheim. She was also a young American living in Paris who began working for Girodias in 1963 and left in late 1965. She later rejoined him in New York to help set up the office and stayed with him for six months. Her memories of the Paris office, like Holly Hutchins's, remained vivid and were vividly expressed:

"It was extremely staid—staffed mostly by down-to-earth women who took no shit from anyone, especially when Arabs would turn up expecting orgies. Most of the business with authors was done in Girodias's apartment or in cafés. The accounting was terrible, filled with as much fantasy as the novels themselves." Did Girodias know? "Sometimes I thought he did; sometimes I thought he didn't. I never saw or made out a royalty statement during my entire time there. He never paid French social security payments, and the authorities went after him for that too. He ended up owing the government, he told me, eighty million francs [$1.6 million]. Being a secretary for Maurice was unlike being anyone else's secretary. He wrote incredibly long letters to lawyers, authors, and publishers . . . rehearsing legal arguments for future court appearances."[6]

WHILE HE TRIED to keep his businesses afloat, Girodias retained enough celebrity status to be invited to a few special functions. One event was a Foyles Literary Luncheon at the Dorchester Hotel in London, where he was the guest of honor. He took with him his old friend Michel Gall, who discarded his multiple and less reputable identities—"Humphrey Richardson" and "Homer & Associates"—for the occasion. Holly Hutchins and Victoria Reiter were also drafted.

It was a gala affair with writers Edna O'Brien, John Braine, Angus

Wilson, and Auberon Waugh and publishers Frederic Warburg, Anthony Blond, and John Calder at the head table. Calder made a graceful introduction, but Girodias was the worse for drink and mumbled a long and rambling speech. Holly Hutchins remembers one disappointed elderly lady in a hat saying she had been under the impression that the meeting was about the Olympic Games. To which her neighbor, a disappointed elderly lady in gloves, responded: "I thought we were going to be listening to a Greek scholar."[7]

The next day the group went to Oxford for a debate at the Oxford Union on censorship, where Girodias was pitted against the British film censor. Victoria Reiter and Michel Gall warned him it was a serious affair and begged him to prepare himself and to lay off the booze. But the night before in London, he was drunk and out of control. On arrival in Oxford, they were given a reception and served sherry with everyone mumbling polite welcomes. Then they were taken into a vast hall and dined at high table with, Victoria Reiter remembered, "marvelous wines and food that sucked."

Girodias, who had sunk a couple of whiskies before he arrived, drank a lot of wine. When he came to speak he had to hold on to the podium to steady himself and rambled on about his life, a recital of his autobiography—exactly what his companions had warned him not to do. "The audience sat quietly through it," said Victoria Reiter. "Initially, one could feel their distress, but later it turned into a quiet sneering." Girodias's side won, but it would have been hard to lose on such a topic in the middle of the permissive 1960s. After that, it was back to Paris—to the dust, the rejected manuscripts, and the used syringes at number 7 rue Saint-Séverin.

Less than a year later, Girodias was at the Biddle Continuation Center in Bloomington, Indiana, a guest of the Kinsey Institute. In a letter addressed to "Miss Olivia Pringle" in Paris, Girodias described the adventure to Holly Hutchins. "Bonjour de Biddle-Continuation-Center," he began, "it's a very funny trip. . . . I saw the Kinsey gang, or part of it. Naturally all dreamy, shy, retiring creatures with their teeth falling off [sic] and creaking kneecaps. The librarian is a dream of a spinster, lording over miles of hysterical pornography, with a gentle, preoccupied air. I am invited to dinner tonite with someone called Professor Rabkin who's been working one year on a history of the Olympia Press and who is dying to see me. . . . [The director] thought that he had to warn me about his appearance, which he said was ludicrous. What can that be!?"[8]

• • •

OLYMPIA'S first proper office in New York was a grand apartment on Gramercy Park. Girodias lodged himself in the Chelsea Hotel and called up Victoria Reiter in Paris to come and join him. "He said he was ready to open in New York," she remembered. "What did that mean? It meant he was *emotionally* ready."

Girodias had managed to borrow some money from a printer from Arizona whom he had met on a plane: "Gobs of money came in, including a ten-thousand-dollar cashier's check for some urgent need," Reiter said. "Another time Girodias needed cash *now* and went berserk. I got the money for him from a banker friend, but he was in over his head and I decided to leave."[9]

Another American who had worked for Olympia in Paris rejoined the colors in New York. This was Gerry Williams, who had been an editor and translator in France and had later run an Olympia affiliate in Holland. Williams said that the key money man behind the New York Olympia was the business manager, David Young, an enormously fat man who was a member of the right-wing John Birch Society. The need to find a good distribution network led Girodias into strange company. Williams remembered men in camel-hair coats, gold cuff links, and Florsheim shoes coming into the office and putting their feet up on the desk as if they owned the place—which they probably did.[10]

Notwithstanding all the problems, Girodias managed to publish a large number of books during his time in New York. Some were reprints of old titles, but many were new books by new authors. The mixture was as before—deliberate pornography, novels that had erotic scenes but also pursued other concerns, and a few that had nothing to do with sex at all.

The style was different, however, and the quality, for the most part, inferior to the Paris list. The pornographic books were, with a few exceptions, harder, cruder, more direct. There was less invention and little humor. Girodias also took into account the growing and much more open homosexual market in the United States and catered to it. "In Paris the writers had style, story lines, imagination, and wrote quite well," said Victoria Reiter. "They were fueled by desperation. . . . All this was very different from the gynecological pornography scene in the States."[11]

Furthermore, Girodias had been surrounded by his writers in Paris, and much of the best work that he published there reflected this interaction. In the United States, cultural diversity and geography distanced Girodias from his authors. No heroic discoveries were made, as they had been in France, with unheralded masterpieces landing on the publisher's desk. One reason was that Paris Olympia had done its work too well. The censorship in the United States and Britain that had nourished it for fifteen years was breaking down. The new Millers, Becketts, Nabokovs, Donleavys, and Burroughses could go elsewhere. Other reasons were that Girodias was not widely known in New York, made little effort to cultivate the literary scene, and did not understand how the American publishing world worked.

Girodias was aware of these changes: "The discovery of freedom invariably provokes an explosion of dismal pornography—the direct effect of that discovery on the semi-literate masses, the shock caused by the sudden disintegration of so many taboos, the need for a total purge-by-obscenity, the realization that, in vice and in weakness, all men are truly born equal."[12]

Girodias noted that when he had started the Olympia Press in Paris in the early 1950s his primary object had been to "dismantle censorship." In New York, "with the sexual revolution well on its way, our aim is to normalize the situation, and help integrate the erotic side of life in creative writing, as being one of its most natural and essential components."[13] A worthy goal, but Girodias did not seem to appreciate that he was no longer the leading player in the game. Gone were the good old bad days when Olympia stood alone and the writer-rebel had no alternative but to knock at Girodias's door. Dozens of doors stood open, and inside was more money, more know-how, and more reliability than Girodias with his shoestring operation—not to mention his threadbare reputation—could provide.

Olympia USA turned out a curious mixture of books. There was Diane di Prima, perhaps the best-known female Beat poet, who wrote about her erotic adventures with Jack Kerouac, Allen Ginsberg, and others in *Memoirs of a Beatnik*. She also wrote some sex scenes for two other Olympia books, according to Olympia bibliographer Patrick Kearney. Diane di Prima later described what it was like working on commission for the Prince of Porn, an experience that bore an uncanny resemblance to that of Anaïs Nin writing erotica to order for a private client.

"Gobs of words would go off to New York whenever the rent was due, and come back with 'MORE SEX' scrawled across the top page in Maurice's inimitable hand, and I would dream up odd angles of bodies or weird combinations of humans and cram them in and send it off again."[14]

There was Marco (actually Fred) Vassi, who wrote erotica well and fast, and Ronald Tavel and "Angelo d'Arcangelo," two writers who specialized in homosexual erotica. There was "Vlas Tenin," the pseudonymous author of *Moscow Nights,* which Girodias said was the first pornographic novel out of the Soviet Union to be published in the West. The author was reputed to be a Soviet journalist resident in Western Europe. Convinced that "a tremendous market" existed in the Soviet Union, Girodias planned to sell bushels of books to Soviet sailors, who would smuggle them into their homeland.

And then there was Norman Singer, the Marcus van Heller or, as Girodias used to call him, "the Balzac" of Olympia USA. Singer, who lived in San Francisco, had made a living for years mainly as a ghostwriter but also produced novels, short stories, and nonfiction. Beginning with *Curtain of Flesh,* he racked up nine DBs for Girodias in five years, making him the press's most prolific writer. He had no compunction about using his real name. "I was unashamed, I didn't care. I had written for many years without getting published, so when I finally did [by Olympia], I wasn't going to hide it." He got on well with Girodias, although they occasionally had disagreements over titles.[15] Once Girodias wrote to him with the following suggestions:

"I am really impressed by the overall results and I am certain the success of the book will reward you for the enormous expenditure of energy. On the other hand, I find you have displayed somewhat less talent in the selection of a title than in the writing of the book, if I may say so. *Naked Enemies,* forsooth! What about *The Flesh of Dreams* or *Verily No Greater Ecstasy* or *The Rape of the Statue, A Curtain of Eyes*? Let me know if any of those suits you as I may use the leftovers for other titleless books."[16]

WHILE HE WAS LIVING at the Chelsea Hotel in 1967, Girodias became friendly with one of the residents, a young woman called Valerie Solanas. "Her clothing was invariable, the same old jeans and sweater, and the cap sitting straight on the top of her head," Girodias noted. "Her fixed expression was that of a Douanier Rousseau personage frozen in wooden immobility against its picture-book background; and yet one could vaguely sense the sunken dreams fermenting inside. She could have been attractive, but obviously did not want to be. There was something slightly hostile in her long jaw and stubborn forehead, as in her drab, sexless clothes. She hardly spoke to anyone, watched the mail rather intensely, and seemed in constant trouble with the management about her rent."[17]

Girodias discovered that Valerie Solanas, who appeared to be a lesbian, had written a virulently anti-male play called *Up Your Ass* and a tract in the same vein entitled *The S.C.U.M. Manifesto* (Society for Cutting Up Men). Girodias thought the play "rather clever . . . amusingly wild." He was more impressed with the manifesto, however, which was "conceived more or less along the lines of Swift's *Modest Proposal,* although it was marred by weak or over-frenzied developments." But he found "the tone of strident aggressivity . . . quite enjoyable" and felt she "definitely had a point." He offered her a contract to write an autobiographical novel, with an advance of $2,000 paid in installments, and she accepted.

The friendship continued, and one afternoon she took Girodias around to Andy Warhol's studio to see a rough cut of his new film, *I, a Man,* in which Valerie played an improvised role based on her own life. Girodias said she seemed very relaxed and friendly with Warhol, "whose conversation consisted of protracted silences and whose silver-dyed hair, I noticed, was turning back to its original mousey color on the sides."[18]

Gradually, things began to fall apart for Valerie. She was ejected from the Chelsea Hotel for failing to pay her rent, she started pestering Girodias for more money in an aggressive way, and her novel appeared to be grounded. At the same time she started to complain bitterly about Warhol: "He was a thief, he wanted to exploit her, he was a vulture." Girodias said he heard that she was saying the same thing about him to Warhol. And Barney Rosset, who never actually met her, said he heard that she was saying similar things about him behind his back.[19]

Valerie finally asked if Girodias would publish the *S.C.U.M. Manifesto* instead of the novel. He agreed, and, after some initial hesitation, she wrote him a letter from California saying that the manifesto "is now yours, to have and to hold—forever." Letters and telephone calls followed, some dealing with corrections and changes in the manifesto, others more personal and abusive.[20]

In early June 1968 Girodias went to Montreal for a few days. The day after he left New York, Valerie Solanas walked into Andy Warhol's studio in Union Square and fired three bullets from a .32 revolver into him, seriously damaging his spleen, stomach, liver, esophagus, and both lungs. She walked out, and a few hours later, as Warhol was undergoing five hours of surgery in the hospital, gave herself up to a policeman in Times Square. Warhol survived, and Solanas was sent to a mental hospital for tests. The story resonated through the media but disappeared when, less than forty-eight hours after the shooting, Sirhan Sirhan assassinated Robert Kennedy in Los Angeles.

The story behind the story appears to be that Warhol was not Solanas's first target. Number one in her sights was Maurice Girodias. She went round to his offices in Gramercy Park first, found he wasn't there, and then walked down the street to Warhol's studio. Did Girodias know she was on the warpath? Barney Rosset thinks he had a premonition and took the opportunity to make his business trip to Canada at that moment. Rosset also said that Solanas was gunning for him, and, after the Warhol shooting, she came round to his office with an ice-pick but was arrested by a policeman. "My ice-cubes remained intact," Rosset said.[21]

Girodias visited her in the hospital several times and sent her money. She wrote back, addressing him as "Toad." Meanwhile, Girodias moved quickly to publish *The S.C.U.M. Manifesto*. While he had been committed to publishing it before the shooting, he capitalized on her sudden notoriety. In an advance press release, Girodias quoted what she had told the police, that her reasons for shooting Warhol were "very involved but best understood if you read my manifesto." The book's front cover bore her photograph and extracts from *Time* magazine ("Warhol . . . the ultimate voyeur . . . felled by S.C.U.M.") and *Newsweek* ("A diatribe of fanatical intensity . . . savage shrewdness and wit.") The back cover carried a reproduction of the front page of the *New York Post* the day after the shooting with the headline: ANDY WARHOL FIGHTS FOR LIFE.

Valerie Solanas, who was thirty-two years old when she shot Warhol, had a disturbed childhood, her parents separating when she was a girl. She was educated at the University of Maryland and graduated with honors. She began graduate studies but dropped out and worked as a prostitute for a time, ending up in New York. A year after the attack on Warhol, she was sentenced to three years in prison. She died from emphysema in 1988.[22]

IN PARIS, things were going from bad to worse. A hurried move of the Olympia office had taken place to smaller and cheaper premises at number 6 rue Séguier. The building had been a religious publishing house in the seventeenth century, and its windows were blacked on the inside. The Olympia staff had dwindled to two people—Holly Hutchins and a bookkeeper.

Girodias spent most of his time in New York writing urgent letters to Holly in Paris. Once when she was going on vacation to the United States, he asked her to bring some Olympia books on microfilm to New York. Holly had them processed in Paris and packed film of about twenty books in her suitcase. On her arrival in New York by ship, the U.S. Customs singled her out, found the film, and confiscated it. Girodias immediately launched a lawsuit without consulting her: Hutchins versus the State of New York.[23]

The transatlantic correspondence reflected the deepening crisis.

· *New York, January 16, 1967:* Girodias, fighting the pirates, asks Holly for books, copyright notices, and other evidence to be sent over— "it's becoming quite imperative to find a copy of the first volume of the pink cover print edition of *120 Days of Sodom* (July 1954). Leon [Friedman] only has Volume II. Can you write to some of the *oldest* fans? . . . Say hello to Vicky [Victoria Reiter]. . . . And keep up the old banner of pornography."

· *New York, summer 1967:* "I have a lot of unavoidable expenses and I'm wasting an awful amount of time and energy because of lack of funds. . . . However, money will start pouring out from all kinds of directions, and this is our last difficult passage. . . . It's wet and stifling and the noise of the air conditioning becomes part of the subconscious. What a city! However, that's where our fortune lies, so I have to take it."

· *New York, December 20, 1967:* "I found things here in a state of great confusion. More books pirated, and my New York distributor is getting more and more difficult. I am secretly negotiating a new deal with another and much bigger distributor. . . . I have to cut down expenses to a bare minimum. Shall I go on? Well, even if it kills me to do so, I have to." (Echoes of Beckett: "I can't go on, I'll go on.") "Can you find yourself some other job?" Girodias suggests she work a few hours a week for five hundred francs. "Unless you have a better idea, like opening a tearoom in rue Séguier with your own money, or a laundromat, or a fortune teller's office."

· *Paris, December 26, 1967:* Holly commiserates with him over his troubles. "But it's been a great experience, I would not have had it otherwise for anything! And who knows perhaps someday 6 rue Séguier could be a *librarie-bar ou quelquechose* and with me under the counter (in a plain brown wrapper of course)." She says she will gladly continue working part-time and ends: "Many thanks for everything and all best wishes for a Happy New Year, and *merde* as we say over here!"

· *New York, December 31, 1967:* "Your letter came as a great relief. . . . So you don't hate me too much for letting you down. . . . Well, of course I knew that you were too good to hate people even when you had the semblance of a reason to; but I must say I felt, and feel, very bad about the whole thing. . . . my whole Paris establishment has now become a ruinous burden which I have to liquidate. . . . Love and Superwishes, MG." This letter has a handwritten postscript: "And what of those fucking Danes? The books! Money!"

· *New York, December 11, 1968 (gap of a year):* Girodias talks about Lamy [owner of number 6 rue Séguier], who appeared to be repossessing the premises. "As Lamy has now made the irreparable mistake of suing me to collect the key money I had undertaken to pay him . . . he has given me the weapon I needed to exercise my REVENGE— which will be swift, terrible and absolutely ruthless. It's for the cops now to put their well-shaped noses in that dung heap."

At the end of the letter he asks about Maria, who Holly told him is living in France, a fact that came "as a major surprise." (Maria was a German woman Girodias had met in Frankfurt. They had an affair, and she had his son after they separated.) "She has not written me in a long time, and sometimes I look at the picture of that little boy and I feel the tears creeping up to those beautiful orbs. . . . You see what I mean? I'm sure you do. Say hello to your Mammy and your Pappy."

· *New York, April 6, 1969:* A new business partner had emerged, a "comic books and girlie magazine publisher, millionaire, lover of *le beau sex* in a very healthy direct manner, and a very good guy although slightly incapacitated brainwise—which is a damned good thing as I have a completely free hand editorially, and get half of the take. . . . Tomorrow I see the editors of New American Library to whom I offered my unwritten book [Girodias's autobiography] for $75,000 advance. They are very hot, and it may work—for a little less than what I am asking, but I won't sign for less than $60,000, so don't fret."

· *Chelsea Hotel, New York:* Girodias writes about contracts, copyrights, and copies of old Olympia books. "I badly need copies of *The Watcher and the Watched, A Gallery of Nudes, Intimate Interviews, Darling, Innocence* (Daimler—very old), *Whip Angels* (very old), *Gaudy Image, Until She Screams, Sin for Breakfast, Father Silas.* . . . I'm sitting here covered with unpaid bills and hungry as hell."

· *New York, June 24, 1969:* Girodias reports that he is dabbling with the notion of collaborating with a Swiss publisher to do fancy art books with an erotic flavor. But he doubts whether the publisher he has in mind is suitable, "his clientele being somewhat Helvetic and turgid." Girodias asks for a first edition of *Story of O* for his lawsuit against Pauvert and has settled another suit with James Sherwood (a Paris Olympia author who wrote *Stradella*). . . . "I am now *winning* all my lawsuits. I am very soon to win against Donleavy. Isn't that a scream! As to Mr Lamy's goose, it is being cooked with most tender care and attention. Hah."

· *New York, May 27, 1970:* He commiserates with Holly over continuing problems with the landlord of Olympia's Paris office, but new dreams are replacing old miseries: "From Finland to Italy, from France to Japan, from Turkey to Venezuela, from England to Israel (and soon also . . . Russia!) Olympia is now reigning *Über Alles*." He says he will be coming over to Paris soon—"if you are a good girl you will get an invitation to a . . . party to launch le Prix Olympia [a literary prize that never materialized]."

At about the same time Girodias wrote to an old girlfriend in Paris asking her for a loan. He talks about his approaching success. "You will have the great pleasure of knowing a new Girodias, a well-to-do, opulent Girodias, with a gardenia in his buttonhole and a greyhound as white as snow at his feet, a thousand dollar cigar between his lips."

Aʟᴀs, it was not to be. If the second half of the 1960s had given Girodias a roller-coaster ride with some upward swoops to balance the downward plunges, the first half of the 1970s was virtually all downhill. Ominously, the decade opened with the reappearance of Girodias's dogged nemesis, J. P. Donleavy.

The last act in the vendetta between Girodias and Donleavy came unexpectedly, yet appropriately, in Paris:

"In 1966 I had bought back the debts so that it [Olympia] was nominally on its feet again," Girodias recalled. "But in 1968 the French administration tripped it for good, and it was re-bankrupted. All right, since I was unable to keep it out of bankruptcy, which I was doing only in order to continue the litigation against Donleavy on both the French and the British fronts, I would keep fighting through the receiver (who profited copiously by it), feeding more and more money to the lawyers in Paris and London; all this from my command post in New York, and through a Swiss holding company."[24]

At this critical stage, Girodias won a judgment against Donleavy in a French court. Donleavy's lawyers immediately appealed the decision, and the case moved up to a higher court. But Girodias was jubilant. "All those patient and passionate efforts were not in vain," he wrote. "The time . . . [had come] when the final victory was at last in sight. In case of success the judgment of the Paris court would become applicable internationally, and I could then force Donleavy to pay me one half of all the subsidiary sales he had made unilaterally over the past 14 or 15 years, plus interest, plus eventual punitive damages: hundreds of thousands of dollars. Half of his castle, half of his seventy-five heifers and other cattle, tractors, limousines, the lot.

"But the question was, how to recover that fortune myself? To do so I had to buy the bankrupt company with the help of the receiver and of course for a nominal amount. But such a sale could only be carried out by way of a public auction; and it . . . cost me a high price in bribes to have this public auction conducted in the most private manner possible.[25]

"So I bribed the receiver some more to organise a public sale of the assets of the bankrupt company, to be the buyer of the company, and to do it in such a secretive manner that this public auction at the Tribunal de Commerce, I should be the only one to be at this auction, nobody else should know about it. It is done in such a way that the legal publicity [notices] for it is immediately torn down from the walls."[26]

Back in his Irish "castle" in the spring of 1970, Donleavy caught wind of the auction from his Paris lawyers. It came in a casual aside during a telephone conversation: "Oh, by the way, the Olympia Press is up for auction the day after tomorrow," the French lawyer said. Donleavy was then living with his second wife, a young American actress called Mary Wilson Price (now Mary Guinness), whom he had met in New York. She immediately volunteered to go over to Paris to see if she could buy the press. "It was completely spontaneous," she remembered. "We figured it out that the simple thing to do was to buy the Olympia Press to stop all the litigation. If we bought it, everything would end."[27]

Accompanied by Donleavy's secretary, Phyllis MacArdle, who spoke some French, Mary Donleavy jumped on a plane. ("They were two stunning-looking women," said Donleavy.) In her handbag was $15,000, in cash. On arriving in Paris, she avoided Donleavy's French lawyers and hired a lawyer who specialized in bankruptcy proceedings, one Émile Achille Jules Paul Plez. In his early sixties, Monsieur Plez was a small, unassuming man who could easily have been mistaken for one of the bureaucrats with whom he dealt every working day. With only twenty-four hours to prepare for the auction, Mary Donleavy scurried from office to office, Monsieur Plez in tow, in a desperate race against the clock.

"You had to have a guaranteed check deposited in the bank before the bankruptcy auction took place," she said, adding: "No foreigners were allowed to buy these bankrupt companies. I didn't realise how severe the law was until the day after the auction. But somehow or other, by some unbelievable fluke, I managed to convince someone to give me special permission. He signed this piece of paper about four-thirty in the afternoon the day before the auction. We rushed over to the bank and deposited the fifteen thousand dollars. It was a miracle. You know how once in a while something happens, that all the red tape is brushed aside. It was an absolute miracle."[28]

The next day, Wednesday, April 29, the two young women and their lawyer arrived at the Tribunal de Commerce in good time for the auction, which was due to begin at 2:15 P.M. It was a fine spring day, and in the park outside the building birds were singing. They sat down in the center of the room and looked around. The auctioneer sat behind a high desk at the end of the room. On the desk were three unlit candles. Rows of benches filled the rest of the room. A number of bankrupt companies were up for sale, and there were about thirty people present.

Mary Donleavy recognized Girodias almost as soon as she entered the room. He was wearing a raincoat loosely over his shoulders in the French style. "I had never seen him before," she said, "but I knew immediately who he was from his attitude. He was so sure of himself, waltzing around the benches with his lawyer beside him."[29]

The Olympia Press auction was second on the list, so she had a chance to see how the system worked before their turn came. French auctioneering practice in those days favored candles for the final countdown. Not for the French the singsong chant of the fast-talking American auctioneer or the crude British "Going, going, gone," ending with the whack of a hammer. In France, auctions had an almost religious air. The auctioneer would light the first candle when the bidding slowed. Each candle had a short-burning wick, and when the first one went out, assuming there were no more bids, the auctioneer would light the second candle and then, if nothing further happened,

on to the third. The sale was final when the third candle went out.
Monsieur Plez was to do the bidding and had been carefully instructed
by his youthful principal.

After the first auction, Girodias came over and took a seat a little
bit in front of and to the right of the two young women and their
lawyer. "Girodias's lawyer started bidding," Mary Donleavy said,
"and our little man came up with '*plus cent*' [a hundred more]. Each
time Girodias raised his bid, Plez looked up for an instant, repeated
'*plus cent,*' and put his head down again. Girodias, taken aback, spun
round. It was clear that he did not know that someone had made a
last-minute deposit the previous day and was putting in a serious
challenge. He bid again, and once more from behind him came the
softly spoken '*plus cent.*' There was a pause, and the auctioneer lit the
first candle.

"It was a very dramatic thing because you could see the bidding,"
Mary Donleavy continued. "In a British auction you don't know
where the bidding is coming from or who is doing it." As the struggle
went on, the people in the auction room began to sense the drama.
"They didn't know what was at stake, but they knew that they were
watching something special. There was total silence."

After a dozen or so bids and counterbids, the action slowed. The
second candle began to sputter, and the auctioneer ignited his taper
from it and lit the third. Girodias bid again. Again "*plus cent.*" "He
turned around and glowered because he didn't know who we were,"
Mary Donleavy said. "He didn't know what we were made of."
Finally, Girodias could go no higher. "*Plus cent*" rang out for the last
time, and the third candle was extinguished. All that remained of
Girodias's hopes of retaining his beloved press, of extracting a fortune
from Donleavy, and of savoring victory over his old enemy was a
wisp of smoke and the faint aroma of wax.

There was a collective gasp from the onlookers, followed by a
round of applause. "They wanted me to get it in the end because
they could see that Girodias was behaving in a more and more volatile
fashion and glaring back at us," Mary Donleavy said. "When he lost
it, he jumped up out of his seat and stormed angrily across the room.
He threw open the door and rushed out. I never saw him again."[30]

The auction had taken about half an hour, and the final price for
the Olympia Press was Frs. 40,100 (about $8,000). Donleavy recalled
the sweet moment of triumph as he heard it later from his wife.
"Girodias flew into a rage," he said. "He didn't know who had
bought the press, but he knew that he had lost it."[31]

"Poor old Girodias," said Mary Donleavy. "I actually felt sorry for him when he went out of the room. It was very sad because he had been a man of such enormous influence and power . . . if he had only been straight. . . . But I am not a vindictive winner, let me put it that way."

The day after the auction, Mary Donleavy received an angry telephone call from her husband's French lawyer. "He started yelling down the phone at me like nothing I had ever heard before. He said, 'Who do you think you are, what do you think you are doing? Just because you are a young attractive woman you think you can break all the laws in France. You are going to go to jail.'

"He was really threatening me. He was sure I had ruined his case representing Donleavy. After he had calmed down I told him I did actually get special permission and he could check that. He rang back about half an hour later, full of apologies, and said he had never heard of anything like it before in his life. But he said, 'you are right, it is absolutely amazing.'"

She knew that the lawyer was jubilant because purchasing the press would end the litigation. "Donleavy had a very shaky case, actually," she said. "I mean he had no case if the truth is to be known. He had sold those rights without the permission of his original publisher. He would have fought it until he was blue in the face, but he would have lost at the highest level—in France, in New York, and in England. He didn't think he could have lost, but I know that in the end—I had seen enough of the papers—he had actually sold all those rights to Girodias. So, you see, it saved an awful lot, it saved an awful lot."[32]

Donleavy denied that he sold the English rights to *The Ginger Man* without Girodias's consent. They were sold, he said, "with the verbal agreement of Girodias made on my visit to Paris," an agreement that the publisher chose "to repudiate as non-existent." If Girodias's case had been so clear-cut in Britain, "he could have obtained an injunction" and "prosecuted the case for damages." But after fourteen years, it was "struck out for want of prosecution." Girodias failed to bring an action in the United States, Donleavy pointed out, and the judgment he won in France was reversed when the writer appealed. His former wife's observations concerning his legal position were "her subjective opinion" and were "speculative and without validity."[33]

Mary Donleavy eventually divorced her husband after more than twenty years of marriage and married a member of the Guinness family. Sitting in the sunlit living room of her London home in Holland

Park, she looked back at this curious episode in her life. Was Donleavy's purchase of the Olympia Press also an act of vengeance?

"I genuinely don't think it was anything other than a practical issue," she said. "Although, subconsciously, there could have been a serious element in it. You know that Irish streak of hatred where they hate forever, they love to hate. . . . Carrying the grudge, the heavy grudge that makes them feels so good. . . . I'm not sure that there isn't a bit of truth in it [the notion of revenge], but at the time it was really practical. I'm pretty practical, and I saw it—if it could possibly be done—as a way out."³⁴

Mary Guinness spends most of her time in her family's country house but comes up to London nearly every week. "I like going to auctions," she said with a winner's smile.

Girodias also had vivid, if bitter, memories. On entering the auction room, he and the friend who was to bid on his behalf were surprised to see a group of people there, apparently foreigners. "We thought they had gone astray, that they were looking for the Sainte Chapelle and had wound up in this Tribunal de Commerce."³⁵

"But then these people start bidding against me!" he continued. "I wasn't prepared for that, you know. I could only go as far as the money I had on me. That was eight thousand dollars. . . . So I had to stop. . . . I looked at the group of three people who were bidding. The man was obviously a Paris lawyer, and the two women were obviously crazy American ladies. I couldn't understand who would do this, you see. Who would benefit? I thought it was a silly rich American girl who wanted to have the name of the company and then make me an offer to run it. I didn't know. So I started thinking about it and looking for answers, accusing some people of being behind it. . . . I got into a great deal of trouble that time."³⁶

Donleavy, with the Olympia Press scalp in his belt, said it took Girodias some time to work out who had taken it. "I heard that he suspected Mason Hoffenberg, one of his own authors, of being behind it. Girodias wrote to him, 'Dear Mason, why have you done this terrible thing to me? What have I ever done to you . . .'" Then, realizing he was mistaken, he wrote to the mysterious Mary Price at the New York address she had given the auctioneer. Donleavy remembered the letter that he called the most "astonishing of all time." "'Dear Miss Price,' it began. 'I understand you have bought my old Paris firm. Would you be interested in publishing my memoirs?'" Finally, "The awful bombshell dropped and exploded when he found out who owned the Olympia Press."³⁷

Donleavy reiterated that his main reason for buying the Olympia Press was to protect himself from Girodias's seemingly endless litigation. When he bought the press at the auction, the legal battle between the two phantom companies—The Little Someone and Eratomique—was still in progress. "The difference after the purchase," said Donleavy, "was that I now owned both of them and I was fighting myself."

Girodias was down but not out. "You would have thought that I had learned my lesson at last? Not quite yet. I then floated a theory in the Paris courts according to which the income accruing to the company prior to the date of the public sale should be considered as the property, firstly, of the creditors and, secondly, of the shareholders, i.e. myself. If I won we would be back to square one, and Donleavy would have to return half of his ill-gotten gains. This was seen as a daring, ingenious novelty by the lawmen, and this titillated their Cartesian minds to the point that, at last—*enfin!*—they handed me a handsome victory. Think of Donleavy's face.

"But of course the decision came from the lower courts and, as I expected, Donleavy appealed the judgment. I was prepared for it, and quite confident that my tactics would be just as good before the higher judges. So confident, indeed, that after a well-irrigated lunch, I took my then mistress with me to watch the proceedings, just as one would take a lady to the races for a bit of excitement and fresh air.

"She was eighteen and of very mixed blood, a chain pot-smoker of the Lower East Side school, a liberated urchin with a remarkable physique and lissom [*sic*] amber dusky skin. She was sitting next to me, the gent with the silver hair, high up on the steep amphitheatre reserved for the public. Looking up from their lower station I could see the bulging eyes of the three august judges in their robes converging on her dimpled knees, which were fully displayed since her robes were far shorter than their own. They could probably decipher the title of the comic book she was reading, for her only available remedy against *ennui,* and she was simultaneously nudging me so that I could disencumber her of a reefer which was burning her fingers.

"I espied Leo's [Matarasso] face, my attorney, and what I found there was best described as extreme frustration and disgust. It was too late, I had done it again. It seems that I had offended the court by unwittingly, and indirectly, stirring their gonads. Now I had lost the contest with Donleavy finally and completely, would I ever learn?"[38]

For Donleavy the end came on March 20, 1978, almost twenty-five years after he had first written to Girodias asking him if he would be interested in seeing the manuscript of *The Ginger Man*. Donleavy's French lawyers wrote to him reporting that Girodias's last appeal had been rejected. To celebrate, Donleavy wrote one of the brief verses that he sprinkled through his writing:

> *Anyone can be a friend*
> *So long as you don't get to know him too well.*
> *And anyone can be an enemy;*
> *You get to know him better than most.*[39]

THE $8,000 that Donleavy paid for the Olympia Press was, as his rival conceded, far cheaper than the costs of further litigation. A backlist of some 285 titles came with ownership of the press, but most of these titles had been lost to other publishers, either through inadequate protection of their copyrights or the result of simple piracy. Girodias had also transferred as many rights as he could to New York to set up his American operation. Donleavy noted that Girodias was fond of saying that the Olympia Press amounted to nothing but sand in the desert that would fall through your hands.

While partly accepting that verdict, Donleavy put some store in the value of the press's archives. "Someone in Paris must have their hands on them," he said, "and should they ever come to be sold it would mean that I would be waiting to do something about it." He laughed. "And God knows how valuable they will be after you publish your book." A louder laugh. "It's a matter of publicity, of attention."[40]

Ownership of the Olympia Press is still in the name of Donleavy's former wife, Mary Wilson Price Donleavy Guinness. The matter is under a court seal, said the ever-watchful Donleavy, and documents are being prepared for the transfer of the company into his own name.

As Donleavy read aloud extracts from the document that took the Olympia Press out of Girodias's hands, it was like hearing the story of Girodias's life: "The rights to *Candy* and *The Ginger Man* are subject to litigation" and so on. It was also perhaps a comment on the unusual character of the Olympia Press that mixed up in the papers was a page of technical instructions entitled "How to Re-Light the Aga."

Girodias reflected on the denouement in his memoirs. "It took me weeks to discover [that the buyer of the Olympia Press] was Donleavy's wife. Donleavy had money from his foreign rights to fight me. He could hire the best lawyers . . . in Paris. So, he became the owner of the Olympia Press, which is a mythical entity. Donleavy makes it sound like a prosperous outfit because he's looking for a sucker to buy it."[41]

One of the ironies of Donleavy's ownership of the Olympia Press is that he reversed roles and became Girodias's publisher. In the mid-1960s Girodias had written an introduction and explanatory notes for *The Olympia Reader,* a collection of extracts from the press's most famous books that was published by Barney Rosset at Grove Press. The collection did well and was reprinted several times. After Donleavy bought the Olympia Press, Rosset found himself sitting on royalties that he felt should be shared equally between Girodias and Donleavy. Rosset suggested that the writer (Girodias) and the publisher (Donleavy) split the money, which amounted to about $40,000. Donleavy refused, and Girodias was not happy with the idea. Rosset says he tried hard to find a compromise but failed, and the money went into Grove's coffers instead. "Enough was enough," said Rosset.[42]

THE TWO MEN were destined to meet for a third and final time. It was in the early 1970s, not long after Donleavy had acquired the Olympia Press. The Donleavys were in Paris, the guests of a wealthy friend. Donleavy was having lunch at the Coupole with his host and at one point went to the men's room. "I was walking down one of those pathways," he said, "and there sitting facing me at a table was Girodia*ss*. He said: 'Hullo, J. P.' I ignored him and walked back to my table. He'd caused so much distress in one's life and was a bully in doing it. . . . I had no sympathy for the man at all."[43]

In his memoirs, Girodias comments that Donleavy was known to be writing "his own version of *our* story, ensconced in his splendid castle, as a tax-exempt resident of Ireland; and I am happy to see that the melodrama we share will survive when we die, in his version as well as in mine, for the edification of the generations to come."[44]

When Girodias died, the funeral took place at Père Lachaise cemetery in Paris, France's last resting place for its own literati as well as for a sprinkling of foreigners, including Oscar Wilde. When I mentioned to Donleavy that Girodias had been cremated, Donleavy looked startled. A great lover of graveyards, he recalled how he had visited Père Lachaise over twenty years before. Tessa Sayle was with him, and, as they were strolling around, she looked into a room where a workman in blue overalls was having his lunch. She struck up a conversation, and Donleavy joined them. Biting into his baguette, the man told them he was in charge of the ovens and explained how the bodies were burned with sticks and gas heat. Offering them a swig out of his bottle of vin rouge, he showed them around the ovens and took a special pride in the grinder used for pulverizing the bones after incineration.

Donleavy looked pensive while telling this story. Then he brightened. "What a pity Girodias is in a box," he said. "I could have given his bones a kick!"

THREE BOOKS were largely responsible for the downfall of Olympia USA, Girodias's last publishing venture. The first was a typical Girodian piece of invention that went disastrously wrong. Patrick Kearney has pieced together the story. In September 1969 Simon & Schuster was to publish a book called *The Seven Minutes,* by Irving Wallace, a bestselling novelist, for which the author was paid an unusually large advance of $500,000. The story dealt with the events surrounding the trial of a Los Angeles bookseller who was accused of selling a fictitious and obscene novel called *The Seven Minutes*, by J J Jadway. This book, according to the story line, had originally been published in Paris in the 1930s by an English-language publisher specializing in erotica. The plot of the book-within-the-book revolves around a seven-minute act of sexual intercourse of such tedium that the female character was driven to review all her previous sexual experiences by way of a diversion.

It appeared that Wallace consulted Girodias when he was researching his novel. Later, Girodias was tipped off by Michael Bernet, an Israeli writer and friend, who told him that he, Girodias, was in Wallace's book, thinly disguised as "Christian Leroux," the sleazy French erotica publisher responsible for the original Paris edition of the pornographic and fictional *The Seven Minutes*. Bernet suggested that, if they moved fast, he could write and Girodias could publish a novel purporting to be Wallace's erotic book-within-the-book in time to coincide with the publication of the novel itself.

Girodias jumped at the idea and, with typical speed and panache, produced a book called *The Original Seven Minutes* by none other than J J Jadway—in real life, of course, Michael Bernet. The cover design closely resembled Wallace's novel and carried a startling foreword by Girodias. It claimed that *The Original Seven Minutes,* "the last and greatest underground erotic masterpiece . . . on which Irving Wallace based his bestselling novel," had been bought from J J Jadway by Jack Kahane in Paris in 1934 but had never been published. Jadway was a real person, Girodias continued, and not a figment of Wallace's imagination. Unfortunately, Jadway had not finished the novel, so the "present version has been largely amended, coordinated and edited by a writer whose talent is at least equal to Jadway's."

Girodias energetically promoted the book, but before he could make a fortune out of sales, Wallace's publisher obtained a court injunction, a case followed, and Girodias lost. He was ordered to destroy the entire print run, which he said was 150,000 copies, and pay all legal costs. He recouped some of his losses later by reissuing the book as *The Seven Erotic Minutes*. Jadway's name was replaced by "Anonymous," the cover design was changed, and the foreword was dropped. But the text was identical with that of the suppressed original. Nevertheless, valuable time and resources had been lost.[45]

The second book was *Sir Cyril Black* by Benjamin Grimm, an erotic novel that appeared under the Ophelia imprint in New York in 1969. The author's real name was Spencer Lambert, one of Girodias's regulars, whose previous works included *Conception of the Beast* and *Celebration of the Flesh*. Nothing happened until 1975, when the real-life Sir Cyril Black, a seventy-three-year-old former Conservative Member of Parliament in Britain who had been alerted by a friend in New York, sued the Olympia Press for libel. Demanding a million dollars, Black said he had originally been under the impression that the book was a biography of himself. Then he discovered that it was "a pornographic novel in which the principal character was named Sir Cyril Black, portrayed as a most evil person engaged in perversions of various kinds, and guilty of practices of an unspeakable nature." The story was about a sadist, who had "long legs and grey eyes, like me." He won the case and was awarded $100,000, a public apology, and his costs.

Black was a devout Baptist who, during twenty years in Parliament, had established a reputation as a relentless campaigner against pornography, homosexuality, alcohol, and miniskirts. His most prominent campaigns had been against the legislation that legalized homosexuality in Britain in 1967 and the prosecution of Hubert Selby's avant-garde novel *Last Exit to Brooklyn,* which had a homosexual theme.

It was no accident that the Olympia Press book bore Black's name as its title. Girodias accepted "full responsibility" for this kamikaze act. The reason, he said, was that he was upset about the prosecution of Selby's novel, which had been published by his "close friends" John Calder and Marion Boyars. "The case was an outrageous demonstration of what I have fought against for a full lifetime. My joke was pretty stupid, I confess, but it was hardly more than that. . . . Some people blow up banks to express their discontent; my method is more peaceful, even if the results are less spectacular."[46]

The third strange book that Girodias published in New York was a more ambitious and self-destructive affair because it attracted the unfriendly attention of the United States government without making the publisher rich or famous. While it brought Girodias a degree of notoriety, which he probably relished more than wealth and fame, it did not last long. The book was the publisher's last hurrah. It had a title that was hard to miss and, once seen or heard, impossible to forget: *President Kissinger*.

In 1973 Olympia USA had filed for bankruptcy, but Girodias managed to relaunch himself as the Venus-Freeway Press with a small young staff consisting of three people: Humphrey Evans, who brought in Ed Ferraro, who recruited Ann Patty. None of them was full-time and salaries depended on cash flow, but they all seemed to have enjoyed the experience. "Getting paid was an adventure, an event," said Ferraro. "Working for Girodias was not business as usual. Come to think of it, it wasn't business at all."[47]

Humphrey M. Evans III was a brilliant composer of music, a child prodigy who was given a retrospective at the Smithsonian in Washington at age fifteen. He came to New York as a young man and teamed up with Girodias because he needed a job and because Girodias was notorious and glamorous. Evans was a homosexual who liked rough trade, a heavy drinker, and an outlandish dresser who could command attention in Manhattan's midtown restaurants by lifting his head and flaring his nostrils. He was witty and bitchy, loving and loved, and he possessed an uncanny insight into people and their motives. He ran Girodias's office and became indispensable to him. While still in his early thirties, Evans died of cirrhosis of the liver in a New York hospital, surrounded by his grieving friends.

Ed Ferraro, tall, witty, and eloquent, was just as wild in a less dramatic way. "It was not easy to be poor in New York in those days but we thought you'd be out of your mind to live any other way. Better Girodias and no money than uptown and a paycheck." He joined Girodias as production manager and for the first six months Ed Ferraro was the unhappiest production manager in New York. Nothing was produced.[48]

Ann Patty was a young Californian, recently graduated from Berkeley, who decided to seek her fortune in New York's publishing world. She got a job as a typist at Knopf and then met Humphrey and Ed at a party at the Gotham Book Mart. "I thought they were the two coolest guys I had ever met, and I wanted to be with them. They said, 'Don't work for Girodias unless you have a trust fund.'" She did not have a trust fund, but she finished up working for Girodias anyway and having an affair with Ed. "It was crazy," she said. "We pretended to have jobs, Maurice pretended to have a company. It was existential publishing."[49]

Venus-Freeway did not publish a great number of books, but once again the selection was curious. The list included a book on kung fu, *An Astrological Guide to Living in the Age of Aquarius, The Office Workers' Manifesto, Pyramid Power,* a slew of pornographic novels (*Sea of Thighs, Mama Liz Tastes Flesh,* reprints of three "Harriet Daimler" books, and one by the ever-reliable Norman Singer, *The Lay of the Land*), *President Kissinger,* and a slim illustrated volume on Muhammad Ali, the boxer.

The Ali book was put together by two young writers, Victor Bockris and Andrew Wylie, who had spent time with the boxer as he prepared to fight George Foreman in Zaire. The idea was that the book would appear at the time of the fight and if Ali won and regained his world heavyweight crown—as the authors confidently expected he would—the book would sell madly.

The book was ready on time, Ali won, and Girodias took the jubilant authors out to a fancy lunch to celebrate and plan their brilliant future. But their book did not sell, and their publisher could not pay for the lunch.

Undeterred, Wylie and Bockris came up with another idea: Adolf Hitler in training for *his* comeback (World War II) as reported by the writers who had just brought back Muhammad Ali. The title was *Springtime for Hitler,* borrowed from Mel Brooks's movie *The Producers.* Girodias loved it and signed them up with a $200 advance, the down payment bouncing when they tried to cash the check. But a double writer's block slowed things down, and then Venus-Freeway went bankrupt, effectively ending Maurice Girodias's publishing career.[50]

His troubles, however, did not end. Instead, they got worse, especially when *President Kissinger,* his last book, was published in 1974. Calling the book "a political science fiction," Girodias blended current events, science fiction, and pornography, convinced that he was creating a blockbuster. "This is going to be an extremely sensational and readable book, very original in form," he told a British publisher. Five people wrote various bits of it, including Girodias himself, although it appeared under only two of their names.

The story starts off by establishing that a change in the American constitution allows a foreign-born citizen to become president. Henry Kissinger wins the election, and the yarn gathers momentum. Marco Vassi, one of Girodias's regular writers, was assigned to add some sex scenes. One of the wildest has Kissinger cavorting with a German girlfriend who is wearing her brother's SS uniform while the statesman is in a frilly French maid's outfit. He is on his hands and knees while she straddles him, whacking him with a riding crop. Other scenes include Kissinger having an affair with a Radcliffe girl at the Paris Ritz Hotel and with a strapping Prussian noblewoman in a Heidelberg inn.

The book was printed and sent to a warehouse, whereupon Girodias's distributor, Kable News, refused to handle it. Girodias decided to distribute *President Kissinger* himself, and staff and friends spent long hours in his office pasting new stickers on every copy. At this point he was called in by U.S. immigration officials and asked to show his passport, which revealed that his American visa had expired. The State Department had, apparently, received an anonymous complaint. *The New York Times* picked up the story, with Girodias complaining that he was being victimized by the U.S. government.

Girodias was then living with Lilla Cabot Lyon, the daughter of a diplomat, who was at medical school studying to become a doctor. They had been thinking of getting married in France, but bureaucratic difficulties intervened. Girodias's immigration problems made a decision more urgent, and the couple were married in New York in the summer of 1974. The drama heightened when Girodias was arrested on a pier at Port Newark, New Jersey, and charged with "trespass on property without legitimate purpose" and "possession of a Controlled Dangerous Substance"—marijuana in this case. He was taken there by a beautiful woman who came to his office professing interest in his legal problems and promising to help him through her connections. She whisked him out to New Jersey, where she planted the pot on him. He was booked and put on probation since it was a first offense.

Girodias tended to see a conspiracy behind every misfortune, but on this occasion he believed he had good grounds for identifying the source. In 1973 he had published a serious investigation of the Church of Scientology called *Inside Scientology: How I Joined Scientology and Became Superhuman,* written by Robert Kaufman, a former member. The group was enraged and tried to have the book banned in Britain. Girodias successfully defended it, the court refusing the Scientologists' application for an injunction. The judge said that the passages in the book the cult complained of as breaches of confidentiality were "nonsensical mumbo jumbo."

At the time of the book's publication, some five thousand booksellers and business associates of Girodias in Britain received letters on the Olympia Press letterhead informing them that the press was out of business when it was not. Girodias believed this was the work of the Scientologists. When the trouble began with the U.S. government, he became convinced that the Scientologists were behind it. After his arrest, his suspicions fell on a young woman whom he had once hired. She used to work long hours in the office when everyone else had gone. After she resigned, Girodias discovered that a number of files were missing, and believed she had passed them on to the Scientologists. (Lilla Lyon later found her name on an official list of Scientology members.) Girodias suspected that material from those files was used as the basis of an anonymous letter to the State Department denouncing him and triggering an investigation into his immigration status.

Leon Friedman obtained a copy of the letter through the Freedom of Information Act. Addressed to Henry Kissinger at the State Department, it warned him about the impending publication of *President Kissinger* and pointed out that Girodias was being investigated for tax evasion and visa violations. Describing him as an "un-American activist," the letter urged that Girodias "should be stopped" before any more mud was slung at the government. It was signed: "A PATRIOT."[51]

14

The Loneliness
of the
Long-Forgotten Publisher

GIRODIAS WAS fifty-five years old when his last publishing venture collapsed. He was to live for another sixteen years, in New
York, Boston, and finally in Paris, trying to lift new projects off the
ground, writing his memoirs, and dreaming impossible dreams. During that time his second marriage broke up, he had operations on his
eyes and for cancer of the colon, and he became virtually destitute,
depending on handouts from family and friends. Forgotten by the
publishing world and ignored by the media, the Frog Prince—his
name for himself—took a wrong turning and disappeared from public
view.

After the debacle of the Kissinger book and the collapse of Venus-
Freeway Press, Girodias stayed on in New York for a time trying to
sort out his legal and financial problems. Although he was threatened
with expulsion from the United States, the threat was never imple-
mented, and he finally acquired resident status. He started writing his
memoirs, for which he expected a large advance; after several rebuffs
he settled with Crown Publishers for a more modest—and realistic—
sum.

During this time he and Lilla were living in a small apartment and feeling the pressure build up on their lives. He had hardly any money and was trying to return to a profession that he loved; she was scraping by while struggling to complete her medical training. Girodias wrote to a friend around this time: "I am paying a heavy karma for all I did to the race of writers. . . . I have lost most everything I had brought here with me; not just the authors, but faith in myself, the belief in the game itself, and the ability to cope with so much atrocious vulgarity. If I make a come-back, it must be an educated one, as I cannot afford another failure. I'd rather carry my wife's thermometer or continue doing the dishes. And fortunately, the only thing I have left, but that's a lot, is my little old wifie, who belongs to a race of backwoods New England heroes tinged with New Age futurology (is that a way to describe one's wife?) One of the rare pleasures is to see women liberating themselves; some do it well, some botch it up, but God, it is a stimulating spectacle!"[1]

In 1977 Lilla finished medical school in New York and they moved to Boston for two years so she could do an internship and residency. Girodias hated Boston, feeling more removed than ever from the world of publishing. When they returned to New York, the marriage, which had started with "*un coup de foudre*" [love at first sight] on Lilla's part and seen many happy times, began to unravel. He was deeply depressed, money problems worsened, and she became exhausted. "Have you ever lived with someone who is depressed?" she asked me. "I just got *completely* worn out."[2]

They initially separated in New York in 1979 but remained close, living together, on and off, in New York and Paris until 1985. A final reunion took place in London in 1990, ten days before he died. Lilla, a physician in the New York medical system, is loyal to his memory while aware of his faults. "Life with Maurice was an endless series of legal problems," she said. "He really liked to fight. But it wore him out and depleted his resources, and this is where we used to argue. Being a cautious, prudent New Englander, it seemed to me that you take reasonable precautions. You don't get into cars with strange women and drive to Newark, New Jersey, which is what he did when he was arrested for possession of marijuana. He was also very stubborn, he never listened to anybody. But he was totally fearless and totally uncowed by authority, and that's what I admired about him."[3]

Girodias spent most of the last decade of his life in his hometown, Paris. He moved, as he had always done, from apartment to apartment, restaurant and bar to restaurant and bar and, less frequently, from woman to woman. He worked on the second volume of his memoirs and produced a huge number of new ideas for publishing and other projects. They included a *Love-Hate Anthology* (a collection of love and hate letters); a project on beauty; a proposal for welcoming tourists to Paris; *Zoë,* "an international collection of books of the future" that embraced studies on the "rights of minorities," the "future of the Red Empire," the "duty of intelligence," "a re-examination of Freud and Marx," and the "hand-gun (pistol)"; a design for an illuminated fountain that he hoped to put on the market; and, finally, the Spiral, a mystical creation that was supposed to provide the answer, among more philosophical considerations, to perpetual motion.

At one stage Girodias had an apartment overlooking Père Lachaise cemetery. From his window he could see the smoke rising from the crematorium. Then the bailiffs came and evicted him, and he moved to his penultimate resting place, an apartment that his brother, Eric, found for him in Montparnasse.

In the spring of 1990, Éditions de la Différence published his memoirs in two volumes. They were well reviewed, and Maurice Girodias found himself on the circuit once again with radio and television interviews, a reading at the Village Voice bookshop, and old friends and colleagues calling on the telephone. He wrote to Lilla in New York: "In the space of 3–4 weeks, my story has become so fashionable in this country that I could sell my toenails for a million each."

On July 3, 1990, he went to do another interview on a small radio station, Radio J. After the session, he complained of not feeling well, had a heart attack, and died. In a small irony that he would have appreciated, the Frog Prince of publishing—a man who had never accepted organized religion or his own Jewishness—left this life expounding his universal ideas on a radio station targeted to Jewish listeners.

MAURICE GIRODIAS carved out a memorable niche in the history of the written word. How is he to be judged? Girodias was a strange man, a mixture of contradictory and conflicting elements that often produced a Jekyll and Hyde effect. On the sunny side basked the charm, the wit, a lively mind excited by—and full of—ideas, loyalty to family, great generosity, and an intuitive compassion.

Miriam Worms remembered the compassion. After she left Olympia in 1961, she worked for *Jeune Afrique,* an anticolonial, left-wing magazine in Paris. A terrorist group, the OAS (Organisation de l'Armée Sécrète), which was fighting to keep Algeria French and trying to kill President de Gaulle, set off a bomb in the magazine's office. The explosion destroyed her left eye. Girodias rushed round to see her in the hospital in a terrible state. He apparently felt responsible for her leaving Olympia and wanted to make up for it.

But in the shadows of his personality lurked a depressive, cruel, destructive streak that could appear and reappear with disconcerting speed. "Something would snap in his poor head," Miriam Worms said, "and he could be lethal." Depression was never far from the surface. "He was not a joyous person. There was no gaiety to his laugh, although he had amusing ideas." She also saw something that most people did not associate with the urbane, amusing, high-living publisher. "He could be very boring, catatonically boring," she said. "Girodias was not as interesting in real life as he may appear in people's memories," she warned. "Or in your book."

Although Girodias was protective of his family and loyal to them, he was not "a family man." His daughters, Valérie and Juliette, suffered from his lack of interest in them. "He was rather cold with us, almost as if he were embarrassed by having children," Juliette said. He saw them infrequently when they were young, although he would occasionally shower them with presents. Laurette Kahane said he would take them out "for an expensive dinner or to a nightclub when what they really needed was new shoes."[4]

A steady social life was foreign to him, and he did eccentric things. He once stood for hours in Barney Rosset's Long Island swimming pool on a blazing summer's day until his torso was burned red. After that self-inflicted, inexplicable ordeal, Girodias merely grunted, left for the airport, and caught a plane back to Paris. On another occasion he took Rosset and his wife to a famous lesbian nightclub in Paris. It was packed, and, as they were waiting for the cabaret to start, Girodias, who was angry with Rosset for some reason, jumped up and started to strip and throw his clothes at the couple. Two powerful lesbian bouncers rushed forward, picked him up, and tossed him out into the street, followed by his clothes and his bewildered guests.

He had a combative spirit that carried him through perilous times. "He thought everyone was a *con* [bastard]," said Miriam Worms. "I'd tell him that there were armies of them out there, but not everybody was one. His favorite expression, which he used nearly every day, was *on les aura* [let's get them]. Yes, he had a fighting spirit, but much of it was employed against an unknown enemy."[5]

Ricki Levenson, an American psychologist and teacher, had an affair with Girodias in the late 1960s that was important to them both. After it ended she wrote to him saying that she thought his greatest enemy was himself. "I hear and feel the self-hate. I also hear the self-overestimation . . . an external denial of some deep disappointment you've experienced and turned against yourself."[6]

Girodias's early interest in Eastern religions, especially the teachings of Sri Aurobindo, continued throughout his life and intensified in its closing stages. It was another aspect of this unusual publisher-pornographer that did not fit the conventional mold. "I rather liked him, but he was a strange person," said Austryn Wainhouse. "He had a very *low* temperature, he was calm, almost somnolent. He was mystical, a theosophist, a very mysterious man." Laurette Kahane said that Girodias spent "a lot of time in his dreams and interior being. He was not a businessman at all."[7]

Girodias had a special attraction to, and affinity with, women. He loved women in a profound sense that transcended their beauty and their sexual magnetism. He loved their company, their style, their intuition, their differences, everything that made them distinct from the male of the species. "He loved us as individuals," said Lilla Lyon. "He didn't have some preconceived, standard *Playboy* image of us. . . . He never felt women had to have a single role. He enjoyed their ability to do things. I met a lot of his old girlfriends, and he retained good relationships with them. I don't think he left a lot of bitterness behind him."[8]

Ann Patty was struck by his elegance, his gentleness, and his charm. "There was nothing sleazy about him. Not many men truly love women, but Maurice was one of them. He appreciated them as women, and all women recognize that kind of man when they meet him."[9]

IN HIS PROFESSIONAL LIFE, Girodias was a real publisher, an unusually good publisher, at times a brilliant publisher. He had an intimate knowledge of the technical side—the quality and heft of paper, the use of illustrations, the printing process, and so on. Girodias read, he loved books, and he knew about literature. He had a publisher's eye for the good and the bad, what would work and what would not.

Austryn Wainhouse, who later became a publisher himself, considered Girodias's record. "If a publisher spots five great books out of five thousand, it's not bad. He had an educated, subtle Frenchman's understanding of good writing, and he was very mainstream in his taste."[10]

Girodias made no bones about being a pornographer. "I am an active and conscious pornographer," he used to say, declaring that the function was no more shameful than selling food or clothing. Since sex was a central part of human activity, publishing pornography was not only morally defensible but had socially redeeming qualities by helping to release sexual tensions in a harmless way. Journalists often called Girodias "the Prince of Porn" or, more flatteringly, "the Lenin of the Sexual Revolution." He gracefully accepted both titles as his due.

"If Maurice was a pornographer, it was a very special kind," said Barney Rosset. "People like Terry Southern, Norman Rubington, and Marilyn Meeske (a real Maurice Girodias person) were closest to Maurice's kind of taste. I could always spot a Girodias book—it would have an intellectualized sexual and political style. *Candy* was the quintessential Girodias book."[11]

The other side of Girodias's publishing persona was his delight in attacking the establishment—the Anglo-Saxon establishment, the French establishment, any establishment that raised its head over the parapet. *On les aura!* Let's get 'em! "I would never have launched into [the Olympia] phase of my publishing career had I not acquired over the years an urge to attack the Universal Establishment with all the means at my disposal," he wrote. "To fight one head of the beast rather than the other had no real importance; to fight French intolerance or Anglo-American moral conventions really came to the same thing."[12]

Girodias, it is clear, was a terrible paymaster. By design or accident, authors were paid late, less than they should have been, or, quite often, as in the case of the patient William Burroughs, waiting for his American royalties, not at all. "On a personal level I found Girodias very charming," said Dick Seaver. "But he was a totally unscrupulous guy. He would not pay royalties."[13]

Women authors tended to be more tolerant. "Girodias was a compassionate person who would help you out if he could," said Marilyn Meeske. "Apart from [failing to register] copyright, he was no worse than any other publisher." Iris Owens's view was that "Gid was the most appreciative and uncritical publisher imaginable for a fledgling novelist. I'm not at all sure he ever read a word I wrote after accepting those first twenty-five pages I submitted that ultimately became *Darling*. I sometimes think I could have plagiarized Mother Goose and the manuscript would have gone automatically into print. I'll always be grateful to Maurice, that generous scoundrel, generous often with money he owed you, that ended up in the pockets of restaurateurs. He taught me about food and wine and other bon vivant attributes, but not, sadly, how to protect or hold on to earnings."[14]

Girodias remained an outsider to the end of his days. He was never accepted by the publishing world, in France, Britain, the United States, or anywhere else—the Olympia Press was bad news. For some publishers, Girodias was just a pornographer and a crook—a man not to be trusted—and his imprints had no standing. With the exception of one or two personal friends like John Calder, no publishers came to his funeral.

It was different with Barney Rosset and John Calder, who were also outsiders. The three men presented an interesting contrast in background, publishing taste, and personal style. Girodias, the Anglo-French, Protestant-Jewish Parisian; Rosset, the Jewish-Irish Chicagoan-turned–New Yorker; and Calder, the Scottish–French-Canadian Londoner, achieved much together in their common fight against censorship in the Anglo-Saxon world. But they were too much alike, and too individualistic, to get on well. Although they respected each other, there was never a real chance of them forming an alliance that would have channeled their talents and resources more effectively.

Girodias was not a businessman. He was scornful of money and people who had money, especially institutional people like bankers. He constantly sabotaged promising deals, partly because he had difficulty identifying where his true interests lay and partly because he never wanted to put himself in a position where someone else could tell him what to do. *Le Monde,* reviewing his memoirs, called him "a kamikaze publisher."

Like many publishers, Girodias was a writer manqué, although he went further than most with his overdeveloped proprietorial sense. Iris Owens put it down to his ego: "When he published something, he thought he wrote it."

His true talent was one that would have drawn acclaim in the eighteenth century. He was a wonderful writer of letters. Laurette Kahane, his first wife, noticed this early on, and Lilla Lyon, his second, confirmed it later. Any propensity that Maurice Girodias might have had to be catatonically boring in face-to-face encounters shut off when he picked up his pen. His letters, sometimes written by hand in an elegant, cursive script, were invariably interesting, full of ideas, unexpected twists and turns, humor, spiky descriptions of people, and candid admissions of his own failings.

Girodias published the first volume of his autobiography in the late 1970s, maintaining his touch with titles—*J'Arrive* in French and *The Frog Prince* in English. In the 1980s he revised it a little, added two chapters, and wrote a second volume. Both volumes were then published in French under the collective title *Une Journée sur la Terre* [*A Day on Earth*]. A third volume never materialized, but he left a large collection of essays, articles, monographs, interviews, and, best of all, letters.

While his writing was invariably entertaining, he was often cavalier with the factual, if not emotional, truth. He was fond of recounting an incident by re-creating it in a dramatic way, complete with sparkling dialogue and sharply etched pen portraits, and then reflecting on what he thought had happened. Parts of a story, where he had not been present or had forgotten, would be imagined. He was careless with dates, sequencing of events, and when he touched on his bogeymen (Donleavy, Nabokov, Rosset, et al.) his paranoia would surface. "His life, like his memoirs," said Miriam Worms, "needed editing."

Books HAD POWER, Iris Owens said, and the powerful books that she and others wrote emerged because publishers like Jack Kahane and Maurice Girodias were ready to put them into print. For some of the writers in Paris, the exercise was a joyful, liberating experience, a lot of fun, but, in the end, not to be taken too seriously.

For others, however, it was a matter of life and death. Writing was a compulsion, inseparable from breathing. Miller, Durrell, Beckett, Nabokov, Donleavy, Burroughs, and Dominique Aury had something inside them that had to come out, whether anybody read it or not. It was their misfortune that, in addition to the natural difficulties of being published as unknown writers, they had to contend with censorship. This increased their anguish and made them more desperate, more paranoid, than they might have been.

Obelisk and Olympia brought salvation. But publication did not necessarily bring peace because Maurice Girodias was also a driven man. While his compulsion enabled the writers to be published, the flaws in his character destroyed their trust in him and shook, for a time, his faith in himself. Ironically, Girodias spent the last decade and a half of his life the way that many of his writers had begun theirs: impoverished, rejected, increasingly paranoid—and desperate to be published.

But finally, like them, he *was* published, and his day on earth ended with his spirits soaring and his words enshrined on the printed page.

Epilogue

Girodias was cremated and buried in Père Lachaise, where his old enemy James Patrick Donleavy once inspected the ovens. On his tombstone, Eric Kahane inscribed the words "*Une Journée sur la Terre.*" Booklegger Jack and his writers have all gone. Several of the Olympia group departed earlier than their publisher, most notably Samuel Beckett, Vladimir Nabokov, Alexander Trocchi, and Mason Hoffenberg; Norman Rubington left shortly afterward; Terry Southern died last year.

The rest have scattered, Paris a distant memory. Baird Bryant turned to making films, is off junk, and had two more marriages after Denny and Jane. "I've been married longer than I've been alive," he says. Marilyn Meeske is still writing, as well as teaching, her sense of humor a constant companion. Iris Owens wrote a critically acclaimed novel called *After Claude* and is toying with the idea of writing a brand-new liberating "Harriet Daimler" DB. John Stevenson returned from the trenches of pornography in France to become a respectable civil servant in Britain and has since retired from both professions.

Austryn Wainhouse is a publisher in Vermont. Barney Rosset sold Grove to Ann Getty and George Weidenfeld and remained head of the firm for a year before being ousted by the new owners. He still publishes, however, under his own Blue Moon imprint. Similarly, John Calder continues to publish and sell his own books in many countries. He also writes obituaries of literary figures, while they are still mortal, for *The Independent* in London; when last seen he had just dispatched Larry Adler and was busy on publisher George Weidenfeld.

Sinclair Beiles, alias "Wu Wu Meng," returned to South Africa, but before going he sent a postcard to André Malraux, then Minister of Arts and Culture in France, saying that he, Beiles, had finally decided to buy the Palace of Versailles. William Burroughs and Allen Ginsberg have continued working and turned themselves into corporations. Gregory Corso remains an inimitable solo act. Christopher Logue, no longer suicidal, writes poetry, has written *Accounts of the Iliad* for the stage, regaled *Private Eye* readers with true stories from far and wide, and is preparing his autobiography. Walter Minton, who, after leaving publishing, became a lawyer, continues to live in "the house that Lolita built."

Ed Ferraro lives in New York, where he works as an editor. Ann Patty and Carol Southern became successful in the New York publishing world. Victor Bockris is a well-known writer, notably of biography, and Andrew Wylie is a prominent literary agent. John Coleman, a distinguished cinema critic for *The New Statesman* for twenty-five years, says he is a hermit, "but not a Trappist."

Muffie Wainhouse, now Mary Briault, runs a bed-and-breakfast inn in New Mexico and, like Girodias, writes marvelous letters. Holly Hutchins still lives in Paris and has become a painter. Miriam Worms has never left either and lives with her husband within hailing distance of the rue de Nesle, the Olympia Press's first proper home. Victoria Reiter, now a writer herself, lives in New York, and Gerry Williams, editor and teacher, is there too and mourns his former employer.

Over in England, Mary Wilson Price Donleavy Guinness still enjoys a good auction.

Notes

Preface

1. Philip Larkin, "Annus Mirabilis," *Collected Poems* (London: Faber & Faber, 1974).

1. Booklegger Jack and the Obelisk Press

1. Jack Kahane, *Memoirs of a Booklegger* (London: Michael Joseph, 1939), p. 260.
2. Hugh Ford, *Published in Paris: American and British Writers, Printers, and Publishers in Paris, 1920–1939* (New York: Macmillan, 1975), p. 345.
3. Kahane, p. 9.
4. Ibid., pp. 20–21.
5. Ibid., p. 182.
6. Ford, p. 348.
7. Kahane, p. 217.
8. Ibid., p. 218.
9. Ibid., pp. 218–19.
10. Ibid., p. 219.

11. Ibid., pp. 219–20.
12. Ibid., p. 220.
13. Sylvia Beach, *Shakespeare and Company* (Lincoln: University of Nebraska Press, 1991), pp. 132–33.
14. Interview with author.
15. Interview with author.
16. Beach, p. 93.
17. Kahane, pp. 225–26.
18. Ford, p. 354.
19. Maurice Girodias, *The Frog Prince: An Autobiography* (New York: Crown, 1980), pp. 88–89.
20. Kahane, p. 227.
21. Ibid., pp. 240–41.

2. *Lesbian Love and Male Fantasy*

1. Kahane, p. 233.
2. Ibid., pp. 235–36.
3. Ford, p. 359.
4. Ibid.
5. Radclyffe Hall, *The Well of Loneliness* (New York: Doubleday, 1990). Also Michael Baker, *Our Three Selves: A Life of Radclyffe Hall* (London: GMP, 1992). This is a fascinating and sensitive biography.
6. Baker, p. 223.
7. Ibid.
8. Ibid., pp. 226, 231.
9. Ibid., pp. 231–32.
10. Radclyffe Hall, "Commentary" preceding *The Well of Loneliness*.
11. Baker, p. 239.
12. Ibid., pp. 241, 243.
13. Ibid., pp. 243–44.
14. Kahane, p. 257.
15. Baker, pp. 252–53, 255–56, 353.
16. Beach, p. 91.
17. Vincent Brome, *Frank Harris: The Life and Loves of a Scoundrel* (New York: Thomas Yoseloff, 1960), p. 9.
18. Ibid., pp. 5–6.
19. Ibid., from the dust jacket.
20. Ibid., p. 5.
21. Ibid.
22. Ibid., p. 231.
23. Philippa Pullar, *Frank Harris: A Biography* (New York: Simon & Schuster, 1976), text on dust jacket.
24. Ibid., p. 10.

25. Ford, p. 360.
26. Kahane, pp. 54–55.
27. Leo Hamalian, "The Secret Careers of Samuel Roth," pamphlet, p. 89.
28. Pullar, p. 11.

3. Henry, Anaïs, Larry & Co.

1. Kahane, pp. 261–62.
2. Ford, p. 364.
3. Ibid.
4. Mary V. Dearborn, *The Happiest Man Alive: A Biography of Henry Miller* (New York: Simon & Schuster, Touchstone, 1992), p. 156.
5. *A Literate Passion: Letters of Anaïs Nin & Henry Miller, 1932–1953* (New York: Harcourt Brace Jovanovich, 1987), p. 109.
6. Ford, p. 364.
7. Dearborn, p. 11.
8. Ibid., p. 15.
9. Robert Ferguson, *Henry Miller: A Life* (London: Hutchinson, 1992), p. 229.
10. Dearborn, p. 171.
11. *The Journals of Anaïs Nin: 1931–1934* (London: Peter Owen, 1966), pp. 319–20.
12. Dearborn, pp. 171, 175.
13. Henry Miller, *Tropic of Cancer* (Paris: Obelisk Press, 1934), Preface.
14. Maurice Girodias, Preface to *The Original Seven Minutes* by J J Jadway (New York: Olympia Press, 1970).
15. Kahane, p. 263.
16. Ford, p. 368.
17. Ferguson, p. 240.
18. *The Times,* February 17, 1986.
19. Kahane, p. 39.
20. *The Durrell-Miller Letters 1935–80,* ed. Ian S. MacNiven (London: Faber & Faber, 1989), pp. 2–3.
21. Ibid., p. 3.
22. Ford, p. 376.
23. *Durrell-Miller Letters,* p. 35.
24. Ibid., p. 55.
25. Ibid., p. 62.
26. T. S. Eliot, dust jacket of *The Black Book* by Lawrence Durrell (London: Faber & Faber, 1973).
27. *Durrell-Miller Letters,* p. 56.
28. Ibid., p. 80.
29. Ibid., p. 124.
30. Kahane, pp. 268–69.
31. Lawrence Durrell, *The Black Book* (Paris: Olympia Press, 1959), pp. 7, 9.

32. David Gascoyne, *Independent,* November 10, 1990.

33. John Unterecker, *Lawrence Durrell,* Columbia Essays on Modern Writers, No. 6 (New York: Columbia University Press, 1964), p. 12.

34. Henry Miller, "The Durrell of *The Black Book* Days," essay in *The World of Lawrence Durrell,* ed. Harry T. Moore (Carbondale: Southern Illinois University Press, 1962), p. 98.

35. Kahane, pp. 265–68.

36. Ford, p. 373.

37. Edward De Grazia, *Girls Lean Back Everywhere: The Law of Obscenity and the Assault on Genius* (New York: Random House, 1992), p. 367.

4. *Enter Maurice Girodias*

1. Girodias, *The Frog Prince,* p. 309.

2. *The Olympia Reader,* ed. Maurice Girodias (New York: Grove Press, Black Cat ed., 1983), p. 16.

3. Girodias, *The Frog Prince,* pp. 38–40.

4. Ibid., pp. 60–63.

5. Ibid., pp. 85–86.

6. Ibid.

7. Interview with author.

8. Girodias, *The Frog Prince,* pp. 89–90.

9. Ibid., p. 350.

10. Ibid., pp. 370–75.

11. Ibid., pp. 341–42.

12. Maurice Girodias, *Une Journée sur la Terre, I: L'Arrivée* (Paris: Éditions de la Différence, 1990), p. 410.

13. Interview with author.

14. Girodias, *Une Journée sur la Terre,* vol. I, p. 408.

15. Pascal Fouché, *L'Édition Française sous l'Occupation* (Paris: Bibliothèque de Littérature Française Contemporaine, 1987), p. 247, footnote 2.

16. Girodias, *Une Journée sur la Terre,* vol. I, p. 443.

17. Ibid., pp. 421–22.

18. Fouché, p. 210.

19. Girodias, *The Frog Prince,* p. 384.

20. Interview with author.

21. Interview with author.

22. Interview with author.

23. Interview with author.

24. Letter to author.

25. Interview with author.

26. Interview with author.

27. Girodias, *The Frog Prince,* pp. 329–30.

28. Ibid., p. 330.

29. Ibid., p. 333.
30. Fouché, pp. 210–11.
31. Letter from Muffie Wainhouse.
32. Michael Neal, interview with author.
33. Girodias, *Une Journée sur la Terre*, vol. II, pp. 56–62.
34. Interview with author.
35. Girodias, *Une Journée sur la Terre*, vol. II, p. 61.
36. Interview with author.
37. Interview with author.
38. *The Olympia Reader*, p. 21.

5. Great Books, Dirty Books: Olympia Gathers Steam

1. *The Olympia Reader*, p. 15.
2. Samuel Beckett, *I Can't Go On, I'll Go On: A Samuel Beckett Reader*, ed. and introd. Richard W. Seaver (New York: Grove Weidenfeld, 1992), p. xi.
3. Ibid., pp. xiv–xv.
4. Christopher Sawyer-Lauçanno, *The Continual Pilgrimage: American Writers in Paris, 1944–1960* (New York: Grove Press, 1992), pp. 133–35.
5. Girodias, vol. II, p. 236.
6. Letter to author.
7. *The Olympia Reader*, p. 23.
8. Letter to author.
9. Letter to author.
10. Girodias, vol. II, p. 234.
11. Letter to author.
12. Letter to author.
13. Interview with author.
14. *The Olympia Reader*, p. 297.
15. Ibid., pp. 578–79.
16. Interview with author.
17. Paul Bowles, *Without Stopping* (London: Peter Owen, 1972), pp. 354–55, and interview with author.
18. Marilyn Meeske, "Memoirs of a Female Pornographer," *Esquire*, April 1965, p. 113.
19. Correspondence with author.
20. Correspondence between "Angela Pearson" and Maurice Girodias, November-December 1988.
21. Ted Morgan, taped interview with Maurice Girodias, transcript from Special Collections, Arizona State University Library, Tempe, Arizona.
22. Interview with author.
23. Philip Toynbee, *Observer*, October 16, 1960.
24. Interview with author.

25. Interview with author.

26. Interview with author.

27. Letter to author.

28. Interview with author.

29. Letter to author.

30. Letter to author.

31. Austryn Wainhouse, "On Translating Sade," *Evergreen Review,* August 1966, p. 56.

32. Meeske, *Esquire,* p. 112.

33. Interview with author.

34. Pullar, *Harris,* p. 413.

35. Girodias, vol. II, pp. 244–51, and *The Olympia Reader,* pp. 336–41.

36. Interview with author.

37. Wainhouse, *Evergreen Review,* p. 53.

38. *The Olympia Reader,* p. 457.

39. Interview with author.

40. Harriet Daimler, *Darling,* Introduction (New York: Grove Press, Black Cat ed., 1983), pp. 2–3.

41. Harriet Daimler, *The Organization* (New York: Olympia Press, 1968), p. 1.

42. *The Olympia Reader,* p. 176.

43. Interview with author.

44. Interview with author.

45. Interview with author.

46. Interview with author.

47. Interview with author.

48. Interview with author.

49. Letter to author.

50. Count Palmiro Vicarion, *Lust* (Paris: Ophelia Press, 1959), p. 218.

51. Letter to author.

52. *Count Palmiro Vicarion's Book of Bawdy Ballads* (Paris: Olympia Press, 1962), p. 2.

53. *Count Palmiro Vicarion's Book of Limericks* (Paris: Olympia Press, 1962).

54. Interview with author.

55. Meeske, *Esquire,* p. 114.

56. Interview with author.

57. Wainhouse, *Evergreen Review,* p. 54.

58. Letter to author.

59. Interview with author.

60. Interview with author.

61. Letter to author.

62. *The Olympia Reader,* p. 23.

63. Interview with author.

64. Interview with author.

65. *The Olympia Reader,* p. 23.

66. Interview with author.
67. Interview with author.
68. Interview with author.

6. *The Wild Ginger Man*

1. *The Olympia Reader,* p. 25.
2. J. P. Donleavy, *The Ginger Man* (London: Penguin, 1993), back cover.
3. Maurice Girodias, unpublished English draft of second volume of autobiography, chapter on "Gingermania," p. 13.
4. Ibid., p. 14.
5. Interview with author.
6. Morgan, taped interview with Girodias, transcript pp. 1–2.
7. Girodias, unpublished autobiography, p. 15.
8. Letter to author.
9. Interview with author.
10. Interview with author.
11. Interview with author.
12. Letter from Mary Wainhouse Briault to Maurice Girodias, April 5, 1968.
13. Interview with author.
14. J. P. Donleavy, *The History of the Ginger Man* (London: Viking, 1994), p. 409.
15. Girodias, unpublished autobiography, p. 14.
16. Interview with author.
17. Interview with author.
18. "The Art of Fiction LIII: J. P. Donleavy," *Paris Review,* vol. 16, no. 63, Fall 1975, pp. 127–28.
19. Letter to author.
20. Girodias, unpublished autobiography, p. 15.
21. Ibid., p. 16.
22. Interview with author.
23. Letter to author.
24. Girodias, unpublished autobiography, p. 16.
25. Ibid., pp. 16–17.
26. Terry Southern, "Flashing on Gid," *Grand Street,* no. 37, Fall 1991, pp. 233–24.
27. Spencer Vibbert, "True Adventures of an X-Rated Publisher," *Boston Globe Magazine,* January 18, 1981, p. 21.
28. Interview with author.
29. J. P. Donleavy, *The Ginger Man* (London: Corgi, 1963), p. 101.
30. Girodias, unpublished autobiography, pp. 17–18.
31. Ibid.
32. Ibid., pp. 18–19.
33. Ibid., pp. 20–21.

34. Ibid., p. 21.
35. Ibid.
36. Maurice Girodias, *Les Jardins d'Éros* (Paris: Éditions de la Différence, 1990), p. 326.
37. Interview with author.
38. Girodias, unpublished autobiography, pp. 22–23.
39. Interview with author.
40. Interview with author.
41. Girodias, unpublished autobiography, pp. 23–24.
42. Interview with author.
43. Extracts from the dust jacket of *The Singular Man* by J. P. Donleavy, published by The Bodley Head, London, 1964.
44. Girodias, unpublished autobiography, pp. 25–26.
45. Interview with author.
46. *Paris Review,* pp. 135, 137.
47. *Paris Review,* p. 134.
48. *Paris Review,* p. 143.
49. Interview with author.
50. Girodias, unpublished autobiography, p. 27.
51. Interview with author.
52. J. P. Donleavy, *J. P. Donleavy's Ireland* (London: Penguin, 1988), p. 121.
53. Girodias, unpublished autobiography, p. 25.
54. Interview with author.
55. Letter to author.
56. Interview with author.
57. Morgan, taped interview with Girodias, transcript pp. 10–11.
58. Interview with author.

7. *Light of My Life, Fire of My Loins: The* **Lolita** *Saga*

1. Girodias, vol. II, pp. 293–5 (author's translation).
2. Girodias, unpublished autobiography, p. 11.
3. Vladimir Nabokov, "On a Book Entitled *Lolita,*" *The Annotated Lolita,* ed. Alfred Appel, Jr. (New York: Vintage Books, 1991), pp. 311–12.
4. Ibid., pp. 313–14.
5. *Rotten Rejections: A Literary Companion,* ed. André Bernard (Wainscott, N.Y.: Pushcart Press).
6. Erica Jong, "*Lolita* Turns Thirty: A New Introduction," *Lolita* (New York: 1988), quoted in De Grazia, pp. 251, 729 footnote.
7. Nabokov, "On a Book Entitled *Lolita,*" p. 313.
8. Vladimir Nabokov, *Selected Letters 1940–77,* ed. Dmitri Nabokov and Matthew J. Bruccoli (London: Vintage, 1991), pp. 142–43.
9. De Grazia, p. 247.
10. Nabokov, *Selected Letters,* p. 153.

11. Ibid.
12. De Grazia, p. 247.
13. Ibid. and *New York Times Book Review,* July 3, 1988.
14. De Grazia, p. 261 and footnote.
15. Nabokov, *Selected Letters,* p. 154, and ibid.
16. Interview with author.
17. Interview with author.
18. De Grazia, p. 251.
19. Ibid., p. 245 footnote.
20. Vladimir Nabokov, "*Lolita* and Mr. Girodias," *Evergreen Review,* February 1967, pp. 37–38.
21. Letter to author.
22. Interview with author.
23. Girodias, *Evergreen Review,* September 1965, pp. 44–45.
24. Maurice Girodias, "Pornologist on Olympus," *Playboy,* April 1961, p. 68.
25. Girodias, vol. II, pp. 298–99.
26. Ibid., p. 299.
27. Ibid., p. 300.
28. Nabokov, *Selected Letters,* pp. 166–67.
29. Girodias, unpublished autobiography, p. 13, and *Evergreen Review,* p. 38.
30. Ibid.
31. Nabokov, *Selected Letters,* pp. 174–75.
32. Appel, introduction to *The Annotated Lolita,* p. xxxiv.
33. Ted Morgan, *Literary Outlaw: The Life and Times of William S. Burroughs* (London: Pimlico, 1991), p. 278, and taped interview with Girodias.
34. Interview with author.
35. De Grazia, p. 259, and *Sunday Express,* January 29, 1956.
36. Brian Boyd, *Vladimir Nabokov: The American Years 1940–77* (Princeton: Princeton University Press, 1991), p. 295.
37. *Evergreen Review,* p. 45.
38. Ibid., p. 40.
39. De Grazia, p. 261.
40. Nabokov, *Selected Letters,* pp. 197–98.
41. *The Olympia Reader,* pp. 27–28.
42. Boyd, p. 301.
43. *Evergreen Review,* p. 46.
44. Nabokov, *Selected Letters,* pp. 199–201.
45. Ibid., p. 203.
46. Nabokov, *Selected Letters,* p. 204.
47. Ibid., pp. 210–11.
48. *Evergreen Review,* p. 40.
49. Interview with author.
50. Interview with author.
51. Nabokov, *Selected Letters,* p. 245.

52. *Evergreen Review,* p. 47.

53. Ibid., p. 47.

54. Interview with author.

55. Boyd, p. 356.

56. *Evergreen Review,* p. 45.

57. De Grazia, p. 264.

58. Nabokov, *Selected Letters,* p. 217.

59. De Grazia, p. 248 footnote.

60. *Evergreen Review,* p. 46.

61. Ibid., p. 38.

62. Ibid., p. 37.

63. Ibid., pp. 39–40.

64. Ibid., p. 46.

65. Ibid., p. 39.

66. Ibid., p. 41.

67. Ibid., p. 40.

68. Nabokov, *Selected Letters,* pp. 205–6.

69. Boyd, p. 305.

70. Nabokov, *Selected Letters,* pp. 219–20, 223–24, 227.

71. *Evergreen Review,* p. 61.

72. Ibid., p. 40.

73. Nabokov, *Selected Letters,* p. 224.

74. Interview with author.

75. Nabokov, *Selected Letters,* p. 225.

76. Interview with author.

77. *Evergreen Review,* p. 40.

78. Brian Boyd, "The Year of *Lolita,*" *New York Times Book Review,* September 8, 1991, p. 1.

79. Ibid., p. 31.

80. Ibid.

81. Ibid.

82. Ibid., p. 32.

83. Interview with author.

84. Boyd, *Vladimir Nabokov,* pp. 386–87, 404, 466.

85. Ibid., p. 466.

86. De Grazia, p. 268.

87. *The Times,* January 23, 1959, and De Grazia, p. 268.

88. *The Times,* July 5, 1990, Girodias's obituary.

89. De Grazia, pp. 268–70.

90. *Evergreen Review,* p. 91.

91. Ibid., p. 90.

92. Ibid.

93. Ibid., p. 41.

94. Girodias, vol. II, pp. 457–60.

95. Boyd, *Vladimir Nabokov,* p. 394 footnote.
96. Interview with author.
97. Interview with author.
98. De Grazia, p. 271; *Nabokov's Fifth Arc: Nabokov and Others on His Life's Work,* ed. J. E. Rivers and Charles Nicol (Austin: University of Texas Press, 1982), p. 191.
99. *Evergreen Review,* p. 38.
100. Nabokov, *Selected Letters,* p. 223.
101. *Evergreen Review,* p. 40.
102. Boyd, *Vladimir Nabokov,* pp. 265–66.
103. Interview with author.
104. Boyd, *Vladimir Nabokov,* p. 376.
105. Girodias, unpublished autobiography, p. 13.
106. Girodias, vol. II, p. 302.
107. Ibid., p. 301.
108. *Evergreen Review,* p. 90.

8. *Good Grief, It's Candy!*

1. Girodias, vol. II, p. 311.
2. Southern, "Flashing on Gid," pp. 230–31.
3. Letter from Terry Southern to Maurice Girodias from Geneva, December 10, 1956.
4. Letter from Girodias to Southern, December 11, 1956.
5. Letter from Southern to Girodias, December 18, 1956.
6. Interview with author.
7. Interview with author.
8. Interview with author.
9. Girodias, vol. II, p. 311.
10. Ibid.
11. Ibid., pp. 308–9.
12. Interview with author.
13. Paul Spike, ear-witness.
14. Interview with author.
15. Letter from Southern to Girodias, February 15, 1957.
16. Letter from Girodias to Southern, February 6, 1957.
17. Interview with author.
18. Letter from Southern to Girodias, February 15, 1957.
19. Ibid.
20. *The Olympia Reader,* p. 361.
21. Girodias, vol. II, p. 422.
22. Letter from Southern to Girodias, September 11, 1958.
23. Terry Southern, first page of chapter 1, *Candy,* by Terry Southern and Mason Hoffenberg, paperback edition (New York: Putnam, 1965).

24. Letters from Girodias to Southern, September 11 and October 1, 1958.
25. *The Olympia Reader,* p. 362.
26. Letter from Southern to Girodias, June 2, 1959.
27. Interview with author.
28. *The Olympia Reader,* p. 363.
29. Contract between Girodias, Southern, and Hoffenberg, May 9, 1961.
30. Letter from Sterling Lord to Maurice Girodias, August 3, 1962.
31. Photocopy with author.
32. Letter from Mason Hoffenberg to Maurice Girodias, September 23, 1963.
33. Letter from Howard A. Singer to Maurice Girodias, November 25, 1963.
34. Letter from Girodias to Southern, November 29, 1963.
35. Letters from Singer to Girodias, December 6 and 31, 1963.
36. Interview with author.
37. Interview with author.
38. Extracts from reviews printed in *Candy,* paperback edition.
39. Letter from Girodias to Southern, March 10, 1964.
40. Photocopy with author.
41. Letter from Terry Southern to Seymour Krim, March 29, 1964.
42. Interview with author.
43. Interview with author.
44. Interview with author.
45. Interview with author.
46. Interview with author.
47. Interview with author.
48. Interview with author.
49. Letter from Maurice Girodias to Claire S. Degener of the Sterling Lord Agency, October 1, 1965.
50. Letter from Girodias to Claire Degener, October 18, 1965.
51. Letter from Maurice Girodias to Mark A. Lillis, Copyright Office, Library of Congress, Washington, D.C., October 25, 1965.
52. Letter from Girodias to Hoffenberg, November 22, 1965.
53. Letter from Barbara A. Ringer, Assistant Register of Copyrights for Examining, Copyright Office, Library of Congress, to Maurice Girodias, December 14, 1965.

9. *Good Grief, It's* Still *Candy!*

1. Letter from Leon Friedman to Maurice Girodias, January 21, 1966.
2. Letter from Girodias to Friedman, February 2, 1966.
3. Letter from Friedman to Girodias, February 7, 1966.
4. Letter from Girodias to Friedman, February 10, 1966.
5. Letter from Friedman to Girodias, February 14, 1966.
6. Interview with author.
7. Letter from Michael Rubinstein to Maurice Girodias, April 25, 1966.

8. Letter from Girodias to Friedman, April 28, 1966.
9. Letter from Friedman to Girodias, July 18, 1966.
10. Letter from Girodias to Friedman, July 18, 1966.
11. Letter from Friedman to Girodias, July 25, 1966.
12. Letter from Friedman to Girodias, August 2, 1966.
13. Letter from Girodias to Friedman, August 4, 1966.
14. Letter from Friedman to Girodias, August 10, 1966.
15. Telegram from Girodias to Friedman, August 22, 1966.
16. Letter from Friedman to Girodias, August 22, 1966.
17. Letter from Girodias to Friedman, August 24, 1966.
18. Letter from Girodias to Friedman, August 26, 1966.
19. Letter from Friedman to Girodias, August 27, 1966.
20. Letter from Girodias to Friedman, September 1, 1966.
21. Letter from Seymour Litvinoff to Maurice Girodias, September 7, 1966.
22. Interview with author.
23. Interview with author.
24. Letter from Girodias to Degener, September 9, 1966.
25. Letter from Rubinstein to Friedman, September 28, 1966.
26. Letter from Friedman to Girodias, October 5, 1966.
27. Telegram from Friedman to Girodias, undated.
28. Letter from Girodias to Friedman, October 8, 1966.
29. Telegram from Friedman to Girodias, November 9, 1966.
30. Letter from Girodias to Friedman, November 12, 1966.
31. Letter from Girodias to Friedman, November 10, 1966.
32. Letter from Southern to Hoffenberg, supplied by Nile Southern.
33. Letter from Maurice Girodias to John Watson, November 18, 1966.
34. Letter from Girodias to Degener, November 22, 1966.
35. Letter from Friedman to Girodias, November 29, 1966.
36. Telegram from Girodias to Friedman, November 30, 1966.
37. Letter from Walter Minton to Maurice Girodias, December 5, 1966.
38. Letter from Friedman to Girodias, December 5, 1966.
39. Telegram from Girodias to Friedman, December 7, 1966.
40. Telegram from Friedman to Girodias, December 7, 1966.
41. Telegram from Girodias to Hoffenberg, December 7, 1966.
42. Letter from Girodias to Friedman, December 7, 1966.
43. Letter from Girodias to Friedman, December 8, 1966.
44. Letter from Friedman to Girodias, December 9, 1966.
45. Interview with author.
46. Letter from Leon Friedman to Gideon Cashman, December 19, 1966.
47. Letter from Girodias to Friedman, December 16, 1966.
48. Letter from Girodias to Friedman, December 23, 1966.
49. Telegram from Friedman to Girodias, December 29, 1966.
50. Letter from Friedman to Girodias, January 3, 1967.
51. Letter from Girodias to Friedman, January 6, 1967.

52. Letter from Cashman to Degener, copied to Friedman, January 11, 1967.
53. Document with author.
54. Interview with author.
55. Interview with author.
56. Interview with author.
57. Memorandum from Claire Degener to Leon Friedman, Gideon Cashman, Seymour Litvinoff, and Robert Montgomery, February 8, 1967.
58. Interview with author.
59. Interview with author.
60. *Monthly Film Bulletin,* British Film Institute, Index 1969, vol. xxxvi, nos. 420–31, p. 80.
61. Interview with author.
62. Interview with author.
63. David Streitfield, "Terry Southern: Back to His Texas Roots," *International Herald Tribune,* March 24, 1992.
64. Interview with author.
65. Interview with author.

10. Une Lettre d'Amour: *The True Story of* Story of O

1. Pauline Réage, "A Girl in Love," published in *Return to the Château* (New York: Grove Press, 1971), p. 8.
2. Interview with author.
3. Interview with author.
4. Interview with author.
5. Réage, "A Girl in Love," pp. 4–5.
6. Ibid., p. 7.
7. Ibid., pp. 7–8.
8. Ibid., pp. 10–11.
9. Ibid., p. 9.
10. Pauline Réage, *Story of O* (New York: Ballantine, 1983), pp. 9–10.
11. Interview with author.
12. Réage, *Story of O,* p. 195.
13. Interview with author.
14. Réage, "A Girl in Love," pp. 11–13.
15. Interview with author.
16. Réage, "A Girl in Love," pp. 9–10.
17. Interview with author.
18. Interview with author.
19. Interview with author.
20. Interview with author.
21. Interview with author.
22. Interview with author.
23. Interview with author.

24. Interview with author.
25. Interview with author.
26. Interview with author.
27. Interview with author.
28. Interview with author.
29. Interview with author.
30. Interview with author.
31. Interview with author.
32. Letter from Girodias to Friedman, February 22, 1966.
33. Interview with author.
34. Extracts in the Ballantine edition of *Story of O,* New York, 1983.
35. Edwin A. Roberts, Jr., "The Controversial *Story of O:* What's Left for the Other Toilers in this Well-Trampled Vineyard," *New York Times,* 1965.
36. Sabine d'Estrée, "Translator's Note" to *Story of O* by Pauline Réage (New York: Grove Press, 1965), pp. xi–xii.
37. Interview with author.
38. Interview with author.
39. Interview with author.
40. Interview with author.
41. Interview with author.
42. Letter from Maurice Girodias to Holly Hutchins, June 24, 1969.
43. Interview with Pauline Réage by Jacqueline Demornex, *Elle,* no. 1498, September 2, 1974, pp. 4–7.
44. Régine Deforges, *O m'a Dit: Entretiens avec Pauline Réage* (Paris: Jean-Jacques Pauvert, 1975), pp. 17–19.
45. Ibid., p. 22.
46. Ibid., p. 163.
47. Peter Fryer, *Secrets of the British Museum* (New York: Citadel Press, 1966), pp. 123–4.
48. Interview with author.
49. Interview with author.
50. Dingwall-Holloway Correspondence, Dingwall Bequest, Harry Price Library, University of London.
51. Interview with author.
52. Interview with author.
53. Letter from Richard Seaver to Eric Larrabee, June 28, 1965.
54. Correspondence between James Price and Richard Seaver, June 21 and 30, 1966.
55. Letter to author.
56. Letter to author.
57. Interview with author.
58. Interview with author.
59. Interview with author.
60. Interview with author.

61. Interview with author.
62. Interview with author.

11. *What William Burroughs Saw on the End of His Fork*

1. Morgan, *Literary Outlaw*, p. 281.
2. *The Olympia Reader*, pp. 25–26.
3. Morgan, taped interview with Girodias.
4. Southern, *Grand Street*, pp. 231–32.
5. Interview with author.
6. Morgan, *Literary Outlaw*, p. 281.
7. Ibid., p. 287.
8. De Grazia, p. 254.
9. Ibid., p. 362.
10. Girodias, vol. II, pp. 433–34.
11. Ibid.
12. *The Letters of William S. Burroughs 1945–59* (London: Picador, 1993), p. 419.
13. De Grazia, pp. 343–44; Morgan, *Literary Outlaw*, pp. 14–41; Barry Miles, *William Burroughs: El Hombre Invisible* (London: Virgin Books, 1992), pp. 19–32.
14. Morgan, *Literary Outlaw*, pp. 238–39.
15. Ibid., p. 244.
16. Interview with author.
17. *Letters*, p. 337.
18. Morgan, *Literary Outlaw*, p. 247.
19. De Grazia, p. 348.
20. Miles, p. 69.
21. Interview with author.
22. Morgan, *Literary Outlaw*, p. 265.
23. Interview with author.
24. *Letters*, pp. 367–68.
25. Ibid., pp. 369–71.
26. Ibid., p. 376.
27. Interview with author.
28. Mary McCarthy, *New York Review of Books* (February 1963).
29. Miles, p. 95.
30. Herbert Gold, *New York Times*, November 25, 1962.
31. Miles, p. 95.
32. De Grazia, pp. 487–88.
33. George Steiner, "Night Words" in *Language and Silence: Essays 1958–1966* (London: & Faber, 1990), pp. 93–94.
34. Morgan, *Literary Outlaw*, pp. 349–50.
35. Chris Peachment, *Observer*, January 30, 1994, Arts Section, p. 6.
36. Morgan, taped interview with Girodias.

37. Interview with author.

38. Barney Rosset, who was present, in interview with author.

39. Morgan, *Literary Outlaw*, pp. 348–49.

40. Morgan, taped interview with Girodias.

41. Ibid.

42. Interview with author.

43. Miles, p. 48.

44. Ibid., pp. 88–89.

45. William S. Burroughs, *Naked Lunch* (New York: Grove Weidenfeld, Evergreen ed., 1992), pp. ix, x, xvi.

12. *Glorious Nights, Weary Days*

1. Thomas Quinn Curtiss, *New York Herald Tribune*, August 7, 1960.

2. *The New Olympia Reader*, ed. Maurice Girodias (New York: Olympia Press, 1970), p. 861.

3. Interview with author.

4. Interview with author.

5. Interview with author.

6. Interviews with author.

7. Interview with author.

8. *The New Olympia Reader*, p. 861.

9. Robert Sage, *New York Herald Tribune*, 1959.

10. *The Olympia Reader*, pp. 637–38.

11. *Observer* and *Esquire*.

12. Interview with author.

13. *The Olympia Reader*, p. 687.

14. Peter Singleton-Gates and Maurice Girodias, *The Black Diaries of Roger Casement* (New York: Grove Press, 1959), pp. 9–13.

15. Interview with author.

16. Henry Popkin, *New York Times Book Review*, April 17, 1960.

17. *The Olympia Reader*, pp. 687–88.

18. Interview with author.

19. *The New Olympia Reader*, p. 861.

20. Interview with author.

21. *The Olympia Reader*, p. 21.

13. *Olympia USA*

1. Interview with author.

2. Letter from Girodias to Friedman, February 10, 1966.

3. Interview with author.

4. Interview with author.

5. Interview with author.

6. Interview with author.

7. Interviews with author.

8. Letter from Maurice Girodias to Holly Hutchins, March 1967.

9. Interview with author.

10. Interview with author.

11. Interview with author.

12. *The New Olympia Reader,* p. 10.

13. Ibid., p. 890.

14. De Grazia, p. 272 footnote.

15. Interview with author.

16. Letter from Maurice Girodias to Norman Singer, February 8, 1968, and interview with author.

17. Maurice Girodias, Publisher's Preface to *S.C.U.M. Manifesto* by Valerie Solanas (New York: Olympia Press, 1968), pp. 11–12.

18. Ibid., pp. 14–16.

19. Interview with author.

20. *S.C.U.M. Manifesto,* pp. 17–18, and letter from Valerie Solanas to Maurice Girodias, February 19, 1968.

21. Interview with author.

22. Mary Harron, interview with author.

23. Interview with author.

24. Girodias, unpublished autobiography, p. 29.

25. Ibid., p. 30.

26. Mike Golden, "Chez Lolita, Candy & The Ginger Man Make Too," *New York Writer,* Spring 1989, p. 70.

27. Interview with author.

28. Interview with author.

29. Interview with author.

30. Interview with author.

31. Interview with author.

32. Interview with author.

33. Letter to author.

34. Interview with author.

35. Morgan, taped interview with Girodias.

36. *New York Writer,* p. 70.

37. Interview with author.

38. Girodias, unpublished autobiography, pp. 29–31.

39. Interview with author.

40. Interview with author.

41. Morgan, taped interview with Girodias.

42. Interview with author.

43. Interview with author.

44. Girodias, unpublished autobiography, p. 28.

45. Patrick J. Kearney, *A Bibliography of the Publications of the New York Olympia Press,* privately printed, Santa Rosa, California, 1988, pp. vii–viii, 42–46.
46. Ibid., pp. viii–ix, and letter from Girodias to the editor of *Queen* magazine, April 16, 1974.
47. Interview with author.
48. Interview with author.
49. Interview with author.
50. Victor Bockris, interview with author.
51. Letter with author.

14. *The Loneliness of the Long-Forgotten Publisher*

1. Letter from Maurice Girodias to Patti Welles, November 9, 1975.
2. Interview with author.
3. Interview with author.
4. Interviews with author.
5. Interview with author.
6. Letter from Ricki Levenson to Maurice Girodias, September 9, 1969.
7. Interviews with author.
8. Interview with author.
9. Interview with author.
10. Interview with author.
11. Interview with author.
12. *The Olympia Reader,* p. 22.
13. Ted Morgan, taped interview with Dick Seaver, Arizona State University Library, Tempe, Arizona.
14. Interviews with author.

Chronology

.

1931:   Founding of Obelisk Press in Paris by Jack Kahane.

1933:   Publication of *The Well of Loneliness* and *My Life and Loves*.

1934:   Publication of *Tropic of Cancer*.

1938:   Publication of *The Black Book*.

1939:   Publication of *Tropic of Capricorn* and *The Winter of Artifice*. Death of Jack Kahane. His son, Maurice Girodias, takes over business.

1940:   Collapse of France and German occupation of Paris. Girodias establishes Éditions du Chêne.

1945:   Liberation of Paris and end of World War II. Girodias marries Laurette Buzon.

1953:   Foundation of Olympia Press in the rue Jacob bookshop. Publication of Beckett's *Watt*, Miller's *Plexus*, and works by De Sade, Bataille, and Apollinaire.

1954:   Olympia moves to the rue de Nesle. *Story of O* published in French and English.

1955: Publication of *Molloy* (March), *The Ginger Man* (June), and *Lolita* (September).

1956: French authorities ban twenty-five Olympia books, including *Lolita, The Ginger Man,* and *Story of O.*

1957: Donleavy-Girodias legal duel begins.

1958: Fall of Fourth Republic; De Gaulle takes power. Olympia moves to rue Grand Séverin. *Candy* is published in Paris. *Lolita* appears in the United States.

1959: Publication of Beckett trilogy (*Molloy, Malone Dies,* and *The Unnamable*), *Naked Lunch,* and Roger Casement's *Black Diaries.* French ban on Olympia books is lifted. Launch of French edition of *Lolita* (October). Opening of La Grande Séverine restaurant-nightclub complex.

1961: Launch of *Olympia* magazine; four issues appear over two-year period.

1964: Collapse of La Grande Séverine. Girodias banned from publishing by French government.

1965: Girodias moves to New York. Publication of *The Olympia Reader* by Grove Press.

1967: Opening of Olympia Press in New York.

1968: Final bankruptcy of the Paris Olympia Press.

1970: Auction of Olympia Press in Paris; bought by Donleavy's wife. Publication of *The New Olympia Reader.*

1973: Bankruptcy and collapse of the New York Olympia Press.

1974: Girodias marries Lilla Lyon. Founds Venus-Freeway Press. Venture collapses after publishing *President Kissinger.*

1977: Publication of Girodias's first volume of memoirs in French (*J'Arrive*).

1978: End of Donleavy-Girodias legal battle.

1980: Publication of memoirs in English (*The Frog Prince*).

1990: Publication of Girodias's two-volume autobiography in French (*Les Jardins d'Éros*). Girodias dies in Paris, July 3, age seventy-one.

Olympia Press List (Paris)

The following are the publications of the Olympia Press in Paris between 1953 and 1965. The dates are of the first editions. The list was compiled by Patrick Kearney from work in progress on a complete revision of his 1987 Paris Olympia Press bibliography.

Ableman, Paul	*I Hear Voices*	1957
Angélique, Pierre [Georges Bataille]	*The Naked Beast at Heaven's Gate*	1956
Angélique, Pierre [Georges Bataille]	*A Tale of Satisfied Desire*	1953
Anonymous	*I'm for Hire*	1955
Anonymous	*The Prima Donna*	1960
Anonymous	*Teleny, or, The Reverse of the Medal*	1958
Anonymous [Diane Bataille]	*The Whip Angels*	1955
Apollinaire, Guillaume	*Amorous Exploits of a Young Rakehell*	1953
Apollinaire, Guillaume	*The Debauched Hospodar*	1953
Baron, Willie [Baird Bryant]	*Play My Love*	1960
Beardsley, Aubrey	*Under the Hill*	1959
Beckett, Samuel	*Molloy*[1]	1955
Beckett, Samuel	*Molloy, Malone Dies, The Unnamable*	1959
Beckett, Samuel	*Watt*[1]	1953
Broughton, James	*Almanac for Amorists*[1]	1955
Burns, R. Bernard	*The Ordeal of the Rod*	1958
Burroughs, William	*Naked Lunch*	1959

Burroughs, William	*The Soft Machine*	1961
Burroughs, William	*The Ticket That Exploded*	1962
Carroll, Jock	*Bottoms Up*	1961
Casement, Roger	*The Black Diaries*	1959
Cleland, John	*Memoirs of a Woman of Pleasure*	1954
Cocteau, Jean	*The White Paper*	1957
Corso, Gregory	*The American Express*	1961
Crannach, Henry [Marilyn Meeske]	*Flesh and Bone*	1957
Cutter, Nicholas	*Rogue Women*	1955
Daimler, Harriet and Crannach, Henry [Iris Owens and Marilyn Meeske]	*The Pleasure Thieves*	1956
Daimler, Harriet [Iris Owens]	*Darling*	1956
Daimler, Harriet [Iris Owens]	*Innocence*	1956
Daimler, Harriet [Iris Owens]	*The Organization*	1957
Daimler, Harriet [Iris Owens]	*The Woman Thing*	1958
Desmond, Robert	*An Adult's Story*	1954
Desmond, Robert	*Heaven, Hell and the Whore*	1956
Desmond, Robert	*Iniquity*	1958
Desmond, Robert	*The Libertine*	1955
Desmond, Robert	*Professional Charmer*	1961
Desmond, Robert	*Seeds of the Rainbow*	1957
Desmond, Robert	*The Sweetest Fruit*	1951
Desmond, Robert	*Without Violence*	1962
Dikes, Mickey	*Sarabande for a Bitch*	1956
Donleavy, J. P.	*The Ginger Man*	1955
Drake, Hamilton [Mason Hoffenberg]	*Sin for Breakfast*	1957
Drake, Winifred [Denny Bryant]	*Tender Was My Flesh*	1955
Durrell, Lawrence	*The Black Book*	1959
Edward, Brett	*The Passion of Youth*	1960
Essays	*L'Affaire Lolita*	1957
Farniente, Beauregard de [J.-C. Gervaise de Latouche]	*The Adventures of Father Silas*	1958
Ford, Charles Henri, and Tyler, Parker	*The Young and Evil*	1960
Genet, Jean	*Our Lady of the Flowers*	1957
Genet, Jean	*Querelle* [German text]	1959
Genet, Jean	*The Thief's Journal*[1]	1954
Hammer, Stephen [John Coleman]	*The Itch*	1956
Harrack, Tim	*Dissolving*	1958
Harris, Frank [Alexander Trocchi]	*My Life and Loves, vol. 5, An Irreverent Treatment*	1954
Himes, Chester	*Pinktoes*	1961
Homer & Associates [Michel Gall]	*A Bedside Odyssey*	1962
Jason, Peter	*Wayward*	1961
Jones, Henry [John Coleman]	*The Enormous Bed*	1955
Justice, Jean	*Murder vs. Murder*	1964
Kenton, Maxwell [Terry Southern and Mason Hoffenberg]	*Candy*[2]	1958
Krishnanada, Swami Ram	*Classical Hindu Erotology* [*Kama Sutra*]	1958

Landshot, Gustav	*How To Do It*	1956
Lengel, Frances [Alexander Trocchi]	*The Carnal Days of Helen Seferis*	1954
Lengel, Frances [Alexander Trocchi]	*Helen and Desire*	1954
Lengel, Frances [Alexander Trocchi]	*School for Sin*	1955
Lengel, Frances [Alexander Trocchi]	*White Thighs*	1955
Lengel, Frances [Alexander Trocchi]	*Young Adam*	1954
Lesse, Ruth	*Lash*	1962
Lewys, Peter [Pierre Louÿs]	*The She-Devils* [*Trois filles de leur mère*]	1958
Logue, Christopher	*Wand and Quadrant*[1]	1953
Lunas, Carmencita de las [Alexander Trocchi]	*Thongs*	1956
Mardaan, Ataullah	*Deva-Dasi*	1957
Mardaan, Ataullah	*Kama Houri*	1956
Martin, Ed	*Busy Bodies*	1963
Meng, Wu Wu [Sinclair Beiles]	*Houses of Joy*	1958
Miller, Henry	*Plexus*	1953
Miller, Henry	*Quiet Days in Clichy*	1956
Miller, Henry	*Sexus*	1957
Miller, Henry	*Wendekreis des Krebses* [*Tropic of Cancer*]	1958
Miller, Henry	*Wendekreis des Steinboks* [*sic*] [*Tropic of Capricorn*]	1958
Miller, Henry	*The World of Sex*	1957
Musset, Alfred de [?]	*Passion's Evil*	1953
Nabokov, Vladimir	*Lolita*	1955
Nesbit, Malcolm [Alfred Chester]	*Chariot of Flesh*	1955
Newton, Hilary	*Without Shame*	1958
O'Connor, Philip	*Steiner's Tour*	1960
O'Neill, Peter	*The Corpse Wore Grey*	1962
O'Neill, Peter	*Hell Is Filling Up*	1961
Parkinson, J. Hume	*A Gallery of Nudes*	1957
Parkinson, J. Hume	*Sextet*	1965
Peachum, Thomas [Philip Oxman]	*The Watcher and the Watched*	1954
Pearson, Angela	*The Whipping Club*	1958
Pearson, Angela	*The Whipping Post*	1959
Pearson, Angela	*Whips Incorporated*	1960
Perez, Faustino [Mason Hoffenberg]	*Until She Screams*	1956
Periodical	*Olympia no. 1*	1961
Periodical	*Olympia no. 2*	1962
Periodical	*Olympia no. 3*	1962
Periodical	*Olympia no. 4*	1963
Peters, Soliman	*Business as Usual*	1958
Piombo, Akbar del [Norman Rubington]	*The Boiler Maker*	1961
Piombo, Akbar del [Norman Rubington]	*Cosimo's Wife*	1957

Piombo, Akbar del [Norman Rubington]	*Fuzz Against Junk*	1959
Piombo, Akbar del [Norman Rubington]	*The Hero Maker*	1960
Piombo, Akbar del [Norman Rubington]	*Is That You, Simon?*	1961
Piombo, Akbar del [Norman Rubington]	*Skirts*	1956
Piombo, Akbar del [Norman Rubington]	*The Traveller's Companion*	1957
Piombo, Akbar del [Norman Rubington]	*Who Pushed Paula?*	1956
Pollini, Frances	*Night*	1960
Queneau, Raymond	*Zazie dans le Métro*	1959
Réage, Pauline [Dominique Aury]	*Story of O*	1954
Réage, Pauline [Dominique Aury]	*The Wisdom of the Lash*[3]	1957
Restif de la Bretonne, N.-E.	*Pleasures & Follies [L'Anti-Justine]*	1955
Richardson, Humphrey [Michel Gall]	*The Sexual Life of Robinson Crusoe*	1955
Richarnaud, Ezra de	*The Small Rooms of Paris*	1956
Roques, René	*Ladies at Night*	1954
Roques, René	*Three Passionate Lovers*	1954
Sade, D.-A.-F., Marquis de	*The Bedroom Philosophers*	1953
Sade, D.-A.-F., Marquis de	*Justine*	1953
Sade, D.-A.-F., Marquis de	*The One Hundred & Twenty Days of Sodom*	1954
Sade, D.-A.-F., Marquis de	*The Story of Juliette, vol. 1*	1958
Sade, D.-A.-F., Marquis de	*The Story of Juliette, vol. 2*	1959
Sade, D.-A.-F., Marquis de	*The Story of Juliette, vol. 3*	1960
Sade, D.-A.-F., Marquis de	*The Story of Juliette, vol. 4*	1960
Sade, D.-A.-F., Marquis de	*The Story of Juliette, vol. 5*	1961
Sade, D.-A.-F., Marquis de	*The Story of Juliette, vol. 6*	1964
Sade, D.-A.-F., Marquis de	*The Story of Juliette, vol. 7*	1965
Sherwood, James	*Stradella*	1962
Storm, Ralph A.	*Intimate Interviews*	1960
Street, Harry	*The Gilded Lily*	1959
Talsman, William	*The Gaudy Image*	1958
Underwood, Miles [John Glassco]	*The English Governess*	1960
Van Heller, Marcus [John Stevenson]	*Adam and Eve*	1961
Van Heller, Marcus [John Stevenson]	*Cruel Lips*	1956
Van Heller, Marcus [John Stevenson]	*The House of Borgia*	1957
Van Heller, Marcus [John Stevenson]	*The House of Borgia, pt. 2*	1958
Van Heller, Marcus [John Stevenson]	*Kidnap*	1961
Van Heller, Marcus [John Stevenson]	*The Loins of Amon*	1955
Van Heller, Marcus [John Stevenson]	*Nightmare*	1960
Van Heller, Marcus [John Stevenson]	*Rape*	1955
Van Heller, Marcus [John Stevenson]	*Roman Orgy*	1956
Van Heller, Marcus [John Stevenson]	*Terror*	1958
Van Heller, Marcus [John Stevenson]	*The Wantons*	1957

Van Heller, Marcus [John Stevenson]	*With Open Mouth*	1955
Vicarion, Count Palmiro [Christopher Logue]	*Count Palmiro Vicarion's Book of Bawdy Ballads*	1956
Vicarion, Count Palmiro [Christopher Logue]	*Count Palmiro Vicarion's Book of Limericks*	1955
Vicarion, Count Palmiro [Christopher Logue]	*Lust*	1954
Von Soda, B.	*Abandon*	1958
Von Soda, Bernhardt	*The Beaten and the Hungry*	1962
Wainhouse, Austryn	*Hedyphagetica*[1]	1954
Wilmot, John, Earl of Rochester	*Sodom, or, The Quintessence of Debauchery*	1957
X, Greta	*There's a Whip in My Valise*	1961
X, Greta	*Whipsdom*	1962

[1]Published in association with *Collection Merlin*.
[2]Reissued as *Lollipop* when the book was banned by the French government.
[3]A new translation of *Story of O*.

Bibliography

Baker, Michael. *Our Three Selves: A Life of Radclyffe Hall*. London: Hamish Hamilton and GMP Publishers, 1985.

Beach, Sylvia. *Shakespeare and Company*. Lincoln: University of Nebraska Press, 1991.

Beckett, Samuel. *I Can't Go On, I'll Go On: A Samuel Beckett Reader*. Edited and introduced by Richard W. Seaver. New York: Grove Weidenfeld, 1992.

Bockris, Victor. *With William Burroughs: A Report from the Bunker*. London: Vermilion, 1981.

Boyd, Brian. *Vladimir Nabokov: The American Years 1940–77*. Princeton: Princeton University Press, 1991.

Brome, Vincent. *Frank Harris: The Life and Loves of a Scoundrel*. London: Cassell, 1959.

Burroughs, William S. *The Letters of William S. Burroughs 1945–59*. London: Picador, 1993.

Cross, Paul J. *The Private Case: A History—Essay in The Library of the British Museum. Retrospective Essays of the Department of Printed Books*. Edited by P. R. Harris. London: British Library, 1991.

Dearborn, Mary V. *The Happiest Man Alive: A Biography of Henry Miller*. New York: Simon & Schuster, Touchstone, 1991.

Deforges, Régine. *Confessions of O: Conversations with Pauline Réage*. New York: Viking, 1979.

De Grazia, Edward. *Girls Lean Back Everywhere: The Law of Obscenity and the Assault on Genius*. New York: Random House, 1992.

Donleavy, J. P. *The History of the Ginger Man*. London: Viking, 1994.

Durrell, Lawrence, and Miller, Henry. *The Durrell-Miller Letters 1935–80*. Edited by Ian S. MacNiven. London: Faber & Faber, 1989.

Ferguson, Robert. *Henry Miller: A Life*. London: Hutchinson, 1991.

Ford, Hugh. *Published in Paris: American and British Writers, Printers, and Publishers in Paris, 1920–1939*. New York: Macmillan, 1975.

Fryer, Peter. *Secrets of the British Museum*. New York: Citadel Press, 1966.

Girodias, Maurice, ed. *The Olympia Reader*. New York: Grove Press, 1965.

———, ed. *The New Olympia Reader*. New York: Olympia Press, 1970.

———. *The Frog Prince: An Autobiography*. New York: Crown, 1980. [Éditions de la Différence: *Une Journée sur la Terre: J'Arrive*, Paris: 1977].

———. *Une Journée sur la Terre*. Volume I: *L'Arrivée*, Volume II: *Les Jardins d'Éros*. Paris: Éditions de la Différence, 1990.

Hall, Radclyffe. *The Well of Loneliness*. New York: Doubleday, Anchor Books, 1990.

Kahane, Jack. *Memoirs of a Booklegger*. London: Michael Joseph, 1939.

Kearney, Patrick J. *A History of Erotic Literature*. London: Macmillan, 1982.

———. *The Paris Olympia Press*. London: Black Spring Press, 1987.

———. *A Bibliography of the Publications of the New York Olympia Press*. Privately printed, Santa Rosa, California, 1988.

Miles, Barry. *William Burroughs: El Hombre Invisible*. London: Virgin Books, 1992.

Morgan, Ted. *Literary Outlaw: The Life and Times of William S. Burroughs*. London: Pimlico, 1991.

Nabokov, Vladimir. *On a Book Entitled Lolita: The Annotated Lolita*. Edited by Alfred Appel, Jr. New York: Vintage, 1991.

———. *Selected Letters 1940–77*. Edited by Dmitri Nabokov and Matthew J. Bruccoli. London: Vintage, 1991.

Nin, Anaïs, and Miller, Henry. *A Literate Passion: Letters of Anaïs Nin & Henry Miller, 1932–1953*. New York: Harcourt Brace Jovanovich, 1987.

Perkins, Michael. *The Secret Record: Modern Erotic Literature*. New York: William Morrow, 1977.

Pullar, Philippa. *Frank Harris: A Biography*. New York: Simon & Schuster, 1976.

Réage, Pauline. *Return to the Château* (preceded by "A Girl in Love"). New York: Grove Press, 1971.

———. *Story of O*. New York: Ballantine, 1990.

Sawyer-Lauçanno, Christopher. *The Continual Pilgrimage: American Writers in Paris, 1944–1960*. New York: Grove Press, 1992.

Scott, Andrew Murray. *Alexander Trocchi: The Making of the Monster*. Edinburgh: Polygon, 1991.

Shifreen, Lawrence J., and Jackson, Roger. *Henry Miller: A Bibliography of Primary Sources*. Paris: Alyscamps Press-Karl Orend Publishers, 1993.

Singleton-Gates, Peter, and Girodias, Maurice. *The Black Diaries of Roger Casement*. New York: Grove Press, 1959.

Webster, Paul, and Powell, Nicholas. *Saint Germain des Prés*. London: Constable, 1984.

Index

Grateful acknowledgment is made to the following for permission to reprint unpublished and previously published material:

Blue Moon Books: Excerpts from *The Olympia Reader,* edited by Maurice Girodias, and excerpts from "On Translating Sade," by Austryn Wainhouse (*Evergreen Review,* Summer 1965), and "Lolita, Nabokov and I," by Maurice Girodias (*Evergreen Review,* No. 37, September 1965). Reprinted by permission of Blue Moon Books.

Farrar, Straus & Giroux, Inc., and Faber & Faber Limited: Excerpt from "Annus Mirabilis" from *Collected Poems* by Philip Larkin. Copyright © 1988, 1989 by the Estate of Philip Larkin. Rights outside the United States are controlled by Faber & Faber Limited. Reprinted by permission of Farrar, Straus & Giroux, Inc., and Faber & Faber Limited.

Grove/Atlantic, Inc.: Excerpt from the Introduction by Richard Seaver to *I Can't Go On, I'll Go On,* by Samuel Beckett. Reprinted by permission of Grove/Atlantic, Inc.

Harcourt Brace & Company: Excerpt from *Shakespeare and Company,* by Sylvia Beach. Copyright © 1959 by Sylvia Beach and copyright renewed 1987 by Frederic Beach Dennis. Reprinted by permission of Harcourt Brace & Company.

Henry Holt and Company, Inc.: Excerpt from *Literary Outlaw: The Life and Times of William S. Burroughs,* by Ted Morgan. Copyright © 1988 by Ted Morgan. Reprinted by permission of Henry Holt and Company, Inc.

Hyperion, an imprint of Disney Book Publishing and Virgin Publishing: Excerpts from *William Burroughs: El Hombre Invisible,* by Barry Miles. Copyright © 1993 by Barry Miles. Rights outside the United States are controlled by Virgin Publishing, London. Reprinted by permission of Hyperion, an imprint of Disney Book Publishing and Virgin Publishing.

New Directions Publishing Corporation: Excerpt from *The Durrell-Miller Letters 1935–1980.* Copyright © 1963 by Lawrence Durrell and Henry Miller. Reprinted by permission of New Directions Publishing Corp.

The Paris Review: Excerpts from "The Art of Fiction LIII: J. P. Donleavy" (vol. 16, no. 63, Fall 1975). Reprinted by permission.

Viking Penguin, a division of Penguin Books USA, Inc.: Excerpts from four letters from *The Letters of William S. Burroughs: 1945–1959,* by William S. Burroughs. Copyright © 1993 by William S. Burroughs. Reprinted by permission of Viking Penguin, a division of Penguin Books USA, Inc.

Random House UK: Excerpts from *Henry Miller: A Life,* by Robert Ferguson (Hutchinson). Reprinted by permission.

Michael Rubinstein: Excerpt from a letter to Maurice Girodias dated April 25, 1966, and an excerpt from a letter to Leon Friedman dated September 28, 1966. Reprinted by permission.

Simon & Schuster: Excerpt from *Published in Paris: American and British Writers, Printers and Publishers in Paris, 1920–1939,* by Hugh Ford. Copyright © 1975 by Hugh Ford. Reprinted by permission of Simon & Schuster.

JOHN DE ST JORRE joined the British Foreign Service after the army and Oxford University. He served in several African countries in the heady days of independence and later went to Lebanon to learn Arabic, a challenge he failed to meet. Abandoning a diplomatic career, he became the London *Observer*'s Africa correspondent, covering wars and political crises. He was subsequently the *Observer*'s correspondent in Paris, the Middle East, and New York.

Turning freelance, he stayed on in the United States, writing for newspapers and magazines, editing and lecturing. His nonfiction books include *The Brothers' War: Biafra and Nigeria; A House Divided: South Africa's Uncertain Future; The Guards; The Marines;* and *The Insider's Guide to Spain.* He also co-authored a novel, *The Patriot Game.*

While in New York, John de St Jorre came across writers who had lived in Paris in the 1950s and had written for the Olympia Press. A casual interest turned into a literary quest to track down the colorful band. The trail led to Tangier, England, Ireland, the United States, and Paris. Some people were easily identifiable; others were more elusive, concealed by their pseudonyms. But most were found and entered the pages of this book.

The author now lives with his family in a small mountain village in Mallorca, Spain.

ABOUT THE TYPE

This book was set in Bembo, a typeface based on an old-style Roman face that was used for Cardinal Bembo's tract *De Aetna* in 1495. Bembo was cut by Francisco Griffo in the early sixteenth century. The Lanston Monotype Company of Philadelphia brought the well-proportioned letterforms of Bembo to the United States in the 1930s.